Markets and Politicians

Politicized economic choice

STUDIES IN PUBLIC CHOICE

Series Editor: Gordon Tullock
University of Arizona
Tucson, Arizona, USA

Previously published books in this series:

Bowman, Mary Jean
Collective Choice in Education

Buchanan, James M. and Wagner, Richard E.
Fiscal Responsibility in Constitutional Democracy

McKenzie, Richard B.
The Political Economy of the Educational Process

Auster, Richard D. and Silver, Morris
The State as a Firm

Kau, James D. and Rubin, Paul H.
Congressmen, Constituents, and Contributors:
The Determinants of Roll Call Voting in the
House of Representatives

Ordeshook, Peter and Shepsle, Kenneth
Political Equilibrium

Tullock, Gordon
The Economics of Special Privilege and Rent Seeking

The intersection of economics and politics is one of the most important areas of modern social science. "Studies in Public Choice" is devoted to a particularly crucial aspect of this intersection -- the use of economic methods and analysis on matters which are traditionally political in nature. Prominent scholars, such as Duncan Black, Kenneth Arrow, Mancus Olson, Vincent Ostrom, William Riker, and James Buchanan, have contributed to the development of the study of public choice. The aim of this series is to promote the growth of knowledge in this important and fascinating field.

Markets and Politicians

Politicized economic choice

Edited by

Arye L. Hillman

Bar-Ilan University, Israel

Kluwer Academic Publishers
Boston/Dordrecht/Lancaster

Distributors for North America:
Kluwer Academic Publishers
101 Philip Drive
Assinippi Park
Norwell, Massachusetts 02061 USA

Distributors for all other countries:
Kluwer Academic Publishers Group
Distribution Centre
Post Office Box 322
3300 AH Dordrecht, THE NETHERLANDS

Library of Congress Cataloging-in-Publication Data

Markets and politicians : politicized economic choice / edited by Arye
    L. Hillman.
        p.   cm. — (Studies in public choice)
    ISBN 0-7923-9135-7
    1. Economic policy.   2. Politicians.   3. Social choice.
    I. Hillman, Arye L.   II. Series.
    HD87.M275   1990
    338.9—dc20   90-19545
                                                            CIP

Printed on acid-free paper.

Printed in the United States of America.

CONTENTS

III: INTERNATIONAL ECONOMIC POLICY
A. International Trade

B. International Monetary Transactions

CONTRIBUTING AUTHORS

Robert E. Baldwin, University of Wisconsin, U.S.A.
Mario I. Blejer, International Monetary Fund, Washington, D.C.
James H. Cassing, University of Pittsburgh, U.S.A.
Kang Chen, The World Bank, Washington, D.C.
Wilfred J. Ethier, University of Pennsylvania, U.S.A.
Manfred Gärtner, St. Gallen School of Economics, Switzerland
Joel M. Guttman, Bar-Ilan University, Israel
Arye L. Hillman, Bar-Ilan University, Israel
Manuel Hinds, The World Bank, Washington, D.C.
Peter Holmes, University of Sussex, U.K.
Ngo Van Long, McGill University, Canada
Jun Li, University of Cincinnati, U.S.A.
Wolfgang Mayer, University of Cincinnati, U.S.A.
Martin Paldam, Aarhus University, Denmark
Adi Schnytzer, Bar-Ilan University, Israel
György Szapáry, International Monetary Fund, Washington, D.C.
Marton Tardos, Hungarian Academy of Sciences
Gordon Tullock, University of Arizona, U.S.A.
Heinrich W. Ursprung, University of Konstanz, FRG
Ben-Zion Zilberfarb, Bar-Ilan University, Israel

ACKNOWLEDGEMENTS

Many of the papers in this volume were presented at the Bar-Ilan Conference on Markets and Politicians at Bar-Ilan University, Israel, in June 1989. Joel Guttman was co-organizer of the conference, and Gershon Alperovitch as departmental chairman was also instrumental in organization.

INTRODUCTION

Arye L. Hillman

There has been much economic theorizing directed at providing the politician with guidance in the design of policies that will amend market outcomes in ways that achieve specified efficiency or equity objectives. It has been common practice in economic models to portray the politician who implements the policy recommendations as a mechanistic individual who behaves as would a benevolent dictator to maximize a prespecified conception of social welfare or the utility of a representative consumer. The self-interest and discretion that is attributed to firms and consumers as optimizing agents is absent from the motives of such a politician. Economic policy choice is thereby depoliticized.

How well depoliticized economic theory fares in explaining or predicting economic policy choice depends naturally enough upon how politicized is the economic system in which economic and political agents function. The papers in this volume recognize that politicians may exercise sufficient discretion so as not to behave mechanistically in correcting market inefficiencies or in pursuit of a somehow specified just income distribution. Since politicians are viewed as self-interested optimizing agents, just as are utility-maximizing consumers and profit-maximizing producers, the choice of economic policies is politicized.

Coverage is provided of a broad spectrum of economic policy choice where markets and politicians interact. Section I is concerned with policy determination in western market economies, Section II with the introduction of markets into economies in transition from socialism, and Section III with international transactions.

Heinrich Ursprung (Chapter 1, *Economic policy and political competition*) begins by reviewing how in past literature political influences on policy choice have been integrated into models of representative democracy. The role of political competition in the determination of economic policies is developed in a model of contenders for elective office who make policy pronouncements to maximize the value of their campaign contributions relative to contributions received by opponents, and thereby maximize their probabilities of election. The model encompasses recognition of the public-good nature of the economic benefits and costs associated with candidates' policies. The preferences of voters, or the median voter, do not here directly determine policy outcomes, which are responsive to campaign contributions. The campaign contributions in turn are sought to influence voters' perceptions of the attractiveness of the candidates and the policies they propose.

Joel Guttman (Chapter 2, *Voluntary collective action*) compares explanations for the observed conjunction of cooperation and self-interest in individuals' collective behavior. Such collective behavior is central to the activities of political coalitions of individuals seeking to achieve common economic objectives.

Wolfgang Mayer and Jun Li (Chapter 3, *Factor income taxation in a representative democracy*) demonstrate how individual interests are reflected in political choice of taxes levied on factors of production, when individuals differ with regard to the tax system that they regard as optimal and seek different patterns of expenditures of tax proceeds.

Martin Paldam (Chapter 4, *Macroeconomic stabilization policy: Does politics matter?*) looks at macroeconomic policy. A literature on "political business cycles" has proposed that macroeconomic policies are subject to political manipulation that is directed at maximizing probabilities of reelection of incumbent governments. Two types of business cycles have been described, election cycles over one election period, and partisan cycles that encompass two election periods under different governments. Paldam reviews theories of the political business cycle, and presents empirical results of tests in seventeen countries.

Gordon Tullock (Chapter 5, *Accidental freedom*) uses an historical account to make the case that economic freedom in the U.S. arose fortuitously. The U.S. did not proceed free of attempts to regulate domestic market activity and protect domestic producers. Tullock recounts how the constitutional guarantee of free trade among the states thwarted attempted state-imposed monopolies, including state socialism, and how domestic regulation of economic activity and U.S. international trade policy have been subject to different influences over time.

Peter Holmes (Chapter 6, *Europe 1992: From the common to the single market*) sets out the political motives underlying the economic policies aimed at creating a post-1992 single European market. Since the intent of the policies underlying the post-1992 "single market" is to all intents and purposes the same as that of the Treaty of Rome that sought to establish the "common market", why should the single-market conception succeed when the common market was only realized in a limited way? Holmes addresses this question, demonstrating how the success of the single-market conception is predicated on political credibility.

Manuel Hinds (Chapter 7, *Markets and ownership in socialist countries in transition*) reviews the experience of attempts to introduce markets in a socialist framework and sets out the internal contradictions that arise in such attempts. The question is whether markets can be relied upon to yield efficiency under enterprise self-management and other organizational forms in the absence of private ownership of the means of production. In the context of Eastern European reforms, Hinds considers how market price indicators replace centralized resource allocation; how financial markets function; how individual incentives influence supply responses to market prices; how incentives affect investment decisions; and how fiscal discipline is related to ownership of enterprises. Hinds makes the case that the inadequacies of decentralized market socialism derive from the absence of private ownership, and concludes that, without private property rights to capital, factor markets cannot perform their allocative roles -- so a market economy cannot be established, and paradoxically there is a need for the political allocation from which the socialist economies seek to escape.

Adi Schnytzer (Chapter 8, *Socialism in less than one country*) expands the distinction between socialism "in one country" and "in more than one country" to the dimension of an economy in transition that does not or cannot dispense with a dominant socialist sector notwithstanding the introduction of markets to replace the planner. Schnytzer describes such an economic system and proposes that the conjunction of incentives and economic structure can trap the economy in the transitional system.

With Hungarian "market socialism" as background (Hungary having abandoned central planning but not socialism in 1968), Marton Tardos (Chapter 9, *Restoring property rights*) evaluates various means whereby private property rights might be assigned in the transition from socialism to a western market economy. Tardos notes that market socialism in Hungary did not yield the benefits of efficiency, because of the associated property rights specification that sustained, and was sustained by, political monopoly. Privatization of socialist industry is considered via self-management and assignment of rights to enterprise capital to workers; after noting past experiences in Yugoslavia, Poland, and Hungary, Tardos proposes that this scheme is best confined to theoretical models of the labor-managed firm. Under a "Personal Social Property" conception, individuals would bid for the right to manage social property. Or state property could be directly allocated to citizens without payment.

Alternatively, management of state property could be assigned to state-regulated investment trusts, or ownership transferred to foundations, insurance companies, and pension funds. Consensus on a program is hindered by the income-distribution consequences of the different approaches to assigning property rights.

My paper (Chapter 10, *Liberalization dilemmas*) is concerned with the policy dilemmas that arise, and also the rents that are threatened, when liberalization of international trade and domestic transactions is sought in a market economy with significant workers' collective or socialist industry and wherein preeminence is assigned to workers' job security. Israel here provide the background, although there is comparative reference to the experience of Hungarian market socialism. In private-property-rights market economies, private claims to factors of production underlie protectionist policies; but the absence of such claims does not make for liberal trade policies in "market socialist" systems. The socially conscious enterprise protects its workers from the market, and is itself protected by the state against less socially conscious cost-minimizing competitors.

Two further papers deal with China. Kang Chen (Chapter 11, *The failure of recentralization in China: Interplays among enterprises, local governments, and the center*) recounts the role of local governments in the process of economic change in China. Local officials "captured" decision making power that via decentralization was intended to establish enterprise autonomy. The outcome has been an "aristocratic economy" ruled by "dukes" and "princes" who protect local interests, pursue regional expansion, and bear no consequences of macroeconomic instability. The changes brought about by decentralization and other reform measures reinforced one another in a manner that inhibited both recentralization and further reform.

Mario Blejer and György Szapáry (Chapter 12, *Market-oriented reform and fiscal policy*) adopt a macroeconomic policy perspective on reform attempts in China. The focus is on the manner in which fiscal policy instruments that indirectly affect agents' economic decision making in market transactions come to replace the directives of the planner.

Robert Baldwin (Chapter 13, *The political-economy perspective on trade policy*) begins Section III on international economic policy with a description of the approaches taken by economics and political science to incorporating political discretion into the analysis of choice of trade policies. Baldwin sets out a model that encompasses elements central to both approaches. Economic choice is expressed directly in the market-place, and indirectly by voting and political contributions to secure desired policies. Individuals are "rationally informed" and "rationally ignorant" in the acquisition of knowledge - they acquire the knowledge which they believe to be to their best advantage, and subject to knowledge acquisition make choices under uncertainty. This framework is applied to explaining how economic and political choice interact in the determination of international trade policy.

Wilfred Ethier (Chapter 14, *The economics and political economy of managed trade*) pursues this theme, observing that although the benefits of free trade are almost universally acknowledged, nonetheless Western international trade has become increasingly regulated or "managed", in particular via the instrument of voluntary export restraints that circumvents GATT regulations. Ethier describes the characteristics of managed trade, and formulates models that describe the consequences of such trade in both competitive and imperfectly competitive markets.

James Cassing (Chapter 15, *Changes in trade-policy regimes*) observes that protectionist policies may be introduced as the response to a change in comparative advantage, but when the impetus for change is reversed or disappears, the policies are nonetheless sustained. Policies therefore persist in the absence of the circumstances that gave rise to policy intervention in the first instance. In Cassing's words: "What seems curious is not so much that large shocks engender regime changes, but that the regime thus enfranchised then seems to win the day after the shock has disappeared and to persist in the very same economic environment that had previously supported an alternative policy regime". Cassing demonstrates how such hysteresis in the conduct of international trade policy can occur.

Manfred Gärtner (Chapter 16, *Foreign-exchange markets and central-bank intervention*) examines the incentives underlying intervention by central bankers in foreign exchange markets. In principle, a system of flexible exchange rates implies that exchange rates are to be market-determined. Yet in the post-Bretton Woods flexible exchange-rate regime, central bankers have continued to intervene in foreign exchange markets. Gärtner proposes that the behavior of central bankers can be described with reference to an optimizing objective that combines accommodation of the interests of the domestic constituency with the requirements of international agencies such as the International Monetary Fund. This implies respectively achieving purchasing-power-parity and exchange-rate smoothing. Since these objectives may be contradictory, central bankers in formulating the optimal interventionist policy may be obliged to trade off domestic goals against compliance with international guidelines for permissible exchange-rate intervention. The predictions of the model are compared with the observed behavior of a number of central banks.

Literature on the international debt crisis has had a macroeconomic orientation and has tended to avoid direct confrontation with the question as to how individual agents' motives relate to the "crisis". Ngo Van Long (Chapter 17, *The political economy of the international debt crisis*) introduces self-interest motives of the agents and agencies into an analysis of the "crisis": banks which made the loans in the first instance; the debtor country governments which have the responsibility for repayment; the creditor country governments whose involvement derives from the effect that default would have on their domestic banking system; international agencies as dispensers of policy advice and intermediators; and the domestic interest groups in the debtor and creditor countries who stand to lose or gain from the different proposals for resolution of the crisis. A game-theoretic framework that incorporates discount rates and time horizons is used to analyze the interdependencies among agents' objectives and behavior.

Ben-Zion Zilberfarb (Chapter 18, *Foreign-exchange market liberalization: Anatomy of a failure*) investigates the reasons for failure of policies directed at the liberalization of the foreign-exchange market in Israel subsequent to the change of government in 1977. The new government professed adherence to free-market principles. The underlying economic structure of the economy and precedent confined liberalization possibilities to the foreign exchange market. Zilberfarb describes how inappropriate macroeconomic policy undermined this limited liberalization program, thereby ending the free-market "economic revolution" of the new government and discrediting market-oriented change.

Chapter 1

ECONOMIC POLICIES AND POLITICAL COMPETITION

Heinrich W. Ursprung

Economic policies in a democracy are subject to influence by interested parties or coalitions of individuals who seek outcomes in their favor. Under direct democracy, voters directly determine the choice of policy, and the median-voter theorem and associated conceptions are pertinent. Under representative democracy, voters are in principle the principals who via the ballot box designate economic policies to their elected representatives as political agents. However, in practice this principal-agent ordering may be reversed, as the politician or candidate for political office seeks campaign contributions to facilitate communication of the merits of his policy position or demerits of his opponent to the constituency of voters. Campaign contributions or political expenditures are then central to the outcome of political competition and the determination of policy. To influence the political -- and thereby the policy -- outcome, interested parties have an incentive to make campaign contributions to influence the policy pronouncements of political candidates. In this sense, the politician or political candidate remains the agent, not the principal; but this is not the traditional principal-agent relationship of electoral democracy whereby the voters -- or the median voter -- designate policy outcomes.

The first section of this chapter reviews approaches to modelling economic decision making in a democracy that retain variants of the traditional principal-agent relationship and also variants that have approached endogeneity of economic policy via conceptions of political-support maximization and rent-seeking behavior. Section II sets out a model of policy determination via political competition wherein political candidates' quests for campaign contributions influence the policy equilibrium. Section III demonstrates applications of the model.

I. TRANSACTIONS COSTS AND THE POLITICAL PROCESS
A. Policy Determination in the Absence of Transaction Costs

In the absence of transaction costs, policy decisions are readily endogenized via the Coase Theorem. It follows from the Theorem that independently of the political decision making mechanism, that is, independently of the assignment of political discretion, the political process will yield Pareto-optimal economic policies.[1] Since recontracting or negotiation of compensation is costless by assumption, policies will be agreed upon which are beneficial in aggregate, and are not directed at benefitting special interests.[2] This applies to all political decision mechanisms, whether democratic or not.

In practice, we do observe inefficient policies - protectionism for example - which indicates that the assumption of negligible transaction costs in the political process is inappropriate. I adopt now the opposite extreme of prohibitive costs of recontracting.[3]

B. Prohibitive Costs of Recontracting
(i) Perfect Information

In a representative democracy, let all agents be perfectly informed. Let voters be intimately familiar with the platforms of the competing candidates or parties, and aware of how these platforms, if implemented, would affect their utilities, and let the rival candidates know the preferences of the voters. If the assumption of perfect information is combined with the economic model of behavior, that is, the assumption of utility-maximizing voters and candidates, one arrives at the modelling structure which comprises the median voter model (Black, 1948) and the spatial refinements thereof, the so-called spatial models of voting. The unidimensional version of the spatial model can be traced to Hotelling (1929) and Downs (1957); the general version makes its first appearance in Davis, Hinich and Ordeshook (1970).[4]

The basic structure of the spatial models of voting is depicted in Figure 1 for the two-candidate case. Voters' utilities depend on the policy pronouncements of the competing candidates; a candidate, if elected to

---

[1] If more than one efficient solution exists we may, of course, be left with a bargaining problem.

[2] In the context of international trade policy, see Baldwin (1985), Hillman (1989).

[3] This rules out the familiar phenomenon of logrolling. For a review of logrolling, see Miller (1977).

[4] Reviews of the spatial theory of voting are to be found in Enelow and Hinich (1984) and Ordeshook (1986), chapter 4.

Figure 1

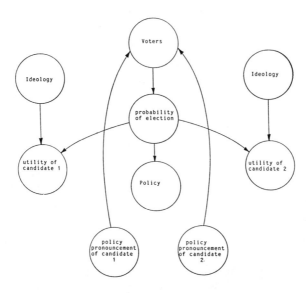

Figure 2

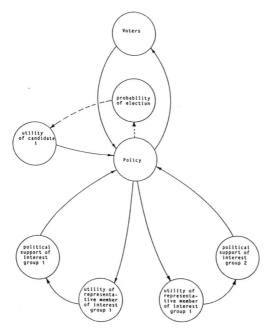

office, is assumed to implement his pronounced policy.[5] As a consequence, each voter votes for the candidate whose policy pronouncement is most favorable for him or her. The individual decisions of the voters are then aggregated to produce the election outcome. The policy pronouncements of the candidates are derived from a utility-maximization calculus. A candidate's utility is assumed to depend for ideological reasons on his pronounced policy, or for more egoistic reasons on the probability of being elected to office. In either case, the expected election outcome influences a candidate's utility.

If, in a unidimensional context, voters' preferences are single-peaked, there exists a unique (Nash) equilibrium.[6] This equilibrium has two noteworthy features. Firstly, the equilibrium is always convergent, that is, competing candidates make the same policy pronouncements, and secondly, convergence does not depend up on whether candidates' motives are ideological or egoistic.[7] The model thus cannot portray the commonly observed characteristic of political polarization.

(ii) Vote Participation Costs and Informational Imperfections

In his seminal contribution Downs introduced policy divergence via voter-participation costs. He proceeded from the assumption that extremist voters would refuse to support of two either candidates if both adopted alike policies - not identical, but merely similar. This assumption was justified on the grounds that for these "alienated" voters voter-participation costs exceed the benefit from voting. Abstention due to alienation in combination with a bimodal distribution of the voters over the uni-dimensional political spectrum can lead candidates' policy pronouncements to diverge. However, this explanation of political polarization is not very convincing, since it is not evident that voter-participation costs systematically influence voter participation,[8] or that the distribution of voters over the political spectrum corresponds to the Downsian assumption.

Another approach to modelling political polarization relaxes the assumption of perfect information. This is done by assuming that the candidates have incomplete information about voters' preferences, or that voters are uncertain about the candidates' policy pronouncements. Uncertainty about voters' preferences is usually modelled via probabilistic voting-decisions (which make their first appearance in Hinich, Ledyard, and

---

[5] This is a heroic assumption, to be sure. In a one-shot game, it implies time-inconsistent behavior on the part of candidates [cf. Alesina (1988)].
[6] See Kramer and Klevorick (1974) for a generalization of this result.
[7] This was observed by Bernholz (1975), p. 21.
[8] See for example Weck-Hannemann (1990).

Ordeshook, 1972). The concept of probabilistic voting has two advantages: Firstly, probabilistic voting guarantees the existence of an equilibrium even in higher-dimensional policy spaces, whereas deterministic voting in general yields no equilibrium; and, secondly, in its biased version, probabilistic voting gives rise to political polarization. If voters are assumed not to be biased in favor of one of the candidates, political polarization can still emerge if the candidates have ideological objectives [cf. Wittman (1983)]. A wedge between the policy pronouncements of the competing candidates is also established if the candidates are perceived by the voters to have ambiguous policy positions. In such a situation, the incumbent has a risk advantage over the challenger as long as he does not substantially alter his established platform. Reputational considerations thus decrease the attraction of the median-voters' preferred policy, and political polarization becomes feasible in equilibrium [cf. Bernhardt and Ingberman (1985)].[9]

C. Information Costs
(i) Traditional Interest-Group Models

The law of demand suggests a negative relationship between voters' information about candidates' policy pronouncements and the cost of information. Since a voter's utility deriving from the consequences of the individual act of voting is marginal in general elections, one can go a step further and postulate that voters are completely uniformed - and rationally so - if information is not entirely free. To be sure, voters may also derive utility from the mere act of making an informed decision. In this case, one has to rely on substantial costs of information to justify the assumption of rationally uninformed voters.

If voters are uninformed, they become susceptible to manipulation via election propaganda. As a consequence, politicians are not bound by the preferences of voters and the median-voter policy loses its attraction. This decoupling provides the politician with discretionary power which he or she can use to create and distribute rents. Thus, politically contestable rents enter the picture[10] as well as interest groups competing for these rents. As compared to the voting-theory approach, the picture has changed dramatically. It is no longer the voter who commands the driving seat of the political vehicle, but the politician and the rent-seeking interest groups

---

[9] For completeness, another body of literature should be mentioned in this context of incompletely informed voters, political business-cycle theory. See the paper by Paldam in this volume. Nordhaus (1975) is the classic paper in this field. A survey of the literature is to be found in Mueller (1989), chapter 15.

[10] See Hillman and Riley (1989).

who seek political redistribution.[11]

The traditional interest-group approach to endogenous policy determination focuses on the interaction between interest groups and the elected politician or the government. The approach has two versions, the political-support-function approach and the rent-seeking approach. In the first version, which originates in the theory of regulation [cf. Stigler (1971), Peltzman (1976)], the elected politician pursues a policy which maximizes his political support. Political support is maximized subject to the gains and losses of the those directly affected by the policy. The approach is one of constrained optimization; that is, interest groups are not modelled as economic agents who strategically interact with the policy-maker in the sense of game theory.[12]

The rent-seeking models which can be traced back to Tullock (1967) introduce interest groups as economic agents[13] who by making lobbying outlays can influence political decision-making. The expected gains from lobbying depend on the lobbying efforts undertaken by the competing interest groups. The contest between the interest groups thus replaces the maximization framework of the political-support-function approach. The policy maker now however has a passive role; the rent-seeking approach portrays the policy maker's behavior in the terms of an ad hoc contest-success function.

The two versions of the interest-group approach thus focus on different aspects of the one relationship - the first on the economic calculus of the policy maker, the second one on the economic calculus of interest groups or rent seekers.

The basic structure of the interest-group approach is depicted in Figure 2. Candidate 1 represents the incumbent who in the political-support version determines policy, which in turn affects the utility of the members of the interest groups, and perhaps the utility of voters, while candidate 2 does not play an active role. In the rent-seeking models the interest groups actively intervene in the political process by means of lobbying activities. In both versions, the policy maker's objective is to maximize political support to secure the election. In the rent-seeking models, however, the policy-maker's maximization calculus is not explicitly modelled.

---

[11] See also Magee, Brock, and Young (1989).

[12] An application to international trade policy is to be found in Hillman (1982). The "Dutch School" [cf. van Winden (1983) and the literature quoted in Renaud (1989)] is also based on this approach.

[13] The rent-seeking literature is surveyed in Tollison (1982). Two representative collections of articles are to be found in Buchanan et al. (1980) and Rowley et al. (1988).

In comparing the interest-group models with the voting-theory models, one notices that the first class of models focuses on electoral competition and neglects interest-group activities, whereas in the second class the converse is true. A well-balanced interest-group model should incorporate the aspect of electoral competition, if only for reasons of consistency. An acceptable interest-group model also needs to portray the interest groups - better yet, the individual members of the interest groups - as rational, that is, utility maximizing agents. The rent-seeking models satisfy this requirement; but the underlying contest-success functions lack a sound microeconomic foundation. This can be overcome by replacing the contest-success function with a framework of political competition.

(ii) Interest Groups and Electoral Competition

The interest-group-cum-electoral-competition models represent an extension of the rent-seeking approach. The main difference is that in the traditional rent-seeking models lobbying has a direct effect on policy, whereas in the extended version political support has an effect on the competing candidates' probabilities of election. The interest groups' political support for candidates takes the form of campaign contributions, which depend on the stakes of the rent-seeking interest groups via the policy pronouncements of the competing candidates, who in turn are assumed to maximize the probability of being elected to office. The voters as a rule are not explicitly modelled[14] but appear in disguise in the functional relationship linking campaign contributions to election probabilities. The basic structure of the interest-group-cum-electoral-competition approach, which has been used by Young and Magee (1986), Austen-Smith (1987) and Hillman and Ursprung (1988), is depicted in Figure 3 [the dotted arrows will be elaborated upon in the next section].

D. Barriers to Entry

If there exist barriers to entry for prospective candidates, electoral competition becomes imperfect, and the possibility arises that the candidates, if elected to office, will use their discretion - which is due to the informational problems described in the previous section - to appropriate rents for their own benefit. Excluding for the time being illegal transactions (by assuming perfect monitoring), this can be achieved either by withholding rents which could otherwise be exchanged for political support, by transforming campaign contributions into personal benefit, or by simply accepting gifts from interest groups. In each case, the politician's behavior will, ceteris paribus, result in a loss of political

---

[14] An exception in this respect is Austen-Smith (1987).

support which is balanced against the direct gain from rent appropriation. Here income maximization replaces political-support maximization as the primary objective of the candidates.

The above-mentioned activities may be legal, but as a rule are not desirable,[15] since the rent-seeking politicians neither follow a political ideology nor are guided in their behavior by electoral objectives (i.e. in the final analysis by the preferences of their constituencies). One can speak in this context of personal corruption.[16] If the competing candidates are personally corruptible, the basic structure of the approach described in the previous section is only slightly altered. In Figure 3 the added dotted arrows indicate that, in addition to the indirect influence through the probability of election, there now also exists a more direct channel through which interest groups can express their political support.

E. Monitoring and Law-Enforcement Costs

The dividing line between personal and official corruption is difficult to make out in day-by-day politics.[17] However, from a theoretical point of view the distinction is quite clear. In the case of personal corruption, the first move in the rent-seeking game is via the politician's policy pronouncement. In the second move the interest groups respond by determining their political support. In such a situation the politician takes on the role of a Stackelberg leader. In the case of official corruption the sequence is reversed. The interest groups move first by offering to "buy" a certain policy. If the bid is successful, the politician responds in a second move by accepting the offer, which implies that he implements the sought-after policy. Thus personal corruption is characterized by the politician's commitment preceding the activities of the interest groups; inofficial corruption, the opposite is true.

Since official corruption is illegal, it can only occur if monitoring of rent-seeking behavior is imperfect. The higher monitoring costs, the larger is the margin for official corruption. If politicians take bribes the indirect influence of political support on politicians' behavior (i.e. the influence which operates through the probability of election) disappears, and we are left with the direct influence introduced in section 1.D [cf. Figure 3].

---

[15] Cowen and Glazer (1990) show however that rent-seeking politicians can increase the efficiency of the political process.
[16] Personally corruptible politicians make their appearence in the rent-seeking literature in Appelbaum and Katz (1987). An interest group model with competing candidates who are personally corruptible is to be found in Ursprung (1990).
[17] Cf. Stern (1988), chapter 8.

Figure 3

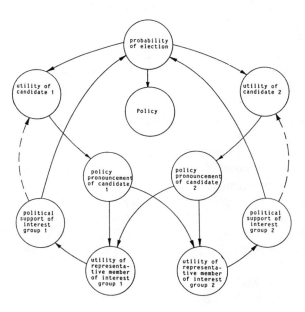

Figure 4

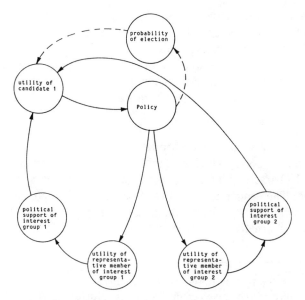

Elected politicians are more likely to be offered bribes than candidates competing for election. Models portraying official corruption are therefore models of government behavior. The basic elements of this type of model are depicted in Figure 4.

To an extent, official corruption can exist in all political systems. In some, it is so prevalent as to dominate the political process. Yet the political-economy literature dealing with the phenomenon of corruption is scanty.[18]

High monitoring costs certainly increase political discretion. Many laws, however, by their nature are easily monitored. As long as these laws can be enforced, politicians are constrained in their actions. The state of law can only break down if the political system is afflicted with substantial costs of law enforcement. In the extreme case, the political system degenerates to an autocracy in which the ruler neither faces a reelection constraint, nor legal or constitutional constraints; he has only to consider the ever-present revolution constraint. There exists a small body of literature on the political economy of autocracies and revolutions.[19]

II. THE BASIC MODEL

I now set out the basic model portraying the relationship between interest groups and candidates competing for public office. Political-economy models analyze the influence over policy exerted by the gainers and losers from redistributional policy proposals. My objective in this section is to focus the analysis on political relationships, in particular on the public-good characteristics which are inherent in many redistribution policies. For this purpose, the economic component of the basic model is cut down as much as possible. Applications via models which use the political relationships of the basic model but are endowed with a richer and thus more interesting economic structure are presented in the last part of the paper.

A. The Structure of the Basic Model

The simplest policy which gives rise to income redistribution exhibiting public-good characteristics is the political allocation of a group-specific public good. The economic part of the basic model thus portrays a political incumbent who has the discretion to allocate a given budget of size X between two alternatives yielding public-good benefits to members of two

---

[18] The classic in the field is Rose-Ackermann (1978).
[19] Gordon Tullock is to be given credit for having initiated research in this field [cf. Tullock (1971) and (1987)]. A short summary of the literature is to be found in Mueller (1990), sections 9G and 14G.

groups. Although individuals in each group share a common interest in influencing budgetary allocation, they do not cooperate.

Let θ denote the fraction of the budget that is used to provide the first group with the group-specific public good. Denoting the number of members of group 1 by m, the utility which a representative member i of interest group 1 derives from the provision with the group-specific public good is

(1a) $$U_i = \mu(\theta X/m)^{\frac{1}{2}}.$$

The respective expression for a representative member j of interest group 2 is given by

(1b) $$U_j = \mu((1-\theta)X/n)^{\frac{1}{2}}.$$

The economic part of the model consists of the above utility functions.

The political part of the model portrays an election contest with two candidates. In a first move, the two candidates announce their policy platforms regarding budgetary allocation. Individuals respond to the policy platforms by making campaign contributions to influence the outcome of the election. The more campaign contributions a candidate collects compared to his opponent, the higher is his probability of election. If L_1 and L_2 denote total campaign contributions collected by candidates 1 and 2, the probability w of candidate 1 winning the election is given by the following contest-success function which is standard in the rent-seeking literature:

(2) $w = L_1/(L_1 + L_2)$ if $L_1 + L_2 > 0$
      $w = 0.5$ if $L_1 + L_2 = 0$

If the two candidates make different policy pronouncements, the members of the two groups have an incentive to influence the election outcome by making campaign contributions to the candidate who promises to do more for them. Campaign contributions yield public-good benefits for the respective interest groups because what matters for the election outcome is total campaign contributions. Denoting the policy pronouncement of candidate k (k=1,2) by θ_k and an individual agent h's campaign contribution by L_h, the expected utility of individuals in group 1 and 2 is

(1a*) $EU_i = w\mu(\theta_1 X/m)^{\frac{1}{2}} + (1-w)\mu(\theta_2 X/m)^{\frac{1}{2}} - L_i$

(1b*) $EU_j = w\mu((1-\theta_1)X/n)^{\frac{1}{2}} + (1-w)\mu((1-\theta_2)X/n)^{\frac{1}{2}} - L_j$

The direct effect of L_h ($h=1,2$) on EU_h is linear because campaign contributions are assumed to constitute only a small part of the rent seekers' disposable incomes.

The candidates are Stackelberg leaders who maximize expected income. A candidate's expected income depends on (i) the salary associated with elected office and income reflecting opportunity cost of political activity, respectively denoted by Y_p and Y_a, (ii) the probability of being elected to office, and (iii) in the case of the successful candidate, a rent that varies positively with political support as measured by total contributions to the successful candidate's campaign. This last component incorporates the notion of personal corruption [cf. section ID]. The expected income of the two candidates is thus

(3a) $EY_1 = w(Y_p + \alpha L_1) + (1-w)Y_a$
(3b) $EY_2 = wY_a + (1-w)(Y_p + \alpha L_2)$

where α is a measure of personal corruption.

The basic model can be summarized as follows. Acting as Stackelberg leaders, that is, taking into account the reactions of the two interest groups, the candidates maximize their expected incomes as given in equation (3) by announcing policy platforms. Observing the policy pronouncements, individuals maximize expected utility as given in equation (1^*) by choosing campaign contributions. The latter then enter into equation (2) which specifies the winner of the election. The overall structure of the basic model is thus described by a Cournot-Nash contest between the two candidates, and a Cournot-Nash contest within as well as between the two interest groups. The two Cournot-Nash games are connected by the Stackelberg relationships linking the behavior of the candidates with the behavior of their respective constituencies. Figure 5 is a graphical representation of this structure.

B. Rent Dissipation and Political Polarization

In a first step of the analysis, the policy pronouncements θ_1 and θ_2 of the two candidates are taken as given in order to focus the analysis on the public-good nature of the contested rent. Let $\theta_1 \geq \theta_2$. In this case members of interest group 1 contribute exclusively to the campaign of candidate 1 and the members of interest group 2 exclusively to the campaign of candidate 2, i.e. $L_1 = \Sigma L_i$ and $L_2 = \Sigma L_j$. Solving the game played by the individual rent seekers yields

(4) $w = a/(a + b)$ and $L_1 + L_2 = ab/(a + b)$

Figure 5

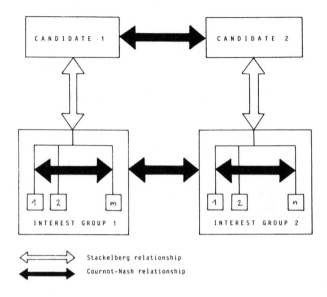

CANDIDATE 1

CANDIDATE 2

1 2 m

INTEREST GROUP 1

1 2 n

INTEREST GROUP 2

Stackelberg relationship
Cournot-Nash relationship

Figure 6

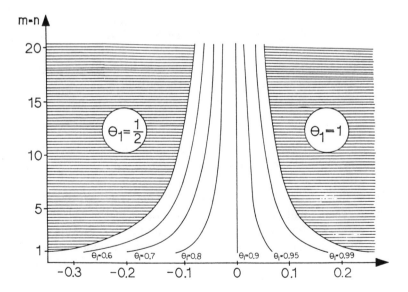

where a $\equiv \mu[(\theta_1 X/m)^{\frac{1}{2}} - (\theta_2 X/m)^{\frac{1}{2}}]$ and b $\equiv \mu[((1-\theta_2)X/n)^{\frac{1}{2}} - ((1-\theta_1)X/n)^{\frac{1}{2}}]$ denotes the stakes of the individual rent-seekers of interest group 1 and 2.[20] The political outcome as well as rent dissipation are thus directly linked to the stakes of the individual rent-seekers. These stakes, in turn, depend on group size: The larger the group, the smaller the individual stake. Equation (4) shows how the political outcome depends on the relative size of the two groups. An increase in the number m of individuals in interest group 1, for example, decreases the individual stake a, and as a consequence also decreases the electoral prospects w of candidate 1, the representative of interest group 1. This result is readily explained. An increase of the number of individuals contributing in a group has two effects. The first is to increase the total value of the rent which, ceteris paribus, increases contributions. The second effect is to increase the incentive to easy-ride which, ceteris paribus, decreases individuals' contributions. In the case of a congestable public good, the easy-riding effect dominates the stake effect.[21] Hence:

Proposition 1:
An interest group's ability to influence the political process varies positively with the stake of its members. If the politically allocated prize is a congestable public-good, the interest group's ability to influence the political process thus varies negatively with its size.

Equation (4) also indicates that an increase in group size reduces total lobbying outlays $L_1 + L_2$, since $\delta(L_1 + L_2)/\delta a > 0$ and $\delta a/\delta m < 0$. Interesting in this respect is the size of total lobbying outlays in comparison with the stakes of the individual rent seekers. Dividing total lobbying outlays in equation (4) by the average stake of the individual rent-seekers yields $(L_1 + L_2)(ma + nb)/(m + n) < 1$. Thus we have

Proposition 2:
If the politically allocated prize is a public good, the average stake of an individual is an upper bound to the total political outlays.

Since the average stake of the individual rent seekers is in all probability very small relative to the total value of the contested prize, proposition 2 implies marked underdissipation, and thus provides an explanation for Gordon Tullock's "puzzle of why the total expenditure on

---

[20] For a derivation see Ursprung (1990).
[21] In the case of a pure public good the two effects neutralize one another, i.e. the political outcome does not depend on the number of rent seekers.

seeking special favors in Washington, immense though it is, is still rather small compared to the value of the favors."[22]

In order to establish the upper bound to total political outlays, an individual's stakes in the outcome of the political contest will now be endogenized. Given X, m, and n, the stakes a and b depend only on the policy pronouncements θ_1 and θ_2 of the two candidates. The more polarized are the policy pronouncements, the larger are individuals' stakes in the outcome of the political contest. Endogenizing the individual stakes a and b thus entails endogenizing the policy pronouncements θ_1 and θ_2 in the manner detailed in section IIA.

The basic model consisting of the two nested Cournot-Nash games as depicted in Figure 5 gives rise to three types of equilibria, depending on the underlying parameter constellation: (1) convergent equilibria in the sense of Hotelling and Downs $(\theta_1 = \theta_2)$, (2) completely polarized equilibria $(\theta_1 = 1, \theta_2 = 0)$, and (3) partially polarized equilibria $(0 < \theta_2 < \theta_1 < 1)$. Figure 6 provides a graphic representation of the parameter constellations giving rise to the three types of equilibria for the special case where the two interest groups are of equal size (m=n). In this symmetric case the equilibrium policy pronouncements obviously satisfy the condition $\theta_1 = 1 - \theta_2$. Thus only the iso-θ_1 curves are depicted in Figure 6. Via these iso-θ_1 curves one can readily derive

Proposition 3:
Let m=n and let the political equilibrium be partially polarized. The policy pronouncements then satisfy $\theta_1 = 1 - \theta_2$ and the following comparative static results hold:
1. $\delta\theta_1/\delta Y_p < 0$ and $\delta\theta_1/\delta Y_a > 0$
2a.   *If* $Y_a > Y_p$: $\delta\theta_1/\delta\alpha < 0$, $\delta\theta_1/\delta X < 0$, and $\delta\theta_1/\delta m > 0$
2b.   *If* $Y_a < Y_p$: $\delta\theta_1/\delta\alpha > 0$, $\delta\theta_1/\delta X > 0$, and $\delta\theta_1/\delta m < 0$
2c.   *If* $Y_a = Y_p$: $\delta\theta_1/\delta\alpha = 0$, $\delta\theta_1/\delta X = 0$, and $\delta\theta_1/\delta m = 0$.

In the general case where m is not equal to n, the comparative-static properties are only slightly altered.[23] The main difference is that in the general case the equilibrium policy pronouncements of the two rival candidates are biased towards the policy sought by the smaller interest group. That is,

---

[22] Cf. Tullock (1988), p. 470-71. For a review of other causes of rent under-dissipation, see Hillman (1989), chapter 6.
[23] For a detailed analysis see Ursprung (1990).

Proposition 4:
If interest group 1 is larger (smaller) than interest group 2, i.e. if m > n (m < n), the equilibrium policy pronouncements of the candidates favor interest group 2 (interest group 1) in the sense that $\theta_1 < 1-\theta_2$ ($\theta_1 > 1-\theta_2$). There is only one exception to this rule, to wit maximum divergence.

The reason for the bias described in Proposition 4 is understood as follows. According to Proposition 1, a candidate's probability of election varies negatively with the number of individuals who provide him with political support. Increasing the number of individuals in a candidate's constituency thus, ceteris paribus, weakens his electoral prospects which he can only counter by converging toward his opponent's political stance.

In summary, the basic model has the following properties:
(1) The equilibrium depends exclusively on the stakes of the individual rent-seekers.
(2) If the prize in the political contest is a congestable public good, the political influence of the competing interest groups varies negatively with their respective number of members.
(3) The model demonstrates how underdissipation can be associated with public-good characteristics of politically contestable rents. In particular, the average stake of the individual rent seekers is an upper bound of the total rent-seeking expenditures.
(4) If the rival candidates seek rents on their own, this may drive a wedge between the candidates' policy pronouncements.

Personal corruption thus gives rise to a novel explanation of political polarization -- an explanation which is not based on the theory of voting but rather on the interest-group approach.

Properties (1) - (3) will reappear in the following section which expands the economic side of the basic model.

III. APPLICATIONS
The raison d'être of the economic side of a political-economy model is to identify the gainers and the losers from policy proposals, and to measure the respective gains and loses. In the basic model this task is performed by the utility functions of the individual rent seekers. The distributional effects of most policy proposals cannot however be portrayed via a single functional relationship. Political-economy investigations as a rule call for a more complex structure of the economic part of the model.

I now demonstrate how two aspects of international trade policy can be analyzed using the interest-group cum electoral-competition approach. For this purpose, the economic part of the basic model is extended while the political part is simplified by assuming that personal corruption can be neglected.

A. Voluntary Export Restraints and the New Protectionism

Protection in the developed countries has in recent years often taken the form of voluntary export restraints (VERs) rather than tariff restrictions. In this section the political motives underlying this shift in the choice of the means of protection are investigated. The exposition is based on Hillman and Ursprung (1988).

The economic part of the model portrays an import-competing industry producing a homogeneous good which is imperfectly substitutable in domestic consumption for imports. The domestic demand functions for the domestic good and imports are

$$(5a) \qquad\qquad P = a - bx + \tau P^*$$
$$(5b) \qquad\qquad P^* = a - bx^* + \tau P$$

where x and x^* denote quantities of domestically produced and foreign goods, and P and P^* are the respective domestic prices of the two goods; τ is a constant with values $0 \leq \tau < 1$ which measures substitutability in consumption between domestic and foreign goods.

The domestic industry consists of m identical profit-maximizing Cournot firms. Each firm makes a campaign contribution L_i to influence the outcome of an electoral contest between two candidates, one of whom is predisposed to a protectionist and the other to a liberal trade policy. Firms' per unit production costs are a constant c. A domestic firm chooses output and a campaign contribution to the protectionist candidate to maximize profits given by

$$(6) \qquad\qquad \pi_i = (P - c)x_i - L_i.$$

The foreign industry consists of n Cournot firms also seeking to influence domestic trade policy. Foreign firms have the same per unit cost of production as domestic firms. When a tariff is the means of domestic protection, a foreign firm chooses output and a campaign contribution to a liberal candidate to maximize profits given by

$$(7) \qquad\qquad \pi_i^* = (P^* - c - t)x_i^* - L_i^*,$$

where t is a specific tariff. Alternatively, with an export restraint V, foreign firms maximize profits given by

$$(8a) \qquad\qquad \pi_i^* = (P^* - c)x_i^* - L_i^*$$

subject to the coordinated market sharing condition

(8b) $x_i^* \leq V/n.$

The economic part of the model thus consists of the equations (5), (6) and either (7) or (8) depending on the trade-policy regime. These are the equations which replace the equations (1*) of the basic model.

The structural equations portraying the political relationships are the contest-success function (2), i.e. $w = \Sigma L_i/(\Sigma L_i + \Sigma L_i^*)$, where w now denotes the protectionist candidate's probability of election, and the conditions (3) of expected income maximization. These conditions reduce to the maximization of the probability of election since the coefficient of personal corruption is assumed to be zero. Hence we are in the world of section IC(ii).

Let the policy pronouncements of the candidates be denoted by t_p and t_l in the tariff regime and V_p and V_l in the VER regime, where p and l stand for "protectionist" and "liberal" trade policy. Consequently we have $t_p \geq t_l$ and $V_p \leq V_l$. For given trade policy pronouncements the stakes of the domestic and foreign firms correspond to the difference in the firms' profits associated with the rival candidates' policy pronouncements:

$$d\pi_i = \pi_i(t_p) - \pi_i(t_l) \quad \text{or} \quad d\pi_i = \pi_i(V_p) - \pi_i(V_l)$$
$$d\pi_i^* = \pi_i^*(t_l) - \pi_i^*(t_p) \quad \text{or} \quad d\pi_i^* = \pi_i^*(V_l) - \pi_i^*(V_p).$$

Using the properties of the basic model [cf. equation (4)] we can immediately infer that the candidates' political objectives depend on the firms' stakes via

(9) $w = d\pi_i/(d\pi_i + d\pi_i^*).$

Total rent dissipation also exclusively depends on the firms' stakes,

(10) $L_1 + L_2 = d\pi_i d\pi_i^*/(d\pi_i + d\pi_i^*)$

and is smaller than the average stake of the firms. Consider now the equilibrium policy pronouncements. According to (9), each candidate has a political interest in maximizing the gains which his constituency secures from his announced policy, relative to the gains that his political opponent's constituency secures from the opponent's policy. To be sure, an increase in protection proposed by the protectionist candidate increases π_i, but at the same time also increases π_i^*. One cannot therefore presume that the protectionist candidate will necessarily announce a prohibitive tariff or a prohibitive VER or that his rival will announce free trade. The equilibrium outcome depends on the trade policy regime.

Proposition 5:
The equilibrium platform combination when candidates make policy pronouncements in terms of tariffs is characterized by the protectionist candidate's announcing a prohibitive tariff and the liberal trade-policy candidate's announcing a policy of free trade. When the candidates choose levels of export restraints the political equilibrium is characterized by the announcement of a common policy.

A tariff regime thus gives rise to political polarization whereas a VER regime induces political concordance. Both equilibrium constellations turn out to be extreme, that is, there is either complete convergence or complete divergence of the rival candidates' policies. The protectionist candidate's trade policy pronouncement can be mellowed by assuming that, via the voters' influence, his probability of election ceteris paribus decreases as the proposed trade policy becomes more restrictive.[24] Complete convergence of the candidates' policy pronouncements can be avoided by introducing personal corruption.

The choice between an export restraint and a tariff is a choice between assigning rents to foreigners or revenue to the government. The specification of political optimization supposes that individual candidates for political office do not themselves value the revenue derived from any tariff which they might propose. However, while the candidates have limited scope for allocation of tariff revenue, their announced export-restraint policies directly influence the allocation of rents between domestic and foreign interests. The rent creation and rent allocation is reflected in campaign contributions received. Political preference in the choice of the means of protection is thus established. When candidates have the choice of making policy pronouncements in terms of export restraints or tariffs, both candidates choose export restraints.[25]

B. Direct Foreign Investments and International Trade Policy
The model can also be applied to an analysis of the relationship between the multinational firm and protection.[26] Direct foreign investment can take the form of acquisition of a foreign firm, or the establishment of

---

[24] Cf. Young and Magee (1986), equation (3).
[25] For elaboration, see Hillman and Ursprung (1988).
[26] Hillman and Ursprung (1990).

a new production facility abroad.[27] In both cases national enterprises are transformed into multinational firms.

Multinational activity can entail horizontal or vertical integration of production across national borders. Vertical integration appears quite unambivalently to give the multinational firm reason to favor liberal international trade policies, since protectionist policies applied to traded intermediate goods can but add to the firm's costs of internally provided inputs. The focus is accordingly on the relation between the horizontally integrated multinational firm.

To investigate this relation the model presented in the previous section is slightly modified. The model is extended to encompass two countries; the goods produced in the two countries are assumed to be homogenous; and the rival candidates are restricted to make their policy pronouncements in terms of tariffs. Multinational firms are introduced which service markets exclusively from the output of their local production facilities, whereas national firms - trade policies permitting - engage in international trade, servicing foreign markets with exports.

The structure of the economic part of the model is portrayed by the following equations:

$$P_1 = a - bQ$$
$$P_2 = \alpha - \beta X$$
$$\pi_i = (P_1 - c)q_i + (P_2 - c - t_2)x_i \qquad i=1,\ldots,m\text{-}s$$
$$\pi_j^* = (P_1 - c - t_1)q_j^* + (P_2 - c)x_j^* \qquad j=1,\ldots,n\text{-}s$$
$$\pi_k^m = (P_1 - c)q_k^m + (P_2 - c)x_k^m \qquad k=1,\ldots,s$$

P_1 and P_2 denote domestic prices in the two segmented national markets and Q and X are respective domestic sales in country 1 and country 2. π_i, π_j^* and π_k^m denote respectively the profits earned by national firms producing in country 1 and country 2, and by multinational firms producing in both countries. Total sales in each market are: $Q = \Sigma q_i + \Sigma q_j^* + \Sigma q_k^m$ and $X = \Sigma x_i + \Sigma x_j^* + \Sigma x_k^m$. There exist m-s national firms in country 1, n-s national firms in country 2, and s multinational firms.

The political part of the model consists of two electoral contests, one in each country. As in the previous model, the candidates' probabilities of electoral success are determined by the contest-success function (2). Rival candidates maximize their respective probabilities of election by announcing tariff policies.

---

[27] Acquisitions have been the dominant source of multinationalization in the United States. Construction of new "greenfield" production facilities have played a minor role. Cf. Graham and Krugman (1989), p. 17.

The structure of political support derives from profit-maximizing objectives and is straight forward. National firms support the protectionist candidate at home and the liberal trade-policy candidate abroad. Multinational enterprises, on the other hand, own local import-competing production facilities at home and abroad and have an interest in protection in both markets. Multinational firms thus provide political support only to the protectionist candidates. By way of a corollary to Proposition 5 we can immediately conclude that in each electoral contest the protectionist candidate announces a prohibitive tariff $t_i^p = t_i^a$, whereas the liberal trade-policy candidates announce free trade $t_i^l = 0$ ($i = 1, 2$). The probabilities of election associated with these policy pronouncements also follow directly from the basic model[28] and permit establishment of the expression for w_1, the protectionist candidate's probability of election in country 1,

$$w_1 = 1 - \frac{\pi_i(0, t_{2\alpha})}{\pi_i(t_{1\alpha}, t_{2\alpha})} = 1 - \left[\frac{m+1}{m+n-s+1}\right]^2 \qquad (11)$$

and in country 2,

$$w_2 = 1 - \left[\frac{n+1}{m+n-s+1}\right]^2. \qquad (12)$$

Hence the stakes of the individual rent seekers depend entirely on market structure, that is, on the number of production plants located in each economy and on the distribution of ownership of these plants between national firms and horizontally integrated multinational enterprises. Relations (11) and (12) permit an answer to the question: Does the multinationalization of the world economy exert a liberalizing or protectionist influence on international trade policy?

A change from national to multinational ownership of production facilities can take place either via foreign acquisition of a plant by a previously national enterprise, or by direct foreign investment that results in the establishment of an additional foreign plant. This implies in the first case an increase in s while m and n remain unchanged, whereas in the second case s and n are increased while m again remains unchanged. The respective comparative-static results are summarized in the following propositions.

---

[28] Needless to say, the rent-dissipation result [cf. Proposition 2] carries over as well.

Proposition 6:
A foreign acquisition by a national enterprise, or equivalently a merger between two national enterprises to create a multinational enterprise, exerts a liberalizing influence on trade policy by increasing the likelihood that political competition will yield a free-trade outcome in both economies.

Proposition 7:
The establishment of a multinational firm via direct foreign investment that results in a new plant abroad exerts a liberalizing influence on the determination of trade policy in the recipient economy where the new plant has been established and leaves unchanged the trade-policy equilibrium of political competition in the source economy.

Since horizontally integrated multinational enterprises have an interest in protecting domestic import-competing production in two markets, whereas national firms have an interest in free-trade at least in their export markets, multinational firms are intrinsically more protectionist than national firms. At a first glance, the above propositions might therefore appear to contain an element of paradox. The paradox, however, is resolved as soon as one observes that it is not the political coalition structure which determines the political economy outcome but the stakes of the individual rent seekers. The following example elucidates this point.

Consider a two-country world with nine firms, three horizontally integrated multinational firms and three national firms in each country. In a first Gedankenexperiment we merge two national firms to create a fourth multinational enterprise. How does this merger change the stakes of the individual firms? In the initial situation the three foreign firms lobbying for access to the domestic market stand to gain or lose a share of 1/9 of the domestic market. The domestic national firms and the multinational firms, on the other hand, try to exclude the foreign firms from the domestic market, and together stand to gain or lose a share of 1/3 of the domestic market. Since there are six firms in this protectionist coalition, the individual stakes amount to 1/18. After the merger has taken place there remain only eight firms, two of them being foreign nationals. These two firms are now competing for a share of 1/8 of the domestic market, the other six firms together for a share of 2/8 = 1/4 which yields an individual stake of 1/24. The individual stakes of the supporters of the free-trade candidate thus increase from 1/9 to 1/8 whereas the individual stakes of the supporters of the protectionist candidate decrease from 1/18 to 1/24. The merger thus changes the incentives to make political contributions to the advantage of the domestic free-trade candidate. Since the model is perfectly symmetric, the same conclusion applies to the foreign election contest.

In a second Gedankenexperiment again proceed from the initial situation. Now, however, let one previously national firm producing in country 1 set up a new production facility in country 2. To analyze the consequences of this kind of multinationalization, notice first that in country 1 there still exist six import-competing firms which confront three potential importers. The fact that four instead of formerly only three of these import-competing firms are now producing in both countries has no consequences for the political contest in country 1; the stakes of the individual firms do not change and neither does the political outcome. In country 2 however we have now seven import-competing firms, three national and four multinational ones. These seven firms confront two potential importers, the two national firms of country 1. The stakes of the potential importers remain the same; they are still competing for 1/9 of the market. The seven import-competing firms, on the other hand, compete together for a market share of 2/9 which yields individual stakes of 2/63. The individual stakes of the supporters of the protectionist candidate thus decrease from 1/18 to 2/63 whereas the incentives of the supporters of the free trade candidate remain unaltered. As a consequence, the free-trade outcome becomes more likely in country 2.

References

Alesina, A., 1988. "Credibility and Policy Convergence in a Two-Party System with Rational Voters," *American Economic Review*, 78, 796-805.

Appelbaum, E. and E. Katz, 1987. "Seeking Rents by Setting Rents: The Political Economy of Rent-Seeking," *Economic Journal*, 97, 685-699.

Austen-Smith, D., 1987. "Interest groups, campaign contributions, and probabilistic voting," *Public Choice*, 54, 123-139.

Baldwin, R.E., 1985. *The Political Economy of U.S. Import Policy*, Cambridge, MIT Press.

Bhagwati, J., 1987. "VERs, quid pro quo DFI, and VIEs: Political economy theoretic analysis," *International Economic Journal*, 1, 1-14.

Bernhardt, M.D. and D.E. Ingberman, 1985. "Candidate Reputations and the Incumbency Effect", *Journal of Public Economics*, 27, 47-67.

Bernholz, P., 1972. Grundlagen der Politischen *Ökonomie*, Band 1, Tübingen, Mohr.

Bernholz, P., 1975. *Grundlagen der Politischen Ökonomie*, Band 2, Tübingen, Mohr.

Black, P., 1948. "On the Rationale of Group Decision Making", *Journal of Political Economy*, 56, 23-34.

Buchanan, J.M., R.D. Tollison and G. Tullock, editors, 1980. *Toward a Theory of the Rent-Seeking Society*, College Station, Texas A&M Press.

Cowen T. and A. Glazer, 1990. "Rent-Seeking Promotes the Provision of Public Goods," Paper presented at the annual meeting of the *European Public Choice Society* in Meersburg, 18-21 April.

Davis, O.A., M.J. Hinich and P.C. Ordeshook, 1970. "An Expository Development of a Mathematical Model of the Electoral Process", *American Political Science Review*, 64, 426-448.

Downs, A., 1957. *An Economic Theory of Democracy*, New York, Harper and Row.

Enelow, J.M. and M.J. Hinich, 1984. *The Spatial Theory of Voting*, Cambridge, Cambridge University Press.

Graham, E.M. and P.R. Krugman, 1989. *Foreign Direct Investment in the United States*, Washington DC, Institute for International Economics.

Hillman, A.L., 1982. "Declining Industries and Political Support Protectionist Motives," *American Economic Review*, 72, 1180-87.

Hillman, A.L. and H.W. Ursprung, 1988. "Domestic Politics, Foreign Interests, and International Trade Policy," *American Economic Review*, 78, 729-445.

Hillman, A.L. and J. Riley, 1989. "Politically contestable rents and transfers", *Economics and Politics*, 1, 17-39.

Hillman, A.L. and H.W. Ursprung, 1990. "The Multinational Firm and International Trade Policy," Paper presented at the annual meeting of the *European Public Choice Society*.

Hinich, M., P. Ledyard and P. Ordeshook, 1972. "Nonvoting and the Existence of Equilibrium under Majority Rule", *Journal of Economic Theory*, 14, 144-153.

Hotelling, H., 1929. "Stability in Competition", *Economic Journal*, 39, 41-57.

Kramer, G.H. and A.J. Klevorick, 1974. "Existence of a Local Cooperative Equilibrium in a Class of Voting Games", *Review of Economic Studies*, 41, 539-547.

Magee, S.P., W.A. Brock, and L. Young, 1989. *Black Hole Tariffs and Endogenous Policy Theory: Political Economy in General Equilibrium*, Cambridge University Press.

Miller, N.R., 1977. "Logrolling, Vote Trading, and the Paradox of Voting: A Game Theoretical Overview", *Public Choice*, 30, 51-75.

Mueller, D.C., 1989. *Public Choice II*, Cambridge University Press.

Ordeshook, P.C., 1986. *Game Theory and Political Theory*, Cambridge, Cambridge University Press.

Peltzman, S., 1976. "Towards a More General Theory of Regulation," *Journal of Law and Economics*, 19, 211-40.

Renaud, P.S.A., 1988. *Applied Political Economic Modelling*, Berlin, Springer-Verlag.

Rogoff, K., 1990. "Equilibrium Political Budget Cycles", *American Economic Review*, 80, 21-36.

Rose-Ackermann, S., 1978. *Corruption*, New York, Academic Press.

Rowley, C.K., R.D. Tollison and G. Tullock, editors, 1988. *The Political-Economy of Rent-Seeking*, Boston, Kluwer Academic Publishers.

Stern, P. M., 1988. *The Best Congress Money Can Buy*, New York, Pantheon.

Stigler, G.J., 1971. "The Theory of Economic Regulation," *Bell Journal of Economics and Management Science*, 2, 137-146.

Tollison, R.D., 1982. "Rent-Seeking: A Survey," *Kyklos*, 35, 575-602.

Tullock, G., 1967. "The Welfare Costs of Tariff, Monopolies and Theft," *Western Economic Journal*, 5, 224-232.

Tullock, G., 1971. "The Paradox of Revolution," *Public Choice*, 11, 89-100.

Tullock, G., 1987. *Autocracy*, Boston, Kluwer Academic Publishers.

Tullock, G., 1988. "Future directions for rent-seeking research," in G.K. Rowley, R.D. Tollison and G. Tullock, editors, *The Political Economy of Rent Seeking*, Boston, Kluwer Academic Publishers, 465-480.

Ursprung, H.W., 1990. "Public Goods, Rent Dissipation, and Candidate Competition," *Economics and Politics*, 2, 115-132.

van Winden, F.A.A.M., 1983. *On the Interaction between the State and Private Sector*, Amsterdam, North-Holland.

Weck-Hannemann, H., 1990. "Protection under Direct Democracy", forthcoming in *Journal of Institutional and Theoretical Economics*.

Wittmann, D., 1983. "Candidate Motivation: A Synthesis of Alternative Theories", *American Political Science Review*, 77, 142-157.

Young, L. and S.P. Magee, 1986. "Endogenous Protection, Factor Returns, and Resource Allocation," *Review of Economic Studies*, 53, 407-419.

Chapter 2

VOLUNTARY COLLECTIVE ACTION

Joel M. Guttman

Economists and political scientists, in recent years, have joined sociologists and social psychologists in the study of voluntary collective action. To economists and like-minded political scientists (notably those allied to economists within the growing "public choice" field), the most problematic aspect of voluntary collective action is its very existence. The prediction of the conventional economic theory of the voluntary provision of collective goods is that such goods will not be voluntarily provided at anything approaching their socially optimal levels. This prediction of the conventional theory expresses what economists call the "free-rider problem", i.e., the problem that self-interested individuals will not find it worthwhile to contribute voluntarily either time or money to the provision of collective or "public" goods.[1] Such goods have the characteristic that individuals cannot be excluded from receiving their benefits, whether or not those individuals have contributed to their provision. Conventional thinking asserts that self-interested individuals, particularly but not exclusively in large groups, will prefer to "free ride" on the contributions of others, and thus the voluntary provision of public goods will be suboptimal from the standpoint of the group.

Economists have responded to the theoretically troubling, pervasive

---

[1] This statement should be made more precise. The conventional theory predicts that an individual will contribute to the provision of public goods only if the quantity provided by other individuals is less than the quantity that he individually demands (i.e., where his marginal rate of substitution between the public good and each private good equals the respective price ratios of the two goods). This individual demand is, generally, considerably less than the Pareto optimal quantity of the good, which is characterized by equality between the *sum* of all individuals' marginal rates of substitution, and the relevant price ratio.

existence of voluntary collective action in four ways. The first (and, perhaps, most common) response is to deny that voluntary collective action exists, or to go on refining the conventional theory as if it such collective action did not exist. Thus, experimental studies have been made which have found that voluntary provision of public goods decreases with increasing experience on the part of the experimental subjects [e.g., Kim and Walker (1984), and Isaac, McCue and Plott (1985)]. On the theoretical level, interesting elaborations of the conventional Cournot-Nash theory have been made by Warr (1982, 1983), Kemp (1984), and Bergstrom, Blume and Varian (1986). The fact that this theory predicts a grossly unrealistic degree of nonprovision of public goods has been largely ignored by these writers.

The second response of economists has been to devise ad-hoc explanations of voluntary collective action in specific settings. The "by-product solution" of Olson (1965) and the "asymmetry solution" of Stigler (1974) fall into this category. Both of these "solutions" introduce a degree of "privateness" into the public good, either by suggesting that the public good is produced jointly with a private good (Olson), or by arguing that public goods can take on highly varied characteristics appealing differently to the various individual beneficiaries of the good, and that such beneficiaries contribute in order to influence the character of the good (Stigler). These solutions implicitly concede the conventional prediction of highly suboptimal provision of pure public goods.

The third response has been to reject the underlying assumptions of the conventional Cournot-Nash theory (and, incidentally, of all neoclassical economic theory in its usual formulation). It is asserted that individuals are altruistic in some degree [e.g., Margolis (1982)], or that they are not completely rational. (One should note, in passing, that irrationality and altruism are not at all the same. The assertion that people are altruistic is an assertion about their "tastes", i.e, preference structures, of which economists have no *a priori* knowledge. The assertion that individuals are irrational, or "boundedly" rational, implies that -- *given* their tastes, which may be selfish -- individuals do not maximize their well-being. The latter assertion is more radically discordant with conventional economic theory.)

The fourth response is less radical, because it does not jettison the basic assumptions of economic theory, but only a more technical, specific assumption of the conventional Cournot-Nash theory. That assumption is that individuals take the contributions of their counterparts to the provision of the public good as *given*, and maximize their well-being given the contributions of their counterparts. As we shall see, the rejection of this assumption allows us to understand voluntary collective action, within the framework of conventional economic theory.

This paper surveys two, related approaches that have been suggested to explain voluntary collective action: the theory of strategic matching [Guttman (1978, 1987)], and the theory of reciprocity of Sugden (1984). These two theories make similar, but nevertheless subtly differing predictions about the voluntary provision of public goods. We then examine experimental evidence bearing on these two approaches.

I. COURNOT BEHAVIOR

Before describing the theories of strategic matching and reciprocity, it is well to begin by outlining the conventional economic theory of voluntary collective action, the Cournot model. This model, which was first popularized by Buchanan (1967) and Olson and Zeckhauser (1966), has become the standard approach to the economic analysis of voluntary collective action, despite the fact that it conflicts rather dramatically with the evidence. Both the theory of strategic matching and the reciprocity theory attempt to modify or replace the Cournot model with a theory more closely consistent with empirical evidence.

In the Cournot theory, each beneficiary of the public good allocates his personal resources between a (voluntary) contribution to the provision of the public good x and other, private consumption (symbolized by a single, composite private good y). The public good and the private good are treated symmetrically; both are continuously variable goods which can be purchased by each individual at a given price. If there were no other contributions to the provision of the public good, the individual (call him i) would allocate his resources between the public good and the private good just as he would allocate his resources between any two private goods. He would determine an individually optimal quantity of the public good, x^*, by equating his marginal rate of substitution between the two goods with the price ratio of the two goods. Now let another individual j also make a contribution to the provision of the public good. Let us assume, momentarily, that our individual i's demand for the public good is independent of his income. Then, according to the Cournot theory, i would take j's contribution x^j as given, and would now supply only the difference between his own, private demand x^* and the contribution of actor j. The reason is simply that, by the definition of a public good, nothing prevents individual i from benefiting from j's contribution, in effect taking a "free ride" on that contribution. Actor i thus may redirect those resources which (in the absence of j's contribution) he previously devoted to the purchase of the public good, to private good consumption. Since i's x^* is independent of actor j's contribution, this redirection of his resources is optimal for i. Thus, for the present, we immediately reach two conclusions: (a) the contribution of actor i will be reduced, dollar for dollar, with an increase in the contribution of another actor, and, therefore, (b) the total level of contributions is unaffected by the contribution of actor j. These two conclusions are correct, strictly speaking, only so long as actor i's contribution remains positive. If actor j contributed so much as to make actor i's contribution zero, then further increases in x^j would indeed increase the quantity of the public good (assuming, of course, that there are no other contributors).

The reader may well ask, in view of conclusion (b), why should actor j contribute at all, if he cannot affect the quantity of the public good? The answer is that actor j does not, according to the Cournot theory, take into account the reduction in actor i's contribution that will be induced by his making a contribution. Actor j is assumed to take the contribution of all other actors as given, and to maximize his utility given the contributions of other actors.

A standard criticism of this assumption, particularly in the literature on the oligopoly problem (in which the Cournot model was first formulated), is that actor j can learn from his experience that the contributions of other actors are not, in fact, invariant to his own contribution. The standard answer of game theorists to this criticism is that we are analyzing a one-shot interaction or "game", and therefore there is no such "experience" from which to learn. This of course is a purely formalistic answer, since the social processes in which we are interested usually are not, in fact, one-shot games. The game theorist then would answer, "fine, then let us model the problem as a repeated game." Unfortunately, the literature on repeated games has offered us a rather unhelpful pair of predictions. If the public goods contributions "game" is repeated a finite number of rounds, the theory predicts the same result as that which would have obtained in the one-shot game. On the other hand, if the game is repeated infinitely (or finitely with a sufficiently uncertain endpoint), the result is that anything can occur (the so-called "Folk Theorem"). Contributions can be those of the Cournot equilibrium or they can be optimal from the viewpoint of the group (Pareto optimal), or anything in between. Thus theorists have been led to develop models which retain the formal structure of the one-shot game but nevertheless lead to outcomes that are preferable from the standpoint of the group, in an effort to explain observed voluntary collective action.

Let us return to the Cournot model. A further implication of the model, under the assumptions we made above, is that the total provision of the collective good is unaffected by the size of the group. This results from the fact that no individual contributes more than the amount required to make the total quantity of the good equal to what he would have purchased in isolation, x^*. If, as we assumed, x^* is independent of the individual's income, the addition of any number of identical beneficiaries of the good (and contributors to its provision) will not change x* and the quantity of the good will remain x* regardless of the number of contributors.

If we relax the assumption that each individual's demand is independent of his income, the conclusions reached above change somewhat. If x is a normal good, the individual's demand will increase when his income increases. Now, the contributions of other actors are, in effect, gifts in kind made to each individual who benefits from those contributions, and thus effectively increase his "full" income (the term "full income" is due to Becker, 1974). Thus, when individual j increases his contribution from zero to some positive quantity, individual i's full income increases, and so does his demand for the public good. This keeps i from decreasing his contribution dollar-for-dollar with the increase in j's contribution, in contrast to conclusion (a) above. But, unless i's income elasticity of demand for the good is very much higher than unity, he will nevertheless reduce his contribution -- albeit not dollar-for-dollar -- when j increases his contribution. Under these conditions, individual j can indeed increase the quantity of the public good (in contrast to conclusion (b) above), but it will cost him more than a dollar to increase the quantity of the good by one dollar. Of course, according to the assumptions of the Cournot model, j is unaware of this fact, and instead takes i's contribution as given, implying that he can always purchase a dollar's worth of the public good for a dollar. Moreover, when the public good is a normal good, increases in group size will increase the quantity of the good, since additional beneficiaries, who also make contributions to the provision of the good in equilibrium, increase the full incomes of the incumbent members and thus increase their demands for the good. Thus x* increases with group size, and with this increase in x*, the quantity provided of the good increases as well. This is in contrast to the third conclusion of the Cournot model under zero income effects, noted above. However, it is easily shown that, for reasonable values of the income elasticity of demand for the public good, the quantity of the public good becomes essentially constant at small group sizes, e.g., 20 individuals.

II. NON-NASH MODELS

The failure of the Cournot model to predict -- even with reasonable income effects -- existing levels of the voluntary provision of public goods led to the development of "non-Nash" or "non-Cournot" models of voluntary collective action. The common feature of these models is that actors are not assumed to take each other's contributions as given when determining their own contributions. Here we must distinguish between two types of models. The first group of non-Nash models assume, as in the Cournot-Nash model, that the only decision variable of the individuals is their contribution to the provision of the public good (this, of course, determines also their private good consumption through the familiar budget constraint). The deviation from the Cournot model is only that individuals now form non-zero "conjectural variations" regarding the responses of their fellow actors to changes in their contribution levels. These conjectural variations may be "consistent" -- i.e., they may equal the actual reaction rates arising from the other actors' maximizing behavior -- or they may "inconsistent". Given these conjectural variations, the individuals choose their optimal contributions. This type of interaction was called by Guttman and Miller (1983) a "passive" interaction. It has been studied primarily by Cornes and Sandler in a series of papers (1983, 1984). The second group of models assumes that individuals, in addition to their choice of contributions levels, also choose *reaction rates* which determine how they will react to changes in the contributions of other actors. These reaction rates are correctly perceived by other individuals and become their (consistent) "conjectural variations". This type of interaction, called by Guttman and Miller (1983) an "active" interaction, is analyzed in the theory of strategic matching.

Models of "passive" interactions have proved disappointing for two reasons. First, it is easily shown that *consistent* conjectural variations (again, under reasonable assumptions regarding the income elasticity of demand for public goods) are negative. Moreover, as group size increases, each individual's consistent conjectural variation, which (correctly) predicts the combined reaction of all other individuals to a change in his own contribution, approaches -1. A rational actor, with a conjectural variation of -1, would not contribute unless all other contribution levels are zero, since any increase in his contribution above zero would only lead other actors to reduce their combined contributions by the same amount as he increased his contribution. Thus the introduction of passively determined, consistent conjectural variations has only aggravated the problem of explaining voluntary collective action [see, e.g., Sugden (1982)]. The second difficulty with this approach is that, as formulated, the conjectural variations (even if they are consistent) are purely *ad hoc*. Since the "game" being analyzed is one-shot, actors have no opportunity to observe other actors' reactions, and, indeed, such reactions are impossible, since there is no second round in which they can take place. In such a world, the "naive" Cournot assumption seems more reasonable than the "consistent" conjectures predicted by the passive interactions literature.

Given these difficulties with models of "passive" interactions, we now turn to a model of *active* interactions.

III. STRATEGIC MATCHING

In the theory of strategic matching, contributions to the provision of the public good are chosen only indirectly, as the outcome of a two-stage game. In the first stage, actors choose "matching rates", which can be positive or negative. These matching rates are undertakings to match other actors' "flat" contributions, which are determined in the second stage of the game. Each individual's final contribution is his flat contribution, plus the product of the vector of his matching rates offered to each of his fellows, times the vector of the flat contributions chosen by his fellows. The equilibrium in each stage of the game is a Nash non-cooperative equilibrium: each actor's matching rate is his best response to the matching rates of his fellows, and likewise for his flat contribution. The matching rates are chosen by predicting the equilibrium of the second stage, when the flat contributions are chosen, and by choosing a vector of matching rates that maximizes the individual's utility, given the other actors' matching rates and given the outcome of the second stage which will result from any choice of matching rates by the individual in question. In the case of identical actors, the vector of matching rates chosen by each individual is assumed to be a scalar, i.e., one matching rate offered to all other actors.

This type of non-Nash model is immune to the two criticisms of the passive interactions models, made in the preceding subsection. First, the "reaction rates" that are rationally chosen in a (non-cooperative) equilibrium of the game are positive, and in fact lead to a group-optimal provision of the public good. Thus the "active" interactions theory succeeds in predicting voluntary collective action. Second, the conjectural reactions are no longer *ad hoc*, but are based on the "matching rates" chosen in the first stage of the game. These matching rates are then implemented after the "flat contributions" are chosen in the second stage of the game. Thus the conjectural variations in the theory of strategic matching are not merely hypothetical conjectures by an actor of what would happen if he were to change his contribution (this conjectured response cannot occur in the one-shot game of the passive interactions approach), but rather equal the actual matching that occurs after the flat contributions are chosen.

The individual's motive for choosing positive matching rates is to provide an incentive to his fellows to contribute toward the provision of the public good. "Matching behavior" occurs, for example, in philanthropic fundraising when a major contributor offers to match the contributions that the "receiving" institution raises from other sources. Another example of matching behavior is the use of matching grants by the Federal government in the United States, in contributing to the funding of public investments by state governments that have appreciable external effects on other states (e.g., interstate highway investments).

In the case of identical actors [Guttman (1978, 1987)], the equilibrium matching rate is unity (this equilibrium *exists* whether or not there are income effects, but its *uniqueness* is guaranteed only when such effects are absent). In the case of non-identical actors [Guttman (1984)], the equilibrium matching rates equal the ratios of the marginal benefits of the public good of the relevant actors. As each individual's marginal benefit increases relative to that of his fellow actor, so does his matching rate. In either case, these matching rates effectively set up "Lindahl prices" for each actor -- i.e., effective prices (which take account of the reactions of the other actors) which lead to a group-optimal provision of the public good. For example, with two identical actors, the equilibrium matching rates of unity imply effective prices of 1/2 times the price of acquiring the public good. This is because each actor, by increasing his flat contribution by one dollar, purchases two dollars' worth of the public good, once the reaction of his fellow is taken into account.

IV. RECIPROCITY

Sugden (1984) has proposed an alternative model which also produces a kind of "matching". In his model, individuals' motives in matching each other's contributions are not strategic but ethical. Sugden suggests that individuals are indeed egoistic, but wish to maximize their utility under a constraint that they meet their moral "obligations". These obligations are met only if they contribute to the provision of public goods to an extent commensurate with the contributions of other actors.

More specifically, Sugden defines the "obligation" of any individual as the *minimum* of: (a) the (equal) contribution of "effort" toward the provision of the public good required of each individual for Pareto optimal provision of the good, and (b) the maximum of the "effort" contributions of the other members of the group, if such contributions are less than those required by Pareto optimality. Thus, even if every individual in the group is meeting his obligations, the group can fall short of Pareto optimal provision of the public good, since it is enough (from each individual's viewpoint of his obligation) to contribute at least as much as everyone else in the group contributes. But there is also the possibility that the group will achieve Pareto optimal provision of the public good, in which case each individual is meeting his obligation by contributing the amount of "effort" required by (a) above. (It should be noted in passing, that Sugden uses the term "effort" rather than simple monetary or monetary-equivalent contributions, in order to allow for "contributions" to be understood in *relative*, rather than absolute terms. For example, "equal effort" may mean equal contributions relative to income.)

Sugden defines an equilibrium as a vector of effort contributions such that each individual is making the smallest effort contribution consistent with his obligations, given the contributions of the other actors. He proves, given his broad restrictions on the production function of the public good and on the utility functions of the individuals, that such an equilibrium exists. Not surprisingly, every such equilibrium is characterized either by Pareto optimality or by undersupply of the public good. Thus Sugden succeeds in proving the *existence* of a Pareto optimal equilibrium, but not its uniqueness. (The model of strategic matching, in contrast, yields a unique Pareto optimal equilibrium with identical actors and zero income effects, as noted above.)

Sugden also obtains a result akin to matching behavior with regard to the *interaction* of the individuals' contributions. Specifically, if initially two individuals are making equal effort contributions, and individual 1 increases his contribution, then individual 2 will either increase his contribution or keep it constant, but will not decrease his contribution. While this behavior is similar to matching behavior -- albeit in a "weak" sense (individual 2, according to the model, may also keep his contribution constant) -- it is limited to the case in which the two individuals initially made equal effort contributions. In the case in which actor 1's contribution initially exceeded that of actor 2, Sugden's model predicts that individual 2 will not change his contribution in response to a change in 1's contribution. Finally, if individual 1's contribution *after* he increased his contribution is less than what individual 2 contributed *initially*, then individual 2 may respond either by *decreasing* his contribution or by keeping it constant. These latter two cases obviously conflict with the prediction of matching behavior made by the model of strategic matching.

If we combine this result of Sugden with still another result, we obtain an even sharper contrast between the predictions of the two models. Sugden's Result 3 states that, the greater an individual's marginal benefit from the public good (his marginal utility of the good relative to the marginal disutility of effort), the more he will contribute to the provision of the good. This result, by itself, is completely consistent with the model of strategic matching. But if we combine Results 3 and 4, we are led to expect that individuals with a relatively large demands for the public good will tend to respond to increases in the contributions of their fellow actors by decreasing their own contributions, while individuals with relatively small demands will tend not to respond at all. This is because an individual with a relatively large demand for the public good will tend (in interaction with a fellow actor with more average preferences) to fall into the third case discussed at the end of the previous paragraph, while an individual with a relatively small demand will tend to fall into the second case discussed above. In contrast, the theory of strategic matching predicts that individuals with relatively large demands for the public good will tend to choose relatively large matching rates.

We may note an additional difference between the two theories, of a methodological nature. The theory of strategic matching makes no special assumptions regarding individuals' tastes. The individuals assumed by that theory are no different from those usually assumed by economic theory. Sugden makes a much bolder, one might say "sociological" assumption about people's tastes, which is equivalent to assuming that they have an inflexible, "inelastic" demand to meet their "obligations". While we may grant that "morality" (roughly as Sugden defines the term) is indeed a good demanded by individuals, it seems more realistic to assume that most people want to be moral only if it is not too expensive, just as they relate to any other good. Thus the kind of behavior discussed by Sugden would seem to operate only when the stakes are relatively low, that is, when being "moral" is relatively cheap. For example, in large groups, when the contribution demanded from each individual is relatively small, being moral is cheap, and Sugden's theory will be relatively applicable. Precisely in large groups, strategic matching would presumably be less extensive. The information assumed by the theory of strategic matching to be possessed by each individual (which includes information on other individual's matching rates) would become less perfect in large groups, since this information is presumably revealed only by experimenting with one's contribution and observing others' responses. Such "experiments" would be difficult in the relatively noisy environment of large groups of individuals simultaneously changing their contributions.

V. A SURVEY OF THE EXPERIMENTAL EVIDENCE

We now look briefly at the experimental evidence bearing on the two theories, strategic matching and "reciprocity". In the previous section, we noted a limited similarity between the predictions of the two theories, and also noted some important differences between their predictions. We need not survey the vast experimental literature on public goods and on the Prisoner's Dilemma, since nearly all of this literature examines only the *levels* of cooperation or (in the case of the experimental public goods literature) of contributions to the provision of a public good. Since both theories are consistent with the fairly high levels of cooperation usually observed, the bulk of this literature cannot discriminate between the two theories.

The evidence that can discriminate between the two theories concerns the interaction between the contribution levels of different actors in a setting in which they may contribute private resources to the provision of a public good. The direction of the interaction usually obtained is positive: if actor

1 increases his contribution, actor 2 is likely to respond by increasing his own contribution. This result was obtained in a number of different experimental settings:

1. Social psychologists have noted, in a series of studies, the phenomenon that the "helping" behavior of one individual leads other individuals to help in response. For example, an experimental stooge contributes money to a Salvation Army appeal in a department store, and the response of other, passing shoppers is noted, in comparison to a control situation in which no such helping behavior is displayed by a stooge. The result obtained in such situations is that helping behavior stimulates other individuals to help as well (Bryan and Test, 1967). Many, if not all such settings can be analyzed as situations in which a public good is provided. In the example of the Salvation Army appeal, the public good is the welfare of the recipients of the charity.

2. Lave (1965), in a Prisoner's Dilemma experiment, allowed human subjects to play together with a "robot" who played a pre-programmed behavioral pattern (the subjects, of course, thought they were playing with a human subject). One such pattern was the "Khruschev" pattern, which consisted of generally non-cooperative play interspersed with random lapses of cooperative moves. The response of the human subjects was to follow the cooperative moves of the robot with cooperative play, until it became apparent that these cooperative lapses were truly random. Following this realization, the subjects ceased to "match" the robot's cooperative play. Hoggatt (1967, 1969) performed similar, "robotized" experiments in an oligopoly setting, and obtained similar results. The similarity between the Prisoner's Dilemma, the oligopoly problem, and the free-rider problem is well-known.

3. Emshoff and Ackoff (1970) performed Prisoner's Dilemma experiments without robots, and examined which of several models of interactive behavior best fit the behavior of the experimental subjects over time . The best-performing model was "tit-for-tat", which is essentially the same as the behavior predicted by the strategic matching and reciprocity theories.

4. I have performed experiments in which subjects could contribute part of a $5 or $7 endowment to the provision of a public good, which was simply called a "common pool". The payoff of the subjects in a given round of the game was an increasing, concave function of the size of the common pool, minus their own contribution to the pool, plus their endowment. The payoff from participating in the experiment was the average of the payoffs obtained in all the rounds of the game. The exact number of rounds was unknown to the subjects in advance. The payoff functions were constructed so that the Cournot equilibrium of total

contributions (i.e., the sum of contributions which makes the individual's marginal net payoff of contributing equal to zero, taking the other players' contributions as given) was $9. The number of players in any game varied from 2 to 6.

The "matching rates" of the players were estimated by two methods. The first method was to isolate changes in the contribution of an actor which did not follow changes in the previous round in the contribution of any other actor, and which were not accompanied, in the same round, by changes in the contributions of other actors. Such changes were called "signals", since they are best interpreted as autonomous changes in a contribution level which may have been intended to "test" the response of other actors. The changes in the contributions of the other actors in the following round were then examined, and if such changes occurred, they were interpreted as responses to the signal of the previous round (recall that, by definition, there was no more than one signal in any given round). The ratio of such a response to the signal was taken as an estimate of a matching rate. The second method was to run regressions, in which the change in the contribution of an actor in round t was regressed on the changes in the contributions in previous rounds.[2] By both methods, the result was that the matching rates were usually positive or zero (see Guttman, 1986). The frequency of positive matching rates was greater in the smaller group sizes.

These results, from four rather different types of evidence, strongly reject the Cournot model, in which reaction rates are predicted as being negative (except in the rare cases of super-luxury public goods). Do they support, to the same extent, the strategic matching model and the reciprocity model? Both models are consistent with positive reaction rates. But there are two points to be noted, which tend to support the strategic matching model more strongly than the reciprocity model. First, the reciprocity model predicts a positive reaction by one individual to an increase in another individual's contribution only in the special case in which their contributions initially were equal. But we observe, in these four sets of evidence, a general tendency to positive reactions, irrespective of the initial levels of contributions. Second, the decreasing frequency of

---

[2] More precisely, the regressors were the residuals between the observed changes in the other actors' contributions and predicted values of these changes, based on the lagged changes in the contributions of the counterparts of these "other actors" in previous rounds of the game. This use of residuals rather than the observed changes themselves was motivated by the fact that only "autonomous", and not "induced" changes in the contributions of the other actors will be matched, according to the matching theory.

positive reaction rates as group size increases is difficult to explain in terms of the reciprocity model, but easily explained by the strategic matching model once extended to allow for imperfect information.

Returning to the first point, we noted (in the previous section), that the reciprocity model would lead us to expect the positive matching rates to occur most frequently when the individual demands for the public good of the two individuals (the "actor" and the "reactor") are equal, and that the reaction rates should tend to be negative when the demand of the "actor" was less than that of the "reactor". The theory of strategic matching, in contrast, predicts relatively large, positive matching rates precisely when the reactor's relative demand for the public good is large. The results of my experiments clearly support the model of strategic matching on this point. In one set of experiments, the payoff functions of the players differed from each other. There were actors with a "high" (total and marginal) payoff, and individuals with a "low" payoff -- half of the high payoff. In the middle of the experiments, the payoff functions were switched between the actors. The players with "high" payoff functions then received "low" payoff functions, and vice-versa. The payoff functions of all actors were common knowledge to the players. According to the theory of strategic matching, the matching rates should be positively correlated with the relative marginal payoff of the reacting player (i.e., relative to the marginal payoff of the player whose change in contribution is being matched). This prediction was supported by most of the regression results. Of 11 significant changes in matching rates, 8 were in the direction predicted by the theory of strategic matching, while 3 were in the opposite direction (that implied by the reciprocity theory).

VI. CONCLUDING REMARKS

The experimental evidence is not entirely consistent with the reciprocity theory, while it is very consistent with the theory of strategic matching. We should note, however, that matching theory is expected to perform best in small groups -- precisely those forming the basis for the laboratory experiments surveyed here.[3] It may be, as we noted in Section 2, that strategic motives are dominant in small groups, while the semi-altruistic motive of meeting one's "obligations" is dominant in large groups when the

---

[3] The studies of Bryan and Test (1967) and others of a similar nature were not laboratory experiments and, in fact, are consistent with the reciprocity theory, because the initial contributions levels of the "actor" and "reactor", before the actor's -- the stooge's -- act of "helping", were both zero.

cost of meeting one's obligations is sufficiently small.[4] Thus the two theories may complement each other, providing an explanation of voluntary collective action in both large and small groups.

References

Bergstrom, T., Blume, L., and Varian, H., 1986. "On the private provision of public goods," *Journal of Public Economics*, 29, 25-49.

Bryan, J.H. and Test, M.A., 1967. "Models and helping: naturalistic studies in aiding behavior", *Journal of Personality and Social Psychology*, 6, 400-7.

Buchanan, J.M., 1967. "Conflict and cooperation in public goods interaction", *Western Economic Journal*, 5, 109-21.

Cornes, R., and Sandler, T., 1983. "On commons and tragedies", *American Economic Review*, 73, 787-92.

Cornes, R. and Sandler, T., 1984. "The theory of public goods: non-Nash behavior", *Journal of Public Economics*, 18, 367-79.

Emshoff, J.R. and Ackoff, R.L., 1970. "Explanatory models of interactive choice behavior", *Journal of Conflict Resolution*, 14, 77-89.

Guttman, J.M., 1978. "Understanding collective action: matching behavior," *American Economic Association Papers and Proceedings*, 68, 251-5.

Guttman, J. M., 1986. "Matching behavior and collective action: some experimental evidence", *Journal of Economic Behavior and Organization*, 7, 171-98.

Guttman, J. M., 1987. "A non-Cournot model of voluntary collective action", *Economica*, 54, 1-19.

Guttman, J.M. and Miller, M., 1983. "Endogenous conjectural variations in oligopoly", *Journal of Economic Behavior and Organization*, 4, 249-64.

Hoggatt, A.C., 1967. "Measuring behavior in quantity variation duopoly games," *Behavioral Science*, 12, 109-21.

Hoggatt, A.C., 1969. "Response of paid student subjects to differential behavior of robots in bifurcated duopoly games", *Review of Economic Studies*, 36, 417-32.

Isaac, R.M., McCue, K.F., and Plott, C.R., 1985. "Public goods provision in an experimental environment", *Journal of Public Economics*, 26, 51-74.

---

[4] Sugden, in a 1985 personal communication to the author, suggested this hypothesis.

Kemp, M., 1984. "A note on the theory of international transfers", *Economics Letters*, 14, 259-262.

Kim, O., and Walker, M., 1984. "The free-rider problem: experimental evidence", *Public Choice*, 43, 3-24.

Lave, L.B., 1965. "Factors affecting cooperation in the Prisoner's Dilemma", *Behavioral Science*, 10, 26-35.

Margolis, H., 1982. *Selfishness, Altruism, and Rationality*, Cambridge: Cambridge University Press.

Olson, M., 1965. *The Logic of Collective Action*, Cambridge, Mass.: Harvard University Press.

Olson, M., and Zeckhauser, R., 1966. "An economic theory of alliances", *Review of Economics and Statistics*, 48, 266-79.

Stigler, G.J., 1974. "Free riders and collective action: An appendix to theories of economic regulation", *Bell Journal of Economics and Management Science*, 5, 359-65.

Sugden, R., 1982. "On the economics of philanthropy", *Economic Journal*, 92, 341-50.

Sugden, R., 1984. "Reciprocity: The supply of public goods through voluntary contributions", *Economic Journal*, 94, 772-87.

Sugden, R., 1985. Personal communication to the author.

Warr, P., 1982. "Pareto optimal redistribution and private charity", *Journal of Public Economics*, 19, 131-138.

Warr, P., 1983. "The private provision of a public good is independent of the distribution of income", *Economics Letters*, 13, 207-211.

Chapter 3

FACTOR INCOME TAXATION
IN A REPRESENTATIVE DEMOCRACY

Wolfgang Mayer and Jun Li

During the past decade, economists have paid increasing attention to the political process of redistributing income. The public finance literature, led by Romer (1975), Roberts (1977), Aumann and Kurz (1977, 1978), and Peck (1988), focuses primarily on the endogenous formation of linear income tax schedules. In addition, Meltzer and Richard (1981, 1985) offer an endogenous theory of government size, as measured by the share of income redistributed, and a theory of income redistribution through negative income taxes or transfers in kind. International economists, in an even more voluminous literature as surveyed by Baldwin (1984), Hillman (1989), and Nelson (1986), have looked at the formation of trade policies through the political process.

The purpose of this paper is to employ a political economy model to explain differences in factor tax rates and to show how the political choice of factor taxes depends on the characteristics of the population, the economy's production structure, and the specific political process through which social choices are made.[1] The voters of this economy decide on both the absolute level of taxes to pay for a public good and the way different factors are taxed. The voters' preferences for tax policies are, however, not exogenously given, as generally assumed in the voting literature,[2] but are derived from their characteristics as consumers and factor owners.

---

[1] Writing on democratically chosen linear income tax schedules emphasizes the form of the tax schedules which come about without discussing whether different factors are going to be taxed at the same or different rates. Meltzer and Richard (1985) examine in a two-good economy how goods are taxed and in what fractions they are redistributed, but they do not go into the issue of differential factor taxation, as labor is the only factor of production.

[2] See Ordeshook (1986).

Specifically, we allow people to differ with respect to initial factor ownerships, preferences for work, and tastes for public good consumption.[3] How such characteristics of people translate into policy preferences also depends on the economy's structure, such as the degree of factor mobility, the variability of factor supplies, the existence of externalities, and the level of competitiveness. Once each person's policy preferences are determined, they represent the inputs for formulating social choices. In general, society's choices are not determinate unless one specifies the political institutions and rules under which they are made. We assume that tax policies are set by a representative of the people who is elected through majority voting in a two-candidate election and that all voters believe that the policy platform of the winning candidate will be enacted.

I. THE ISSUES

Our analysis highlights three issues. First, we show how each person's preferences for tax policies and their "ideal" points in particular are shaped by the underlying characterization of people in terms of factor ownership, preferences for work, and tastes for public goods, and by the specification of the economy in which they are acting. Specifically, we discuss this in a small, open economy model under alternative assumptions about the variability of labor supply and the economy's production pattern.

A second issue addressed by the paper is whether knowledge of peoples' characteristics can assist us in determining the tax policy position which maximizes a candidate's probability of election. As was shown by Black (1958), a majority rule equilibrium exists if people vote on one issue only and their preferences are single peaked. When there are more issues involved, a candidate can choose a position which will definitely win only under very special circumstances, such as when the voters' ideal points are in a perfectly symmetric relationship to each other, as shown by Plott (1967), or when two issues are related to each other through a budget constraint, as discussed by McCubbins and Schwartz (1985). We add another restrictive case of using the median-voter result in a multi-issue situation, namely when the voter's ideal position on a variety of issues is linearly related to just one of his characteristics. Since this condition is quite restrictive, we also address the issue of policy choice when there are multiple issues and a median voter equilibrium does not exist. It is in these situations that the specification of the social choice process becomes critical. We employ a two-candidate election which can be described as a

---

[3]Hence, consumer characterizations are more general than in Mayer (1984) where people differ with respect to factor ownership and in Meltzer and Richards (1985) where they differ with respect to labor productivity.

two-person, zero-sum game. Making use of the concept of 'uncovered set', as dealt with by McKelvey (1986), one can gain a general idea of the type of platform which will be pronounced by the winning candidate. The uncovered set, of course, crucially depends on the characteristics of the population and how these characteristics are distributed. Furthermore, the location of the uncovered set is sensitive to eligibility criteria for voting. Eliminating certain classes of factor owners, say young people or migrants with no or very little land ownership, from the voting process will lead to a definite repositioning of the set of possible outcomes in a two-candidate election.

Finally, we raise the issue of consistency between the usually made assumptions about the behavior of economic agents and their preferences in political decisions. Our results, as well as those of much of the literature on majority voting, crucially hinge on the assumptions that with one issue political preferences are single peaked and with many issues utility functions, with political choices as arguments, are quasiconcave. It is shown that the usual assumptions made by economists, namely that preferences with respect to commodities are quasiconcave, do not eliminate the possibility that people have preferences with respect to political issues which are not single peaked and quasiconcave. Consequently, the restrictiveness of majority voting results must be kept in mind.

II. THE MODEL
A. The Political Process

Consider a country in which firms use land and labor as inputs in the production of commodities. There are I people who supply these factors of production in varying combinations to the market and receive factor incomes in return. Only $G < I$ of the people are eligible voters, as residency requirements and age restrictions eliminate certain factor owners from participation in the election process. The eligible voters are faced with the task of determining how much should be spent on public goods and at what rate land and labor income recipients be taxed. Tax revenues can be used for expenditure on the public good, as well as income redistribution purposes. Voters are assumed to make their choice of a tax program by electing a representative who is expected to implement the tax program as promised during the election.

Two candidates or two political parties compete for votes. Each is assumed to know the characteristics of voters, and each candidate adopts a position which maximizes the expectation of election. The candidate with the majority of votes wins the election.

B. Characteristics of voters

In the economy under consideration, land and labor are the only factors of production, and two private goods, leisure, and a public good are commodities consumed. Each person is characterized by three features: land ownership, preferences for leisure, and preferences for public goods expenditure. People differ from each other with respect to one or more of these features.

A person's utility (U^i) is assumed to depend on income available for the acquisition of private goods (y^i), leisure (H^i), and the amount of public goods provided (S), where $i = 1, ..,I$ refers to the ith person. Specifically, we postulate the utility function:[4]

(1) $U^i = y^i + a^i g(H^i) + b^i v(S)$,

where $g' > 0$, $v' > 0$, $g'' < 0$, and $v'' < 0$ for $H^i \leq Z$. The functions $g(.)$ and $v(.)$ are the same for every person, but the values of $a^i > 0$ and $b^i > 0$ are specific to individual i.

The ith person earns income from the supply of land T^i and labor L^i. While each person's land ownership is fixed, his supply of labor is chosen to maximize utility, where

(2) $L^i = Z - H^i$.

Given the ith person's supply of land and labor, his expenditures on private goods are equal to his factor income net of factor taxes:

(3) $y^i = w(1 - t_L)L^i + r(1 - t_r)T^i$,

where w and r are the returns on labor and land respectively, and $t_L \leq 1$ and $t_r \leq 1$ are the corresponding tax rates. Substituting (2) and (3) in (1) and maximizing the obtained utility expression with respect to L^i yields the first-order conditions:

(4) $g'(Z - L^i) = w(1 - t_L)/a^i$.

Since $g'' < 0$, one can see that the ith person's supply of labor is directly related to the wage rate, and inversely to the wage tax and the preference parameter for leisure. Importantly, if net compensation, $w(1 - t_L)$, becomes

---

[4]The specification in (1) implies that a person's labor supply is independent of his income. Hence individual labor supplies differ only because of differences in preferences for work and not because of differences in land ownership.

zero, no labor is supplied.

C. The Economy

This is a small economy, which takes world prices of commodities as given. Its production side is described by a two-industry, two-factor model, in which one factor, labor, is variable in supply, while the other factor, land, is fixed. Each industry employs both factors and production functions are homogeneous of degree one in inputs. The commodities are produced in competitive industries, there are no externalities or distortions, and there is full factor mobility between industries, but complete immobility between countries. Given these assumptions, firms of this country produce either two (incomplete specialization) or just one (complete specialization) commodity; the form of specialization depends on relative factor supplies and world prices of commodities. If specialization is incomplete, factor returns depend on world prices only and are independent of factor supplies,

$$(5) \qquad w = w(p_i, p_j) \qquad \text{and} \qquad r = r(p_i, p_j),$$

where p_i and p_j refer to the prices of two alternative commodities currently produced by the country. Under complete specialization, on the other hand, factor prices depend on both world commodity prices and domestic factor supplies:

$$(6) \qquad w = p_j F_{Lj}(L,T) \qquad \text{and} \qquad r = p_j F_{Tj}(L,T),$$

where F_{Lj} and F_{Tj} are the marginal products of labor and land in the production of commodity j.

In an analysis of factor taxes under variable labor supply we have to consider the possibilities of both complete and incomplete specialization. Factor supplies respond to factor taxes and sufficiently large adjustments in factor supplies may move the economy alternately from a production pattern of incomplete to one of complete specialization. As portrayed in Figure 1, at fixed land endowments, factor prices are independent of labor supplies for certain ranges of labor supply while wage rates are inversely and land rentals directly related to labor supplies for other ranges.

III. THE VOTER'S PREFERENCES FOR TAX POLICIES

The literature on voting theory typically assumes that the voter's preferences for issues, such as tax programs, are exogenously given. This section shows how political preferences are related to individuals' personal

Figure 1

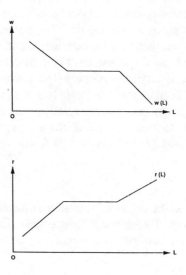

Figure 2

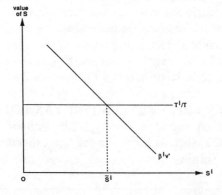

factor ownership and consumption preferences, as well as the economy's production structure.

The ith voter's ideal choices of expenditure on public goods, S, the tax rate on labor income, t_L, and the tax rate on land income, t_T, are determined by maximizing utility, U^i, using (1) and (2):

(7) $$\max_{S,t_L,t_T} \quad w(1-t_L)L^i + r(1-t_T)T^i + a^i g(Z-L^i) + b^i v(S).$$

The voter is aware of the government's budget constraint, which limits expenditure on public goods to revenues collected from labor and land taxes:

(8) $$wLt_L + rTt_T = S.$$

Substituting (8) in (7), the ith voter's choice problem becomes:

(7′) $$\max_{S,t_L} \quad w(1-t_L)L^i + rT^i - (T^i/T)S + (T^i/T)(wLt_L) + a^i g(Z-L^i) + b^i v(S),$$

where the economy's total labor supply depends on $t_L \leq 1$ and factor returns w and r are affected by changes in labor supplies only if there is complete specialization. Differentiating (7′) with respect to S yields:

(9) $$\partial U^i /\partial S = -(T^i/T) + b^i v'(S),$$

where (T^i/T) refers to the ith person's share of land ownership. At a given wage tax, the tax on land is raised to finance the extra public good expenditure. The extra cost to person i is T^i/T, while $b^i v'$ is the extra benefit from another dollar spent on the public good. The ith person's most preferred level of public good provision, $\tilde{S}^i$, is given where $\partial U^i/\partial S = 0$, as illustrated in Figure 2, whereby $\tilde{S}^i$ rises with b^i and falls with T^i/T.

Differentiating (7′) with respect to S yields:

(10) $$\partial U^i/\partial t_L = -wL^i + (T^i/T)wL + (T^i/T)wt_L(dL/dt_L) + \{[(1 - t_L)L^i + Lt_L(T^i/T)][\partial w/\partial L] + T^i[\partial r/\partial L]\}\{dL/dt_L\},$$

where $[w(1 - t_L) - a^i g'] = 0$ from (4). To highlight the impact of the production structure on individually optimal policy choices, we first assume that labor supply is fixed, $\partial L/\partial t = 0$, reducing (10) to:

(10′) $$\partial U^i/\partial t_L = (wLL^i/T)[(T^i/L^i) - (T/L)].$$

In this case, which prevails in the standard Heckscher-Ohlin model, a wage tax raises (reduces) the ith person's utility if his land/labor ratio exceeds (falls short of) that of the average person. Consequently, people with above average land-labor holdings want to see a wage tax raised to the limit of $t_L = 1$, while people with below average land-labor holdings would like wage earners subsidized; $-t_L = (rT - S)/(wL)$ is the maximum attainable subsidy rate, setting $t_L = 1$ in (8). In this standard Heckscher-Ohlin specification of fixed factor supplies, people would either favor complete taxation or maximum subsidization of labor.[5]

In our model, however, the ith person's labor supply is variable. From (4), one can see that the individual's response to a labor tax is:

$$(11) \qquad (dL^i/dt_L) = [w - (1 - t_L)(\partial w/\partial L)(dL/dt_L)]/[a^i g''(H^i)].$$

Summing over all I people in the economy, the country's labor supply response to a tax on labor income is:

$$(12) \qquad dL/dt = \frac{w\Sigma[1/a^i g''(H^i)]}{1 + (1 - t_L)(\partial w/\partial L)\Sigma[1/a^i g''(H^i)]} < 0,$$

since $(\partial w/\partial L) \leq 0$.

Provided the country is incompletely specialized, such that $(\partial w/\partial L) = (\partial r/\partial L) = 0$, the impact of an increase in the wage tax on the ith person's utility, as expressed in (10), can be reduced to:

$$(10'') \qquad \partial U^i/\partial t_L = [(wLL^i)/T][(T^i/L^i) - (T/L)] + [wt_L(T^i/T)(\partial L/\partial t_L)].$$

Under fixed labor supply, all people with above-average land-labor ownership aim for maximum taxation of labor, such that $t_L = 1$. This extreme possibility is eliminated once variable labor supply is introduced. This can be seen as follows: From (4), the supply of labor is zero when the wage tax becomes confiscatory. This implies that:

$$\lim_{t \to 1} (\partial U^i/\partial t_L) = w(T^i/T)(\partial L/\partial t_L) < 0.$$

---

[5]Confiscatory taxation is the outcome if majority voting in a two-candidate election determines the outcome. The situation would however be different if policy choice were made in committees where coalitions can be formed and bargaining can take place.

Utility of the ith person, no matter what his factor ownership, must decline as all wage income is taxed away. Also,

$$\lim_{t \to 0} (\partial U^i / \partial t_L) = [wLL^i/T][(T^i/L^i) - (T/L)],$$

such that the above-average land owner always gains from a small positive wage tax. An interior maximum must exist, although it may not be unique, as shown later. Setting (10") equal to zero, the ith person's optimal tax on labor income is given by:

(13) $t_L^i = [L^i L/T^i][(T/L) - (T^i/L^i)]/[\partial L/\partial t_L].$

Since $(\partial L/\partial t_L) < 0$, the optimal labor income tax rate is positive, but less than one for every person with above-average land-labor ownership. This optimal tax rate rises with T^i, such that people with large land-labor ownership like to see higher labor taxes implemented. Also, it should be noted that the ith person's labor supply is inversely related to the value of a^i, a measure of the willingness to work. Hence, in general the distribution of optimal wage tax rates across the country's population depends on the distribution of both land ownership and willingness to work.

Earlier we demonstrated that under fixed labor supplies all below-average land-labor owners vote for a maximum subsidy of labor income. This again is no longer true with variable labor supply. Although (10") reveals that all below-average land-labor owners become better off when a positive wage tax is reduced, once there is a wage subsidy, $t^L < 0$, the second term in (10") becomes negative as the subsidy is raised, provided the person owns some land. People with very low land-labor ratios may still want extreme subsidization of labor, but this is no longer true for all people with below average land holdings.

So far, incomplete specialization of the economy has been assumed, implying that factor returns remain independent of factor supplies. For large changes in labor supplies, which might be caused by large variations in factor taxes, this is too strong an assumption. Therefore, we examine the impact of a wage tax on a person's utility when there is complete specialization implying that factor returns adjust to labor supply variations. In this case only commodity j is produced and wage rates and returns on land respond to labor supply changes as expressed in (6). Using (6), one can rewrite the part of (10) which includes factor return changes as:

(14) $\{[(1 - t_L)L^i + Lt_L(T^i/T)][\partial w/\partial L] + T^i[\partial r/\partial L]\} =$
          $[L^i L/T][(T/L) - (T^i/L^i)][p_j F_{L_j L_j}][\partial L/\partial t_L],$

where we used the property $F_{TjLj} = -F_{LjLj}(L_j/T_j)$ for homogeneous of degree one production functions. Substituting (14) in (10), yields:

$$(10''') \quad \partial U^i/\partial t_L = [L^iL/T][(T/L) - (T^i/L^i)][w - (1 - t_L)F_{LjLj}(\partial L/\partial t)]$$
$$+ (T^i/T)wt_L(\partial L/\partial t_L),$$

where substitution of (12) shows that $0 < [w - (1 - t_L)F_{LjLj}(\partial L/\partial t_L)] < w$ always. Comparing $(10''')$ with $(10'')$, one can see that the inclusion of factor return responses to labor supply changes makes the first bracketed term smaller. As a result, while the sign of optimal tax rates will be the same as under incomplete specialization, their values will be smaller. Both very high tax and subsidy rates on wage income will not be in the interest of anyone. Hence, variable labor supply imparts a moderating influence on wage taxes as desired by individuals.

IV. THE CANDIDATES' CHOICES OF POSITIONS

Individuals do not vote directly on the magnitude of public-good provision and rates of factor income taxation, but vote for one of two candidates who pronounce policy platforms on these issues. A person votes for the candidate whose position yields him the highest level of utility. Each candidate is assumed to choose his position with full knowledge of voters' preferences, and the candidates' objective is to win the election. Such a two-candidate race can be described as a two-person, zero-sum game, in which the candidates' strategies (s_A, s_B) are their policy positions and the payoffs for candidate A, $\pi(s)$, can be defined as:

$$(15) \quad \pi(s) = \begin{cases} 1 & \text{if } s_A \ P \ s_B \\ -1 & \text{if } s_B \ P \ s_A \\ 0 & \text{otherwise.} \end{cases}$$

where 1 (-1) indicates win (loss) and P stands for majority preferred.

The two-candidate game has a pure strategy equilibrium if and only if there is a majority rule core point; that is, if there exists a policy position which cannot be defeated by any other policy position. Such a majority rule core point exists only under special circumstances. Best known is the single-issue case with single-peaked voter preferences (Black, 1958); the winning candidate adopts the median voter's ideal point. When there are more issues, a median voter equilibrium can be found only under very restrictive conditions, such as where highly restrictive symmetry conditions prevail (Plott, 1967), or when there are two issues and a linear budget constraint confines the choice to just one issue, (McCubbins and Schwartz, 1985).

This section adds another case for a majority rule core point under multiple issues, namely when the voters' ideal positions are linearly related to just one of their characteristics, such as land ownership, and policy indifference curves are circular.   Since these conditions are highly restrictive, one cannot use this method in general to determine the precise nature of the winner's policy platform. However, one still can describe the general nature of the set of policies from which the winning candidate's position will come. This choice set's size and position are shown to be quite sensitive to voter eligibility criteria.

In order to make these points, we will consider the selection of public good provision and form of taxation in a two-candidate contest under a variety of assumptions about the characteristics of voters. It should be recalled that initially there are three issues, namely S, t_L, and t_r, but that use of the government budget constraint reduces the choice to a two-issue problem concerning S and t_r. Also, we note that each person is characterized by his land ownership, T^i , taste for leisure, a^i, and preference for the public good, b^i.

A. Voters differ with respect to land ownership only

First, consider an economy in which voters are homogeneous except for their initial land holdings; hence, $a^{in}=1$ and $b^i=1$, while $0 \leq T^i \leq T^{max}$. Although people differ only with respect to one characteristic, each person still has different ideal levels of public goods provision, S^i, and wage tax, t^i_L, as is apparent from (9) and (13). The higher a person's land ownership, the smaller his demand for public goods and the larger the optimal wage tax. Figure 3 marks the ideal combinations of S and t_L for each person with a given land ownership. Starting at $t_L = t^{max}_L$ and $S = S^{min}$, point A describes the ideal policy choice for people with the highest land ownership, who desire a minimal amount of public goods and a high tax rate on labor income. Generally, these tax revenues from labor income will pay not just for the public good, but also for subsidies to land owners. Moving along the pp-line in a north-west direction, people with gradually lower land ownership desire more of the public good and less taxation of labor, until labor becomes more and more subsidized. The pp-line is linear if a person's optimal choices of s and t_L are linearly related to land ownership.

Although there are two issues under consideration, the two-candidate game still has a pure strategy equilibrium if each voter's indifference curves are circular, as drawn. The winning candidate's position will be the ideal point of the median land owner among voters, such as point 2. There is no other point which can defeat this position. The position of the median voter, in turn, can be influenced by setting restrictions on who is allowed to vote. Residency requirements are more likely to be met by people with some land ownership. Age requirements also tend to favor land owners, as wealth accumulation over a person's life frequently takes the form of land acquisition. The most extreme restriction, of course, is the requirement that a person must own a minimum amount of land to be eligible. Casual empiricism suggests that past and present restrictions on voter eligibility had a pro-land owner bias, thus making a wage tax more likely than a wage subsidy.

B. Voters differ with respect to all characteristics

When voters differ with respect to all three characteristics, T^i, a^i, and b^i, or the restrictive assumptions of linear dependence on characteristics and circularity of preferences are not satisfied, it no longer is possible to reduce majority voting to one dimension. The ideal points of voters in the S-t_L plane of Figure 3 are no longer systematically related to each other. The candidates for election, therefore, cannot determine the winning position by just identifying the median voter in the characteristics space.

In order to illustrate the problem faced by candidates when they have to identify their positions, Figure 4 shows the ideal points and indifference curves for three different voters. The ideal points are derived from (9), when set equal to zero, and (13), and the indifference curves are obtained from (7′). Without stating slope and curvature expressions for these indifference curves explicitly, a few comments are in order. First, these indifference curves generally are not circular, although this is frequently postulated in the voting literature. Second, strict quasiconcavity in multi-dimensional voting situations is the equivalent to single-peakedness in the presence of one issue. However, as shown in the next section, strict quasiconcavity of the direct utility function for commodities does not imply strict quasiconcavity of the indirect utility function for tax policies. Additional restrictions must be imposed to assure strict quasiconcavity of the indirect utility function. In the paper, we just assume that these functions are strictly quasiconcave. Figure 4 clarifies that there is no tax policy position which cannot be beaten by some other position. For example, given the ideal points of three voters, 1,2,3, and their indifference curves, if candidate A chooses position X, then candidate B can adopt a majority-preferred position by selecting position Y. In fact, all points in the shaded areas are majority preferred to X. However, even though position Y allows candidate B to defeat candidate A if the latter adopted X, there are other positions, such as Z which, in turn, would beat Y. Consequently, there is no determinate outcome of the election game.

Although a majority rule core point does not exist, one still can reduce the set of choices from which the winning candidate selects his position by excluding all dominated policy positions. More precisely, if s_A and q_A are

Figure 3

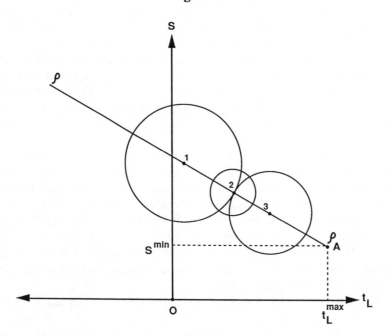

Figure 4

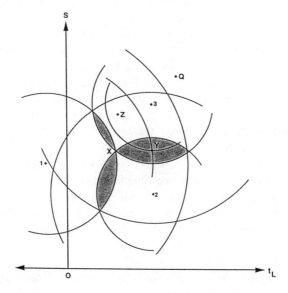

possible position choices for candidate A and the payoffs are such that $\pi(s_A, s_B) \geq \pi(q_A, s_B)$ for all position choices of candidate B, then s_A dominates q_A. In an election game, this means that candidate A realizes that if he adopts position s_A he can be beaten by some strategies of B, say $\tilde{s}_B$. The same position $\tilde{s}_B$ would, however, also beat q_A. On the other hand, there are many other positions which candidate B might adopt which would still be majority preferred to q_A but not to s_A. Figure 4 shows that point Q is dominated by point X. Point X is majority preferred to point Q, and all points in the shaded area, which are majority preferred to X, are also majority preferred to Q.

In a two-candidate election, the winning candidate's position must come from the uncovered set, which differs from the set of game-theoretically undominated positions by at most a measure of zero. McKelvey (1986) shows that in the case of circular preferences there exist some definite bounds on the uncovered set. Cox (1987) has extended the analysis to the more general case of strictly quasi-concave preferences. The basic conclusion is that the uncovered set takes a central location in the distribution of voter ideal points and that it tends to be smaller the more symmetric this distribution is.

When the social choice process is restricted to a two-candidate election and the candidates pick positions from the uncovered set, the location of the uncovered set and, therefore, the general nature of tax and expenditure policies will be affected by eligibility criteria. This is illustrated in Figure 5 for the case of circular preferences. Using McKelvey's (1986, p. 301) technique, we start with five voters and determine the bounds on the uncovered set. Then we add more voters - people who own very little or no land - and find out how the bounds of the uncovered set change.

In order to determine these bounds, one must identify the ideal points for each of five voters, marked by 1,2,3,4,5. Then we draw some median lines, which are defined as lines such that at least half of the voters are on or to one side of the line and at least half are on or to the other side of the line. In the case of just five voters, the limiting[6] median lines are the dashed lines of Figure 5. Next, we identify the smallest circle which intersects all median lines, which is marked by C_5. The bounds on the uncovered set are described by UC_5, a circle with the same origin as C_5, but four times its radius. Next, we liberalize the voting eligibility criteria and add two more voters in locations which indicate that they are people with very low land holdings, preferring high labor subsidies and high expenditure on public goods. These voters have ideal points 6 and 7. To

---

[6]There are many more median lines. For example, all lines which connect point 4 and any point on a line between 3 and 2 would also be median lines.

avoid cluttering, we have not drawn any more median lines for seven voters. We only draw the smallest radius which intersects all median lines, C_7, and the bounds on the uncovered set when there are seven voters, UC_7. As shown, the positioning of the bounds changes, moving towards a more pro-labor position. Hence, the candidates' positions on tax programs shift towards the group which has just become eligible to vote.

V. POLICY PREFERENCES AND ECONOMIC BEHAVIOR

The results of section IV rest on highly restrictive assumptions. Most importantly, we implicitly postulated that ideal points are unique and that indifference curves in the policy plane are circular. In determining a median voter equilibrium in the presence of many issues, the additional restriction was imposed that a person's optimal policy choices are linearly related to his land ownership. The purpose of this section is to warn the reader that these restrictions, so commonly made in the voting literature, are in no way innocuous. The economist's standard assumptions about consumers and firms do not preclude the possibility of multiple ideal points and indifference curves with convex segments.

Let us look at the question of uniqueness of ideal points first. For a given person i, the ideal point is described by a combination of S and t_L which satisfies (9) and (10) when set equal to zero. Figure 2 illustrated that $\bar{S}^i$, the ith person's optimal public-good expenditure, is unique since $v'' < 0$. A problem, however, arises with the uniqueness property of the individually optimal wage tax, t^i_L. In order to illustrate this problem in the simplest possible way we assume that incomplete specialization in production prevails for all relevant rates of t_L and that all individuals have the same preference for work, such that $L^i = L/I$. In this case, (13) can be reduced to:

$$(16) \qquad -t_L(\partial L/\partial t_L)/L = [1 - (T/T^i)/I].$$

The right-hand side of (16) is positive (negative) if a person's land ownership is above (below) average; that is $T^i > (<) T/I$. More importantly, it is independent of the value of t_L. The left-hand side of (16), on the other hand, is positive (negative) for $t_L > (<) 0$. The possibility of multiple solutions arises since the left-hand term is not necessarily increasing everywhere, as $\partial^2 L/\partial t^2_L$ is indeterminate in the absence of restrictions on the utility function's third derivatives. And even if $\partial^2 L/\partial t^2_L$ were equal to zero, the left-hand term may still decrease with t_L for $t_L < 0$. This is illustrated in Figure 6. The relationship between the left-hand term and t_L is the same for every person, as represented by the W-function.

Figure 5

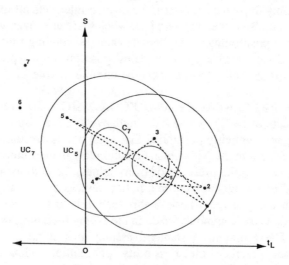

Figure 6

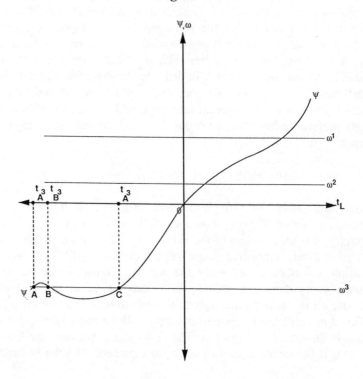

The right-hand term's position depends on land ownership; we consider three possible positions, w_1, w_2, and w_3, where $w_i = [1 - T/(T^i/I)]$. If the W-function has at least some decreasing portions in the relevant range, then there will be some people with multiple locally optimal wage tax rates, such as individual 3 at points A, B, and C.

In Section IV we employed the commonly made assumption that indifference curves in the policy plane are circular. Again, this is a very restrictive assumption which does not follow from the underlying assumptions about economic behavior. Not only are these indifference curves generally not circular, but the assumptions about economic behavior do not even assure that they are quasiconcave. This can be shown as follows. Writing a person's utility function as $U = U(S, t)$, the slope of the indifference curve is given by $(dS/dt) = -U_t/U_s$, where expressions for U_s and U_t are stated in (9) and (10) respectively. Since $U_{st} = 0$ under our specification , the curvature of an indifference curve can be expressed by:

$$(17) \qquad d^2S/dt^2 = -[U_{tt}U_s^2 + U_{ss}U^2t]/U_s^3.$$

While U_s is positive (negative) for any S below (above) the person's optimal value of S and $U_{ss} < 0$, U_{tt} is not necessarily negative. For example, in the incomplete specialization case, where

$$(18) \qquad U_{tt} = w\{[(2T^i/T) - (1/I)][\partial L/\partial t] + (T^i/T)(t/L)(\partial^2 L/\partial t^2)],$$

$U_{tt} > 0$ for an individual with no or very little land ownership evaluated in the neighborhood of $t=0$. Consequently, when S is below a person's optimal value of S, such that $U_s > 0$, d^2S/dt^2 may be negative, implying that indifference curves are not concave everywhere.

Finally, it must be pointed out that in general ideal points, even if unique, are not linearly related to the characteristics of a voter. This can be clearly seen from (9) and (10), when set equal to zero to solve for the ith person's ideal values of S and t_L.

VI. CONCLUSIONS

In the political choice of taxing incomes from various factors of production and of spending tax revenues on public goods, a voter's ideal point for political issues has been shown to depend not only on his characteristics as a consumer and factor owner, but also on the type of economy he is working in. If, as usually postulated in small, open economy models, labor supply is fixed, ideal points for people with above-average land ownership call for confiscatory taxation of workers while ideal points of below-average land owners are associated with below-average land ownership. Under variable labor supply, on the other hand, the preferred tax on labor is never confiscatory. Indeed, the ideal wage tax depends not only on a person's land ownership, but also on how responsive labor supply is to changes in wage taxes.

We have also pointed out that the commonly made assumptions that ideal points are unique and policy indifference curves are circular or, at least, concave, do not follow from the underlying assumptions about voters as consumers of goods and leisure. This has important implications for just about any voting results, whether in a direct or representative democracy.

When additional restrictions are imposed on voters' policy preferences and on the relationship between voter characteristics and their preferences, one can precisely determine what the social choice will be or one can at least describe the general nature of the policy platform which will be adopted. The set of policy platforms from which a winning candidate will choose is shown to hinge on eligibility criteria for voting. If more people with low land ownership were allowed to vote the pronounced policy would favor higher expenditure on public goods and less taxation of labor.

References

Aumann, R.J. and M. Kurz, 1977. "Power and Taxes," *Econometrica*, 45, 1137-61.

Aumann, R.J. and M. Kurz, 1978. "Power and Taxes in a Multi-Commodity Economy (updated)," *Journal of Public Economics*, 9, 139-161.

Baldwin, R. E., 1984. "Trade Policies in Developed Countries," in R. Jones and P. Kenen, editors, *Handbook of International Economics*, Amsterdam: North Holland, 571 - 619.

Black, D., 1958. *The Theory of Committees and Elections*. Cambridge: Cambridge University Press.

Cox, G.W., 1987. "The Uncovered Set and the Core," *American Journal of Political Science*, 31, 408-22.

Hillman, A.L., 1989. *The Political Economy of Protection*, London and New York: Harwood Academic Publishers.

Mayer, W., 1984. "Endogenous Tariff Formation," *American Economic Review*, 71, 970 - 985.

McCubbins, M.D. and T. Schwartz, 1985. "The Politics of Flatland," *Public Choice*, 46, 45-60.

Meltzer, A.H. and S.F. Richard, 1981. "A Rational Theory of the Size of Government," *Journal of Political Economy*, 89, 914-27.

Meltzer, A.H. and S.F. Richard, 1985. "A Positive Theory of In-Kind Transfers and the Negative Income Tax," *Public Choice*, 47, 231-65.

McKelvey, R.D., 1976. "Intransitivities in Multidimensional Voting Models and some Implications for Agenda Control," *Journal of Economic Theory*, 12, 472-82.

McKelvey, R.D., 1986. "Covering, Dominance, and Institution-Free Properties of Electoral Competition," *American Journal of Political Science*, 30, 283 - 314.

Nelson, D., 1986. "Endogenous Tariff Theory: A Critical Survey," *Working paper, The World Bank.*

Ordeshook, P.C.,1986. *Game Theory and Political Theory*, Cambridge: Cambridge University Press

Peck, R.M., 1988. "Power, Majority Voting, and Linear Income Tax Schedules," *Journal of Public Economics*, 36, 53-67.

Plott, C.R., 1967. "A Notion of Equilibrium and Its Possibility under Majority Rule," *American Economic Review*, 57, 787-806.

Roberts, K.W.S., 1977. "Voting over Income Tax Schedules," *Journal of Public Economics*, 8, 329 - 340.

Romer, T., 1975. "Individual Welfare, Majority Voting, and the Properties of the Linear Income Tax," *Journal of Public Economics*, 4, 163-185.

Schofield, N., 1978. "Instability of Simple Dynamic Games," *Review of Economic Studies*, 65, 575-94.

Chapter 4

MACROECONOMIC STABILIZATION POLICY:
DOES POLITICS MATTER?

Martin Paldam[1]

A very neat picture of the role of macroeconomics is the Tinbergen view of the (wise and benevolent) government trying to control economic fluctuations being generated in the private sector of the economy.[2] In this view (we) economists are to provide the analysis allowing the government to manipulate the economy so as to maximize its welfare function. The realism of this idyllic picture has often been disputed.

One of the strongest objections originates from the literature on Political Business Cycles. The key idea in this literature is that the very institutions of the political system are such as to generate fluctuations. Hence, instead of stabilizing an inherently unstable private sector the public sector might be a destabilizing agent in the economy - another matter is if the private or the public sector is the most volatile sector. Public sector fluctuations occur not just by accident, or as a result of bad policies. They occur as a consequence of the institutions, and they have a systematic component, and hence deserve the name of "cycles". Such cycles may be of two types:

(a) Deliberate cycles generated by the government for its own purpose, i.e. cycles occur as a result of a macro-optimization. Two purposes

[1] Flemming Nielsen has provided research assistance. I have benefitted from discussions with Jan Rose Sørensen, Jan Trosborg (who has re-calculated my analysis, using a more normal regression technique) and, in particular, Doug Hibbs. I am grateful also for help from Viggo Høst, and comments from Alberto Alesina, Michael Beenstock, Sven Berg, Daniel Heymann and Ben-Zion Zilberfarb.
[2] See Tinbergen (1956) for the classical statement of the position and Johansen (1977, 1978) for a newer version including the theoretical development over two decades. Recently there have been developments to a theory analyzing the "time consistency" of a policy, see Persson, Persson and Svensson, (1987).

are proposed in the literature:
(a₁) Reelection, the economy is manipulated to please voters at elections.
(a₂) A party-specific welfare function, which may correspond to the one of the voters of the party.
(b) The result of the endogenous forces set into motion by the institutions, so that they occur without a macro-optimization.

I. TYPES OF POLITICAL BUSINESS CYCLES

Two main types of political business cycles have appeared in the literature: *Election Cycles*, lasting one election period, and *Partisan Cycles*, lasting two election periods under different governments. Both main types of cycles will be presented in two versions. Our main purpose below is to test the first type of Partisan Cycles; but it is worth saying a few words on the other types of political business cycles for comparison.

A. Election Cycles in Theory and Practice

The dominating theory of political business cycles in the literature has till recently been *the Nordhaus-MacRae Election Cycle*, as introduced by Nordhaus (1975) and MacRae (1977).[3] They are cycles of type a_1. The idea is that the government has a much longer time horizon than the voters, who are myopic. The government plans for the whole of the election period, steering the economy so that the voters experience a very good combination of the key economic variables just before the election. The theory assumes that voters reward governments, who create good economic outcomes - i.e. the theory builds on the existence of the *VP-function* - i.e. the Vote and Popularity function giving the support of the voters for the government as a function of economic conditions,[4] and it is not entirely consistent theoretically.[5] This idea has not fared well empirically.

---

[3] The election cycle has also been estimated as a part of a more general econometric politico-economic model, see Frey and Schneider (1978a,b).

[4] The large literature on the VP-function is surveyed in Paldam (1981b) and more recently in Lafay, Lewis-Beck & Norpoth (1987). It is a problem that the VP-function lacks stability; but it is often highly significant, and it often explains about 20 - 30 % of the variation in the vote/popularity.

[5] The theory makes three assumptions as regards time horizons: (i) Voters have myopic adaptive expectations, as is actually found in the VP-function literature. (ii) Wage-setters have adaptive expectations that are "longer" than the voters. (iii) Governments have perfect foresight for the whole of the election period. Several attempts have been made to change the theory so as to include rational expectations into a theory of election cycles, see eg. Minford & Peel (1981) and Cukierman & Melzer (1986).

The main empirical test of the Nordhaus-MacRae theory is found in Paldam (1979 and 1981a). Even when there actually is a (weak) Election Cycle in the main economic aggregates *the Actual Election Cycle* does not look as it should according to the theory. The pattern found in the data shows that the economy is the most expansionary in the second year, then inflation rises in the third year, and finally in the fourth year, where the election takes place, the economy is again brought under control. So the year just before the election is not generally a particularly good year. The explanation of the Actual Election Cycle appears to be of type b̲: a significant fraction of all governments makes promises of an expansionary character during the election campaign and tries to implement the promises until these attempts cause economic problems. This brings us to our main subject:

B. Partisan Cycles, the Effect of Left/Right Ideologies

Recently another type of cycle has appeared (or rather: reappeared) in the literature: *Partisan Cycles*. They are of type a̲₂. The goal optimized is purely ideological. The theory takes the central ideological difference between governments to be *the left/right dimension*[6]: Left governments try to expand the economy to bring down unemployment, and in so doing increase inflation. Right governments seek to bring down inflation, and thereby increase unemployment. Both types of governments loose elections so power keeps changing between the two types of parties. By concentrating on the ideological aspect of policy the Partisan Cycle literature comes to address the old puzzle in political economy known as the *politics-doesn't-matter result*: it is well known that it is hard to find a difference between *average* economic performance under left and right governments.

Note the difference in the main idea behind the two cycles: Election Cycles are, in principle, the same for all governments. They occur because of the pressures the elections impose upon the decision process. Partisan Cycles only need elections to change government; the cycles are caused by governments pursuing different policies, as predicted by the different Partisan Cycles exist in two versions.

---

[6] Hibbs further argues that the reasons for the different ideologies is that parties work for the distributional interests of their voters. To what extent the link from ideologies to distributional interest can be made will not be discussed at the present. The opinion of the author as regards the deeper logic of the left/right ideological cleavage is covered in Høst & Paldam (1990).

C. The Hibbs Non-RE Partisan Cycle: Ideologically Generated Trends
     The first is *the Hibbs Partisan Cycle*, as presented in Hibbs (1977, 1986 and 1987b). The theory assumes that policies can systematically generate the outcomes intended. With the right combinations of parameters and reaction lags it is easy to model this as to generate a cyclical pattern where the cycles last two election periods and necessitates a shift of government between right and left at each election. As will be discussed in more detail in Section II, the Hibbs theory leads us expect to find ideologically determined trends in the variables: unemployment goes down under left governments, etc. as listed in Table 1 in Section II.B below. When exogenous shocks are added, a government may sometimes survive to be reelected and the cycles come to be a bit irregular. The proponents of this type of cycle find a great deal of evidence in the macroeconomic history of the U.S.A. and (to a lesser extent) the U.K. during the last 40 years.

D. The Alesina RE Partisan Cycle: From Trends to Blips
     Hibbs' theory of Partisan Cycles assumes that policies influence outcomes, and it is consequently contrary to RE-theory (where RE stands for Rational Expectations). However, Alesina has shown that only small deviations from a "perfect" world are needed in order for Partisan Cycles to appear even in an RE-model. Hence the second type of the Partisan Cycle, *the Alesina Partisan Cycle*, as presented in Alesina (1987, 1988a,b) and Alesina and Sachs (1988). The basic theory is almost the same as Hibbs' theory; but rational expectations are added and the resultant cycles look different in an highly relevant way. The empirical tests in Alesina (1988b) cover 12 to 20 countries, and reach results which are similar to ours, even when the technique of the tests is different. The Alesina theory leads to much less dramatic differences in the outcomes under governments with different ideologies. All we are likely to observe are short run "blips" in the politically important variables just after the election, as will be further discussed in Section II. The post election blips might last one or two years; but then all variables follow their "natural" paths.

E. The Purpose of this Study and some Additional Points
     The *main purpose* of this study is to examine how significant the Hibbs type of Partisan Cycle is in a large data set. Our data set covers all governments in the 17 main developed countries between 1948 and 1985. It proved easy to classify governments as left (-1), right (+1) and left/right coalition (0). With these data we then study the trends and post election blips in the following economic series: unemployment $u_{i,t}$, real growth $y_{i,t}$, inflation (consumer price rises) $p_{i,t}$, and public consumption growth $c_{i,t}$. In

each case i is a country index and t is time.

One major problem might be the *international elements* in the series. As a certain fraction of each series is internationally generated and not due to domestic policies, one wonders what that implies for the possibility of observing such cycles? To control for this factor we have, corresponding to each series $x_{i,t}$, calculated a series, $x^a_{i,t}$, for the trade weighted "abroad", seen from the point of view of the relevant country i. We have then calculated $x^d_{i,t} = x_{i,t} - x^a_{i,t}$, as the domestic component of x. This procedure is further defined in Section III.A. All trend-tests are made both on:

[s1] the *raw series*: $u_{i,t}$, $p_{i,t}$, $c_{i,t}$ and $y_{i,t}$ and on
[s2] the *domestic components* of these series: $u^d_{i,t}$, $p^d_{i,t}$, $c^d_{i,t}$ and $y^d_{i,t}$.

A second major problem might be that governments are different in seemingly relevant ways - apart from being left and right: Many governments are reelected and so weak that it is dubious if they have any possibility of following a consistent policy at all. Therefore, we make all tests for three types of governments, as will be further discussed below in Section II.E:

[g1] *All* left and all right governments - including minority governments and reelected ones.
[g2] *Stable* left and right governments - including reelected governments.
[g3] *First* left and right governments after a change - including minority governments.

II. PARTISAN CYCLES-THE HIBBS AND ALESINA THEORIES

As already outlined, the theory of Partisan Cycles requires that the following three and one half conditions are fulfilled:

(C1) *Governments change* between parties having different orientations.
(C2) Each government pursues an *ideologically determined policy*.
(C3) An *expectations* condition which allows policies to influence economic outcomes in a systematic way. This condition appears in different versions - (C3.H) and (C3.A) - in the Hibbs and Alesina theories.
(C3$^1/_2$) *There is a minimum of a Phillips curve.*

The three full conditions will be discussed in subsections II.A, II.B and II.C. Then we put together the two versions of the theory in I and II.E. The discussion will concentrate on two variables: unemployment u and inflation p and we take a government period to be 4 years. Later we also include public consumption c and real growth y, and we look at the government periods actually occurring. Bold types are used to indicate the path of the variables over the government period: $\mathbf{u} = [u_1, u_2, u_3, u_4]$ and $\mathbf{p} = [p_1, p_2, p_3, p_4]$. The three conditions are all necessary and together they are

Fig. 1.The path of unemployment, u, in three types of political business cycles.

a. The Nordhaus-MacRae Election Cycle.

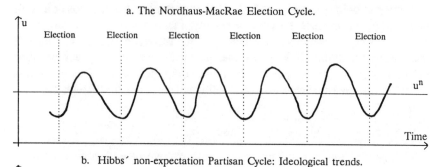

b. Hibbs´ non-expectation Partisan Cycle: Ideological trends.

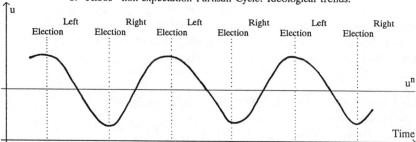

c. Alesina´s rational expectations Partisan Cycle: Post election blips.

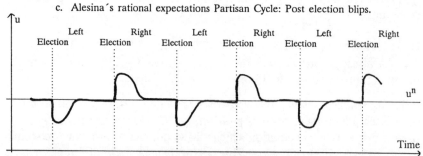

Notes: The inflation path is like the one of u on Fig. a; but symmetrical to u (around u^n) on Figs. b & c.

a.   Cycles are alike irrespective of political orientation of governments.

b.   Cycles last two governments of different orientation, each government following its policy, the economy is controlled by the government.

c.   Cycles shown to last two governments of different orientation (cf. text). All agents have rational expectations. Elections have an element of surprise, and some agents are prevented (by institutions, such as a contractual system) from immediate adjustment to the new information.

u^n the long run average rate of unemployment or the natural rate as appropriate. In theories (a) and (b) a dynamic Phillips curve in the medium term is needed; but there may or may not be a well defined natural rate. In theory (c) there is a natural rate.

(with some minor assumptions to be mentioned) sufficient for producing Partisan Cycles. It is easy to check (C1) independently; but (C2) and (C3) are both quite controversial, and a lot of evidence exists *pro et contra*, allowing different people to hold different, but well substantiated, opinions. We shall therefore concentrate on these conditions below.

The half condition (C3$^1/_2$) is that both versions of the theory need a minimum of a Phillips-curve: if a left government reduces unemployment, u↓, by increasing public spending, c↑, then we should get increasing inflation, p↑. Conversely, if a right government reduces inflation, p↓, and public spending, c↓, then unemployment should rise, u↑. Note that all we need is that this mini-Phillips curve holds within one government period. Nothing is assumed as to the dynamics of the Phillips-curve outside one election period.

A. (C1) The Government Change Condition

We know from many studies that the average government looses votes. In Paldam (1986) the loss from ruling is analyzed for our cross country sample. It appears that the average government looses 1.6 % of the vote; the loss has a standard deviation of 4.5 %. The distribution of the losses from ruling is remarkably stable over time and across countries. It does not appear to depend upon the voting system, the party system, the size of the vote for the government at the last election.[7] It is not really clear why there is a loss like this;[8] but several hypotheses exist.

One theory which explains the cost of ruling, in a highly relevant way, is the theory of the "kick-the-rascals-out" asymmetry in the voter reactions, found by Mueller (1970) and Bloom and Price (1975). Voters punish governments more for the "bad" outcomes they produce, than they reward them for the "good" outcomes produced. Mueller also coined the colorful name for the effect: the *kick-the-rascals-out* asymmetry.

Hence, let us imagine two outcomes produced by two governments termed the left and the right: [u^l, p^l] and [u^h, p^h]. The left outcome pushes down unemployment, so that u^l gets a downward trend, but in the process an upward trend occurs in p^l, the rate of inflation. For the right government, the important goal is to reduce inflation, so p^h gets a downward trend, and consequently u^h gets an upward trend. The kick-the-rascals-out asymmetry says that the right government is punished more

---

[7] The loss has a larger standard deviation in presidential systems (i.e. in the USA), than in parliamentary systems.

[8] If, for a moment, we look upon the average loss in a RE-perspective it appears logical that the average government rules exactly as the rational voter must have expected. Hence, it is illogical that it should loose 1.6 % of the vote.

for the high unemployment it produces than it is rewarded for the low inflation produced, while the left government is punished more for the inflation it generates than it is rewarded for low unemployment. Hence, it is clear that there will be fairly regular changes between left and right wing governments, if the kick-the-rascals-out asymmetry is true. However, this is a rather dubious theory empirically.[9] We do not, fortunately, need the kick-the-rascals-out asymmetry in order to get Partisan Cycles. All we need is the simple, extremely well established fact, that governments loose votes by ruling. It is easy to check the data and see that power does change between parties in most of the 17 countries.

It should be noted that the Alesina version of the theory is less dependent upon actual changes taking place as upon the *surprise element* in the election outcome (as will be discussed in a moment). However, it is unlikely that the agents will continue being surprised by the election result if the government is always re-elected.

B. (C2) The Ideologically Determined Policy Condition - from Ideology to Policy

The ideological dimension in politics we shall apply in the present study is the *left/right-dimension*. It will be assumed that this is, by far, the most important ideological dimension in politics. For three of the variables - u, p and c - it is clear what the dimension predicts. This is indicated in Table 1. However, it is less clear what a left/right dimension lets us believe about real growth, y. Maybe, the left ideology will automatically raise y as u goes down as per Okun's law; but on the other hand it is right to be pro-business, and hence to promote growth in the private sector.

Research (see for example Castles, 1981) shows that the averages of the key economic variables $A(u)$ and $A(p)$ are not significantly different under governments of different orientation. The result is both standard in time series and in cross section covering local governments. It is known as the *politics doesn't matter result*. Some people dislike this result - and it surely flies in the face of a lot of casual observation. Politicians from different parties certainly claim that they pursue rather different policies. Party programs are different, the discussion at party conferences are different, etc. However, two arguments have been presented to explain the politics-doesn't-matter-result:

---

[9] The kick-the-rascals-out asymmetry has not fared well in subsequent research. It has actually (almost) disappeared in the subsequent large literature on the VP-function, as discussed above in note 15. It is interesting to note, however, that the VP-function in the particularly flexible form modeled by Hibbs produces a result consistent with the kick-the-rascals-out asymmetry.

Table 1. **Expected trends in the variables according to ideology.**

Series:	Left government	Right government
u, unemployment	downwards	upwards
p, inflation	upwards	downwards
c, growth in real public consumption	upwards	downwards
y, real growth rate	??	??

(1) The *Median Voter Theorem* says that when the two parties (blocks) fight for the majority they end up contending for the same "middle" voter. Consequently, both parties come to follow the same policies, which are those most appealing to the median voter. A lot can be said both for and against this explanation; but it is worth pointing out that the politics-doesn't-matter-result is the main empirical evidence for the median voter theorem, so there is some circularity in the proofs.

(2) The RE-theory, in its extreme version, argues that even when policies may be different this is unlikely to make outcomes different when everybody recognizes that governments keep changing. That brings us to the last condition:

C. (C3) The Expectations/Actions Conditions - From Policy to Outcome

A key result in the RE-literature is the policy inefficiency result (see Begg, 1982).[10] It is an extreme result appearing if:

(i) all reactions in the economy are symmetrical,

(ii) expectations are rational, in the sense that the agents consider the costs of improving their expectations to be very small relatively to the gains they may win from the improvement.

(iii) From (i) and (ii) it follows that all information that exists in the market is quickly disseminated to everybody.

The gist of the argument is that under RE all agents in the economy take every predictable future policy change into consideration in their

---

[10] Depending upon the pay off from having expectations improved, one obtains a whole spectrum of RE-models: the adaptive pattern of expectations formation is the extreme case where the pay off from improved expectations is small relative to the cost. We follow the tradition of concentrating on the reverse extreme, where the costs of improving ones expectations are small relative to the pay off. We shall reserve the name RE for that case.

actions, and the effect of any systematic policy therefore shows up as a discrete jump in the relevant endogenous variables at the time the information that such a policy will be pursued becomes available and is believed. Election results are never fully predictable, so on election day new information becomes available. However, to the extent that the cycles are fully predictable, they are already taken into consideration in advance.

So under RE we should therefore expect jumps in the relevant variables at election day; as the series adjust to the levels that are "natural" under the said regime. On the other hand, the voters cannot fail to know that the government elected will only rule for a limited period. Hence, the jump at election day may only be a short time blip in the series before it returns to its long run "natural level". The sizes and directions of the *post election blips* are what Alesina (and Sachs) have tried to model.[11] The more perfect and symmetrical the economy is, the *smaller* the blip. However, there is one good reason to expect the blip to be significant: It is the fact that many agents are constrained by contracts or adjustment costs to act except at certain points in time. The key example of a constrained group of agents is the unions/workers who have wage contracts covering, in the typical case, a two year period. Most other adjustment constraints have a shorter period; but it appears reasonable to look for blips lasting one to, at most, two years.

D. Assembling the Hibbs Theory

At the start of the section I listed three conditions (C1), (C2) and (C3) for a Partisan Cycle. The Hibbs theory uses a strict version of (C3):

(C3.H)   An *anti-RE* condition: Policies influence economic outcomes systematically throughout the full governmental period.

It is worth pointing out that there has gradually emerged a large amount of sample evidence about the way people actually form expectations (see Jonung and Laidler, 1988 for a brief introduction to the Swedish evidence). The evidence is differently interpreted, but it would be hard, indeed, to claim that the evidence is strongly in support of the RE-theory. The patterns observed show an amazing variation between the expectations of different people, adding up to something that on average looks a lot like fairly myopic, adaptive expectations. Hence it is not difficult to argue that the manner in which people form expectations is far different from that

---

[11] A literature analyzing this idea is already quickly emerging (though most is available only as working papers as this is being written), see e.g. the references in Sørensen (1988).

proposed by RE theory.[12]

The shape of the cycles depends upon the details of the models used. Hibbs' original version of the model contains no expectations at all. Here the adjustment starts immediately after the victory of the new government. However, Hibbs (and common sense) suggests that there are some lags involved. This gives the general shape of the cycle shown in Figure 1b. It is easy to amend the model with adaptive expectations. If expectations are sufficiently myopic, we still have the same shape of the cycle; but normally adaptive expectations move the maxima and minima of some of the variables (especially p, the inflation rate) to be lagged somewhat after the election.

In the basic version of the Hibbs model it is however clear that the key prediction is that we should find "ideological" *trends* in the variables mentioned. The exact form of the cycles is heavily dependent upon the details of the model. To test the general idea of Partisan Cycles we have therefore developed a *non-parametric testing procedure* which is *very sensitive to trends* in the variables, while it is *insensitive the exact path* of the trend. The test is presented in Section III.C, while the results are given in Section V.

E. Assembling the Alesina Theory

The Alesina version of the theory uses conditions (C.1) and (C.2), but now (C.3) becomes:

(C.3A)   All agents have RE, but they are not all able to adjust immediately to major pieces of new information, such as an election result.

The results are, as already explained, post election blips lasting one to, at most, two years. The government elected immediately starts to pursue its ideologically determined policy, and as the agents manage to take the policy into consideration, the effects of the policy disappear. The size of the blips depends on three factors:

(i)   The size of the surprise; that is, if the election outcome has been predicted with a great probability, then all agents have already had time to adjust, but if the surprise has been great, then the blip will be great.

---

[12] Another formulation would be to claim that most people can gain very little from having improved expectations, and that it is time consuming to improve one's expectations, so that it is entirely rational to have myopic, adaptive expectations on the mass level. And as we know that politicians, trade union leaders etc. have to sell their policies to their clients at the mass level, then surely the mass level must influence policymaking at the top level too.

(ii)   The institutional system of contracts, etc.

(iii) The difference between the ideologies of the parties.

The direction of the blips is clear to predict in the Alesina theory. The variables jump in the direction desired by the government. This gives the picture depicted on Figure 1c. In Paldam (1990b) a test is developed for Alesina Cycles. The test results are briefly summarized in Section VI below.

When the two types of the Partisan Cycle are compared, something interesting emerges: The *trends in the variables reverse* in the two versions of the cycle. Consider the path of unemployment under a left government: If the Partisan Cycle is of the Hibbs type, unemployment is adjusted from the former high level to the new low level, so the trend is negative. If the Partisan Cycle is of the Alesina type unemployment jumps down immediately and then rises to the natural level as the agents manage to adjust. Hence, the trend is positive.

F. The Three Types of Governments - Definitions and Relevance

We have, as already mentioned, classified governments as left (-1), mixed coalitions (0) or right (+1). Using this classification we distinguish between three types of left and right governments:

[g1] *All* left and all right governments - including minority governments and reelected ones.

[g2] *Stable* left and right governments - including reelected governments. Two criteria have to be fulfilled for a government to be stable: {1} It should have a majority - i.e. the parties in the government should have a majority in the main chamber (in the US both chambers) of the parliament. {2} It should rule for a normal election period, i.e. the full statutory period minus half a year.

[g3] *First* left and right governments after a change - including minority governments. A change is defined as either of the two possibilities: {1} from left (-1) or mixed coalition (0) to right (+1), or {2} from right (+1) or mixed coalition (0) to left (-1).

When going through the two theories it appears that the most relevant type of government is [g3]. However, it is not clear whether the other two types are irrelevant. In the Hibbs theory a reelected government may very well adjust its goals. By increasing support it may implement a more ideological policy. In the Alesina theory, the size of the surprise is crucial, and it may very well be that a reelection comes as a big surprise and then we get a blip to the same side as the last blip; but if a government keeps getting reelected, the surprise must decrease. Hence, it is interesting to run the tests for all three types of governments.

III. THE DATA AND THE KENDALL TREND SCORE

The data covers all government periods, as defined in sub-section VI.A, from 1948 to 1985, for the following 17 OECD-countries:

(1) Australia, (2) Austria, (3) Belgium, (4) Canada, (5) Denmark, (6) Finland, (7) France, (8) Germany, (9) Holland (the Netherlands), (10) Ireland, (11) Italy, (12) Japan, (13) New Zealand, (14) Norway, (15) Sweden, (16) U.K., and (17) the U.S.A. In the following the index $i = 1, \ldots, 17$ refers to the countries.

A. The Four Economic Series: the "Raw" Series and the "Domestic" Component

p   inflation rate, i.e. the % rise in the CPI of the country. It is calculated as the implicit deflator for private consumption as found in the OECD tables of National Accounts.

p^d $= p - p^a$, domestic component of price rises. Here p^a denotes trade weighted price rises abroad.[13]

u   unemployment rate, in % of labor force (OECD Labor Force Statistics).

u^d $= u - u^a$, domestic component of unemployment. Here u^a is trade weighted unemployment abroad.

c   the % rise in general government consumption (OECD Tables of National Accounts).

c^d $= c - c^a$, domestic component of increases in public consumption. Here c^a is trade weighted increases in public consumption abroad.

y   the real growth rate, i.e. the percentage increase in the gross domestic product in base/factor prices, from the OECD tables of National Accounts.

y^d $= y - y^a$, domestic component of real growth. Here y^a is the trade weighted real growth rate abroad.

The idea behind the domestic versions of the series is that all economic time series contain international elements (see Paldam, 1983). To see how a government influences the economy one therefore has to adjust the series to "take out" the international element and consider the domestic component only. The way we have obtained the domestic component is somewhat crude; but it nevertheless should give an approximation to the desired

---

[13] The trade weights are constructed with five years apart, using a matrix giving all the sum of all import and export from/to each of the 17 countries to/from each of the others. By setting the rest of the world to zero, and normalizing each row in the matrix to sum to 1, we have the weights used. The years in between are reached by linear interpolation. The construction is further discussed in Paldam (1989)

series.

B. The Political Data: Governments, Periods, Left/Right and Majority Measures

For each election period we include the last *government* $G_{i,j}$ before the election,[14] except in (a few) cases of short run governments of civil servants appointed with the sole purpose of providing "neutral" rule while an election takes place.

For each government we define the *government period* $T_{i,j}$, by using the "division point" of the 1st of July: if the government is appointed before the 1st of July of a certain year this is the first government year, if the appointment is later the following year is the first government year. The same principle is used to define the last government year. In Australia and New Zealand where the statistics are compiled using a different year the division point is adjusted accordingly. Hence, for each government $G_{i,j}$ we obtain a government period $T_{i,j}$ of 1, 2, 3, 4 or (in a few cases) 5 years. To speak of a trend we need a $T_{i,j}$ lasting at least 2 years, so governments with a period of less than 2 years are excluded.

For each of the included governments - of which there are n_i in country i - we have collected the following data:

$T_{i,j}$ government period, constructed as explained.

$L_{i,j}$ = -1, 0 or +1. The left/right variable, defined relative to the political spectrum of the country. It is -1 if the government is left, 0 if it is a left/right coalition, and +1 if it is right. The variable is discussed in Høst and Paldam (1990).

$M_{i,j}$ = 1 or 0. Indicates if the government has a majority or not. In all countries (except the USA) the government can be formed only if there is no majority against it in the parliament. However, this does not necessarily mean that a government had an actual majority that it could rely upon.

$M_{i,j}$ = 1 if the party/parties in the government form a majority in the (main chamber of the) parliament.[15]

C. The Main Principles of Kendall's and the Trend Score

For these eight series we construct a "Kendall" *trend scores* $\underline{m}$. The scores are made using the technique of Kendall's $\underline{s}$. The trend-score $\underline{m}$ for one government is simply $\underline{s}$, between the series and a trend: Let us

---

[14] This means that we exclude a few governments which break down, presumably because they fail to agree upon a policy.

[15] In the USA a majority demands a majority in both houses in our definition.

Table 2. The possible result for the Kendall counts

Section 1 For two years, T=1					Section 2 For three years, T=3					Section 3 For four years, T=6				
N_+	N_-	S	D	P	N_+	N_-	S	D	P	N_+	N_-	S	D	P
1	0	1	+1	.5	3	0	1	+3	.167	6	0	1	+6	.042
0	1	1	-1	.5	2	1	2	+1	.333	5	1	3	+4	.125
		$\xi = 2$			1	2	2	-1	.333	4	2	5	+2	.208
					0	3	1	-3	.167	3	3	6	0	.250
							$\xi = 6$			2	4	5	-2	.208
										1	5	3	-4	.125
										0	6	1	-6	.042
												$\xi = 24$		

Note:

N_+ is the number of pairs in rising
order. N_- is the number of pairs in falling
order. T is the number of pairs compared. S is the
number of orders where the $\{N_+,N_-\}$-score of the line occurs.
$D = N_+ - N_-$. P is the probability of obtaining the said $\{N_+,N_-\}$-score
given that the x´es in x are randomly drawn numbers from the same distribution.

consider the four observations $x = [x_1, x_2, x_3, x_4]$ of the variable, for a certain 4-year government period. We term $\{(l,k,j,i)\}$ the order of x, if $x_i < x_j < x_k < x_l$. Four observations can stand in 4! = 24 different orders, and they contain $\underline{T} = 6$ pairs: $[\{x_1,x_2\}, \{x_1,x_3\}, \{x_1,x_4\}, \{x_2,x_3\}, \{x_2,x_4\}, \{x_3,x_4\}]$.

Next we count the number of pairs in rising order N_+ and the number in falling order N_-, and reach $[N_+, N_-]$. We further calculate the difference $D = M_+ - N_-$. There might be ties, as for example $x_2 = x_3$. So $N_+ + N_-$ need not sum to $\underline{T} = 6$; but let us for the moment disregard the ties. Section 3 of the Table shows the $N+$, $N-$ counts, the D's and $\underline{T}$, for all $\underline{n}$ = 24 possible orders in which the four numbers may stand. There is only one case where $\{N_+,N_-\} = \{6,0\}$, so that D = +6. It is the order $\{(1,2,3,4)\}$, where $x_1 < x_2 < x_3 < x_4$. But there are 6 cases, such as e.g. the orders $\{(3,1,4,2)\}$, and $\{(2,4,1,3)\}$, where $\{N_+,N_-\} = \{3,3\}$, so that D = 0. If all cases are equally probable, i.e. if x is perfect white noise, we reach the probabilities P calculated in Table 2, for the different outcomes.

Kendall (1970) has developed tables and approximations (for high values of $\underline{T}$), for $\underline{s} = \underline{s}(\underline{a},\underline{T})$, where $\underline{a}$ is the significance level (such as 5 %), allowing us to see if a $\underline{s}$ calculated from a set of observations exceeds the test value $\underline{s}(\underline{a},\underline{T})$ for the desired level of significance $\underline{a}$. Table 3 is a summary of Kendall's tables. To see if a certain expected trend is significant we can just calculate the Kendall trend score and look up the probability that the said D-score (or something even better) might have occurred accidentally.

Let us imagine that we examine whether a trend is positive in the rate of inflation during a certain left wing government and here find $\{N_+,N_-\} = $

{4, 2}, so that D = +2, and $\underline{m}$ = +2/6 = +0.33. By looking in Table 2, we see that the cumulative probability that this is accidental is .042 + .125 + .208 = .375 or 37.5 %. However, if the $\{N_+, N_-\}$-score is {6, 0}, so that D = +6, so that $\underline{m}$ = +6/6 = +1.00, then the P-value that this is accidental is 0.042 or 4.2 %, and we can therefore reject the possibility that the x´es are randomly distributed at the 5 % level of significance. Obviously, it is hard to obtain significance when we have four observations only, and in the cases where x has three elements only even a D-score of +3 has a P-value of 16.7 %.

D. Combining Results from Many Governments

Test results can be combined in different ways;[16] but remember that the logic of the Kendall $\underline{s}$ is to calculate $\underline{s}$ = D/$\underline{T}$, the number of pairs in the right order minus the number of pairs in the wrong order, divided by the total number of pairs compared. The comparisons should be made for all pairs comparable.

Hence, if we want to test if there is an upward trend in the inflation rate under left governments in X-country, we have to see how many of all possible pairs $\underline{RT}$, we are allowed to compare, are going up $\underline{RN_+}$, minus the ones going down $\underline{RN_-}$. And the difference $\underline{RD}$ = $\underline{RN_+}$ - $\underline{RN_-}$, now gives a perfectly ordinary $\underline{m}$ = RD/$\underline{RT}$. Imagine that we have four such governments, where D/$\underline{T}$ = (+4/6), (+4/6), (-1,3) and (+4/5), none of which is significant, even when the total evidence looks fairly strong. We can test the combined evidence simply by adding the four nominators, 4 +5 -1 +4 = 12, and the four denominators, 6 +6 +3 +5 = 20. Hereby we obtain an aggregate $\underline{m}$ = ($\underline{RD}$/$\underline{RT}$) = (11/20) = +.55. Table 3 shows that this (just) passes the 5 % significance limits, which is $\underline{s}$(5 %,$\underline{T}$) = +.54.

The reader will note that to the extent we can take the data sets for different governments to be *independent*, we can simply add the D´s and the $\underline{T}$´s, and then we have a very simple test using Table 3. Another key reason to try to purge the series of the international elements is that this allows us to test across countries. That is, we can test whether the trends in all left governments in inflation are positive, etc.

Finally it should be mentioned that when we test if there are trends in y, where our theory is indeterminate, we have to use the two-sided tests.

---

[16] The reader should note that if there are ties, then the number of ties reduces the number of pairs counted in both nominator and denominator. The Kendall test procedure used is equivalent to using R.A. Fishers Omnibus procedure for combining the results of independent tests.

Table 3. Percentage points for $\underline{s}$, calculated from Kendall (1970).

T	Significance level				T	Significance level				T	Significance level			
	5	2.5	1	0.5		5	2.5	1	0.5		5	2.5	1	0.5
6	.70	-	-	-	30	.48	.55	.64	.70	60	.36	.44	.52	.56
10	.62	.80	.80	-	35	.45	.51	.61	.67	80	.33	.41	.48	.53
15	.58	.73	.73	.87	40	.43	.49	.59	.64	100	.32	.38	.45	.49
20	.54	.68	.72	.82	45	.42	.47	.56	.60	150	.29	.34	.40	.45
25	.51	.59	.67	.76	50	.40	.46	.54	.58	200	.26	.31	.37	.41

Note: The table is for the one sided tests, it is symmetrical for $T < 0$. Two sided tests are made by taking the "2.5%-column" as the 5% level, and the "0.5%-column" as the 1% level.

This enyails multiplying the $\underline{a}$´s by two, as explained in the note to the table.

IV. THE AVERAGE PATHS OF THE FOUR VARIABLES DURING ALL LEFT AND RIGHT GOVERNMENTS

The purpose of this Section is to examine the paths of the four series over the period of the average left and right government, as indicated in the 16 curves drawn on the 8 sub-figures of Figure 2.

The statutory period for a government is between 3 and (in two countries) 5 years in the 17 countries. In most countries it is possible to call an early election, and this frequently happens. Therefore only very few government periods extend to 5 years, so this possibility is disregarded in the calculations underlying Figure 2. However, there are enough data so that we can draw the 4-year periods (sub-figures A to D) separately from the 3-year periods (sub-figures a to d). In both cases we have added two years to both sides of the government period for comparison.

The reader should note that the figures are all cross-country averages covering the cases found, irrespective of the years and countries. All that matters is that it is a left government lasting four years, a right government lasting four years, etc. Hence, the reader should disregard the levels of the curves on all the graphs. However, it is interesting and relevant to look at *the development in each curve over time*.

A. Discussing Figure 2

The paths depicted on Figure 2 present a fairly unclear picture in the sense that one can see different cycles in the different series and for the government periods of different lengths. Consider first unemployment in the two cases: here a clear Hibbs Cycle appears in the paths of the right governments, but it is difficult to see a pattern like the ones predicted by either of the two types Partisan Cycles in the paths of unemployment under the left governments.

Fig. 2. The paths of the four variables over all left and right governments.

Paths under left ▬ and right ▬   the E´s are the election before and after the government.

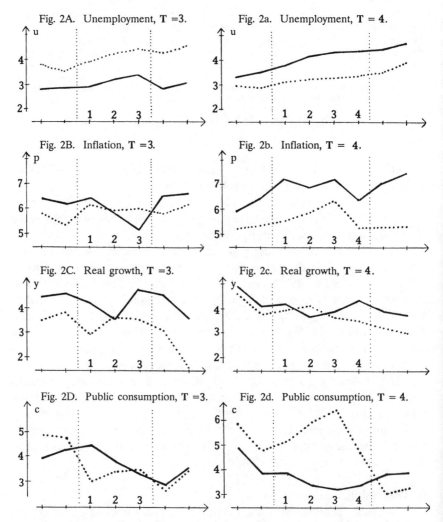

Fig. 2A. Unemployment, T = 3.

Fig. 2a. Unemployment, T = 4.

Fig. 2B. Inflation, T = 3.

Fig. 2b. Inflation, T = 4.

Fig. 2C. Real growth, T = 3.

Fig. 2c. Real growth, T = 4.

Fig. 2D. Public consumption, T = 3.

Fig. 2d. Public consumption, T = 4.

Note: Sub-figures with capitals A to D cover averages of the all governments ruling 3 years, i.e. T = 3. There are 15 left and 36 right governments, with T = 3. The corresponding graphs with small letters a to d cover the 26 left and the 29 right governments, where T = 4.

For the inflation rates the paths are rather mixed: Under the left 3-year and right 4-year governments there are Alesina-blips, but the other cases look like Hibbs-trends. Therefore it is hard to draw any conclusion.

For the real growth rate the picture is even more unclear, and in the next two sections we fail to find strong results here. However there is a tendency for the trend to be upward under the right governments and down under the left governments. Also there might be an Alesina Cycle in the left 3-years governments and the right 4-year governments.

Of more interest are the paths of public consumption. Here there seem to be no clear cases either; but for the 3-year governments there appears to be something almost like a reverse Partisan Cycle. And, furthermore, the picture for the 3-years-governments looks very different from the picture under the 4-year governments.

All in all it is therefore very difficult to reach firm conclusions from Figure 2. We have also made the similar drawings for the domestic components of the series; but the pictures found are not clearer. The next two sections test the two types of cycles separately. It is perhaps not surprising - considering Figure 2 - that we do find a significant number of both cycles in the data.

V. THE RESULTS: TESTS FOR THE HIBBS PARTISAN CYCLE

Tables 4 to 6 contain our tests of the Hibbs Cycle. In Japan all governments during the period examined have been Right,[17] so we have not included Japan in the tests. In the other sixteen countries we have at least two of the three possible types of governments: (-1) Left governments, (0) Left-Right coalition governments and (+1) Right governments. In Belgium, Finland (where the socialist period starts too late for our study), France, Italy and the Netherlands we have only the possibilities (0) and (+1).

In each of the tables there are three sets of three columns for our *three types of governments: [g1] all* governments, *[g2] stable* governments and *[g3] first* governments. *If* a government has ideologically determined permanent targets for the variable, *if* the different goals pursued are time consistent, and *if* it can implement these targets in one government period, *then* we expect that the variable stays constant in the second (and all later) governmental period(s), of the same party - i.e. only [g3] is relevant. However, all these qualifications are dubious, and, in particular, it is likely that governments learn from rulingthat targets are less consistent that they

---

[17] The first and only socialist government in Japan ruled from 1949 to 1952. However, during that period Japan was also ruled by the US military government of Douglas MacArthur.

thought (or were induced by the competitive political process to promise) when they were in opposition. Hence, policies of repeated governments will change, perhaps in a systematic way as to converge to the long run paths of the variables.

In theory dealing with human behavior, it is however a central theme that targets are relative. Hence, it is possible to argue that we should include all governments. Also, it is arguable (see Hibbs, 1977) that much of the seemingly ideologically induced difference between the countries has emerged only in the long run. It is, for example, a strong result that countries with relatively large public sectors and peaceful labor markets have large and old Social Democratic parties. Therefore, it was *a priori* possible that either [g1] or [g2] provided the more interesting and relevant tests.

The three sets of columns are each divided into three columns:

{C1} $\underline{T}$ gives the number of relevant pairs compared, i.e. the denominator in the calculation of $\underline{m}$. If there is a 4-year and a 3-year left government $\underline{T} = \binom{4}{2} + \binom{3}{2} = 6 + 3 = 9$. Note that it is irrelevant for the calculation if the two governments are adjacent or many years apart.

{C2} $\underline{m}(x)$ gives the test results for the raw series x.

{C3} $\underline{m}(x^d)$ gives the corresponding test results for the domestic component x^d.

To indicate the level of significance we use the following signs:

*   If at least one of the tests is significant, in the direction expected, at the 5% level.

(*)   If at least one of the tests is significant, in the direction expected, at the 10% level.

!   If at least one of the tests is significant, but in the wrong direction, at the 5% level.

(!)   If at least one of the tests is significant, but in the wrong direction, at the 10% level.

A. Discussing the Test Results

The tables are large and contain a lot of information, of which little is really clear-cut. If we start by looking at the results for unemployment under the left governments, the first thing to note is that the $\underline{R}$-line shows no signs of significance whatsoever. There are some significant results; but there are also significant results with the wrong signs. Really convincing results throughout are found for the USA only. However, when turning to the lower half of the table, which gives the results for the right governments, the $\underline{R}$-line gives significant results in the direction expected;

Tab. 4.   Tests for the Hibbs non-RE Partisan Cycle in unemployment u.

Left governments/expected signs for $v(u)$ and $v(u^d)$ is negative

	All governments			Stable governments			First governments		
	T	$v(u)$	$v(u^d)$	T	$v(u)$	$v(u^d)$	T	$v(u)$	$v(u^d)$
1. Australia	1	1.00	1.00	1	1.00	1.00	1	1.00	1.00
2. Austria	15	0.60	-0.73 **	15	0.60	-0.73 **	6	0.67	-1.00 *
3. Belgium	-			-			-		
4. Canada	35	0.37	0.54 !	33	0.45	0.64 !	13	0.23	0.85 !
5. Denmark	16	0.00	0.13	9	-0.56	-0.56(*)	6	0.67	1.00 !
6. Finland	-			-			-		
7. France	-			-			-		
8. Germany	15	0.07	-0.47(*)	15	0.07	-0.47(*)	3	1.00	1.00
9. Holland	-			-			-		
10. Ireland	10	0.20	-0.60(*)	10	0.20	-0.60(*)	10	0.20	-0.60(*)
11. Italy	-			-			-		
12. Japan	-			-			-		
13. New Zealand	6	0.00	-0.33	6	0.00	-0.33	6	0.00	-0.33
14. Norway	31	-0.03	-0.10	18	0.00	0.67 !	12	0.17	-0.33
15. Sweden	25	-0.44	-0.12	7	-1.00	-0.43 *	9	-1.00	-0.11
16. U.K.	13	0.23	0.54(!)	13	0.23	0.54(!)	13	0.23	0.54(!)
17. U.S.A.	24	-0.58	-0.50 *	18	-0.56	-0.56 *	18	-0.56	-0.33 *
Σ	191	0.02	-0.05	145	0.06	-0.02	97	0.03	-0.03

Right governments/expected signs for $v(u)$ and $v(u^d)$ is positive

	T	$v(u)$	$v(u^d)$	T	$v(u)$	$v(u^d)$	T	$v(u)$	$v(u^d)$
1. Australia	25	0.28	0.28	25	0.28	0.28	5	0.60	0.20(*)
2. Austria	6	0.00	-0.33	6	0.00	-0.33	6	0.00	-0.33
3. Belgium	19	0.47	0.26(*)	16	0.38	0.13	19	0.47	0.26(*)
4. Canada	6	0.33	0.33	6	0.33	0.33	6	0.33	0.33
5. Denmark	5	0.20	-0.60(!)	3	-0.33	-1.00	5	0.20	-0.60(!)
6. Finland	4	-1.00	-1.00	1	-1.00	-1.00	3	-1.00	-1.00
7. France	29	0.79	0.03 *	23	1.00	-0.13 *	6	0.00	0.67(*)
8. Germany	12	-0.83	-0.17 !	12	-0.83	-0.17 !	6	-1.00	-1.00 !
9. Holland	20	-0.30	0.10	19	-0.37	-0.05	18	-0.44	0.00
10. Ireland	30	0.13	-0.20	27	0.19	-0.26	15	-0.33	-0.33
11. Italy	17	0.18	0.17	4	1.00	-0.50	4	1.00	1.00
12. Japan	no changes			no changes			no changes		
13. New Zealand	28	0.29	0.21(*)	28	0.29	0.21(*)	7	0.43	0.71 *
14. Norway	12	0.00	-0.33	12	0.00	-0.33	12	0.00	-0.33
15. Sweden	3	1.00	-1.00	3	1.00	-1.00	3	1.00	-1.00
16. U.K.	27	0.41	0.11(*)	27	0.41	0.11(*)	15	0.33	0.07
17. U.S.A.	30	0.20	0.27(*)	12	0.33	0.50(*)	18	0.11	0.11
Σ	273	0.21	0.05(*)	224	0.24	-0.01 *	148	0.07	-0.01

but it is interesting to note that (1) the results are best for the "stable" governments, (2) they are weakest for the "first" governments. Furthermore, it is noteworthy that the cycle is weaker for the domestic component of the unemployment rate than for the raw series.

The results are stronger when we turn to Table 5, covering the Hibbs Cycle in the inflation rate. Here the $\underline{R}$-lines show the right signs and the results are statistically significant in most cases. It is not clear if the results are strongest for the domestic components or for the raw series. Table 6 shows the test results for the $\underline{R}$-lines for all four variables, including the real growth rate y and the growth rate of public consumption c. For the real growth rate none of the $\underline{m}$´s are significant; but the $\underline{m}$´s are significantly different between the left and the right governments. Growth increases more under right governments and decreases under left.

When all the results are considered we can draw the following conclusions:

(H1) Most of the key results are significantly different from zero and the signs are right. However, the trends under left and right governments are significantly different as expected from the theory - very significant for unemployment and inflation and just about significant for the real growth rate. We do have so many observations that it is possible to make rather strong tests.

(H2) When the results for the three types of governments [g1], [g2] and [g3] are compared there is a weak tendency that they are strongest under first governments [g3].

(H3) In most cases the results are more significant for the raw series than for the domestic components.

(H4) The US constitutes an extreme case, in being the country where the results are best throughout.

The country results, apart from the ones for the US, are rather mixed. For two countries Canada and Ireland we have significantly wrong signs for one of the key variables. And in many cases we have no signs of anything. However, thanks to the large number of observations we have established that the Hibbs Cycle is a weak, but significant phenomena.

VI. CONCLUSIONS

The results are easy to sum up: *the trends in some key variables, notably unemployment and inflation are significantly different under left and right governments,* as predicted by Hibbs' theory of NE Partisan Cycles (where NE stands for No Expectations). The cycles are not very strong, except in the USA; but they remain just significant even if the US is excluded from the analysis. The findings for the US and UK are well in accordance with the literature since Hibbs (1977), while the findings for the other 15 countries are new.

One objection to the whole analysis should be mentioned. It is the usual one that the causality may be the reverse. Perhaps it is the trends in unemployment and inflation that cause the shifts between left and right and not vice versa as we have assumed. One such reverse theory would see the economic time series as generated by stochastic shocks combined with a slow regression toward the mean. If economic variables have this structure and the voters react to the economic variables at election times (that are random relative to the shocks) then we may obtain a pattern as observed. It is not easy to reject this possibility; but the results in Paldam (1987) and Høst and Paldam (1990) analyzing the vote function in our data set do not support the reverse causality hypothesis.

In Paldam (1990b) the same data are analyzed for *Alesina RE Partisan Cycles* (where RE stands for Rational Expectations). They should, as explained in Sections I and II above, appear as post-election blips in the series. Since blips give less structure to test, there are fewer degrees of freedom in the tests; but we nevertheless find very significant results for the RE-version of the Partisan Cycle too. The Alesina Cycle is, in fact, a more commonly found phenomena than the Hibbs Cycle. It proved difficult to establish whether the RE-blips last one or two years, but the results are marginally better for one than for two years. As for the Hibbs Cycle it also decreased the significance of the Alesina Cycle when the series were purged of the international elements.

It is worth mentioning that earlier work (Paldam, 1979 and 1981a) using data for 1948 to 1975 only and testing for one period Election Cycles did find that many economic variables have a weak, but significant, cyclicality over the average election period; but, as mentioned in Table 1 this cycle did not look as it should according to the theory.

The Alesina RE-version of the Partisan Cycle looks remarkably different from the Hibbs' NE-version of the theory, as shown on Figure 1. It is clear to see from the detailed results that most often we get either the one or the other in the results for a particular government. In most countries we find specimens of both types of cycles. However, the US data appear to contain only the Hibbs Cycle. This is contrary to the findings of Alesina (see his 1987 and all later papers referred to). Perhaps the explanation is that Alesina obtains the best results for the growth rate of real GDP - our y variable - and that he takes account of the mid-term elections. We find that the results for y are relatively weak, and the mid-term election only appears in our analysis as a factor that may change the stability of the US government (i.e. it only enters in the definition of g2).

Tab. 5.   Tests for the Hibbs non-RE Partisan Cycle in the inflation rate p.

Left governments/expected signs for $\nu(p)$ and $\nu(p^d)$ positive

	All governments			Stable governments			First governments		
	T	$\nu(p)$	$\nu(p^d)$	T	$\nu(p)$	$\nu(p^d)$	T	$\nu(p)$	$\nu(p^d)$
1. Australia	1	1.00	-1.00	1	1.00	-1.00	1	1.00	-1.00
2. Austria	15	0.33	0.07	15	0.33	0.07	6	0.67	-0.67
3. Belgium	-			-			-		
4. Canada	35	-0.14	-0.43(!)	33	-0.21	-0.45(!)	13	-0.69	-0.54 !
5. Denmark	16	0.38	0.50(*)	9	0.33	0.33	6	0.33	0.67(*)
6. Finland	-			-			-		
7. France	-			-			-		
8. Germany	15	0.07	0.20	15	0.07	0.20	3	1.00	1.00
9. Holland	-			-			-		
10. Ireland	10	0.80	0.40 *	10	0.80	0.40 *	10	0.80	0.40 *
11. Italy	-			-			-		
12. Japan	-			-			-		
13. New Zealand	6	0.00	-0.33	6	0.00	-0.33	6	0.00	-0.33
14. Norway	31	-0.16	-0.10	18	-0.33	-0.44	12	-0.67	-0.33(!)
15. Sweden	25	0.04	-0.12	7	1.00	0.71 *	9	0.33	0.11
16. U.K.	13	-0.08	-0.08	13	-0.08	-0.08	13	-0.08	-0.08
17. U.S.A.	24	0.92	0.50 *	18	0.89	0.33 *	18	0.89	0.33 *
Σ	191	0.17	0.02(*)	145	0.19	-0.03(*)	97	0.20	-0.01

Right governments/expected signs for $\nu(p)$ and $\nu(p^d)$ negative

	T	$\nu(p)$	$\nu(p^d)$	T	$\nu(p)$	$\nu(p^d)$	T	$\nu(p)$	$\nu(p^d)$
1. Australia	25	0.04	-0.20	25	0.04	-0.20	5	-0.20	-0.20
2. Austria	6	0.33	0.00	6	0.33	0.00	6	0.33	0.00
3. Belgium	19	-0.47	-0.26(*)	16	-0.50	-0.25(*)	12	-0.47	-0.26(*)
4. Canada	6	-1.00	-1.00 *	6	-1.00	-1.00 *	6	-1.00	-1.00 *
5. Denmark	5	0.20	0.20	3	1.00	0.33	5	0.20	0.20
6. Finland	4	-0.50	-0.50	1	-1.00	-1.00	3	-0.33	-0.33
7. France	29	0.03	-0.24	23	0.22	-0.13	6	-0.67	-0.67(*)
8. Germany	12	0.50	0.17(!)	12	0.50	0.17(!)	6	1.00	0.67 !
9. Holland	20	0.30	0.00	19	0.37	-0.05	18	0.33	-0.06
10. Ireland	30	0.33	0.33(!)	27	0.33	0.33(!)	15	0.20	0.47(!)
11. Italy	17	-0.06	-0.18	4	-1.00	-1.00	4	-0.50	0.00
12. Japan	no changes			no changes			no changes		
13. New Zealand	28	-0.25	-0.43(*)	28	-0.25	-0.43(*)	7	-0.14	-0.43
14. Norway	12	-0.50	-0.33(*)	12	-0.50	-0.33(*)	12	-0.50	-0.33(*)
15. Sweden	3	-1.00	0.33	3	-1.00	0.33	3	-1.00	0.33
16. U.K.	27	-0.33	-0.78 *	27	-0.33	-0.78 *	15	-0.20	-0.73 *
17. U.S.A.	30	-0.47	0.00(*)	12	-0.50	0.33(*)	18	-0.44	-0.22(*)
Σ	273	-0.11	-0.19(*)	224	-0.08	-0.20(*)	148	-0.18	-0.20(*)

Tab. 6. Comparing the sum-line for Hibbs non-RE Partisan Cycles for all four variables.

Left governments

x = u, p, y, c	All governments			Stable governments			First governments		
	T	$v(x)$	$v(x^d)$	T	$v(x)$	$v(x^d)$	T	$v(x)$	$v(x^d)$
Unemployment rate - expected sign negative									
Σv	191	0.02	-0.05	145	0.06	-0.02	97	0.03	-0.03
Price rises - expected sign positive									
Σv	191	0.17	0.02(*)	145	0.19	-0.03(*)	97	0.20	-0.01
Real growth rate y - expected sign unclear									
Σv	191	-0.12	-0.13	145	-0.12	-0.01	97	-0.11	-0.01
Growth in public consumption c - expected sign positive									
Σv	191	-0.15	-0.10	145	-0.21	-0.18(*)	97	-0.21	-0.21(*)

Right Governments

x = u, p, y, c	All governments			Stable governments			First governments		
	T	$v(x)$	$v(x^d)$	T	$v(x)$	$v(x^d)$	T	$v(x)$	$v(x^d)$
Unemployment rate - expected sign positive									
Σv	273	0.21	0.05(*)	224	0.24	-0.01 *	148	0.07	-0.01
Price rises - expected sign negative									
Σv	273	-0.11	-0.19(*)	224	-0.08	-0.20(*)	148	-0.18	-0.20(*)
Real Growth rate y - expected sign unclear									
Σv	273	0.10	0.07	224	0.09	0.08	148	0.19	0.01
Growth in public consumption c - expected sign negative									
Σv	273	-0.03	0.01	224	-0.08	0.03	148	0.03	-0.03

In any case it should be noted that the distribution for the *USA is an outlier*, as is often the case in comparative economic studies.

It is hard to say if one should have expected to find relatively strong or weak Partisan Cycles in the USA. The impression is that the difference between left and right is relatively small in the US, so we expect to find stronger cycles elsewhere. On the other hand, the US economy is relatively closed, and therefore the US series are likely to contain relatively small exogenous international elements, so domestic series should stand out more clearly. However, our attempt to purge the series of the international elements did make the results marginally *weaker* in the average country. Therefore, there are no reasons to expect stronger Partisan Cycles the US.

This leaves us in a situation that is not altogether pleasant. On the one hand, we have found significant Partisan Cycles. On the other hand, we have found that both types of Partisan Cycles are significant. The only real difference between the two versions of the Partisan Cycle is the way in which expectations are formed. It would have been an important result, had such clear difference been found between the number of cases where the two types of cycles appear, that we could have drawn strong conclusions as to how expectations are formed. Our results do give an edge to rational expectations; but it is far from being a clear victory.

Let us finally return to two general questions which has followed us throughout the paper: Does politics matter in the determination of macroeconomic policy? And do policies matter? We can now answer both questions in the affirmative: *yes, politics matters*, and *yes, policies matter*; but we have to add to both answers: *but not all that much*.

References

Alessina, A., 1987. "Macroeconomic Policy in a Two-Party System as a Repeated Game", *Quarterly Journal of Economics*, 102, 651-677.

Alessina, A., 1988a. "Macroeconomics and Politics", *NBER Macroeconomic Annual 1988*, MIT Press.

Alessina, A., 1988b. "Politics and Business Cycles in Industrial Democracies", Conference paper, prepared for *Economic Policy*, no 8.

Alessina, A. and J. Sachs, 1987. "Political Parties and the Business Cycle in the United States, 1948-1984", *Journal of Money, Credit and Banking*, 20, 63-82.

Alesina, A. and H. Rosenthal, 1988. "Partisan Cycles in Congressional Elections and the Macroeconomy", *American Political Science Review*, 83, 63-82.

Begg, D.K.H., 1982. *The Rational Expectations Revolution in Macroeconomics. Theories and Evidence*. Phillip Allen, Oxford.

Bloom, H.S. and H.D. Price, 1975. "The Effects of Aggregate Economic Variables on Congressional Elections", (An article in the discussion on Kramer, 1971), *American Political Science Review*, 69, 1232-69.

Castles, F.C., 1981. "How does Politics Matter?: Structure or Agency in the Determination of Public Policy Outcomes", *European Journal of Political Research*, 9, 119-132.

Cukierman, A. and A.H. Meltzer, 1986. "A Positive Theory of Discretionary Policy, The Cost of a Democratic Government, and The Benefits of a Constitution", *Economic Inquiry*, 24, 367-88.

Frey, B.S. and F. Schneider, 1978a. "A Politico-economic Model of the United Kingdom", *Economic Journal*, 88, 243-253.

Frey, B.S. and F. Schneider, 1978b. "An Empirical Study of Politico-Economic Interaction in the US", *Review of Economics and Statistics*, 60, 174-183.

Hibbs, D.A. Jr., 1977. "Political Parties and Macroeconomic Policy", *American Political Science Review*, 71, 1467-1487 (reprinted in Hibbs, 1987a).

Hibbs, D.A. Jr., 1986. "Political Parties and Macroeconomic Policies and Outcomes in the United States", *American Economic Review*, Papers and Proceedings, 76, 66-70.

Hibbs, D.A. Jr., 1987a. *The Political Economy of Industrial Democracies*. Harvard UP, Cambridge Mass.

Hibbs, D.A. Jr., 1987b. *American Political Economy. Macroeconomics and Electoral Policy in the United States*. Harvard UP, Cambridge Mass.

Høst, V. and M. Paldam, 1990. "An International Element in the Vote? A comparative study of 17 OECD countries 1946-85", *European Journal of Political Research*, 18.

Johansen, L., 1977 and 1978. *Lectures on macroeconomic planning. Volume 1 1977, Volume 2 1978.* North-Holland, Amsterdam.

Jonung, L. and D. Laidler, 1988. "Are Perceptions of Inflation Rational? Some Evidence from Sweden", *American Economic Review*, 71, 1080-87.

Kendall, M.G., 1970. *Rank correlation methods.* (First 1948, fourth ed.), Griffin, London.

Kramer, G.H., 1971. "Short-Term Fluctuations in US Voter Behavior, 1896-1964", *American Political Science Review*, 65, 131-43.

Lafay, J.D., M. Lewis-Beck and H. Norpoth, editors, 1990. *Economics and Elections in United States and Western Europe,* Michigan U.P.

MacRae, D.C., 1977. "A Political Model of the Business Cycle", *Journal of Political Economy*, 85, 239-63.

Minford, P. and Peel, 1981. "The political theory of the business cycle", *European Economic Review,* 17, 253-70.

Mueller, J.E., 1970. "Presidential Popularity from Truman to Johnson", *American Political Science Review*, 64, 18-34.

Nordhaus, W.D., 1975. "The Political Business Cycle", *The Review of Economic Studies*, 42, 169-90.

Paldam, M., 1979. "Is there a Election Cycle? A Comparative Study of National Accounts", *Scandinavian Journal of Economics*, 81, 323-342.

Paldam, M., 1981a. "An Essay on the rationality of economic policy. The test-case of the election cycle", *Public Choice*, 37, 287-305.

Paldam, M., 1981b. "A Preliminary Survey of the Theories and Findings on Vote and Popularity Functions", *European Journal of Political Research*, 9, 181-199.

Paldam, M., 1983. "The International Element in Economic Fluctuations of 20 OECD-Countries 1948-75", *Regional Science and Urban Economics*, 13, 429-454.

Paldam, M., 1986. "The Distribution of Election Results and the two Explanations of the Cost of Ruling", *European Journal of Political Economy*, 2, 5-24.

Paldam, M., 1989. "Wage Rises and the Balance of Payments. A Study of the Reaction Lags", Working Paper, Institute of Economics, Aarhus University.

Paldam, M., 1990a. "How Robust is the Vote Function ? A Comparative Study of 197 Elections in the OECD Area 1948-85", in Lafay, Lewis-Beck and Norpoth (1990).

Paldam, M., 1990b. "Politics Matters After All (1). Testing Alesina's Theory of RE Partisan Cycles on Data for 17 countries", Forthcoming in N. Thygesen and Velupillai, editors, *Recent Developments in Business Cycle Theory - Methods and Empirical Applications*, MacMillan, London.

Persson, M., T. Persson and L.E.O. Svensson, 1987. "Time Consistency of Fiscal and Monetary Policy", *Econometrica*, 55, 1419-1431.

Sørensen, J.R., 1988. "The Political Business Cycle in a Rational Expectations Model with two Political Parties", Paper for the European Public Choice Meeting 1989.

Tinbergen, J., 1956. *Economic Policy: Principles and Design.* (2nd edition 1964). North Holland, Amsterdam.

Chapter 5

ACCIDENTAL FREEDOM

Gordon Tullock

The gradual change of England from a weakly mercantilistic state at the time Adam Smith wrote his book to almost pure free trade by 1850 is one of the great examples of the triumph of ideas in history. It is, of course, true that England was already much freer economy than most of the world but, still, the change was very significant. Unfortunately, I am unable to claim similar influence for ideas in the United States.

It is true that the United States was influenced by Smith and that many of our leading officials were under his sway, including a number of presidents and congressmen. Indeed, his influence at various times on our history had considerable effect. Interestingly, Alexander Hamilton -- probably the most brilliant of our economic managers -- understood Mr. Smith perfectly and rejected his advice.

Basically, however, we are more the fortunate product of a series of accidents rather than of careful thought. To explain this, I am going to present a desperately brief and oversimplified account of our history in this area.

In the first place, the colonies themselves were essentially appendages to England. There was an active coastal trade along the coast of the thirteen colonies, but, in general, the trade between England and the colonies was more important than the intercolonial trade. At the time of the American Revolution, there was a very thin layer of settlement running along the coast with few people living very far inland, so they made little use of land transportation. The general population density was not great enough to support canals although a number were built in the early nineteenth century. It was not until the introduction of the railroads that overland transportation in the United States became reasonably good.

There is here, however, a rather important modification, which is that during the winter the northern part of the United States gets very cold. At this time, the muddy roads become hard as rock and a good deal of the movement of heavy objects was carried out by using special equipment for operating in snow and ice. In this respect, the situation was rather similar to that of Russia. The existence of many streams, together with the fact that in those distant days even a rather small boat was a suitable method of getting things around, meant that inland citizens were not as cut off from the world as one might think.

I. THE BEGINNINGS

But to return to the pre-revolutionary situation, the colonies were subject to a good deal of economic regulation from England and almost all of this regulation had the specific purpose of benefiting various English interests.   The English, after all, were represented in the House of Commons and the colonies were not.   Still, the total volume of such regulation was not gigantic.[1]

These regulations were simply abandoned the moment that the colonies broke off from England. No one in Virginia was interested in retaining the monopoly of certain products in Virginia by English merchants. This was particularly true since during the Revolution we were allied with France and Spain and, if anything, would be likely to give their goods priority. Thus, what we had in the way of major regulations were more or less terminated by the Revolution itself, and there were very few such regulations at the time the Constitution was set up. This, again, is not the result of careful thought but the result of historic accident.

Now, this deals with what we may call major regulation. The states and local governments actually followed the custom of their day by having a very large number of minor regulations such as maximum prices on bread, and so on.   Those regulations, however, although certainly uneconomic in their character, do not seem to have done a great deal of damage, partly because they were not very well enforced. The principal enforcement mechanism in most of the United States, after all, was an elected sheriff, who normally would be quite reluctant to imprison a prominent local merchant. Also, the geographic scope was too small.

At that time, the average American citizen was a farmer who, if he was not completely autarkic, nevertheless produced himself a large part of his consumption. Insofar as he was engaged in trade, he was usually trying to sell agricultural commodities, hopefully in Europe. Quite naturally, he was not interested in anything which would depress their price.

---

[1] Indeed, I have always wondered why the Revolution occurred. The view that the colonies were severely repressed by England is absurd, even though, of course, there are various ways our condition could have been improved.

Undoubtedly, he would have liked price controls on those things that he did buy, but such regulations were likely to simply deprive him of any access to iron, horseshoes, and so on.

In the larger cities, and it must be emphasized that the larger cities were not very large at that time, there was more in the way of regulation, but, again, it does not seem to have been a major matter, not because people were in principle against it (they were in principle in favor of it) but because there was relatively little opportunity.

In addition, there were certain institutions which automatically were going to make rent seeking difficult. First, as Tollison (1988) pointed out, it is, on the whole, harder to make a deal with a legislature of many people than with a hereditary monarch; hence, democratic governments are apt to have less of rent seeking than authoritarian governments. The American government was for its day an extreme example of democracy. If we did not have universal manhood suffrage, it was nevertheless true that most men could vote.

A second argument (my own) is that the jury as a legal method of law is singularly inappropriate for enforcing the type of regulation that rent seekers normally want. In the first place, juries are never much impressed by the law when it conflicts with their own ideas of ethics, and, in the second place, juries tend to favor the smaller of the two parties. Lastly, they do not, in general, like monopolies of anything except labor. In sum, they are a weak reed for monopolists to lean on. Of course, if monopoly cannot be enforced, there is not much point in investing resources in seeking to monopolize an industry.

II. COMPETITION AND THE FEDERAL SYSTEM

But the basic factor that led to a fairly free economy in the United States, without anyone particularly planning it, was simply the federal system. As a general statement, the American states frequently have favored all sorts of rent seeking to benefit various small groups of their citizens. Some of the western states, settled by Germans and Scandinavians in the late nineteenth century, were actually formally socialist. They set up cooperative or state-owned grain elevators and various types of retail organizations. We had free trade, however, and by that time the railroads were in existence.[2] Their cooperative stores simply could not face the mail order competition of Sears Roebuck and Montgomery Ward.

The collective grain elevators found that their customers were shipping the grain across the state borders to private grain elevators. Internal free

---

[2] They also had a trial at regulating the railroads but after some experience came to the conclusion that unregulated railroads were better than no railroads.

trade made all of this quite possible. Such regulations were not particularly new. The early nineteenth century had the same kind of thing; the states enacting a great deal of mercantilistic regulation most of which promptly broke down because of free interstate trade. Of course, in the early days when internal transportation was very poor, the trade across state boundaries was not very sizable, but those were the days when there literally was not a great deal of trade, and, again, controls by local states were not very helpful.

The federal system here made it impossible for the states to put direct controls on interstate shipments. Further, in general, a given state that attempted to put some kind of indirect restriction on imports would immediately find that several other states were annoyed and these other states had a) a perfect right to sue them in the federal courts under a specific provision of the Constitution, and b) the right to have their senators and congressmen do various nasty things to the offender in Washington. Under the circumstances, this just did not pay.

In Switzerland, this kind of thing goes farther down because the communes have a good deal of independent power. In the United States, local governments -- the cities and counties -- have always done a large part of the total amount of the "governing." From the standpoint of our present discussion, however, the fact that the local governments are the "creatures of the state" legally means that a cartel of all the municipal governments in a given state enforced by the state legislature is possible. But as we have been pointing out, state sponsored cartels could not ban imports from other states; hence, they had very little scope.

It might be thought that the adoption of the federal system showed great forethought, but in both the United States and Switzerland, it arose from the pre-existing situation and not from careful thought. The states and cantons both already existed and the federal constitution was, in effect, a treaty among these previously existing governments. In order to get unanimous agreement, it was necessary to find the lowest common denominator, which meant a minimum transfer of power to the central government.[3]

---

[3] In practice, the state has not enforced cartels on the local governments for more than a limited number of subjects. A small corporation with which I am associated recently decided that it should build a small factory employing about 80 unskilled laborers. It simply solicited bids from 30 small towns in the immediate vicinity of its headquarters. The final arrangement is that we will rent a factory built for us by a town of about 1200 population with advantage for both us and the town. Whether such deals are actually desirable from society's interest is a much disputed point. They do show rather well, however, the competition between government

III. THE FEDERAL GOVERNMENT

Let us consider the federal government, which is not subject to all of these difficulties. The first thing to be said is that until about 1900, the national government did not do much of anything except run the post office and small military forces. Indeed, it seems likely that the United States was able to get off to such a good start, because the wars of the French Revolution and Empire broke out almost immediately after the signing of the Constitution, and distracted the European powers.

In a mild way, we did get into those wars. Our first war -- a very minor one -- was fought with France under the republic. Our second war,[4] a pretty major one, and, in fact, the first war that we lost, was fought beginning in 1812. We entered that world war on the side of Napoleon while he was marching on Moscow. Our objective was essentially to take Canada and we failed totally, but at the end of the war England was so exhausted -- not by fighting us, but by fighting Napoleon -- that she did not feel in the mood to undertake the difficult task of conquering the United States.[5]

In any event, our central government got off to its start as an extremely weak organization. It had little power or revenue. Interestingly, for the first seventy or eighty years of the American independent government, one of our major sources of revenue was not a tax. The western lands were held by the federal government and sold for revenue. This was such a major source of revenue that occasionally the federal government actually could not spend all its receipts and made gifts to the states.

Other than this land sale item, the main revenue was, of course, tariffs on imports, but there were some internal excises, one of which set off what came very close to being the first revolution against the American government.[6] The small revenues that were derived were used primarily to maintain military forces and to some extent domestic improvements.

---

units which makes government cartel management difficult.

[4] I am not counting our difficulties with the Barbary pirates as a war.

[5] It is not obvious she could have won. Her failure in the war of the American Revolution came not from the hard fighting of the colonists but because she was fighting France, Spain, and the armed neutrality, with the American fighting very much of a sideshow. By 1815, however, the population of the United States was nearly as large as that of England and conquest would have been extremely difficult. A joint project of England, France and Spain to partition the colonies in, say, 1795, would have been completely different. It was apparently fear of such a coalition which led to the Constitution.

[6] Washington marched out personally in charge of the militia to put the uprising down but it was successfully suppressed without significant fighting.

This was, however, a very minor matter and the domestic improvements were, in general, of a minor character.

Canals and railroads, and what toll roads there were in the United States, were put up primarily by private companies, sometimes with considerable aid from state and local governments and occasionally with aid from the federal government.[7] It would appear that the federal government was absorbing 2-3 percent of GNP in peacetime years throughout the nineteenth century. Since the United States was, of course, growing quite rapidly, this does not mean that the absolute size of the federal government was unchanging.

The general lack of central control is perhaps best illustrated by the fact that for the twenty years from 1843 to 1863 there was no centralized money system. Insofar as we were not using gold or silver coins (many of which were privately minted), the circulating medium was notes issued by private banks chartered by the states. The states had very little control over these banks and what rules they imposed were largely perverse.[8] This period has never been thought to be much of an advertisement for free banking, but it was showing signs of becoming more stable towards the end.

The end of this system came because the federal government wanted to make use of the money system as a way of raising funds to pay for the Civil War. The result was a switch to money still issued by private banks but now under fairly stringent federal government control. Until the founding of the Federal Reserve System just before World War II, most paper currency in the United States was issued by individual banks rather than by some central agency.

Insofar as there was central control, it was carried out by a federal government official called the comptroller of the currency and stabilization of the economy; insofar as it was done, it was carried out by J. P. Morgan. It does not seem like a very good system by present standards, but the economy was more stable during this period than during the first thirty years of the Federal Reserve System. Whether it was more stable than since World War II is the subject of a rather complicated historical debate.

But that has been a digression. The basic point here is that there was really little in the way of federal government activity and what there was

---

[7] After the Civil War, the federal government made some rather large land grants to railroads crossing the Rocky Mountains. Since several of these railroads proceeded to go bankrupt, one can assume that these grants were not all that generous.
[8] The banks were compelled to keep reserves in state bonds which were highly unstable. This led to numerous bankruptcies.

had to do with such traditional government activities as the military and the road system. The states attempted various rent-seeking activities, as I suppose would be expected, but, in general, were unsuccessful because of internal free trade.

IV. PROTECTIONISM

There was one area where the federal government had considerable power and used it detrimentally -- foreign trade. Under the Constitution, export taxes were prohibited but not import taxes. This was put through essentially by the Southern states who at that time were already major agricultural exporters to Europe. It seems that the Southern states feared that Congress might put export taxes on their crops.

Alexander Hamilton, however, saw things differently and he is the source of intellectual backing for what we now think of as protective tariffs. He seems to have all by himself invented the infant industry argument, although I cannot be sure. In any event, List, like Tocqueville, came to the United States to study new methods. List came for the purpose of studying how the American government was encouraging industry. He quickly realized that the American government was simply succumbing to various special interests. It can be said that when he went back and set up the Zollverein in Germany, he also succumbed.

Hamilton wanted to set up a major set of protective tariffs and he had the support from incipient industrial interests in the North. But his problem was the Southern agricultural exporters who had very early in the republic become primarily exporters of cotton; thus, they had an interest in preventing import tariffs from rising. Since in those days they were about half of the country, the period from 1788 to 1860 is one of fluctuating tariffs going up or down depending to a large extent on fluctuations in the political power of different parts of the country.

The tariff was, in many ways, an easier type of control than more sophisticated mercantilistic means. In the first place, the Constitution provided, and then the courts enforced, a number of things that made collecting tariffs easy. For example, it is not necessary to have a search warrant if a customs inspector wishes to search any person in the general vicinity of a dock. It is also not necessary for a jury to deal with most cases of evasion of duties. The fact that the tariffs were imposed only around the perimeter of the country also meant, of course, that one could have a much smaller tax collection force than required to collect an excise tax inside the country.

V. SIZE OF GOVERNMENT

I have pointed out, however, that the federal government was not collecting or spending a great deal of money and it had an alternative source of revenue in the form of the land sales. Under the circumstances, American tariffs developed a tendency which was unkindly referred to by some Europeans as a prohibited list and a free list. This is, of course, an exaggeration but it is, nevertheless, true that American tariffs have frequently not covered at all items where a lot of revenue could be obtained -- for example, coffee. At the same time in other areas we had taxes so high that no revenue was obtained. It has, of course, never been true that there were no tariffs that actually raised considerable amounts of revenue.

The result of all of this is that the United States, as of, say, 1855, had an extremely free and open economy.[9] The Civil War raised government expenditures very sharply. In a real sense, the American Civil War was the most severe war we ever fought. At its end a number of costs continued. An army of occupation, admittedly a small one, was maintained in the South for a period of time and there were war veteran pensions.

Further, one of the results of the Republican ascendancy had been the more or less complete abandonment of land sales as a source of revenue. The Homestead Act provided land that could be obtained freely by anyone who simply occupied it. Thus, at the end of the war, the government collected something like 6 percent of GNP in taxes. There was a steady fall in this amount until about 1900, at which time the federal government was absorbing about 2 percent of GNP -- again, for military and rather minor domestic improvements. Even our minor wars with Spain and the Philippines did not have much affect on this very low budget. It is interesting that at this time the sum of local government budgets was considerably larger than the federal budget but still did not add up to more than 6 percent of GNP.

But there were some signs of difficulties to come. In many ways, this was the heroic period of American development. The compound and then the triple condensation steam engine lowered the fuel consumption of steam engines to the point where trans-atlantic steamers became a much cheaper mode of transportation than the sail boats that had dominated the traffic up to that time. This led to an influx of people from Europe, mainly coming from Eastern Europe rather than Western Europe where we had previously drawn our immigrants.

Western Europe at this time was also rapidly growing. In 1870, per

---

[9] The Southern slaves may not have thought of it as free but economic freedom in this case means something different from political or human freedom. From present day standards, it is ironic that Southern slaveholders like Jefferson and Jackson were the principle defenders of low tariffs and Northern abolitionists normally favored protection.

capita income was higher in a number of European countries than it was in the United States. From the Russian Empire and from parts of the Austro-Hungarian Empire, however, there was a flood of people seeking improvement in their living standards which, in general, they achieved. Some of them, of course, were also fleeing political repression and a good many of them just did not want to be drafted.

Some of these immigrants settled in the West and others were much of the labor force for the expansion of industry which led to American economic dominance in much of the world. Looking back on this, we see a gigantic free trade area, the largest one in the world at that time by a wide margin, with governments mainly doing things that Adam Smith would have approved of. Much of our present-day world comes out of this period. Edison, Ford, Bell, and Burbank all were Americans and all true revolutionaries.

Politically, however, we were now moving toward changes which I regard as undesirable, but which many people would regard as straightforward progress. Indeed, it was called the "Progressive Movement" at the time. Kolko, a representative of the far left, refers to this whole period as the triumph of capitalism because the government regulations that were enacted were generally for the benefit of special interests. But it should be said that they were mainly sold as democratic efforts to help the poor, a camouflage which has continued.

Now, in all of this, the United States was far behind developments in Europe. Bismarck invented the welfare state and it spread rapidly in Europe. But it was not until the 1930s that it began to have any significant effect in the United States.

With respect to the tariff, the situation at the end of the Civil War was that the tax system had been designed to raise money for the military establishment maintained by the federal government. As this was disbanded, the taxes were steadily reduced, and year after year there were bills to "reduce the revenue" introduced in Congress. The tariff became even more to resemble a free list and a prohibited list, since the congressmen quickly realized they could reduce revenue just as readily by raising the import duty on something that their constituents produced as by lowering the tax on something that their constituents consumed.

The rise in tariffs in this time was also probably affected to a considerable extent by the fact that the South had lost its influence. The western states, major exporters of grain, do not seem to have ever been as firmly opposed to tariffs as had been the more traditional Southern states which were now under military occupation.

Nevertheless, although there were events that were forerunners of developments in the twentieth century, very little was actually done in the

nineteenth century. Further, I must repeat my previous remarks about the
evaluation of these changes. Most people then and, indeed, until most
recently, would simply have said that the United States was rather
backward. The new methods of running states for the benefit of the poor
or the people, and (especially) the special interests, had not penetrated very
thoroughly into the United States.

I have mentioned this was the period in which certain western states
attempted to adopt Socialism and failed because of internal free trade. It
is also the period in which many other regulations were established. For
a while, the Supreme Court impeded these developments but it eventually
gave in.

As an example which has absolutely nothing to do with Socialism, the
slaughterhouse case -- a very important case in the history of American
constitutional law -- involved a law passed by the Louisiana State
Legislature under the cover of concern for public sanitation. In fact, it
gave a designated person a monopoly of butchering meat in New Orleans.
This was rather typical of the kind of thing that was being done and the
kind of thing that still was being destroyed, in essence, by free trade. If
we were going to have controls on the economy, if special interest groups
were going to secure significant gains, it would be necessary for the federal
government to come to their aid. In the latter part of the nineteenth century
it began to do so.

But although we do have this development of federal government
control of the economy to the advantage of various special interests, and it
should be said to some extent in the public interest, still it was very mild
compared to what it was and still is in Europe. Our general tax burden is
much lower than that of Europe. Government spending as percent of GNP
in the years 1890 through 1910 was extremely small and this was a period
in which we fought two wars, albeit rather minor ones. Still, foundations
for much greater expansion were laid at this time.

VI. REGULATION

As an indication of what was happening, consider the Interstate
Commerce Commission (ICC). This was an effort to control the railroads,
and it should be said that the railroads at that time did raise some special
problems. In general, getting around the United States then depended on
the use of railroads, which also shipped the bulk of the produce from place
to place. If you wanted to get from one major city to another major city,
you normally had a choice of a number of routes run by different
companies. These companies regularly attempted to organize cartels but
these just as regularly broke down. They were, therefore, interested in
some kind of government control which would prevent the price

competition that they found so painful.

More importantly, however, the inhabitants of small towns were politically important at this time. Usually the small towns had only one railroad running through them. Further, the railroad usually was on a route between two major cities. It might well be true in the periods when the cartels were in disarray that the cost of shipping goods from, say, Chicago to New York by way of Evansville, was less than the cost of shipping them from Evansville to either Chicago or New York. The inhabitants of Evansville naturally objected, and taking the United States as a whole, this still being basically an agricultural country, the inhabitants of these small towns outnumbered the inhabitants of the major cities.

This made possible an alliance between the small town interests and the railroads. The alliance was formed and created the ICC which provided control over railroad rates. Naturally, there is nothing in the act that says the ICC shall enforce cartel arrangements among railroads, and, indeed, in the early years it was not very good at that although certainly there was an improvement. The act purported to have nobler purposes. In addition to the "public benefits", the farmers obtained a ban on higher rates for a short distance on a given rail line than was charged for a longer distance.

Interestingly, although mentioned by the early economists, the cartel aspects of the ICC, and, indeed, of the later government regulatory commissions, rapidly disappeared from the scholarly literature. I think it would be correct to say that by the 1930s, and probably much earlier than that, the general view of most of the regulatory commissions was simply that they were doing good. It was argued that we had natural monopolies and a regulatory commission was necessary to control them. A special branch of law had developed and most of the economists who were interested in this area regularly testified as experts before various control commissions. In other words, they had been co-opted.

As an example of how thorough this idea had become, let me give a little of my own experience. When I was in law school in the early 1940s,[10] I was given a project on the railroads in an antitrust course. I looked at the voluminous data which the ICC published about the railroads and was greatly shocked to discover that the profits of the railroads had actually increased after the ICC had been formed. This raised questions in my mind about the controlling of natural monopoly argument.[11] The reason

---

[10] Before I was drafted.

[11] It should be said that the gains were almost entirely in the early days. Eventually the ICC transferred the bulk of the profits from the owners of railroad stock to the railroad employees. By the 1930s, most of the railroads no longer could pay interest on the bonds which had been used to build their roadbeds.

I was shocked was simply that I had never heard anything about the regulatory commissions except that they prevented monopolist exploitation.

Still, in the 1930s ICC jurisdiction was extended to cover truck and bus line transportation when the railroads ceased to be monopolies. In this connection, my own proposal at the time[12] to abolish all regulation of short railroad trips because the trucks and busses were fully capable of providing competition was regarded with horror by most of my more conventional colleagues.

It is also interesting that about this time, that is in the 1930s, the rapidly developing air transportation system petitioned for and received the organization of the Civil Aeronautics Board (CAB) with the specific argument that without it there would be destructive competition. The CAB, of course, effectively cartelized a naturally highly competitive industry.

Let us return to the 1890s and the early part of the twentieth century when a great many other interventions into the market began. I mentioned earlier that the United States had made considerable revenue out of selling its national lands and then under the Homestead Act had abandoned this revenue. As one moves west in the United States, however, rainfall falls off and the areas cease to be suitable for farming on small plots.[13] Land could still be purchased but the minimum price was high enough to leave a good deal of land in federal hands.[14]

Congress and the government made several rather inept efforts to amend the Homestead Act so that people could simply take larger plots of land in hopes that this would solve the problem, but about 1890 the policy itself was changed. Instead of aiming at transferring as much land as possible into private ownership, a positive conservation policy was adopted for timber land, and later range land, which was kept in government hands. The history of this, again, is rather like the history of railroad regulation, in that policy was announced in terms of general benefit but actually benefitted narrower parties.

It should be said that in this case from the beginning and to the present, the principal beneficiary of the management of the forest lands has been the forest service whose management of the lands has been, I think, pretty unmitigatedly aimed at increasing the total budgetary revenues of the forest service. Rangeland, on the other hand, was distributed to politically powerful ranching interests in the west until recent years when such organizations as the Sierra Club have shown an ability to generate more votes than the ranchers.

---

[12] Not to the government, just around in my class and friends.

[13] 160 acre.

[14] Indeed, some 40 percent of the land area of the United States.

Herbert Hoover, during the 1920s as Secretary of Commerce, and, of course, eventually President, was a great believer in government control of almost everything. Under his leadership, the Department of Commerce grew to the point where it occupied the largest office building in Washington D.C. -- the entire west end of the famed government triangle. Among other things, he is responsible for the development of our present regulatory system for radio (subsequently extended to television).

What happened here is not that the popular attitude towards regulation changed. The behavior of the states, and for that matter the local governments, continued to involve much regulation. It was simply that the switch of activity to the federal government meant that this regulation no longer faced competitive pressure; hence, could, in fact, grow greater.

To name but one example of local regulations, the general adoption of zoning laws in most states and most cities of the United States occurred during this period. These laws greatly increased the power of local politicians which was sometimes used to solicit bribes. Again, the laws had very general intellectual support. I remember being taught in high school what a good thing they were.

It is easy to develop good intellectual and economic rationalization for zoning codes since there is no doubt that what you do on your land generally exerts externalities on your next-door neighbor. But that this assumes that the zoning is, in fact, well run. There is no reason to believe that has been characteristic of our zoning in the United States. Indeed, it seems likely that the principal result of these codes is transfer of large site values back and forth among different real estate owners, depending on the zone classification. It also created a large industry of specialists in zone changes.

All of this has not been as expensive as you might expect because in practice zoning codes do not bind very tightly. Houston has no zoning code and you cannot tell by simply looking at it that it is any different from any other American city. In general, up-zoning -- that is, moving from one zone category to a more valuable category -- is reasonably easy and very widely practiced. Still, it is a waste. Undoubtedly, the ideal system would be an efficient set of building restrictions designed to minimize externalities and run by impartial and highly competent people. The second best probably is no zoning at all and the third best is the zoning we, in fact, have.

VII. GROWTH

It is interesting that the period from 1870 to 1929 was the period in which the United States acquired the highest living standard in the world. In other words, it overtook various European countries. England, in particular, had been relatively better off as late as 1900. It is possible that the explanation for this is simply the development of the Bismarckian welfare state in Europe and that this slowed down growth. Since we did not have it, and England got it late, the data fit.

But having said that this is possible, I should go further and say that it is by no means obvious that this is so. A theory which would imply that this is the explanation for this change would hold that there is a slowing down of growth in a move from a free market to a highly regulated market and in particular to a welfare state, but that once growth has fallen for a while, there is a return to the main trend but at a lower base.

This would imply that the growth of the United States during this period was normal and the growth of most European countries was retarded and then during the period from the 1930s on, when the United States was moving into the welfare state and the Europeans already were there, it was the United States whose growth rate was retarded.

This theory which I used to regard as quite sound is lacking in empirical support. The United States as the richest country in the world does have certain disadvantages in growth since it does have to invent new things, whereas other people who are behind us can to some extent copy us, which is cheaper. But, nevertheless, our relatively slow growth in recent years is conspicuous.

VIII. GOVERNMENT BY 1929

In any event, the United States had relatively light government in 1929. It must be emphasized again that there was a great deal of local government. The school system, for example, is very expensive in the United States and before 1930 was paid for almost exclusively[15] by the local municipal or county governments. State governments built most of the highways, although in this case there were some arrangements under which the gasoline taxes collected by the federal government was in part rebated to them for the building of highways.

The courts and police were, again, almost entirely local responsibilities with the exact division between the municipal and county governments on one hand and the state government on the other, depending on where you were. Having said this, we have covered the bulk of the American government in those days. The federal government maintained a military force with a small army but bigger in air and sea power. It also maintained a number of minor services such as patents, weather service, and so on, and was developing a control bureaucracy in Washington which was, however, still rather small. The pension system for war veterans and the

---

[15] Some of the Southern states were the major exceptions.

fairly elaborate research establishment paid for by the federal government, although actually administered by the states for the benefit of agriculture, were also significant relative to central government expenditures.

IX. THE REGIME SHIFT

We then had a regime shift in the 1930s. The easiest way of explaining this is that the United States' intellectuals had followed much the same course as European intellectuals. When I was in law school just before and just after World War II, most of my colleagues were Socialists of one sort or the other. Indeed, that was the reason that I joined the Department of State. I concluded that personally I could have no future anywhere except in government service, and even I, black reactionary that I was, conceded that the government should run foreign policy.

The Great Depression, an incredible catastrophe of which I have only faint yet nevertheless depressing memories, led to quick internal revolution in which many of these ideas which had been fermenting on the intellectual backboilers of society were put into effect. In essence, what we did was copy the European Bismarckian states and, indeed, in the thirties people would frequently quite consciously refer to Hitler's policies as the kind of thing which we were moving toward. Of course, they referred far more commonly to Russian policies.

Although this change occurred, the total volume of government was still quite small by European standards. The National Recovery Administration (NRA) and the Agricultural Adjustment Administration, in fact, established government sponsored cartels for much of our economy. The NRA was knocked out by the Supreme Court about the time that almost everyone realized that it was failing, but we still have our agricultural program.

Interestingly, the leading lights of the New Deal who had organized the cartels of the NRA almost immediately switched over to radical antitrust policy. Apparently there was no feeling on their part of intellectual inconsistency, probably because in either event there was government control of business.

At this time national old-age pensions were introduced, and we very nearly got a medical program too, although we switched instead to widespread private health insurance.

Almost all of this was rationalized in terms of helping the poor, but as a matter of fact, there is no real evidence that it has particularly done so. Indeed, if it has retarded growth, as I tend to think it has, the poor are probably worse off than they would have been without these programs. There have not been many studies of this particular subject but the studies that we do have indicate that the poor, defined roughly as the bottom 10 percent of the population, were given about as much government aid relatively in 1850 as they were in 1950.[16] The studies of old-age pensions indicate that the poor older people, again, were about as well taken care of relatively in the 1920s as they are now.[17]

Unfortunately, there has not been much research done along these lines. Most people just assume that the program benefitted the poor because the people who advocated it said it did. I would like to have the two sources that I have just footnoted supplemented by at least 100 doctoral dissertations. Those of you who are teachers are in a position to see to it that this particular hard -- in the sense of tedious but not intellectually difficult -- task is undertaken.

The growth of the American government is frequently talked about in military terms but actually this is quite unrealistic. The First and Second World Wars led to increases in government expenditure which vanished more or less after each war. The Korean War led to a smaller increase but the bulk of that increase remained in position. Thus, from the Korean War to the present, we have had fairly sizeable land forces as well as maintaining the traditional large navy and air force.

But, although we have maintained sizeable forces, they have not grown as rapidly as the economy, with the result that their share of GNP has fallen irregularly. There have been at least three cases in which new presidents were elected on a campaign of strengthening the military: Kennedy, Nixon, and Reagan. In all three cases, there was a temporary rise in the military budget followed by continuing decrease as a share of GNP. It is, of course, true that the absolute size of the military budget, on the whole, grew over this period. Indeed, it had to, because it was necessary to raise wages of soldiers in order to keep them in uniform.

Basically, however, the growth has been in transfers of one sort or the other, old-age pensions, increasing medical programs particularly for the poor,[18] and the Aid to Families with Dependent Children (AFDC) program which, in essence, rewards women for having illegitimate children.[19]

The actual expenditures, however, I think are less important in dealing with the freedom of the economy than the regulations. Of course, the two are highly correlated. It is hard to specify a good measure of regulation.

---

[16] Lebergott (1979), p57.

[17] Weaver (1977).

[18] Who also received free medicine before these programs were instituted.

[19] It should be emphasized that by no means are all the women receiving AFDC teenagers fully dependent on AFDC. They do, indeed, exist but there are a good many people who receive this money because, say, a husband has died and who are dependent on it only for a rather brief time.

Measures like number of pages in the Federal Register which have been used have the disadvantage that Congress from time to time decides that a procedure should be more complicated, with the result that everything has to go into the federal regulations again so that many times the same regulation appears four or five times.

Switzerland, another federal state -- in fact, one that is even more federal than we are -- is our only close competitor on share of GNP absorbed by government. Japan, where the government is now growing very rapidly, had a long period with practically no central government controls, essentially because General Douglas MacArthur abolished a large part of the Japanese government during his reign. In addition, the Japanese corporations seem to have a great ability to control the controllers.

Japan, of course, like the four little Asian dragons, is heavily concerned with export markets where they do not have market power. But domestically, one finds government regulations providing protection, in particular agriculture. Interestingly, American efforts to have the Japanese, Koreans, and so on, to benefit their citizens by lowering protective tariffs and hence permitting their citizens to buy goods like oranges at a reasonable price, are objected to by populist groups in all of those countries. The same would have been true in the United States in the 1920s.

One can hope that Europe will go through a reduction in rent seeking, although in the past the Brussels organization has succeeded in partially offsetting reductions in tariffs by cartel arrangements.

The Reagan years have not shown any real reduction in the share of the government expenditures or in regulation, although neither has grown particularly. There are some encouraging areas here, however. We now have free trade agreements with Canada and Israel. In these cases, the economy that we are opening up for free trade is fairly small compared to ours. But a domestic cartel, even supported by the federal government, would confront competitors from these countries. Thus, we may be moving into a period in which a larger free trade zone will provide for the United States as a whole the kind of protection against rent seeking that in the past was given by the federal free-trade zone. It is, of course, a very old economic chestnut that tariffs are the mother of monopoly. This is true whether the monopolies are privately organized or sponsored by the government.

X. LIBERALIZING TENDENCIES

The free-trade agreements are but a small part of the changes in tariffs in the United States over the last fifty years. Before turning to that, however, I would like to mention briefly another development which has made internal trade in the United States much less regulated. The invention of the truck and the development of a large trucking industry in the United States, as I mentioned, was countered by the extension of the ICC regulation to the trucks. Interestingly, from the very beginning there was an exception. The farmers were powerful enough so that they were able to prevent trucks carrying farm produce from being regulated, which would seem to have eliminated the "natural monopoly" argument.

But even a regulated trucking industry provided a great deal of flexibility for shipment within the United States and in recent years the regulations have, for all intents and purposes, vanished. Regulations were also cut back on the railroads, with the result that internal transportation in the United States is now much freer than at any time since the foundation of the ICC.

But to return to the important problem of tariffs. The long period between the Civil War and 1929 was, on the whole, a period of rising protection. Indeed, Senator Pine of Oklahoma, trying to obtain a tariff for his constituents in the Smoot-Hawley tariff said: "We must either build up a tariff on oil or tear down the tariff on steel. The Government cannot deny the equal protection of the law to any of its citizens."[20] Politically, these tariffs were essentially pushed by the Northeast and objected to by the South, but the South was politically weak during this period.

With the rise of the Democratic control in 1932, however, this situation changed, with greatly increasing government control. But President Franklin Roosevelt chose as his Secretary of State a congressman from Tennessee who had been all of his life a free trader. Cordell Hull immediately began a program of reducing tariffs by way of the Reciprocal Trade Act. In the thirties, these reductions were rather small. I think that perhaps the reason that Hull was able to get away with it was at least partially the general antibusiness climate of that government. Another reason for the success was that Hull and his colleagues at the Department of State simply lied about the consequences of such agreements. They alleged that we won on each and every trade in the sense that our exports were benefitted more than our imports.

Hull remained Secretary of State during most of World War II, and continued talking about free trade and succeeded in building it into some of our objectives at the end of that war. Further, there seems to have been a genuine intellectual conversion to free trade on the part of many high government officials, although it is difficult to argue there was much on the part of the common man. We were prosperous after the war and the rather obscure connection between lowering tariffs and keeping the Communists in check was pushed hard by the Department of State and various other

---

[20] Proceedings, Tariff Act of 1929, p. 361.

groups. The result was international negotiations under the GATT and the decline of tariffs in the developed economies. This was accompanied by falls in the costs of international shipping.

XI. PROTECTIONIST SENTIMENT

In recent years, it has become more difficult for the government to resist the common man's view of protectionism. Indeed, Congress seems to be thoroughly under control of this view, and we depend upon the president to resist. Politically, the president in this matter acts essentially as a third house of the legislature. The political motives of a person appealing to the entire United States populace for reelection are different than the political motives of a body of people in the House of Representatives and the Senate, each of whom appeals to a segment of it.[21]

In any event, this fall in the costs of internationally traded goods, whether from reducing tariffs or the fall in transportation costs, has once again had an immense effect inside the United States. Export industries, of course, are relatively uncontrolled and one of the results of the increase in our imports is an increase in our exports. Imports, however, also are subject to relatively little government control provided they can enter the country. It seems likely that the very sharp shrinkage in the American labor union movement has occurred simply because the monopoly held over various products disappeared when imports became possible. I remember hearing an official of the steel union, visiting Virginia Polytechnic Institute and State University for a public lecture, explain that things had changed very sharply in the steel industry and now, instead of simply pushing hard for increase in wages, the union was pushing hard for efficiency to keep Japanese steel from closing down all of their plants. Indeed, they were willing to accept wage cuts if that were necessary to retain jobs. With continuing protectionism, I doubt if this would have occurred.[22]

Protection, again, is the mother of monopoly. The United States, because of its large internal trading area, was less monopolized than other countries. The shrinkage in tariffs reduced monopolies even further. Again, the situation in the United States is, and almost always has been, much freer for the economy than elsewhere. I do not believe that this is because we economists have succeeded in convincing the voters that free trade is a good thing. I think it is the byproduct of other matters.

---

[21] As author of the original logrolling model (Tullock, 1959) I find this readily explicable.

[22] Possibly it would. The introduction of the so-called minimills, which are mainly non-union in the United States, conceivably could have destroyed the power of the steel workers even without the Japanese threat.

Nevertheless, there is everything to be said for continuing vigorously to push the arguments for a free economy. My own experience in this area is that I never lose an argument and I never convince anyone. It is representative of the kind of problem we face, that William Niskanen, Chief Director of Economics for Ford Company, was compelled to resign because he was not willing to sign a statement saying that a high tariff on the import of foreign cars was for the benefit of the American people.

At the very beginning of the paper I pointed out that, in the early nineteenth century, free-trade arguments had influenced policy in England. Perhaps the same can be achieved in the United States. Each individual tariff or quantitative restriction injures many people and benefits a few, whereas protectionist structures, as a whole, injure everyone. We succeeded in the U.S. in considerably reducing special privileges in our Tax Act by stressing such a point a few years ago, and we may be able to do it again with respect to protectionism. The benefits will fall much more strongly on non-American countries than the United States, because as I have pointed out, we already have, and in general have had, more economic freedom than most other countries.

References

Lebergott, S., 1979.   *The American Economy*, Princeton: Princeton University Press.

Tollison, R.D., 1988.   "Why Did the Industrial Revolution Occur in England?" in C.K. Rowley, R.D. Tollison, and G.Tullock, editors, *The Political Economy of Rent Seeking*, Boston: Kluwer Academic Publishers, 409-419.

Tullock, G., 1959.   "Problems of Majority Voting," *Journal of Political Economy*, 67, 571-579.

Weaver, C., 1977.   *The Emergence, Growth and Redirection of Social Security*, unpublished dissertation, Virginia Polytechnic Institute.

Chapter 6

EUROPE 1992: FROM THE COMMON TO THE SINGLE MARKET

Peter Holmes

In this chapter I demonstrate how political motives and political credibility are at the heart of the European Community's single market "1992" Programme. The Programme raises the political stakes of European politicians in implementing econimic policies that will give rise to a competitive internal market in the EC. The aim is to radically alter business expectations about the degree of competition in the internal market.

The most important element in the undertaking consists in establishing the credibility of commitment. The task lies not so much in devising measures which if adopted and implemented would have the effect of unifying the European market, but in persuading the business community that such measures will be adopted and once adopted will be implemented. The means is an attempt by member governments to politically precommit themselves to the unification strategy by entering into broad commitments of principle at the outset and constructing a set of incentives for themselves that raise the price they will pay if they do not fulfil their promises.

The first part of the paper shows how a series of political events led to the gradual erosion of most of the original commitments made in 1957 when the EEC was founded other than the elimination of intra-EC tariffs. I conclude by analyzing the way the new developments in the EC represent an attempt to return to the original European concept, including the original dynamics.

At the start of the European Economic Community, a series of agreements were signed, in which the immediate impact was modest, but which would require broader and deeper agreement on further issues if the initial commitments were not to be abandoned. The Rome Treaty of 1957 was "an agreement to agree" about future matters in ways that could not yet be specified by the architects of the original treaty. Compliance is effectively voluntary at each step in the proceedings, but the EC is unique in that the Rome Treaty signatories makes it impossible to renege on one part of the bargain without imperiling the whole edifice.

Under French pressure, implicit understandings were reached in the 1960s that parts only of the Rome Treaty would actually be implemented by the member states. But this eventually undermined the constitutional commitment to free competition. The 1992 Programme seeks to reverse the understandings. If the plan succeeds a new kind of "United States of Europe" could emerge out of economic contracting with national sovereignty technically recoverable but only at the cost of unwinding all the achievements of the EC system.

I. THE EC AND THE EUROPEAN STATE SYSTEM

The European Community may be in the process of forming a new kind of state-entity, not merely larger than, but different in kind from the separate nations that make its components: its origins are not the direct aftermath of territorial conflict and conquest, but out of a system intended to promote economic strength (if not always totally fine-tuned to this aim).

Richard Rosecrance (1986) in the "Rise of the Trading State" argues that in the past a combination of factors have led to the evolutionary survival of state-systems built on the conquest of territory and relying on military power to survive. By contrast, he sees post-war Japan as an example of a state whose structures are organized to be functional for expansion by trade and he contrasts the survival value of this with more traditional states in the 1980s. The voluntary cession of sovereignty in the EC may be creating a new kind of "contractual" trading state.

Like Rosecrance, the historians Paul Kennedy (1988) and Bernard Porter (1983) have suggested that Britain in the early nineteenth century was an abortive example of a state oriented around the principle of minimizing military expenditure and seeking to profit by persuading its neighbors to keep their markets open -- by offers of trade rather than conquest. But this was simply not consistent with the nature of the other states that had emerged from military conquest in nineteenth century Europe. It is clear that the post-1815 balance of power depended on a coalition of interests among the European powers to preserve the status quo. However, it did not take the form of general and agreed disarmament, but rather of heavily armed empires each distrustful of every other, and ready to cooperate only for the purposes of putting down an attempt by one power alone, or by revolutionary uprisings, to disrupt the equilibrium of the system. The common interest was in maintaining the existing system of "national-territorial" states.

Only Britain oriented its state structures and foreign policies for the purpose of promoting the growth of liberal capitalism, and had a vested interest in the creation and maintenance of a liberal international order without heavy arms spending.   Other state systems, effectively able to obstruct this arrangement, were not willing to cooperate.   There were a remarkable series of proposals for free trade in nineteenth century Europe, including the Anglo-French commercial treaty of 1860 and the plan for a common currency for the members of the Latin Monetary Union.   But the free trade treaties gave way to a new system of bilateral and exclusive alliances that drew even "liberal" Britain into militarized competition with other European states.   The experiences of the first half of the twentieth century certainly demonstrated that even, if free market liberalism in the international order was in the general interest, many states perceived themselves as having an interest in defection in pursuit of zero-sum gains.[1]

In the late 1940s the United States made receipt of Marshall Aid conditional on participation in the Organization for European Economic Cooperation (OEEC) and the European Payments Union (EPU) which required liberalization of trade and payments between member states.   The EPU was a perfect example of a way to break the Catch-22 of foreign exchange shortage; each member was committed to extending credit to every other in the knowledge that defection would be punished by the external force (the USA).   Other attempts to move faster towards economic and political union where the USA was not putting on pressure were aborted in the late 1940s, largely due to opposition from the United Kingdom.

Within continental Europe there was considerable pressure to make such advances, and in the end the opposition of the United Kingdom was ignored.   France and Germany had fought three wars within 100 years. Neither saw gains from another such conflict, but they did perceive an external threat from the Soviet Union that created a desire for cooperation. However, the inability to agree on details without external coercion resulted in the failure of the European Defence Community proposal, but a willingness to participate in the US-led NATO.

II. THE CREATION OF THE EUROPEAN COMMUNITIES

The aim of the proponents of European Integration in the 1950s was to create a system so interlinked and interdependent that military conflict would become impossibly costly for every single potential participant, i.e.,

---

[1] Kindleberger [1987] has suggested that a key element had been missing from the moment that others had perceived the weakness of Britain's resources to act as a liberal hegemonic power. The United States eventually assumed the role of an external actor threatening the European states with sanctions if they did not cooperate with each other. The European Community system can be seen as a device to replace the waning US hegemony.

to build in a set of incentives to decision makers to act like "trading states". The ultimate goal was to create political institutions that would neutralize conflict. But in order to do this economic arrangements had to be in place which were perceived as creating large gains from cooperation and net losses all round from defection.

In the economic sphere the attempts to turn the OEEC into a fuller union were thwarted by the UK, but in 1951 France, West Germany, Belgium, Italy, Luxembourg and the Netherlands agreed to establish the European Coal and Steel Community (ECSC) which put under collective jurisdiction the crucial disputed assets of the Ruhr and Lorraine which had been the occasions for Franco-German conflict. The economic interest is clear, but what is unusual is that under the Treaty of Paris, the ECSC embodies a greater degree of supra-nationalism than was later to be included in the wider EEC. The High Authority of the ECSC was empowered to take executive action without referring back to member governments.

The six governments continued to promote discussions about the creation of a wider economic union and in 1957 signed the Treaty of Rome creating the European Economic Community (EEC). A second Treaty of Rome in 1957 established the Euratom, the European Atomic Energy Community, (EAEC). There are thus three "European Communities" with their own Treaty rules, but since a Merger Treaty in 1965, all are managed by the same Council of Ministers and Commission. The term European Community is often used to described the whole network of arrangements, but strictly the "EEC" is only one aspect of this, albeit so far the most important part.

The British refused to sign, insisting that all that was required was a Free Trade area. The UK continued to promote this idea even after the six had set up the EEC, by establishing its own European Free Trade Area arrangement with Sweden, Denmark, Norway, Austria, Switzerland and Portugal, and also by trying to interest the EEC countries in a looser free trade arrangement that would undermine the attraction of the EEC.

The British distraction proved abortive, but more serious internal divisions undermined the original goal. The Rome Treaty committed its members to creating a "Common Market" with no internal tariffs by 1969. Non-tariff barriers (NTBs) were also to be removed but the mechanism was less precisely delineated. There were also a number of looser commitments which would remain unfulfilled unless the success with the earlier commitments generated the further political will to realize the other aims.

III. THE EEC AND NATIONAL SOVEREIGNTY

The Rome Treaty was an ingenious compromise between the immediate political realities and the grander ambitions. It commits member states to accept the Treaty and subsequent legislation into their own laws and it provides a Court of Justice to interpret Community Law and arbitrate between Community institutions and members. The importance of the Court of Justice has become more evident since the 1970s; at the outset, the focus was on the two central bodies, the EEC Council of Ministers and the EEC Commission. The Commission is the permanent "Civil service". The 17 Commissioners are appointed by member states for fixed terms, and are supposedly bound not to defend national positions. Answerable to them are the 10,000 or so officials also known as the Commission.

In fact the decision-making body for the system is the Council of Ministers, consisting of representatives of member states voting in secret on legislation that is proposed by the Commission and ultimately implemented by the Commission. It is worth remembering that the EC Commission and the Secretariat of the Council of Ministers are two bodies housed in adjacent buildings in Brussels with separate staffs. The two entities are distinct: the secretariat of the Council of Ministers is a bureaucracy which logically cannot have any collective mind of its own independently of its masters, whereas the Commission was originally intended to have such a mind. It was given executive power in a very limited number of areas, notably policing the EEC competition rules, but was never given the opportunity to develop into a European government. (The European Parliament was given a largely consultative role).

On almost every issue, ultimate control was left to the Council of Ministers, under the Rome Treaty, and that body was for most topics to act by unanimity. The Treaty (Article 148) actually specified that, except as otherwise provided for, "qualified majority voting" would be used in the Council. (This meant a roughly two-third majority in a size-weighted vote by ministers). But in fact key areas did specify unanimity, and where it was not the law it became the custom.

The power of the Council of ministers over the constituent members is dramatic. Once Governments in the Council of Ministers have adopted legislative proposals they are then committed to implementation in the form of domestic legislation. The so-called "democratic deficit" arises because the governments can agree amongst themselves in the Council as to what legislation they will then impose on their own legislatures, who have no choice about the content of subsequent secondary national legislation. Decisions upon agreed unanimously by the governments concerned, with no consultation with electors or legislators, can be presented as an exogenously determined requirement of "Brussels". It is clear that, for countries with weak executives and strong parliaments, this system is a boost to the power of the government vis-a-vis its own legislators. This was the case for France when she signed the Rome Treaty and is so now in Italy. The very tight grip the UK executive has over the legislature is reflected, paradoxically both in Britain's exemplary record in implementing EC law, and the UK government's hostility to transferring (pooling) sovereignty into the Council of Ministers.

The Court of Justice has enunciated the doctrine of "direct effect" which states that national laws which violate EC law are automatically invalid. Nevertheless legislation agreed in Brussels will not be obeyed by economic actors until appropriate national laws have been passed under the normal procedures of the country concerned. In practice therefore both the Rome Treaty and other EC law are often neglected.

The thesis of this paper is that the 1992 plan is more about bringing practice in line with formal rules than with changing the formal rules. In 1985 the member states agreed upon the Single European Act (SEA), modifying some of the details after 1987, notably by allowing decisions by qualified majority voting for decisions to create the "Internal Market". The change is a modest one, since unanimity is retained for many other topics including tax harmonization. Moreover, the Council is not obliged to use majority voting. Indeed the crucial failure of the pre-SEA European Community was that there was unanimous agreement by the member states that they would in fact not go by the rules of the Treaty.

The framers of the original Treaty had expected an eventual political union to emerge from the open-ended "agreement to agree" within the Rome Treaty framework. In fact, political realities of the 1960s led to a double failure. The domain of integration was effectively limited to the Customs Union and a Common Agricultural Policy, and all else was left to ordinary state-to-state diplomacy instead of everyone agreeing to be bound by the procedures of the Treaty.

President de Gaulle of France who came to power in 1958 rejected the principles of the Rome Treaty. De Gaulle was in fact attached to the idea of some form of political union in Europe, agreed by new state to state negotiations (see G-H Soutou [1990]). He made a number of proposals for political union. But he was not willing to agree to its emerging from the existing "communities". His main objections seem to have been to the blank cheque that the Rome Treaty appears to have represented, and to the even the limited autonomy of the EC Commission. He demanded that key matters be settled on a state-to-state basis without EC institutions being involved. In fact, after his departure, a European Council of heads of government was instituted and only formally made part of EC law in the SEA.

De Gaulle's nationalism was pragmatic. Under his presidency the French economy opened itself to European trade and implemented the core commitment of the Rome Treaty. He was at the forefront of the bilateral rapprochement with Germany, which if it had any content at all necessarily would lead to France curtailing its freedom of manoeuvre. He accepted the idea of a Common Market and his governments acted as if they were irrevocably committed to the idea, but his rhetoric contributed to a climate of expectations in which it appeared that France would only realize the commitments it had made ex-ante when it appeared in its interests ex-post to do so. His main achievement was to subordinate EEC procedures to state-to-state Realpolitik rather than vice versa. As a result of de Gaulle's opposition to the EEC system, an "agreement" was reached in 1965 known as the Luxembourg compromise under which, where majority voting was specified, member states could claim a right of veto in the Council of Ministers where "vital national interest were at stake". It is worth noting that this did not involve a change in the Rome Treaty, but a political decision not to implement it fully. Perhaps this was inevitable, but it had the ultimately fateful effect of turning the EC system from a rule-based one to one in which the member states could by consensus operate the system however they wished without having to change the treaties. The result was to change the all or nothing character of the incentive for general compliance. The roof did not fall in if member states gradually began to ignore their commitments and appointed Commissioners who would allow them to do so. And yet the result was to bring the whole system into disrepute by the early 1980s and to lead to the need for the SEA to restore the original system. Since the Luxembourg compromise was never written into the Treaties, no-one can say if it has been written out, but this is the logic of the new agreement.

Ironically, the British attitude to sovereignty appears rather similar to that of de Gaulle in the 1960s. The Thatcher government apparently regards the commitment it signed in the preamble to the SEA to "transform the relations between member states into a European Union" as being totally non-binding. But where the UK position differs from de Gaulle is that the UK is prepared to consider as irreversible (as long as it stays a member) all of the commitments it does acknowledge.[2]

---

[2] The distinction between the intergovernmental and supranational components of the EC may appear arcane to economists who are well aware that governments are subject to forces from the world economy which drastically reduce their effective autonomy. It is also customary to treat legal forms as being of very little significance in economic matters. Ironically Coase [1960] by paying close attention to the law probably reinforced most economists in the opinion that original

Continental European governments have for a long time recognized that the myth of absolute sovereignty, and the need to negotiate. In this light, the European Community system economizes on the transactions costs of negotiation, by making for a once-and-for-all agreement to resolve a package of problems in a common way. Individual member states who voluntarily agree to pool their sovereignty hope to achieve more power by having a small stake in a larger entity. What is special about decision-making here is that once the initial voluntary commitment is made to the Community, the member governments cannot go back on commitments without leaving the whole system. Under the Luxembourg compromise, they could claim a right to exercise sovereignty with regard to an issue over which they had originally declared a willingness to cede or pool sovereignty, but given that many issues are likely to be on the table at the same time, use of the veto is likely to provoke a response from others.

Moreover, once a unanimous decision has been made there is no legal method for a government or its successor to withdraw the assent once given, without withdrawing from the Community system as a whole. Insisting on unanimity ensured that when the EC did take decisions they were ones everyone was at least in principle in favor of; the core agreements on the tariff-free market were respected, but there was precious little else where unanimity was really possible. The domain of the EC was thus restricted.

IV. COMPLIANCE WITH EC LAW
A government may choose not to fulfil its legal obligations, but this undermines both the value of the system and the credibility of future promises made. The problem of compliance with the Rome Treaty exists on a multiplicity of levels. The governments must collectively implement the promises made in the Treaty by issuing directives to give them effect, and then the member states must draw up national legislation to implement the community directives; then the EC-originating national law must be

---

distribution of formal legal rights is irrelevant if (horse-)trading is possible. Breton and Scott [1978] argue that if jurisdictions within a federation can freely contract, there is no need to worry about which powers are given to what layers of government. In this perspective it is in fact optimal for all power initially to be given to lower levels who can voluntarily agree to set up ad hoc collective agencies to manage problems which affect all their territories, from defence to interregional highway networks. It could be pointed out that voluntary cooperation between states normally ensures that roads being built across frontiers usually meet by free agreement.

properly enforced. An EC directive is a decision by the Council of Ministers (or exceptionally the Commission) binding member governments to change their laws to achieve a common agreed end. A "regulation" forming one actual common law for the whole EC will still rely on national courts for enforcement.

By signing the Treaty of Rome member states had incorporated into their own domestic law its provisions and those of community legislation made under it, superseding all contrary national laws. Each individual member state agreed in effect to tie its own hands in certain fields for as long as others did the same, though as we have seen the scope of this binding was not as great as originally intended.

The existence of the European Court of Justice (ECJ) allows governments to enforce their rights against other states and EC institutions. There are crucial differences with the equivalent US bodies. The US Supreme Court, though appointed by the executive branch, rights has independent legitimacy arising out of the Constitution. In the European Community, the states which set up the ECJ can by their unanimous wish increase or reduce its powers, or agree unanimously to tacitly ignore it. The key incentive each state has to comply is of course that others will too. EC law does not merely hand over rights of individual member states to their collectivity, but it also directly confers economic rights on citizens vis-a-vis their own and other governments. The complex interplay of economic legal and political forces is illustrated by the fact that though these rights are implicitly and in some cases explicitly written down in the Rome Treaty it has taken a very long period for the actors concerned to act as if the ability to sustain these rights were a legitimate expectation. This is illustrated by the reaction of even more sophisticated elements of UK public opinion to a judgement of the EC Court of Justice in June 1990 affirming that a national court had the right to provisionally suspend operation of a UK statute (pending a final decision) if there were strong grounds to believe that the statute violated EC law. The "Independent" newspaper (June 20th 1990) headline stated that the Court had "re-written the UK constitution." This was quite false: the UK constitution was re-written in 1973 when the European Communities Act came into force. At that point the UK legislators voluntarily bound themselves to ensure that all UK legislation would in future be in conformity with EC law. Such a commitment is valid as long as the UK remains part of the EC.

V. EXTERNAL TRADE POLICY

There are parallels between the EEC regime and the GATT system. In both cases governments bind themselves not to engage in costly protectionism against other states that have also signed the agreement. Domestic demands for protectionism at home can thus be deflected on the grounds that a binding commitment has been made to trading partners which has also been extracted from them in return. The great differences between the GATT system and the EEC rules are that the GATT agreements are far less specific, less far-reaching, and GATT involves no potential sanctions, while the EC rules are part of the internal law of the signatories and the European Court of Justice is a backstop enforcement agency.

With respect to external trade policy, the rules of the Rome Treaty (Article 113) remove sovereignty from individual member states and transfer it to the Council of Ministers (not the Commission). The Rome Treaty committed member states to a common external commercial policy, but did not impose any obligation of free trade with respect to the outside world, merely for trade within the EEC. In fact many non-tariff barriers exist at the level of member states; some are formally incorporated by the EC into its own collective trade policy, e.g. MFA quotas, while others such as VERs are as "grey" under EC rules as under GATT. They are held to be transitional anomalies until the true common commercial policy envisaged by Article 113 is introduced, after 1992. But they exist because the Council of Ministers has so far decided that it would not implement a truly Common Commercial Policy as the Treaty lays down.

It is not clear whether the Ministers acting collectively are likely to be more or less protectionist than acting alone. The politicians forming the council are concerned about re-election and individually unconcerned about the losers in other member states, but collectively they represent a wider coalition of interests than individual states.[3]

VI. COMPETITION POLICY

The failure of the governments to implement the original Rome Treaty probably stands out most sharply in the case of competition policy with the

---

[3] Patterson criticizes the apparent dispersion of responsibility between member states, Council of Ministers and Commission but also suggests that "the Commission if left to itself would be considerably less trade restraining than in fact the Community is," (Patterson [1983], p.230.) But under the rules of the Rome Treaty the Commission cannot be left to itself. The question is whether it is dictated to by the members collectively as the Council of Ministers or as individual states. The Commission has to implement the legislation set by the council of ministers and implement policy in ways that reflects the Council's wishes. The Commission has an interest as a bureaucracy must in maximum autonomy: however it can best achieve this by attempting to implement policy in ways that the council will approve.

greatest economic consequences. Under the Rome Treaty the EC Commission was given direct executive authority to regulate subsidies and control monopolies and restrictive business practices. This represents the most striking area of transfer of sovereignty away from governments, since the Commission could according to the Treaty fine firms and issue directives to governments. It could be argued that the decision to give these sweeping powers to the Commission in the 1950s was premature. In practice there was a tacit understanding that these powers would be used very sparingly, and those appointed to the Commission knew this.

In the event, in the 1960s the tacit agreement not to apply the competition rules did not matter much as the main distortions to markets were tariffs; but after tariffs were abolished, the recession of the 1970s created incentives for states to introduce various NTBs, a situation which led to fears that the gains from the original common market might be compromised.

VII. THE NATURE OF GAINS FROM THE COMMON MARKET: POLITICS MEETS ECONOMICS

The Rome Treaty did achieved its basic aim of a tariff-free Common Market, because this was seen as a Pareto-improvement and a commitment which all could adhere to merely on the condition that others were equally committed to it.[4] The Rome Treaty was a device for breaking an isolation paradox or prisoners' dilemma. The benefits were expected to be universal, and the degree of benefit sufficiently even that little attention was paid to the issue of compensation for gainers and losers and the enforceability of any agreements on that.

Typical estimates suggested that the removal of all intra-EC tariffs would barely raise member states GNP by 1% (see Lipsey [1960], Winters [1986])). The reason for this was that the tariffs being removed were rarely more than 10%, and so if the tariff were the only trade barrier, the improvement to resource allocation would only involve an improvement in efficiency. One risks however underestimating by an unknowable amount the consequences of creating the EEC by assuming that other aspects of economic cooperation would have been as close without the EEC. An intuitive reading of the economic history of Europe in the 1960s in the light of economic analysis makes it hard to believe that trade liberalization had no more than a minor part to play in the rapid economic growth in France

---

[4] J.S. Mill observed that: "Two nations which agreed in everything except their commercial policy would agree also on that", (cited by D.N.McCloskey [1987].) One may well ask: would a set of nations that did not agree on commercial policy agree on everything else?

and Germany in the 1960s. And yet it is hard to pin down the direct effects. Two of the most obvious economic benefits were intensified competition and the exploitation of economies of scale, the so-called dynamic effects.

Skeptics argued that there was no reason to expect the removal of small trade barriers to have anything other than small effects in any respects; in particular, major economies of scale would always be exploited as long as cost reductions exceeded the amount of the tariffs (see Lundgren [1969]). What matters however for investment purposes is not current tariff levels, but expected future tariffs, and here the EEC had created credible future expectations that all tariffs would be removed. There was no provision for selective retention of tariffs to protect individual industries. The OECD [1987] argues that it was not so much the removal of the tariffs that mattered as the "perception that the opening of markets was a largely irreversible process - a perception which re-shaped corporate strategies"(OECD [1987] p.277). This emerges indirectly from the analysis of Owen [1983] who argues that the exploitation of economies of scale and the intensification of competition were much more important in the EEC than had previously been reckoned, generating cumulative gains of 5-6% of GNP by 1980 for the six original states.[5]

However, the data in Owen's study suggest that, for most of his examples, it would have been profitable expanded to supply neighboring markets even if the tariffs had remained. He states: "In the absence of any animal spirits stimulating expansive entrepreneurs, tariffs can be a powerful inhibiting factor on the exploitation of scale through trade" (Owen, p20). But the real force of this observation is that tariff cuts will only have a major effect if they influence expectations, giving the clear signal that trade policy will no longer be an endogenized process that can offset competitive advantage. Such a guarantee could be given for tariff policy, but no such pre-commitments were made on non-tariff policy. This did not matter much in the 1960s when non-tariff barriers were not perceived by firms as a potential threat, but it became important in the 1980s.

VIII. GOVERNMENT-SUSTAINED FIRMS IN THE FRAGMENTED INTERNAL MARKET

Although tariff barriers on industrial goods were abolished, no absolute

---

[5] Owen's thesis is that market opening widened opportunities for economies of scale because it enabled low cost producers at the efficient end of the spectrum of costs to knock out (smaller) producers at the inefficient tail of the spectrum from other countries as well as their own, thus raising the returns from newer lower-cost larger plants.

commitment to complete market opening was established, and during the 1970s oligopolistic industries were able to re-create their positions.[6] The trade barriers sustaining this were the joint creatures of firms and governments. Our thesis here is that the threat of private and public action in concert to restrict intra-EC trade has been more important than actually existing trade barriers in the EC. Research carried out on the actual scope and magnitude of trade barriers in the EC (see House of Lords [1982], Holmes [1987]) actually suggested, that for most industrial sectors existing trade barriers in the EC were small (typically around 2% of costs of consignments) though they were important in public procurement, certain services (especially finance and transport) and some high technology areas.

Calculations of the costs of trade barriers suggested that the direct benefits from lessened administrative burdens would be modest: the main effects would come from secondary effects inducing more competition. Of the 5-6% GNP gain from the "1992" plan reported by Cecchini [1988] and Emerson et. al. [1988], about one half comes from restructuring and intensification of competition.

Price differentials between EC markets far exceed any reasonable estimate of the costs of administrative and other barriers to trade. One can postulate invisible non-tariff barriers, or else in many European industries a certain tacit market sharing and price leadership has become the norm.[7] This observation is consistent with econometric findings of Geroski [1989] that the influence of imports on competition appears less than that of additional entry by domestic producers. Scherer et al found that European firms typically used more multi-plant operations than could be explained by the nature of scale economies.

Hughes (1990, p11) proposes that in some sectors "firms are already operating an implicit spheres of influence agreement." This suggests that import suppliers anticipate that if they encroach too much on the territory of domestic producers they will be subject to retaliation. This may take the form of price-cutting in the entrant's home territory or else of threats to invoke government action in the importer's market.

The threats need only be occasionally implemented to be effective. Notorious examples include the French government's actions at the behest of the Thompson company to change technical regulations on refrigerators to exclude cut-price imports from Italy. While the French government was for a long time willing to subsidize its car producers, especially Renault,

---

[6] Geroski and Jacquemin [1985] have commented that "the root cause of the current industrial crisis in Europe in not the small scale of European firms but rather that they have been too slow in initiating and responding to change" (p.202).

[7] See Holmes [1989], Scherer et. al. [1975].

the UK government preferred to see the state owned car firm Austin-Rover boost revenues from participating in arrangements that led to importers' keeping prices higher in the UK market than in the rest of the EC. Both policies give a clear signal to importers that price competition will be penalized. The EC Commission itself has discovered and fined cartels in the chemical industry.

But there has been intense debate about whether there really are efficiency losses from unexploited economies of scale in the EC. In Holmes [1989] I argue that Scherer's study shows that rational firms may well fail to exploit economies of scale, if closure of plants and concentration provokes rivals to undertake similar action and also to begin price competition. If coordinated behavior permits prices which cover costs, and if importers are persuaded by trade policy to price in an accommodating way, the incentive to restructure to cut costs is severely reduced. Clearly firms have an incentive, other things being equal, to minimize costs, but if cost minimization involves concentration of production in certain member states, it risks destabilizing expectations in such a way that prices may fall more than costs.

Indeed, simulations for the EC Commission suggest that, if the single market plan is realized, prices will fall more than costs (see Emerson [1988]). Much of the debate about economies of scale may well be misplaced: what matters is whether there are unexploited economies of rationalization. If these involve plant closures and concentration of production,[8] this will look as if scale economies are being exploited. Governments and firms acting together have used the threat of employment as reason for slowing rationalization. The chairman of Renault publicly states that he could cut costs by introducing new plants with lower manning levels[9]. His unwillingness to do so is motivated both by his concern for the workers who would lose their jobs, but also by the recognition of inter-dependence between his prices and costs and the strategy of other firms.

The nature of the interplay between private and public anti-competitive practices is best seen in the public procurement sectors where monopolistic and cartelistic arrangements between buyers and sellers have been tolerated and even encouraged by government agencies. Evidence shows that a high proportion of tenders for public procurement contracts had only one bidder and that price was rarely the criterion for choice.[10]

Thus, failure by governments to implement their promises to be bound in all respects by the provisions of the Rome undermined the carrot and

---

[8] Pratten [1988] suggests this is usually the case.
[9] New York Times, April 30th 1989.
[10] Atkins [1988], Cawson et. al. [1990].

stick certainty of market access. The lapse in the political credibility of the European Community was beginning to undermine its central economic purpose as well in the early 1980s.

The European economy was in the doldrums and the EEC itself was seen as redundant. It had abolished tariffs but otherwise appeared to exist largely to administer the increasingly costly Common Agricultural Policy which absorbed two thirds of the EC budget.

The EEC by the early 1980s had thus reached a political impasse where members implicitly agreed not to interfere with one another's non-tariff measures. Even the programme for harmonization of technical standards had almost completely stalled. High levels of unemployment were widely attributed to "eurosclerosis", failure of markets to work as flexibly in the EC as in the United States.[11]

IX. THE EC TOWARDS 1992

Ammunition for the recovery perhaps first began to accumulate in 1978 with a ruling by the ECJ in the Cassis de Dijon case which laid down that West Germany could not exclude the French beverage "Cassis de Dijon" on the grounds that it did not have the minimum alcohol content for labelling as a "liqueur". The Court of Justice declared that the Rome Treaty implied the general principle of "mutual recognition" of standards. Whatever was legally saleable in one state should be saleable in any other subject only to safeguards (allowed for in the Rome Treaty's Article 36 such as reasons of public health). It was, said the Court, up to the Commission and, on appeal the Court of Justice, to decide whether trade bans (as imposed for example on imports of British beef into the rest of the EC in 1990) were reasonable or "proportionate" in the circumstances rather than camouflaged protectionism. The Cassis de Dijon decision in theory merely made explicit what was in the Rome Treaty but actually was an example of judicial activism. But it was a little ahead of its time. Neither economic nor political circumstances were ripe for the EC Commission to rely on the Cassis de Dijon case to short-circuit the whole process of standards harmonization by the Council of Ministers.

With the notable exception of France, the leading European states had right-wing pro-market governments in the early 1980s, and "liberal" solutions were widely supported. At first sight this appeared to exclude collective action to stimulate the European economy. Certainly collective macro-reflation was ruled out politically. But somehow, European political leaders managed to harness the drift towards economic liberalism into a commitment to economic and political integration, including EC-level

---

[11] See for example OECD [1987].

re-regulation. An important element here was the anxiety that the political cohesion of the EC was under threat. Each member state risked adopting its own individual solutions, not merely to trade relations with Japan but to the already altering relationship between Europe and the two superpowers. A further twist was given by the already agreed commitment to admit first Greece then Portugal and Spain to membership. It was clear that if each of them kept a veto, paralysis would risk being total. In terms of our earlier argument the vulnerability of the EC system in the early 1980s may well have been what saved it. It was unanimously recognized that a new incentive had to be created to prevent a potential degeneration into intra-EC "new protectionism." Exaggerated fears of the consequences of government imposed NTBs had a big role to play, as did optimistic estimates of the effects of removing them.

In 1984 Jacques Delors, newly nominated as President of the EC Commission, proposed three alternative plans to reinstate momentum towards "European Union": defence cooperation, monetary union and more institutionalized political cooperation.[12] None of these were accepted: the one project commanding unanimous assent was a programme to remove all remaining trade barriers inside the EC; hence the agreement in 1985 on the Internal Market programme and the Single European Act (SEA) to implement it.

There was a curious convergence of interests on this plan. The Thatcher government in the UK government saw it as an alternative to political integration which would spread the Thatcherite gospel of deregulation across Europe. The French socialist government, after a disastrous flirtation with extreme interventionism in 1981-1983, began to see the merits of external constraints on both monetary policy and the sums that public enterprises could demand in subsidies from the state. They also began to see the advantages of moving France from a dirigiste regime to a system more closely resembling the German social market economy. For the German economy, the Single Market plan was of slight interest, as such trade barriers as there were had not stopped German exports. However, Chancellor Kohl and Foreign Minister Genscher had a genuine ideological commitment to European unity. Only Ireland and Denmark had reservations about the possible implications of the new plans for their sovereignty.

The SEA gave formal institutional recognition to a number of de facto developments in EC affairs, notably meetings of the heads of government as the "European Council" and the system of European political cooperation on foreign policy; it also gave the EC formal competence on environmental matters. Most visibly it committed member states to the creation by

---

[12] See Delors [1988].

December 31st 1992 of "an internal market.. an area without internal frontiers in which the free movement of goods, persons, services and capital is ensured", and a new Article 100a of the Rome Treaty provided for qualified majority voting by the Council of Ministers for legislation to achieve this. The Act amended the Rome Treaty, and had to be agreed upon by every national parliament.

The remarkable point however is how little it contained. The "internal market" was defined in the new Article 8a of the Rome Treaty using phrases already contained in separate parts of the original Rome Treaty to define the "Common Market". Only the commitment to remove "frontiers" was new. Nothing was said about trade policy or competition policy. One interesting twist on the sovereignty notion fits in with the trend we have identified here: the SEA provides that environmental policy (including the "polluter-pays" principle) shall be a Community matter; but decisions are to be by unanimity until such time as the Council of Ministers decides -- by unanimity -- that majority voting can in future be used. The SEA also introduced a number of vague pre-commitments on regional and social policy and technology policy, which served as a way of widening the scope of side-payments that can be made within the system. The EC Commission got no new powers, but subsequent events clearly suggest that the SEA was a signal from the member states that the de jure position laid down in the Rome Treaty was to replace the de facto position, and that the Commission could exercise delegated and Treaty powers to the letter and spirit of the Treaties. The "Luxembourg compromise" of 1965 has not been formally denounced, but the specification of the use of majority voting only makes sense if governments were willing to actually implement it, and this has been done.

The signing of the SEA therefore represents a reaffirmation of the commitment to the original goals of the Rome Treaty. The political and economic hype accompanying it are intended to raise the perceived costs to any member state contemplating reneging on the deal. John Kay has said that "the real significance of 1992 lies in the hype, rather than in the programme itself...it is the sincerity with which governments pursue the ideals of 1992 that matters, rather than the content of the Commission directives themselves."[13]

In 1985 the Council of Ministers gave general approval to the "White Paper" Completing the Internal Market which set out a detailed legislative programme, to be completed by December 31st 1992, of 300 directives necessary for a frontier-free Europe. These measures were thus approved in principle but had to be implemented by the Council before coming into

---

[13] Kay [1988], p1.

effect. The Cecchini Report [1988] argued strongly that for effective credibility every one of these measures had to be adopted (though the list has since been shorted for technical reasons).

In fact a close reading of the contents of the White Paper would leave one totally mystified as to how acceptance of these measures could transform a continent. It distinguished physical technical and fiscal barriers to trade and enumerated those measures most needed to realize the frontier-free Europe and the new Rome Treaty in a technical sense. Thus there are 71 proposed directives on animal and plant health controls, as against 20 on financial services. The White Paper proposed various measures of tax harmonization (still needing unanimity under the unamended Article 99), but tax harmonization was being sought not in such a way as to eliminate distortions, but so as to allow the removal of frontier controls.

The Paper also laid down a series of proposals for directives to extend (by majority voting) the common market to all sectors of public procurement that had been deliberately left out of the legislation passed by the Council of Ministers in 1962. This meant applying the Rome Treaty for the first time in this area, rather than extending it. On external trade policy the White Paper merely said it would be "not unreasonable" to implement a common policy by 1992. If we see the 1992 plan as a new plan, the position is indeed as vague as this, but if we see it as the commitment to realize the original plan, the logic of a truly common external policy is more than "not unreasonable"; it is unavoidable if internal barriers are to be removed.

The measures actually listed in the 300 proposed directives of the White Paper would by themselves do almost nothing to break the system of oligopolistic fragmentation in the EC market described above. This was caused by corporate behavior rather than frontier controls or the few technical regulations not written by industry for industry.

Only a dramatic gesture affecting expectations about political will could establish patterns of economic behavior. The true import for business and politics of what had been agreed in 1985 was apparent to few observers. The new commitment to removing frontier controls was widely advertised. But many observers were skeptical about the member states' new willingness to implement the commitments, for example, to introduce legislation on public procurement that had been deliberately shelved in the 1960s. But what should be the most important part of the programme was hardly mentioned at all, namely the commitment on the part of the Commission to use its powers under the Treaty to enforce competition.

This has led to a striking paradox. Many people are criticizing the 1992 plan as likely to reduce competition through encouragement of cross border concentration. For example, Hughes [1990] has argued that ease of cross border cooperation will further facilitate the kind of oligopolistic collusion that previously caused the fragmentation of EC markets. Others have argued that the stress placed in the Cecchini Report on economies of scale, the promotion of potentially collusive technological collaboration, and the apparent enthusiasm for mega-mergers risks pushing the EC in an anti-competitive direction.[14]

My argument is that these fears are misplaced. The "1992" plan itself contains very little positive substance that could actually make cross-border collusion and concentration easier than it is now.   The new wave of mergers that is occurring in the EC is happening in anticipation of the actual implementation of the "1992" legislation[15] and has not been facilitated by it. Many of the mergers and takeovers are a response to the threats of additional competition brought about by anticipation of the removal of trade barriers. I have argued that the actual trade barriers being removed are modest in importance compared to the behavior patterns of firms. It is self-evident that large firms, for example in public procurement have an interest in establishing the kind of "rings" that have often operated successfully in national markets.

Whether or not the operation succeeds in shifting oligopolistic businesses from collusive to competitive equilibria will depend not on the "1992" legislation but on the credibility of the commitment to competition policy. The EC Competition directorate has recently declared its policy to be: "In its application of the competition rules of the Treaties, the Commission is to a large extent concentrating on dismantling the no-trespassers signs that have been created or re-created by a wide variety of ways and means. They range from the restrictive or abusive practices of undertakings to the hidden protectionism operated by member states, notably in the form of certain state aids, certain financial measures to assist public undertakings or an obvious reluctance to adjust national monopolies of a commercial character. Because of [firms'] strategies, it is increasingly essential to create an instrument to monitor concentrations with a Community dimension in order to keep a closer watch on highly concentrated markets and, if necessary, to prohibit them if they are liable to impede effective competition" (CEC [1989],p16).

The new merger regulation of 1989 gives the EC Commission the right, some would say the obligation, to ban mergers that would reduce competition in the EC market. My point is that increased concentration emanates spontaneously from business, while the input from the policy-makers has been the declared commitment to regulate business. The

---

[14] See for example Geroski [1988].
[15] See the Financial Times Survey of July 2nd 1990.

trick of the 1992 plan has been to create a political imperative for pan-EC pro-competitive reregulation of business, out of an initial situation in which the only possible outcomes appeared to be either the continuation of national champion industrial policies or else haphazard and uneven national deregulation.[16]

The EC Commission in the late 1980s began to reinvigorate its competition policies. It has for example fined illegal state aid in a way that quite clearly surprised the British government, when it had to justify the subsidies to British Aerospace for the sale of Rover; and yet the UK government could not claim the interference was unjustified since it had been complaining of the need for tighter policing of other countries' subsidies.

My argument cannot be that the procompetitive tactic will win. The politics of business behavior are such as to favor the kind of tacit collusion that grew in the 1970s. I would merely observe that the EC's political class has equipped itself with one of the few weapons it could have to resist these pressures, namely an agreement henceforward to respect the quasi-constitutional pro-competitive provisions of the Treaties.

X. CONCLUSIONS: FROM 1992 TO A UNITED FORTRESS EUROPE?

Two basic questions remain. Will the exercise succeed and will it turn in on itself? Recent events have provided greater incentives for the European politicians to carry on with the constitutional binding process. The current German government and its likely successors wish to convince its partners that Germany will be a "trading state" and not another Reich. The EC provides a framework for them to do this, in a way that conforms almost exactly to the perceived economic interests of French politicians. Unlike the 1960s, France sees positive economic value in a policy pre-commitment strategy. The greater the perceived costs of the break-up of the existing system, the greater is the incentive to cement it with steps to a "United States of Europe", including monetary union.

But, as I have argued, there is less in this system to bind the EC with respect to its external free-trade commitments. Nevertheless my own view is that a highly protectionist "Fortress Europe" is an unlikely scenario, despite a number of disturbing signs in the EC's trade policy.[17] Protectionist coalitions no longer take the form they did. The very fact, for example, that

---

[16] Sharp has noted that: "Liberalization and deregulation therefore become an essential complement to collaboration and concentration - the twin tracks to competitiveness" (Sharp, [1990], p.28).

[17] See for example Messerlin [1990].

Japanese firms producing inside EC protection are quietly enjoying the benefits of restrictions on imports from new entrants is making politicians wary of the protestations of "domestic industry". The eventual Communitization of trade policy means that more political and bureaucratic actors have to be won over. Full respect for EC rules would be a constraint on national protectionism. However, the logic of our argument is that if Europe's political leaders are sincere in their wish to keep to a rule-based external trade system and distance themselves from interest groups, they will seek multilateral agreements in which the EC binds itself in the same way that the individual member states bind themselves to the collectivity.

References

Atkins W.S. Ltd, 1988. *The Costs of Non Europe in Public Sector Procurement, Studies on the Economics of Integration, The Costs of non-Europe*, Vol.5, Luxembourg: Commission of the European Communities.

Breton A. and A. Scott, 1978. *The Economic Constitution of Federal States*, Canberra: Australian National University Press.

Cawson, A., K. Morgan, P. Holmes, D. Webber and A. Stevens, 1990. *Hostile Brothers: Competition and Closure in the European Electronics Market*, Oxford: Clarendon Press.

Cecchini, P., M. Catinat and A. Jacquemin, 1988. *1992 The European Challenge*, London: Gower.

Coase, R.H. 1960. "The problem of social cost", *Journal of Law and Economics*, 3.

Commission of the European Communities, 1989. *Eighteenth Report on Competition Policy*, Luxembourg.

Delors J., 1988. Preface to French edition of P.Cecchini et al 1992, *le Defi Europeen*, Flammarion.

Emerson M. et al, 1988. *The Economics of 1992*, Oxford University Press.

Geroski, P., 1988. "The Choice between Scale and Diversity" in: *1992: Myths and Realities*, London Business School.

Geroski, P., 1989. *Barriers to Entry and Intensity of Competition in European Markets*, Luxembourg: Commission of the European Communities.

Geroski P., and A. Jacquemin, 1985. "Industrial barriers to mobility and European industrial policy".

Holmes, P., 1987. "Real and imaginary barriers to trade within the EEC and economies of scale", University of Sussex, mimeo.

Holmes, P., 1989. "Economies of scale, expectations and Europe 1992",
    World Economy, 12, 525-537.
House of Lords, 1982. *Select Committee on European Affairs*, 17th Report
    1981-2, "The Internal Market", London: HMSO.
Hughes, K., 1990. "Competition, competitiveness and the European
    community", Berlin, *Wissenschaftszentrum Berlin fur Sozialforschung*.
Kay, J., 1988. "Myths and Realities", in *1992: Myths and Realities*,
    London Business School.
Kennedy, P., 1988. *The Rise and Fall of Great Powers*, New York Random
    House.
Kindleberger, C., 1987. *The World in Depression 1929-39*, 2nd Edition,
    London: Penguin.
Lipsey, R.G., 1960. "The theory of customs unions: a general survey",
    Economic Journal, 70, reprinted in J.Bhagwati, editor, *International
    Trade: Selected Readings*, London: Penguin.
Lundgren N., 1969. "Customs unions of industrialized West European
    countries", in G. Denton, editor, *Economic Integration in Europe*,
    London, Weidenfeld and Nicolson.
McCloskey, D.N., 1987. "Counterfactuals", in J. Eatwell, M. Milgate and
    P. Newman, editors, *New Palgrave Dictionary of Economics*, London:
    Macmillan.
OECD, 1987. *Structural Adjustment and Economic Performance*, Paris.
Owen, N., 1983. *Economies of Scale, Competitiveness and Trade Patterns
    within the European Community*, Oxford: Clarendon Press.
Patterson, G., 1983. "The European Community as a threat to the system",
    in W.R. Cline, editor, *Trade Policy for the 1980s*, Cambridge, MIT
    Press, 223-242.
Porter, B., 1983. *Britain, Europe and the World*, London: Allen and
    Unwin.
Prate, A., 1990. "Le message economique du general de Gaulle", *Le
    Monde* June 19th.
Pratten C., 1988. "A survey of the economies of scale", in *Studies on the
    Economics of Integration, The Costs of non-Europe* Vol.2,
    Luxembourg: Commission of the European Communities.
Rosecrance, R., 1986. *The Rise of the Trading State*, New York: Basic
    Books.
Scherer F.M. et al, 1975. *The Economics of Multi-plant Operations*,
    Harvard University Press.
Sharp, M., 1990. "The single market and European policies for advanced
    technology", *Political Quarterly*, forthcoming.
Soutou, G-H., 1990. "Le General de Gaulle et le Plan Fouchet", conference
    on *De Gaulle en son siecle*, Paris.

Wallace, W., 1990. *The Transformation of Western Europe*, RIIA/Chatham House.
Winters, L.A., 1986. *Britain in Europe: A Survey of Quantitative Trade Studies*, London: Centre for Economic Policy Research.

Chapter 7

MARKETS AND OWNERSHIP IN
SOCIALIST COUNTRIES IN TRANSITION[1,2]

Manuel Hinds

The fundamental issue in the reform of the Eastern European economies is whether a socialist economy can adopt a market form of organization.[3] That is, can market forces lead to an efficient allocation of resources without extensive private ownership of means of production? This paper addresses this question and reaches a negative conclusion. By forbidding private ownership of means of production, the socialist mode of organization eliminates the factor markets that are essential to the functioning of market economies. A corollary is that the introduction of market forces in socialist economies should be accompanied by large-scale privatization of means of production.

---

[1] The findings, interpretations and conclusions contained in this paper are entirely those of the author and should not be attributed in any manner to the World Bank, to its affiliated organizations, or to members of its Board of Executive Directors or the countries they represent.

[2] This paper is a revised version of sections of "Issues in the Introduction of Market Forces in Eastern European Socialist Economies", EMTTF, The World Bank, January 1990. I have benefitted from ideas presented both verbally and in papers by several EMTTF staff members, especially Roberto Rocha, Fernando Saldanha and David Tarr. They and others, especially Branko Milanovic (EM4CO), also provided substantial comments on an earlier draft.

[3] The word "socialism" is used in this paper meaning a system that forbids the ownership of means of production by private individuals in order to achieve an equal distribution of income. Countries like Sweden, where private ownership exists, are not socialist under this definition, even if they have achieved more uniform income distribution than some socialist countries.

I. BACKGROUND
A. The Introduction of Central Planning

The prohibition of private ownership of means of production has been a fundamental tenet in countries organized in the Marxist tradition. However, the question of whether the economy should be managed in a centralized or a decentralized manner has appeared and reappeared ever since the first writings of Marx and Engels.[4] The issue was settled for decades by the decision of the Soviet Union took in the late 1920s to implement a centrally planned economy. It reappeared when Hungary in 1968 initiated decentralizing reforms while maintaining the socialist nature of the economy and then reappeared more generally in Eastern Europe with the changes of the 1980s.

Decentralized socialism has been attempted before. The Soviet Union went through a decade-long period of decentralization known as the New Economic Policy (NEP) immediately after the nationalization of agricultural land and industry that took place during the civil war of 1917-1921.[5] During the NEP period, the Government intervened in the economy. However, it largely liberalized prices and used profits as the criterion to judge the performance of socialist enterprises.[6]

The Government also restored profit motives in agriculture. One of the primary objectives of the regime was to industrialize fast, by using resources from agriculture for industrial investment. Before the NEP, the government had extracted resources from agriculture by expropriating all but the vaguely defined basic needs of farmers. With the introduction of the NEP, the Government replaced expropriation with a fixed tax, which allowed farmers to sell a substantial part of their surpluses in local markets.

Several schemes were used to decentralize the management of the nationalized industries. Those included "one-man control of state-owned enterprises" (which gave power to individual managers appointed by the state), contracting-out the management of a large portion of small-scale firms, and even the privatization of a minor portion of small firms

---

[4] Marx predicted the ultimate disappearance of the state in the ideal socialist state but mentioned the need for a transitional period (subsequently called the dictatorship of the proletariat) in which the state would play a decisive but largely undefined role in the management of the economy. Lenin took this line in *State and Revolution* (1916) and led a radical move toward centralization in the early years of the revolution. Shortly thereafter, however, he sponsored the introduction of the decentralized New Economic Policy described in the following paragraphs.

[5] The description of this period follows Chapters 2-8 of Nove (1989).

[6] The Government made several attempts to control prices, but these were largely ignored. In 1922, the Government established a system of suggested prices.

(returning the enterprises to their former owners).[7] The government also offered foreign capitalists the opportunity of investing in the Soviet Union under concession arrangements. The private agents working under this system, who came to be called "Nepmen", dominated commerce and produced most of the agricultural output.

The NEP was not unsuccessful in terms of output. Production grew quickly, mainly as slack capacity was put to use. However, the authorities perceived serious inconsistencies between market rules and socialist objectives. The profits of the Nepmen created income differences that were incompatible with a socialist economy. Also, unemployment increased sharply and remained high after the NEP's emphasis on profits led to the elimination of many surplus jobs.

Most importantly, the government's priority objective of developing a large industrial sector was not being accomplished. For most of the period relative prices and taxes were extracting the surplus of agriculture, but resources were not being channelled into investment in heavy machinery. There was little incentive in the system to do that; for, in the absence of private ownership of means of production, the Nepmen had no incentive to invest their profits in capital goods. Throughout the NEP, the state undertook most of the investment.

Moreover, relative prices were inconsistent with socialist income distribution objectives. The government considered product prices excessive relative to wages. Also, the relative prices of agricultural in terms of industrial goods fluctuated greatly.[8] These problems became more acute at the end of the NEP, when a policy of maintaining low prices in the official market led to conflicts with farmers, increased scarcities, and the development of informal markets.

By the end of the 1920s, the NEP gave way to the highly centralized Five-Year Plans. In the early 1930s, the government collectivized farms and reaffirmed its control of industry and transportation. To finance the

---

[7] The large-scale enterprises were organized in conglomerates, called trusts, which had to be profitable and had no obligation to sell to the state (except for trusts in strategic activities, which were subject to a rudimentary central planning).

[8] The early years of the NEP witnessed what was called the "Scissors Crisis". In October 1923, industrial prices were 276% of those of 1913, while agricultural prices were 89%. This crisis was largely caused by the interaction of liberalized prices with the monopolistic structure of industry and the more competitive rural structure of production. Government intervention and improved efficiency in the industrial sector brought agricultural prices back to more reasonable levels. However, throughout the period, relative prices kept on moving substantially, endangering either the survival of the farmers or the development of the industrial sector. See Alec Nove, op-cit, pp. 83-86.

creation of industrial capital, the government introduced direct allocation of resources to extract the agricultural surplus while restricting consumption in the country as a whole.

Thus, the first attempt to use market forces was abandoned in favor of central planning because markets were considered to be incompatible with socialist objectives.

B. Central Planning and Relative Prices

Even under central planning, socialist governments continued to manipulate prices to control income distribution. Imposing distributional objectives on the pricing system created conflicts between prices that covered production costs, and prices that were distributionally appropriate. For products deemed "essential", the distributionally-based price was set. In practice, most prices were set on this latter basis, or were distorted by the pricing of essential materials. Prices therefore in general did not reflect production costs.

However, discrepancies between selling prices and production costs are not important for the allocation of resources in a centrally planned economy. In market economies, prices are the signals that guide resource allocation. In centrally planned economies, resources are directly assigned to uses, and no price signals are required.

The complex system of taxes and subsidies that characterizes centrally planned economies further weakens the role of prices. Most centrally planned countries have had a policy of "flexible tax rates," which allowed tax discrimination among enterprises. Taxes were flexible because of the objective of extracting surpluses from enterprises for central allocation of investment. Enterprises that made losses received subsidies.[9]

C. Prices and International Trade

The distorted relative prices made it necessary to isolate socialist economies from international markets. Tariffs were not an appropriate protectionist instrument because distortions were so great that the required structure of tariffs and exemptions would have been difficult or impossible to estimate. For this reason, socialist countries tended to have very low import tariffs, around 5-10 percent. However, quantitative restrictions on

---

[9] The policy of "Flexible Tax Rates" is being gradually abandoned in the reforming countries. Hungary, especially, has moved a long way in this direction through the establishment of income and value added taxes. However, the subsidization of loss-makers, both from the budget and from the financial system, is still pervasive, despite the fact that its reduction or elimination has been part of every stabilization program attempted in the last decade in Yugoslavia, Hungary and Poland.

trade were pervasive. These restrictions were sometimes explicit, and sometimes implicit in the institutional arrangements.

The isolation from international markets was complicated by the Council for Mutual Economic Assistance (CMEA), the arrangement for socialist international trade.[10] CMEA trade took place at prices which only rarely coincided with either international or domestic prices, and balances were cleared in a non-convertible unit of account. On the export side, prices did not play an important role, except in Yugoslavia and, recently, in Hungary and Poland. A "Price Equalization Fund" taxed and subsidized trade in accord with differences between domestic prices and the prices at which CMEA trade took place. In many countries, the Fund also functioned for convertible-currency exports. This eliminated any role that prices could have played in exports.

D. Price Manipulation, Excess Demand and the Overhang

The use of prices as a distributional devise underlies the creation of the monetary overhang in socialist countries. In a socialist economy, minimum income suffices for the basket of goods considered "essential". However, in practice the basket of essential goods varies across individuals and families. The problem is to ensure that income satisfies diverse "essential needs".

One solution is to tailor incomes individually to exhaust purchasing power. This solution is not practical.

Another solution is to allow currency to be spent only in conjunction with rationing entitlements. Rationing entitlements can be estimated outside the monetary system, so that the objective of directing and limiting the consumption of individuals can be achieved without disrupting the administration of enterprises. In order to function as desired, the system requires that the supply of the monetary component of the composite money exceed the supply of rationing entitlements. Otherwise some people would not be able to exercise an entitlement for lack of money. Thus, with money flows exceeding rationing flows, the accumulation of a monetary overhang is an inevitable consequence of attempting to use prices to divorce consumption possibilities from incomes.[11]

---

[10] The CMEA includes three non-European countries (Cuba, Mongolia and Vietnam), in addition to Bulgaria, Czechoslovakia, the German Democratic Republic, Hungary, Poland, Romania and the Soviet Union. Yugoslavia is not a member.

[11] This problem has reappeared whenever governments have tried to reduce the rate of monetary creation. It seems to be happening now in the USSR, where many people cannot get essential goods not for lack of entitlements but for lack of

In some countries, rationing has taken a more subtle form. Governments have been able to produce basic goods in quantities sufficient to
avoid rationing, but by restricting the variety of goods and services. In
those cases, the income remaining after fulfillment of basic needs cannot be
spent, even if there is no explicit rationing. Also, enterprises become
accustomed to "forced substitution" of inputs. Of course, the quality and
variety of available goods and inputs improves with economic development.

Some socialist countries have sought to set prices at levels that
approximate market prices and have not accumulated excessive monetary
balances. Where accumulated, such balances have not remained idle but
have nurtured the development of informal markets.

Informal markets clear, but in an inefficient way because of the
discrepancy between consumer and producer prices. The seller in an
informal market extracts a rent equal to part of consumer surplus and the
losses of producers. Consumers willingness to pay higher than official
prices is not transmitted to producers, who thus have no incentive to
increase output. The results are quite negative.[12] A class of rentiers arises
with high real incomes, not because of contribution to production but
because of privileged access to entitlements to goods.

E. Enterprise Management

In the classical centrally planned economy, the enterprise is the means
of delivering products in accordance with the plan. Enterprises depend on
Branch Ministries, which receive orders from the Planning Office and
convey them to the enterprises through "associations" or groups of firms
operating in the same or related fields. Managers are appointed by the state
and, in varying degrees, share powers with the representative of the
Communist Party and with local authorities.

Although their overriding concern is delivering the required volume of
production, enterprises are expected to contribute to other objectives such
as full employment. In the late stages of central planning, profitability has
been one of the objectives. However, this objective has been difficult to
achieve for several reasons, including price inconsistencies, the priority
given to deliveries at all cost, and the pervasive shortages of raw materials
and intermediate products.

---

money. This reflects the fact that the monetary overhang is highly concentrated in
a relatively small group.
[12] See Tarr (1989).

II. THE PROCESS OF REFORM

A. The Initial Stages: The Search for Decentralized Socialism

For years before the beginning of reforms, socialist economies had shown signs of severe inefficiency. Rates of growth were low although investment tended to be 35-40 percent of GDP. Also, rationing of essential goods, which was to be only a temporary sacrifice, became a permanent feature of the system. The quality of goods produced was also inferior.

Reforms in Yugoslavia, Hungary and Poland started when governments instituted reforms to move away from central planning but retain the socialist nature of the economy. The aim was to design a system that would decentralize enterprise management without allowing unrestricted private ownership of capital.[13] Prices were to provide efficient signals to producers. However, they should not disrupt the egalitarian distribution of wealth and income consistent with socialism. The feasibility of this combination of objectives is the principal issue in mixing socialist objectives with market forces.

The history of reforms in Eastern Europe centers on Yugoslavia, Hungary and Poland. There have been substantial country differences. Thus, a discussion has to be based on common stylized facts. This is the approach taken in this paper.

The establishment of a decentralized economic system without private ownership of means of production requires delinking the ownership of enterprises (held by the government) from enterprise management. There are two principal varieties of decentralized enterprise. One is that managed primarily by Worker's Councils. The other is that managed by independent managers.

B. The Self-Management System

Theoretically, the objective of the enterprises under this system is to maximize workers' income, which in turn is linked to profits based on market signals. Under self-management, the government transfers the management of the enterprises to the workers, organized in Worker's Councils which have the final word in decisions concerning the appointment of managers, the design and implementation of business plans (including

---

[13] The Soviet Union also made an attempt at partial decentralization in the 1965 industrial planning reforms, which aimed at scrapping gradually the system of material allocation. Managers would gain autonomy and part of their income was to be determined on the basis of managerial bonuses linked to profitability and sales. The 1965 reforms, however, were abandoned quite rapidly, mainly because of the inconsistencies of the mixture of the still strong central control with decentralized management. See Alec Nove, op-cit, pp. 367-368.

determination of wages) and the allocation of enterprise profits (which also can be transformed into wages or other compensation for workers). With those powers, Workers' Councils effectively run companies and decide on the distribution of enterprise earnings.[14]

To provide incentives for efficiency, the model links workers' compensation to profits, so that wages and other workers' benefits can formally be increased only when profits increase. Also, a rudimentary concept of the cost of capital is introduced in the form of a "dividend," a fixed annual payment to the government based on the value of socially-owned capital stock.[15]

The "dividend," however, became weaker with time. It was abolished in Yugoslavia in the 1970s. In Poland, the "dividends" are paid only on the stock of capital existing at a date established by law, December 1983. As a result, the importance of the original stock of capital in total capital diminished as enterprises proceeded to invest. This effect was accentuated in Poland because the original stock of capital was not adjusted for inflation and the "dividend" was equal to the Central Bank's rate of discount: in 1989 this was 46% per year while the rate of inflation was about 55% per month. The enterprises in Poland were therefore increasingly becoming the owners of themselves, a phenomenon that had already occurred in Yugoslavia and, to a large extent, in Hungary.

Lately, some Governments have made an effort to reintroduce the concept of capital cost. As part of the reforms introduced in Poland in January 1990, the dividend was increased and its collection enforced. In the same date, Yugoslavia reinstalled the dividend.

C. The Trend toward Self-Management

In Hungary and Poland the system of independent managers was predominant in the initial stages of reform. However, in both countries, workers have gradually asserted their control over the enterprises--both formally and *de facto*--to the point that the generic term self-management is applied specifically to the labor-management system.[16]

---

[14] In reality, as it is discussed later, the state and the Communist Party also have a strong influence in the management of enterprises and in the appointment of managers.

[15] This system existed in Yugoslavia and exists in Hungary and Poland. It existed for a short while in the Soviet Union in the mid-1960s. It exists in a more flexible form in China, where firms negotiate with the government the portion of profits to be remitted to the state.

[16] This is the usage followed in this paper. The term self-management is used to refer specifically to the system where enterprises are controlled by their workers.

The Polish enterprise reform of the early 1980s established the three "S" principles: enterprises should be self-governed (decentralized and independent of the Associations); self-managed (controlled by the workers); and self-financed (profitable). Initially, the Government appointed most of the managers and, together with the Party, effectively controlled the enterprises. Workers' Councils in each enterprise were given consultative powers on several issues and decisive powers on the approval of the firms' financial plans and on the distribution of profits. With time, self-management (labor control) was asserted throughout most of the economy. Exceptions tended to be strategic enterprises.

Hungary went through a similar transformation. Under the decentralization reforms undertaken prior to 1985, managers were supposed to be autonomous, but were appointed by the Branch Ministries. The 1985 reform introduced full-fledged self-management in 80% of the socialist enterprises. There are two types of such enterprises. In the large and medium-sized enterprises, workers elect an Enterprise Board, which, in turn, elects the managers. In the small enterprises, the workers elect their managers directly. The remaining 20% of the enterprises (mainly utilities, transportation, and defense) have remained administered directly by the state.

In 1985-1987, the Government of the Soviet Union announced a blueprint for the elimination of central planning. The program included *demokratizatsiya*, the election of managers and foremen by the enterprise workers, which effectively would give control of enterprises to workers.[17]

Thus, during the 1980s, decentralization moved the East European countries, both formally and *de facto*, toward some variant of the self-management system of Yugoslavia. In the process, the specification of ownership of enterprises became increasingly vague.

D. The New Ownership Laws: The Creation of Mixed Economies

In Yugoslavia, Poland and Hungary new ownership laws, which are remarkably similar, have removed most of the obstacles that had constrained the private ownership of capital goods and which had limited the private sector to small enterprises. The laws permit private entrepreneurs to create firms of any size, and to compete against each other and against firms in the socialist sector.

This reform in theory transformed the three countries from socialist to mixed economies wherein private and socialist firms can compete for resources and markets. However, the economies have remained largely socialist because most production is in the socialized sector.

---

[17] See Alec Nove, op-cit, chapter 14, pp.379-380, and also Aganbegyan (1990).

E. Creation of Commercial Banks

Under central planning, the banking system is an extension of the Treasury. The Central Bank combines monetary functions with those of commercial banking. The system usually includes an agricultural bank and a savings bank. The role of these institutions is subordinated to the central planners. Financial resources follow the allocation of real resources, providing little more than a unit of account. In order to isolate the flows related to production from the more volatile monetary flows of the population, the government maintains two separate "monetary circuits." Savings banks transact only with individuals and small numbers of small private enterprises, while the rest of the banking system transacts only with the socialist sector (state enterprises and cooperatives). Transfers between the two circuits are not permitted.[18]

The moves toward decentralization have included financial reforms aimed at transforming the financial system into the main mechanism for resource allocation. The Central Banks have created several commercial banks by splitting their loan portfolios, while they have specialized to monetary control. Banks are to introduce financial discipline in the management of enterprises by extending credit only to profitable enterprises.

In Yugoslavia, banking reform was carried out in the 1970s. All banks in Yugoslavia operate as financial agencies of their owners, which in all cases are enterprises (called the "founding members"). Under this arrangement, the objective of financial institutions is not the maximization of their own profits but the provision of financial resources to founding members at minimum cost. Financial institutions cannot accumulate profits. After meeting operating costs and setting aside the mandatory reserves, banks must distribute their surpluses among members and among other entities that make use of the banks' services. As a counterpart, founding members are, in theory, jointly and severally liable for their bank's obligations. This arrangement was to give flexibility to enterprises while imposing financial discipline on the owner-borrowers. However, 20 years after the introduction of this system, financial discipline did not exist in Yugoslavia and most, if not all, banks were insolvent.

The governments of Poland and Hungary decentralized their banking systems in 1987-1988. State ownership of banks was retained, but management was decentralized under a model that resembles that used in the enterprises. The control of banks, however, was not assigned to

---

[18] In Hungary, they are still formally prohibited by a provision deemed to be temporary.

workers, but to managers appointed by the government or the Central Bank. Managers were accountable to the government for the profits and losses of their institutions.[19]

The operation of commercial banks in Poland in 1990 remained hardly distinguishable from previous operations as branches of the Central Bank. Hungarian banks were more autonomous. In both countries, however, the operations of banks were determined by the portfolios inherited from the Central Bank. Given the concentration of industry, these portfolios were also concentrated, to the point that some banks had most of their assets invested in one or two large conglomerates. Also, the share of substandard loans (unrecoverable or recoverable but contracted at very low and fixed interest rates) was substantial in both Hungary and Yugoslavia.[20]

F. Macroeconomic Instability

The reform process was accompanied by a substantial increase in the inflation rate in at least two of the forerunners, Poland and Yugoslavia. In these countries, monetary policy has been overly expansionary to cover deficits, not in the fiscal budget, but in the enterprise and banking sectors. Investment had not been consistent with comparative advantage, and was a source of losses from the onset. Losses were masked by protection, and could be sustained without a decline in the standard of living by maintaining a high rate of growth of nominal domestic demand financed by large external borrowing.

When international lending ceased, Poland and Yugoslavia sought to increase their export foreign-exchange revenues. However, this proved difficult with enterprises that were not competitive on world markets. The rate of growth of nominal domestic demand was increased by subsidization of the losses of enterprises. With foreign borrowing no longer an option, excessive domestic demand was reflected not in large current account deficits but in higher rates of inflation and then hyperinflation.

In 1990 Hungary had a substantial foreign debt, a convertible-currency current account deficit in the balance of payments, and an inflation rate of about 20%, which suggested that excess nominal domestic demand was substantial. Also losses in the Hungarian enterprises and banks were massive. Estimates put the stock of Central Bank losses from external debt valuation differences at about 30% of GDP.

---

[19] In Hungary, the Government has kept 50.5% of the ownership of banks. The rest is widely distributed among enterprises and other bodies.

[20] The indebtedness of Polish enterprises was wiped out by the strongly negative real rates of interest that prevailed for several years, up to, and including, January 1990.

G. The Trend

The economic reforms in Eastern Europe up to the end of 1989 consisted principally of institutional measures: the decentralization of management, the creation of decentralized banking systems, and the removal of restrictions on private ownership of means of production.

In 1990, emphasis has been placed on liberalization of prices (which remained distorted throughout the reform process) and the reduction of the macroeconomic instability that accompanied the reforms. In January 1990, both Yugoslavia and Poland launched economic programs aimed at stabilizing their economies through monetary, fiscal and exchange rate policies. In both countries, the program also included an immediate liberalization of most prices and international trade. Other countries are thinking of similar strategies.

There is a perception that the implementation of these measures will bring the East European countries to something approaching western market economies. Under this view, price liberalization, complemented by decentralized management and the creation of decentralized commercial banks, will create a market economy.

Yet without ownership reform, price reform can only move these economies toward a model that has failed in practice in Yugoslavia. Yugoslavia achieved the highest degree of decentralization among socialist economies. Also, although prices in Yugoslavia were quite distorted, they were less so than in the other East European countries. Thus, with price liberalization, the latter will become something close to Yugoslavia.

Still, Yugoslavia cannot be called a western market economy. Although it has no central planner, Yugoslavia shares with other East European countries most of the problems associated with central planning. Yugoslav savings have been invested in volumes as large as and in ways as inefficient as those of the centralized socialist economies. Overstaffing is as pervasive in Yugoslavia as in Poland and Hungary before and after these countries' moves towards decentralization. After more than 20 years of reforms, Yugoslav enterprises are as much loss-makers as their counterparts in other East European countries.

One of the most important differences between Yugoslavia and the other East European countries, the establishment of a fully decentralized financial system, ended in total disaster. Rather than being a vehicle for improved efficiency in allocation of resources, the financial system of Yugoslavia has become a part of the country's economic problems. One therefore questions the rationale of turning the other countries into something that approximates Yugoslavia.

Furthermore, the experience with the stabilization attempts launched in both Poland and Yugoslavia in January 1990 shows that self-managed enterprises do not react to monetary policies and financial discipline in the same way as private firms in market economies. As is discussed later, enterprises have reacted to the stabilization efforts in ways that threaten the sustainability of these efforts, prompting a heated debate on the need for urgent privatization.

The experience of Yugoslavia and Poland, suggests that the root of the problems of the unreformed economies is not central planning, and that distorted prices are not the main source of the problems of the countries engaged in reform. Instead, it appears that the source of both kinds of problems is the objectives imbedded in socialism, that require either central planning or distorted prices, or both. The following section discusses how the mechanism used to decentralize decision making without extensive private ownership cannot function without substantial government intervention.

III. CAN THE MARKET FUNCTION WITHOUT OWNERS?
A. The Problems of the Self-Management System
The financial system is a capitalist mechanism that allocates resources by influencing incentives confronting owners of capital. When owners of capital react to changes in incentives, the effects are felt in the demand for capital goods and in the labor market. The efficacy of the financial system in affecting economic behavior is as good as its ability to influence factor markets. And that ability relies primarily on affecting capital owners first, then labor. But there are no owners in the self-managed socialist enterprises. In effect, having socialist enterprises owning themselves means that nobody owns them. Thus, there is no advocate for capital in these enterprises. Workers are supposed to be the surrogate advocates, but they have little incentive to preserve and increase their enterprises' capital.

On the contrary, as I shall elaborate, workers have a vested interest in decapitalizing the enterprise and, in the absence of government intervention, can do so. I now consider the implications of enterprise collective self-ownership for the functioning of the market.

B. The Absence of Factor Markets
The lack of an advocate for capital in the self-management system means that there are no capital markets. In turn, this means that there is no market for labor.[21] This introduces at least three difficult problems. First, how to ensure that investment takes place in the right amounts and in the right activities; second, how to avoid free rider problems, both

---

[21] The lack of a labor market is in fact inherent in the self-management system.

within enterprises and among them; third, how to avoid wide divergences in the wage level for similar activities and skills in different enterprises, which would contradict income distribution objectives.[22]

The problem of investment has two dimensions. One is the share of investment in GDP. The other is the allocation of investment among competing alternatives. In centrally planned economies, the government sets both, forcing a high rate of saving and investment. In a pure self-management system, the population and enterprises should be able to substitute for the government in both dimensions. However, the incentives prevailing in the self-management system make government intervention necessary on both counts.

In capitalist economies, investors are entitled to returns from enterprise ownership independently of whether they work in the company. They can sell their entitlement, transforming their claims on real capital into cash, and they can transfer ownership to heirs. That is, they have an assurance that the capital formed with investment, and the returns, benefit them or their heirs.

No such an assurance exists in the self-management system. Under that system, workers have access to the rents of capital via decisions on the allocation of the surplus of production. However, they do not own the capital. This makes an extremely important difference. Incumbent workers run a very high risk that they will not be able to enjoy the benefits of today's proposed investments. Workers can enjoy the benefits of investment only as long as they remain in the enterprise (a condition that they can fail to meet as a result of death, restructuring of the enterprise, or other causes).[23]

Thus, while workers can cotemporaneously appropriate the rents of capital, they cannot be sure that they will be able to do so in the future.[24] Moreover, if workers choose to invest, monitoring of investment performance is required. Workers lack preparation and also motivation in this regard, because of their small share in the returns of the new capital.

---

[22] For an excellent and more rigorous discussion of the problems of self-management see Sandanha (1989). Several of the ideas presented in this section come from that paper.

[23] The difference between the incentives for workers under self-managed enterprises and those prevailing in enterprises totally or partially owned by their workers is fundamental but is frequently ignored. When workers own the enterprise, they become capitalists and act accordingly. Under self-management, there is no capitalist.

[24] The fact that it does not pay to invest in non-owned assets is recognized in East European literature and is called the Furubotn-Pejovic effect.

As a result, the incentive to increase current individual earnings at the expense of the enterprise investment is very strong.

Taken to the extreme, this incentive could push workers to appropriate not only the rents of capital but also the entire stock of capital of the enterprise. They could increase their wages to a point where the enterprise makes losses and is decapitalized. The enterprise would disappear when the last key piece of machinery breaks down.[25] If borrowing is allowed, the best course of action is to borrow to pay higher salaries until the enterprise becomes insolvent. Thus, there are strong incentives encouraging self-liquidation in the self-management system.[26]

In reality, self-liquidation has not taken place. This can be partially explained, even without government intervention, by other forces in the system. One is that, in a strictly socialist economy, there are not many opportunities to invest outside enterprises because the private ownership of capital goods is not tolerated. In these economies, individuals tend to invest their savings in inventories of consumer goods as are obtainable. These goods can be expected to maintain their real value, which is not generally true of local monetary holdings. Another means of storing savings is hoarding convertible foreign exchange.

Thus, workers could increase their consumption substantially through the period of decapitalization of the enterprise, and could provide for some future consumption by buying consumer durables. However, they would not be able to invest their high wages in other activities to ensure future income once the enterprise, and their jobs, disappear. So, it is in their interest to ensure that the enterprise somehow survives as long as they work in it. Also, although managers are in principle subordinated to workers, they are influential and they may push for investment to increase their

---

[25] The optimal path would include some investment to ensure that the maximum value is extracted from the total capital stock. For example, if a key piece of machinery breaks down while a substantial stock of machinery is still useful, it could be optimal to replace it.

[26] This mode of behavior exists in capitalist economies in cases, such as that of many Savings and Loan Associations in the United States, where enterprises are controlled by people who do not own the assets of the enterprise. Such situations may arise when the formal owners realize that their enterprise is bankrupt, so that they have lost their equity and, therefore, no longer own it. The company still has assets, but their owners are the creditors of the enterprise (depositors, in the case of the Savings and Loan Associations). Very frequently, if this situation is not known to creditors or regulators, the formal owners vote themselves huge dividends or large unsecured loans to appropriate the assets of the enterprise before it collapses. This practice is severely penalized in market economies, most frequently with jail.

power vis-a-vis other enterprises.

Within such an environment, and without government intervention, the level of investment would be determined by the resolution of a conflict among several forces only vaguely related to the economic variables that should shape an efficient investment strategy for the enterprise. The outcome would be levels of investment well below both what is optimal. The ownership structure leads workers to multiply the expected returns from investment in their enterprises by a probability lower than one to estimate their expected returns. This probability varies inversely with their age. As a result, the appeal of investment in enterprises declines both relative to consumption and to other ways in which workers can store savings, which, given the restricted options, can be only unproductive assets.

Recognizing this, the government intervenes to foster investment. It does so by compelling firms to set aside for investment a part of net income, either directly (taxation of profits, combined with subsidization of investment or direct investment) or through incentives and regulations (forcing enterprises to allocate a portion of their income to investment funds).[27] This intervention determines the volume of investment, but in an arbitrary way. It also distorts the allocation of investment funds.

Taxation and subsidization returns investment decisions to the government, in the manner of central planning. The alternative solution, forcing enterprises to invest a portion of their profits, provides the government with a lever to control the overall level of investment while leaving with enterprises the discretion to decide on the allocation of investment. But this type of intervention may result in even more rigidity in the allocation of resources than central planning. Resources are retained in the activities wherein they are generated. Enterprises tend to invest in the fields in which they operate because that is the activity managers and workers know. Thus, their personal welfare depends on the development, or at least the maintenance, of that activity. But also, it is easier for workers to appropriate the rents of capital if it is invested in their own

---

[27] Vanek in 1970 wrote that the Furubotn-Pejovic effect does not affect the overall level of investment but only its financing. That is, workers would invest only in fully leveraged investments. However, private banks cannot be expected to consistently finance highly leveraged projects. That is, government intervention in financing is needed to keep investment going. In fact, governments have found it necessary to subsidize investment as well.

company.[28] This dampens substantially the mobility of capital and distorts the allocation of investment. The immobility of capital is confirmed by Fernando Saldanha, who shows that in Yugoslavia capital did not flow from low- to high-return manufacturing branches.[29]

The problem of absence of an advocate for capital is demonstrated in the three countries that have attempted market oriented reform. In Poland and Yugoslavia, the subsidization of enterprises with existing or potential losses (that is, with losses that are masked by the subsidies) was at the root of hyperinflation. In Poland, the inflation tax transferred resources equivalent to 10 percent of GDP to the enterprise sector in 1988. This transfer was in addition to the explicit subsidies granted through the fiscal budget, which were on the order of 10 percent of GDP.[30] In Yugoslavia, the transfer effected by the inflation tax to enterprises in 1988 was around 8 percent of GDP, while arrears in the banking system were mounting.[31] In both countries, wages increased faster than inflation while enterprise losses soared.

Up to 1987, at 20 percent of GDP, Hungary had the highest explicit subsidies to industry among the three reforming countries. The subsidies were subsequently drastically reduced. However, the problem of arrears of enterprises with the banking system was aggravated. Enterprises were not repaying their debts, yet continued to increase wages and fringe benefits. This problem is frequently interpreted as a crisis of temporary illiquidity in the enterprises; but enterprises had enough liquidity to increase wages. The illiquidity appears only when it is time to repay debts.[32]

Thus, although the self-management system is decentralized, its solution to the investment problem is as rigid as that of central planning. In practice, governments of decentralized socialist countries have set investment volume targets not as high as those of the centrally planned economies, but still very high in comparison with the investment rates of

---

[28] Enterprises could become interested in investing in other fields if they could still appropriate the rents of capital. That is, if they invest in firms that are not self-managed. If this happens, it would mean that the currently self-managed companies would become the future big capitalists of socialist countries, with their workers extracting the rents of capital of their own firms and their subsidiaries. In Poland, the Government is thinking of introducing a rule that would force the self-managed parent companies to invest all profits from a non-self-managed firm in the same firm. This would be yet another restriction to the mobility of capital introduced just to avoid the appropriation of profits as wages.

[29] Saldanha, op. cit.

[30] See Sanldana (1990).

[31] See Rocha (1989).

[32] Of course, unrepaid debts become equivalent to subsidies.

comparable western market economies. The results in terms of growth have been disappointing.

Government intervention to ensure enterprise survival removes some of the restraint on workers of the fear of bankruptcy. In fact, almost no enterprise has failed in East European countries. The implicit signal, which the workers seem to have understood only too well, is that, no matter how unrealistic the compensation increases they grant to themselves, the government will avoid the bankruptcy of the enterprise. The more enterprises that act under this assumption, the better the chance that the assumption is right.

The incentive in the self-management system is also to devote as low an effort as possible to work. Although in theory workers have an incentive to monitor the efficiency of others, their share of the benefits of increased efficiency is much smaller than the benefits they can extract from inefficiencies, such as not coming to work. Thus, absenteeism, shirking, and lack of initiative are pervasive in the self-managed enterprise.

The day-to-day apathy of workers increases the power of those whom the workers have elected to manage the enterprise. Enterprise managers can pursue their own objectives as long as the labor force does not realize that decisions are against the workers' interests. In practice, this means that managers are well regarded as long as they fight for increasing the income of the workers. Sometimes, however, managers can act against the interests of the workers, as for example via "spontaneous privatization".

C. The Income Distribution Problem

In western market economies, capital and labor markets tend to equalize wages and profit rates (return on assets) across the economy. Employees working in capital-intensive firms or activities can at times negotiate higher wages than their counterparts in less capital-intensive activities. However, the counterbalancing force of investors who are able to transfer their resources to activities yielding higher returns on assets keeps to a minimum the differences between wages paid to workers with the same skills.[33]

In contrast, in the self-management system, wages depend on the ratio of the absolute level of profits before wages to the number of workers in the enterprise (called net operating income). This ratio varies from firm to

---

[33] A common occurrence is that of firms highly intensive in capital (human or physical, or both) paying higher wages than their industry average not only to those people with special skills crucial to the success of the enterprise but to other workers as well. This seems to be a way to keep internal harmony necessary for a successful operation.

firm depending on capital intensity. As a result, wage equalization cannot occur in the self-management system. Since remuneration for labor is mixed with the rents of capital, workers with the same skills can have widely different wages, depending on the capital intensity of their firm.

In short, the fact that there is no uniform price for capital means that there is no uniform price for labor. Therefore, there are no economy-wide factor markets. If these key markets are missing, the transmission of market signals is interrupted at the core of the economic system.

To moderate the wide differences in wages for the same skills that would prevail in an unconstrained self-management system, the government intervenes to equalize profits in all (or most) enterprises through taxes and subsidies, pricing policies, quantitative restrictions on international trade, and privileged access to inputs and foreign exchange. Firms take advantage of this policy to request tax and other relief when they are running losses or have below-average profits as a result of wage increases. Given the government's concern with income equality, enterprises know that the government is predisposed to oblige in providing transfers to cover losses.

As a result, cross-subsidization is substantial in the reforming countries. In the case of Poland, for example, explicit subsidies alone were around 10 percent of GNP (ignoring price advantages and other subsidization through indirect instruments such as negative real interest rates) which approximates the level of profits after taxes of the consolidated socialist sector (Figure 1).[34] That is, in the aggregate, it is as if the whole volume of profits were reshuffled fiscally.

In the effort to avoid appropriation of the rents of capital within the enterprise, governments themselves appropriate the rents in order to reallocate the proceeds among enterprises. In Hungary, subsidies to enterprises represented the largest item in the budget. In Yugoslavia, the profit-makers were taxed to subsidize loss-makers, or forced to finance them.[35]

In spite of such intervention, wage differentials remain. In the case of

---

[34] This figure includes all subsidies for which payments are made from the budget to enterprises. This treatment differs from that in the budgetary accounts, where a distinction is drawn between subsidies to the enterprise sector and subsidies to the population; the latter are subsidies from which the population is the direct beneficiary even though the corresponding budget disbursement may be to an enterprise. This distinction is not relevant for the current analysis because all these subsidies affect the profits of enterprises, and, therefore, the wages they can pay. The figure underestimates the amount of subsidization because it does not include subsidies intermediated to enterprises by financial institutions.

[35] See Konovalov (1989).

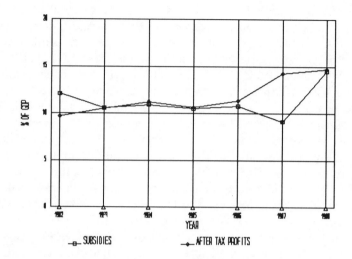

Figure 1 Poland: Subsidies to enterprises compared with after tax profits as proportion of GDP (Source: IMF)

Yugoslavia, these differentials have been wide and have been widening. The coefficient of variation (standard deviation divided by mean) of wage rates in 33 manufacturing branches changed from 0.30 in 1985 to 0.32 in 1986 and to 0.81 in 1987.[36] The rapid increase in 1987, a year in which the rate of inflation increased substantially, suggests that the government's grasp on the enterprises' allocation of surpluses is weakened by macroeconomic instability.

There are at least three explanations for this. One is that not all wage contracts are signed the same month, which can make for important differences in highly inflationary economies. The second, related to the former, is that high inflation leads to greater relative price variability, including wages. The third is that workers are able to appropriate more of the rents of capital of their enterprises as a result of the dilution of taxation caused by inflation; since taxes and subsidies are the main instruments that governments have to equalize wages, the weakening of taxation results in higher wage differentials.

This tendency was confirmed in Yugoslavia in 1985-1987, during which time the real wage remained approximately constant while enterprises' net operating income per worker fell by 29 percent. In 1988 the manufacturing sector as a whole incurred losses, and the wage bill exceeded

---

[36] See Fernando Saldanha, op. cit.

the enterprises' net operating income.

D. Resulting Rigidities

The absence of factor markets is a source of rigidities in the economy. There are incentives for incumbent workers to oppose new hiring, because by diluting profits per worker this would lead incomes of incumbent workers to decline. Therefore labor lacks mobility. Workers who are laid off have little chance of being hired by other enterprises. To counteract this, central and local governments (and the Communist Party) intervene to compel enterprises to hire new recruits. Managers are happy to comply because a larger work force increases their power and status. Such intervention results in overstaffing, which in turn leads to losses and provides a justification for subsidies.[37] Still, substantial overstaffing need not solve the employment problem. In Yugoslavia, overstaffing estimated at 30 percent of the employed coexisted with an unemployment rate of 16 percent.

Moreover, self-managed enterprises are very rigid concerning the size of their labor force. As much as they are unlikely to hire new people voluntarily, they are also reluctant to sack redundant workers. Although there are some rules that could be applied to sack a portion of the workers, such as last to come is the first to go, the political difficulties involved in workers firing fellow workers are likely to be substantial. It has never happened in a large scale.

In Poland in 1990, for example, real output had fallen by 30% and unemployment had increased only from 1.5% in December 1989 to 3.5% in June 1990. Furthermore, these figures exaggerate the rise in unemployment. The latter includes substantial numbers who have registered as unemployed although they were not working before[38] as well as people who quit voluntarily and people dismissed for causes not related to the contraction. At the end of April 1990, out of 351,000 unemployed, 43% had never worked, 48% had quit or were fired for other reasons, and only 7.7% had been laid off.[39] If the figures are corrected, unemployment had increased only by 0.2% from December 1989 to April 1990, by 1% to

---

[37] Thus, the final effect is a combination of the incentives of the self-managed enterprise with Kornai's soft-budget constraint. However, it should be noted that the self-management system cannot exist without the soft-budget constraint, not only because of the employment problem but also because of the tendency to decapitalize the enterprise and the other problems sketched in the previous Sections.
[38] They have done so in the expectation of getting the unemployment benefits that the government is planning to establish.
[39] Source: Freedman and Rapaczynski (1990).

June.

The rigidity is even more spectacular in Yugoslavia. There, reacting to the financial squeeze of the stabilization program, a substantial portion of enterprises have preferred to stop paying wages of all workers than laying off a portion of them. The government estimates that 1.5 million workers were not being paid in May 1990. Obviously, as in Poland, the enterprises are expecting the government to blink first and go back to subsidization.[40]

Self-management also affects the choice of technique. Once profits have been distributed and investment determined, the basis for remuneration of labor biases enterprise investment decisions towards capital-intensive techniques that provide higher wages for the incumbent working force. Investment is also biased in favor of projects that maximize short-term returns.

Self-management is not conducive to the creation of new firms and activities. Potential entrepreneurs' gains from the establishment of new enterprises are limited by the absence of claims to capital. Further, since the remuneration of labor is higher in capital-intensive enterprises (which tend to be the old ones), workers do not have incentives to move to new ventures.

The government favors large enterprises because of management economies. As a result, the industrial structure comprises mostly large socialist enterprises, small scale private workshops, and almost nothing in between. Medium scale enterprises that in other western economies facilitate mobility of real resources are missing. Smaller firms tend to be more flexible in allocation of resources, and are more easily created and destroyed than their larger counterparts.

IV. ARE INDEPENDENT MANAGERS A SOLUTION?

The inefficiencies of socialist ownership in Eastern Europe are frequently attributed to lack of autonomy of managers. In contrast, in other countries--mainly OECD--government-owned enterprises have often functioned adequately under the management of autonomous executives.[41] The latter experiences might suggest greater autonomy of management in

---

[40] This behavior is not new. Using data for 1975-88, Roberto Rocha found that Okun's Law (the rate of change in the unemployment rate is inversely proportional to the rate of growth of output) does not hold in Yugoslavia. The relationship between those variables follows a random pattern, which suggests that non-economic forces are strong in shaping it. See Rocha (1990).

[41] The assertion that public sector enterprises are a success in the developed countries can be challenged. This, however, is not the point of this paper.

Eastern Europe as a direction for reform.

A. Government Enterprises in Western Market Economies

The conditions of management of public enterprises in western countries cannot be reproduced in socialist countries. In the western market economy there has been a separation between ownership rights of the government (which retains control over major decisions, including investment and disinvestment as well as overall control over borrowing) and decentralized day-to-day management by managers. Governments are not involved in day-to-day management because the performance of managers can be judged by comparison with that of private enterprises. This separation is possible because the public enterprises coexist with a strong private sector, which provides a benchmark for public enterprise performance.

In particular, in western market economies public sector enterprises function in an environment in which factor prices are established by factor markets wherein the private sector is a major participant.[42]   Without a benchmark provided by domestic competition, allocation decisions become, as in centrally-planned and self-managed economies, variables that are distinct for each enterprise. If managers are told to make the enterprise profitable, what is the norm for profits? Or for the wage level? The answers to these questions can only be arbitrary. Being arbitrary, they can easily be changed by political means.

Benchmarks could be sought by international comparisons, directly via foreign competition, or indirectly via an average of returns to capital in countries with comparable development. The wage rate would be a residual. Such means need not yield results applicable to the economy and can imply inappropriate choice of relative factor intensities.

B. Accountability and the Unstable Autonomy of Managers

There have been at least four attempts to give autonomy to managers in Eastern Europe: in the Soviet Union, during the New Economic Policy and in the mid-1960s; in Hungary after the abolition of central planning in 1968; and in Poland in the 1980s. In none of these cases did the independence of managers survive for long. It gave way to either a return to central planning or the establishment of labor management.

The failure is often attributed to specific circumstances. That is, the assertion is that the system would have succeeded, if only the government, the Party, or the workers had not interfered. Interference may however

---

[42] Competition for production factors and other inputs exists even if the publicly-owned enterprises are not in the same line of business as the private ones.

have been intrinsic to the system.

The instability of the system derives from the isolation of the manager as a representative of an absent and silent owner. Under a system where the owner (the government) has agreed not to intervene in the management of the enterprise, managers confront powerful forces that fill the void left by the absent owner. Rather than combatting these forces, managers accommodate them. The forces are primarily political. As Tamás Bauer puts it, ..."Enterprise managers as bosses in all forms feel themselves politically weak in reformed planned economies. Thus, they are inclined to give in quickly in any labor conflict, since a strike may endanger their position as subordinates of local (regional) party organs first."[43]   The tendency to accommodate workers' demands leads to equivalence between the system of independent managers and the self-management system.[44]

The pressures to fill the vacuum left by the owner derive from two complementary sources. Managers cannot be totally autonomous; if not accountable to someone,[45] they can appropriate the assets of the enterprise.[46] Also, the power of managers is weak relative to that of governments, trade unions, or owners. Managers represent the interests of others, while workers and owners represent their own interests.

As a reflection of these circumstances, managers lack means of advancing their own interests in case of conflict. Both labor and owners command such means. Workers can strike. A manager who strikes is likely to be replaced. An owner can close a company, or refuse to invest further. A manager cannot make such decisions without consulting the owner. The decision to close a company leaves the owners with at least the net assets of the enterprise. By contrast, the manager taking such a

---

[43] See Bauer (1990).

[44] Bauer, op-cit, quotes Gács (1982), who uses the term "control by consent" to describe the management of these firms, where managers disregard efficiency in order to please pressure groups.

[45] Quite frequently, the system of independent managers is taken as equivalent to the system prevailing in many large capitalist corporations, where professional managers control enterprises for absent (and frequently unknown) owners. This equivalence, however, is misplaced. In capitalist economies, the managers are clearly accountable to the owners (directly or through the price of the shares in the stock exchange), and a committee of owners with relatively high exposure in the exercise of control over the managers through the board of directors. This is true even of public sector enterprises in OECD countries. Enterprises where owners do not exert control exist in these countries, but the lack of control does not last for long.

[46] For further discussion on this possibility, see next Section, on the coexistence of the socialized and private sectors.

decision becomes unemployed. The only weapon that managers can use in conflicts with the government or trade unions is the threat of resignation, which those with whom they are in conflict will be only happy to accept.

In a conflict over compensation, managers will tend to side with the more powerful side. This is likely to be labor in socialist economies. There, the owner is a political entity sensitive to the political pressures that workers can exert. If a manager antagonizes workers, it is easier to get rid of the manager than support him.

The intellectual stream in socialism also stresses the eminence of workers. This position is manifested in theoretical writings throughout the history of socialism. Since the inefficiencies of socialist systems are attributed to ownership by the government and consequent centralism, the workers' position is enhanced, and the government can become reluctant to exercise its formal ownership rights.[47]

In this environment, managers become political beings who survive by appeasing others while furthering their own ambitions in terms of income and power. Workers are appeased by raising wages; politicians by increased hiring; and the larger the enterprise becomes, the better for managers.

In summary, the system of independent managers has not ensured the existence of an advocate for capital.

V. COEXISTENCE OF SELF-MANAGED AND PRIVATE ENTERPRISES

Laws eliminating the restrictions previously imposed on private enterprises limit the above problems to the socialist sector. However, the rigidities on factor mobility constrain growth prospects in the private sector, since the self-management system, in addition to restricting the flow of resources within the socialist sector, also impedes the flow of resources from the socialist to the private sector. As long as the socialist sector remains overwhelmingly larger than the private sector and continues to command most of the capital stock, resource availability to the private sector is constrained.

There has been a presumption that banks will solve this problem by

---

[47] A fourth reason is that, in wage disputes, the interests of managers tend to be closer to those of labor than to those of owners. If a union of managers were to strike over compensation, probably it would do so against the owners rather than against the workers (except when the workers are also the owners). Also, while owners frequently close enterprises temporarily to fight wage increases, it is quite improbable to have managers striking against wage increases demanded by the workers.

receiving deposits from all sectors and competitively reallocating resource access. But there are several obstacles to such financial intermediation in an environment where most enterprises are socialized.

A clear example of this is the agricultural sector in Poland, where 75% of the land is in private hands. However, the sector suffers from severe inefficiencies because it depends on socialized enterprises for the provision of inputs and the commercialization of outputs. Also, banking credit and other funds for investment have gone overwhelmingly to the socialized sector.

Efficient allocation requires interest rates to be market-determined, and requires the imposition of financial discipline by elimination of subsidies and the enforcement of bankruptcy. Market interest rates and an end to subsidies would oblige enterprises to constrain both wage increases and demand for credit.

However, the introduction of financial discipline is quite difficult, if not impossible, under self-management.   There are incentives for enterprises to ignore interest rates, even without subsidies. Self-managed enterprises do not have the instinct for survival that characterizes a private-ownership system.

As I have noted, incentives for workers to decapitalize their enterprise are tempered by the fear of losing their jobs. Under private ownership, workers are able to invest the proceeds of decapitalization. Given access to credit, the socialist enterprise could borrow to increase wages and workers' benefits, so that workers would not have to wait for depreciation of the real stock of capital to appropriate the assets of the enterprise.[48] In this way, the capital of the socialist enterprises would be "privatized". Resources would flow from the socialist to the private sector. The unstable nature of the self-management system would lead to its own dissolution.

This process of privatization however creates a serious fairness problem, since workers secure ownership of a stock of capital that is formally owned by all citizens. Equally important, such "privatization" is costly in terms of the economic and financial disruption caused by spontaneous self-liquidation of enterprises that account for the bulk of an economy's productive capacity.

Appropriation of socialist enterprises' capital has not been only for the benefit of workers. In Hungary, enterprises underwent "spontaneous privatization" whereby assets have been transferred in various ways to the

---

[48] Borrowing to decapitalize an enterprise is not as bizarre as it sounds. This is precisely what happens when firms finance losses with credit, a phenomenon common to all countries in financial distress, including Poland, Hungary and Yugoslavia.

advantage of management, most frequently by selling the socialist enterprise's inventories and leasing the equipment to a new private firm at low prices. Managers receive compensation via stock of the new company and highly paid management positions. The same phenomenon in Poland has been called "uwlascenie nomenklature."

Also, I have noted that wage resistance is fierce in self-managed enterprises. If forced with macroeconomic instruments to reduce expenditures, workers would reduce investment or decapitalize their enterprises (especially now that private ownership is allowed) rather than reduce their own wages. If workers do not believe in the seriousness of the government's stabilization program, their best bet is to keep on increasing their wages to maintain or improve their acquisitive power vis-a-vis the rest of the economy. If they become convinced that the government is serious, and that their company faces bankruptcy (or that they may be fired), their best bet is again to increase their wages to extract as much as they can from the enterprise before they become unemployed. Since enterprises tend to be grossly overstaffed, individual workers would perceive the risk of being fired as very high, which would strengthen their incentive to decapitalize the firm while they still can.

If the government precludes the transfer of assets and enforces strict wage controls, firms would tend to hold tight, reducing production without firing workers, waiting for the government to desist in its attempt to introduce fiscal discipline. This is what happened in Yugoslavia and Poland in the summer of 1990.

In these countries, labor managed enterprises have gone to extremes (like falling in arrears with the banking system and with each other, selling needed assets, giving licenses without payment to their employees and even stopping paying their employees) in order to avoid laying off workers. With these measures, the enterprises avoid the permanent adjustments they need to improve their production methods, on the expectation that the government will eventually bail them out. Such-bail out would end the efforts to stabilize.[49]

VI. REFORMS

There are means of resolving the problems of the self-management system. The government can regain control of the self-managed enterprises by "renationalizing" them, and, in conjunction with day-to-day autonomy

---

[49] Enterprises have powerful weapons to induce the government to desist in their efforts to eradicate subsidies permanently. For example, in summer 1990, food industries in Poland threatened food scarcity if the government did not bail them out.

for managers, the allocation of resources among enterprises can be centralized. The next step is privatization, with the large conglomerates broken up in the process.

A. Improving the Management of Socialist Enterprises

Ensuring capital mobility in the socialist sector requires the government as owner shifting resources among enterprises. Decisions regarding whether to reinvest profits in the same enterprise or elsewhere, whether to liquidate or restructure loss-making concerns, and whether or not to sell enterprises can only be taken by an agent *external* to the enterprise, that is, by the owner. So centralization of investment decisions for socialist enterprises cannot be avoided if mobility of capital is desired.

Socialist enterprises should be assigned objectives of maximizing the return on capital.[50] Consistently, the government should not expect from socialist enterprises any assistance in implementing macroeconomic or other policies, nor in supplying particular goods without regard for costs. Conversely, no privileges should be granted to the enterprises.

The existence of a large number of socialist enterprises thus requires two levels of management, each pursuing the objective of maximizing the return to capital; at the enterprise level managers are responsible for profitable operation; in the holding company the responsibility is to ensure mobility of resources within the socialist sector and to the private sector.

Given the opportunities for fraud and other crimes, a supervisory agency is also needed that is independent of the holding company. The primary tasks of the agency are to ensure that transactions between the holding company and the enterprises, and between the holding company and the private sector, are conducted at arms-length and market terms; that the books of the holding company reflect the true value of the government's capital; and to measure the performance of the holding company by comparing the returns to capital with returns in the private sector.

The corporate tax structure will also require reform, by eliminating *ad hoc* taxation and subsidization, and establishing uniform tax treatment among enterprises that will allow comparisons of profitability.

B. Privatization

Replacing the self-management system with a more efficient form of organization for the socialist enterprises cannot in itself make for factor

---

[50] There may be some exceptions to this general approach, as the Government may choose to keep ownership of some industries deemed as strategic. These industries should be treated as exceptions in ways that minimize the distortions they introduce in the economy.

mobility. Entrepreneurial spirit would still be missing. Privatization of a substantial portion of the socialist enterprises is necessary.

There have been proposals to maintain the self-management system in place while improving factor mobility and incentives. One proposal is requiring payment for the right to work in an enterprise. Paying for the right to work has been successfully applied in some individual cooperative enterprises within market economies. For example, in Mondragon in Spain, workers hold shares in the firm's capital: nobody can own capital without working in the enterprise, and nobody can work in the enterprise without owning its shares. Each new worker is required to buy shares in the enterprise, and to sell his shares when leaving.

Mondragon is a voluntary organization. Coercing enterprises to become Mondragon-type organizations is not conducive to labor mobility. There is a problem in firing workers. This does not mean that the Mondragon-type of enterprise should not be allowed voluntarily to form. Mondragon has however remained an isolated successful case for decades, when nothing has prevented replication of this organizational form in Spain and elsewhere. There are evident disincentives associated with undertaking investments when there is free entry into sharing subsequent gains.

Privatization into conventional joint-stock companies is a prerequisite for decentralization of economic decision making. Privatization via sale of enterprises may, however, take decades to achieve a functional market. An alternative is fast privatization by transferring ownership without payment; since the people already own the socialist enterprises, the government should in principle only charge for the transfer of shares to a subset of citizens.

(i) Transfer Without Payment

Giving away the enterprises to citizens is an appealing solution. Sale of the enterprises would have to await the completion of liberalization, to facilitate capital market valuation, and to avoid misleading investors because of changes in the value of an enterprise in the course of liberalization. Sale of the enterprises is also impeded by insufficient or unevenly distributed purchasing power among the population. These problems are resolved by transfer of titles to ownership to the population without payment. There is no need to value the stock of capital and no purchasing power constraint.

Transferring ownership without payment, however, has its difficulties. The method of transfer must be fair and practical, although the logistics of distributing the shares should not differ from rationing of commodities. More fundamentally, completely dispersed private ownership presents problems similar to self-management. Without a controlling shareholder, management is not monitored. This could be resolved by the transfer of ownership without payment in an initial phase and the sale of shares subsequently. The government could retain a controlling interest to be sold after a market had been established in the freely distributed shares. Better, it could give the management of the enterprises to entrepreneurial groups, paying them with stock options to provide an incentive for them to increase the value of the shares by managing the enterprise efficiently.

It has been proposed that the transfer of shares could be organized through the holding companies transformed into mutual funds. The initial transfer could take the form of distribution of the shares of the mutual funds, which could subsequently be exchanged for shares of the enterprise themselves or of other mutual funds. Or broadly based pension funds could be endowed with the shares of the enterprises. This uses to advantage the preexisting institutional setting that manages the public sector enterprises and establishes institutional investors for the functioning of stock markets.[51]

A source of concern associated with all schemes to create financial capital markets is the potential for individual capital loss in an environment where information on the value of enterprises is very limited. Initial stock trading would inevitably change the domestic distribution of wealth.

The transfer of shares to individuals without payment has been attempted successfully at least in two instances, although not on the scale of an entire economy. In Canada, the Government of British Columbia privatized the British Columbia Resources Investment Corporation by offering free shares to each Canadian citizen or resident of the province for at least one year: a purchase entitlement was also offered. In Chile, the two largest banks were privatized in sales to taxpayers under conditions that effectively reduced the price of shares to zero.

(ii) Directing gross investment toward the private sector

Another prospective privatization strategy, used in the 1950s by South Korea to reduce the size of the public sector, consists of blocking investment in the socialist enterprises to free all gross investment for the private sector.[52] This restricts socialist enterprises to internal financing. The option remains for the socialist enterprises to attract private investors willing to acquire the enterprises' equity capital. This scheme imposes a continued political strain that tests the government's determination. Also, the East European economies of 1990 differ from South Korea in the 1950s, although the relative size of the public sector is similar. Korea's

---

[51] Marton Tardos is among those authors advocating such proposals. See his paper in this volume.

[52] This strategy was proposed by Lawrence Lau from Stanford University in a seminar held in Washington to discuss an earlier draft of this paper.

capital endowment was lower, so that choking public-sector enterprises did not imply writing off the installed productive capacity of the entire industrial sector.

On the other hand, investing in enterprises working under a perverse set of incentives would most likely lead to waste, as happened in the investment drive of the 1970s in both Yugoslavia and Poland. Such investments left these countries with enterprises as inefficient as before but with a much larger external debt. Thus, privatization should be accompanied by a policy restricting socialized enterprises to internal financing.

(iii) Selling the enterprises to workers

Privatization via sale of enterprises to workers on credit raises problems of valuation and monitoring incentives. To whom are the assets to be sold, the workers or their union?

The valuation of assets could be deferred until a capital market had been established. But then inappropriate incentives confront the new shareholders, who gain by decapitalizing the enterprise before the date of valuation. The more they increase their compensation before that date, the lower the future price they will be obliged to pay for current assets.

Selling the enterprise to the union entails transfer of ownership to a body that is subject to political forces inside and outside the enterprise. If the shareholdings are equally allocated (equal number of shares to each worker), problems of control and monitoring reappear. Seeking to establish a controlling interest via sale to a smaller group, such as managers, is subject to incentives for management to appropriate assets or misconstrue asset valuations before the day of valuation.

VII. CONCLUSIONS

The absence of immediate privatization directs the East European countries toward the self-management model. The analysis of the incentives imbedded in this system leads to the conclusion that self-management is inefficient and unstable. The instability then introduces the government intervention that these economies are seeking to replace.

Thus, it seems that, as long as the socialist nature of these countries is kept in place, their governments face a stark choice concerning intervention in economic activity. One option is to reinstate central planning. The other is to intervene to transfer resources between enterprises in an *ad hoc* manner, so as to sustain investment and at the same time ensure an equitable distribution of income. Eliminating intervention altogether is, given the incentives of the self-management system, undesirable. Furthermore, as the experience of Yugoslavia and

Poland shows, self-management makes sustainable stabilization a difficult goal to attain.

If private ownership is introduced while the self-management system is in place, a resource transfer would take place from the socialist to the private sector, but in an inequitable and disruptive way. Rather than confront such choices, it is preferable to privatize immediately, thus replacing the self-management system with a form of ownership that allows efficient and flexible allocation of resources via functioning factor markets.

References

Aganbegyan, Abel, 1990. *Inside Perestroika*, Perennial Library, Harper & Row.

Bauer, Tamás, 1990. *The Microeconomics of Inflation Under Economic Reforms: Enterprises and Their Environment*, presented at the Seminar on Managing Inflation in Socialist Economies, Laxemburg, Austria.

Freedman, Roman and Rapaczynski, Andrzej, 1990. "Privatization in Poland: A new proposal," mimeo.

Gács, Janos, 1982. "The passive purchasing behavior and possibilities of adjustment in the Hungarian economy," *Acta Oeconomica*, 28, 337-349.

Konovalov, Vladimir, 1989. *Yugoslav Industry: Structure, Performance, Conduct,* Industry Development Division, PRE, The World Bank.

Nove, Alex, 1989. *An Economic History of the USSR*, Penguin Books, London, second edition.

Roberto Rocha, 1989. *Structural Adjustment and Inflation In Yugoslavia*, EMTTF, The World Bank.

Rocha, Roberto, 1990. *Inflation and Stabilization in Socialist Countries: Lessons from Yugoslav Experience*, paper presented at the Seminar on Managing Inflation in Socialist Economies, Laxemburg, Austria.

Saldanha, Fernando, 1989. *Self-Management: Theory and Yugoslav Practice*, EMTTF, The World Bank.

Saldanha, Fernando, 1990. *Interest Rates Subsidies and Monetization in Poland: The Year 1988*, EMTTF, The World Bank.

Tardos, Marton, 1990. "Restoring property rights," chapter 9, this volume.

Tarr, David, 1989. *The Welfare Effects of Foreign Exchange Restraints, Shortages and Subsidies in the Polish Auto, Color TV and Butter Markets*, EMTTF, The World Bank.

Chapter 8

SOCIALISM IN LESS THAN ONE COUNTRY

Adi Schnytzer

This paper is concerned with the problem of transition from a socialist centrally-planned economy to a capitalist mixed-market economy. Such a transition has never been made, although, since the mid-sixties, there have been attempts -- mostly failed -- to extend the role of commodity-money relations within a socialist framework. I point out the existence of an economic system which, while apparently representing a transitional stage between central planning and the market, itself introduces difficulties on the path to reform.[1] A transition trap can emerge. I term the economic system of the transition trap "socialism in less than one country".

For a number of reasons, the transition from a socialist centrally-planned economy to a capitalist mixed market cannot be accomplished instantaneously. Most importantly, a planned socialist economy is a politicized economy in which vertical flows of information, formal and informal, between enterprises and the state bureaucracy play an important part in the allocation of resources. In a capitalist market economy, on the other hand, information flows are essentially horizontal and resources are allocated in response to price signals. Depoliticization and the replacement of -- from an economic viewpoint -- arbitrary decision-making by an apolitical invisible hand cannot be accomplished by legislation alone. Time is required for economic agents to adjust to a new set of system rules. To the extent that individuals see themselves as potential losers in the new system, they will attempt to obstruct reform implementation. The probability that they will succeed will be influenced by the time taken to complete the reform. The longer the time taken, the greater the probability that the system will succumb to "reform fatigue".

Centrally-planned economies are characterized by a high degree of

---

[1]Different types of economic systems are described in Bornstein (1985).

industrial concentration.   If the purpose of economic reform is the establishment of an efficient competitive system, then decentralization of economic decision-making alone will not suffice.   However, if high levels of unemployment are to be avoided, industrial restructuring also must take time.

Product markets have existed in some form or other in every society throughout history.   They require no complex institutional framework for relatively effective functioning.   On the other hand, in an industrial economy efficient capital markets require a sophisticated infrastructure, the likes of which are not to be found in a centrally-planned economy.   Privatization of socialist industry also is a gradual process.

Hence, a reforming socialist economy must pass through a transitionary phase.   To characterize this phase, I consider an economic system in which a mix of property-rights structures prevails, a degree of politicization remains because of ownership implications, industrial structure is concentrated, and factor markets are imperfect.   Welfare comparisons between this system and a centrally-planned economy yield ambiguous results.

I. FACTOR MARKETS AND BUREAUCRATIC INTERVENTION

It has been generally the case that economic reforms in a centrally-planned economy have focused on product markets while leaving factor markets other than labor highly controlled.   One reason for this order of sequencing the decentralization aspect of reforms has been the desire to prevent short-run high levels of unemployment.   From the viewpoint of government, continued control over factor markets facilitates the determination of industrial structure.   This control is strengthened by the informal discretionary power accorded to state bureaucrats as a legacy of central planning.

When private enterprises are permitted in a reforming socialist centrally-planned economy, the government will wish to maintain control over new entrants to industry to ensure the desired flow of tax revenues. The legalization of a large part of the black product market in Hungary was undertaken with this in mind.   As in most countries, a system of permit requirements must be established.   In principle, such requirements need not represent barriers to entry if they are spelled out explicitly and state officials have little or no discriminatory power in their granting.   Under socialism in less than one country, such will not be the case.   Economic reform implies a decentralization of economic decision-making power from state officials to enterprise management.   The former will attempt to minimize this loss of authority by adopting discretion in the granting of permits.   Such behavior may be illegal, but legislated reforms cannot eliminate the bureaucratic arbitrariness characteristic of the political culture in a centrally-planned economy. As the Hungarian economic reforms have shown, the formal authority granted to bureaucrats under central planning is converted to discretionary decision-making power by the reform process. This is an important source of barriers to entry. The permit process facilitates government control over the initiation of economic activity.

In a socialist centrally-planned economy, land is owned by the state (although there have been exceptions, for example Polish agriculture). Individual enterprises and agricultural cooperatives are provided with land free of rent for use in accordance with the government's economic objectives. Thus, there is no market for land, and shadow prices are impossible to determine accurately. In a capitalist-market economy, however, the sale of state-owned land dilutes the power of the state in this respect, zoning laws notwithstanding. In the context of economic reform in a centrally-planned economy, decentralization of property rights in land via leasing -- as in recent Soviet proposals regarding agriculture -- will result in an imperfect land market in which the location of economic activity remains largely in the hands of the government.

Unlike product markets, which arise spontaneously even in the context of central planning, an efficiently functioning capital market requires a suitable institutional framework. In capitalist market economies, such institutions have developed over a long period of time. In a reforming centrally-planned economy, the establishment of a capital market must be planned if it is to take place within a time horizon considered reasonable by the authorities. The plethora of government credits and subsidies under central planning also are not given to spontaneous removal, if short-term disruptions are to be kept to a minimum. Hence, the system has a highly imperfect capital market.

II. PROPERTY RIGHTS

The imperfection of factor markets in the system of socialism in less than one country has implications for the structure of property rights. In a socialist centrally-planned economy property rights in domestic enterprises are vested in the state. The essential non-transferability of these rights is a well-known source of inefficiency. Thus, the privatization of economic enterprises is an important element of East European and Soviet reform packages. However, the non-existence of efficient financial markets makes the raising of funds by private individuals for the purchase of state enterprises difficult.

Another impediment to the rapid implementation of privatization programs is the inevitable conflict over income redistribution implied by such programs. For the purposes of defining socialism in less than one country, I will suppose that a stage has been reached in the reform process at which private, mixed and state-owned firms coexist. Given government control over the capital market, joint ventures between the state and private entrepreneurs will be common.

In an analysis of the efficiency implications of mixed enterprises, Eckel and Vining (1985) come to the intuitively appealing conclusion "that jointly owned firms will tend to be more efficient in production than 100 percent publicly owned firms, but less profitable than those totally in the private sector." However, a recent empirical study refutes this proposition. Boardman and Vining (1989) compare the performance of private corporations, state-owned enterprises and mixed enterprises among the 500 largest non-U.S. industrial firms. Econometric estimates of profitability and efficiency reveal that "mixed enterprises perform no better and often worse than state-owned enterprises" in a competitive environment. Partial privatization may thus not be the best strategy for governments wishing to reduce the number of state-owned enterprises. It is suggested that "some patterns of joint ownership appear to generate conflict between public and private shareholders, leading to a high degree of managerial cognitive dissonance".

Given the legacy of bureaucratic discretion in socialism in less than one country, problems related to managerial behavior may be exacerbated relative to the competitive environment studied by Boardman and Vining. Under these circumstances, society may face an efficiency loss owing to partial privatization in the transition from central planning. On the other hand, to the extent that private firms are created, particularly within the context of a competitive environment, reform brings welfare gains. The private small enterprise service sectors of the Hungarian and Polish economies exemplify such gains.

III. PRODUCT MARKETS

A priori, there is no unavoidable reason why socialism in less than one country should not have a competitive industrial sector. Nonetheless, the system has a certain inner logic which would tend to favor the prevalence of concentrated industry. In the preceding centrally-planned economy, political rather than efficiency considerations will have determined the allocation of resources and preference will have been given to projects which fulfill a perceived need in the economy. This tendency will persist in socialism in less than one country on account of continued, albeit unplanned, government control over enterprise establishment. Once an enterprise has been established, there is, from the viewpoint of the state, little inherent reason why new entrants should be permitted or granted scarce government investment finance. Further, the government's stake in extant enterprises may give rise to protectionist tendencies.

A centrally-planned economy has no need for anti-trust legislation. Under socialism in less than one country, such legislation legitimizes government intervention in the market and permits the attempted alleviation of those welfare losses perceived by government as undesirable. On the other hand, given the above arguments, strong restrictive trade practices legislation will not be introduced. In particular, given the large proportion of monopolies inherited from the centrally-planned economy, any new law will need to allow for their continued existence.

Consider, now, one such monopoly and suppose it to be price-regulated. Notwithstanding the constraints on objectives implied by the property rights structure, I assume initially that the firm attempts to maximize profits. This assumption is relaxed below. Suppose also that the firm faces an average cost regulatory constraint.[2] Then the problem faced by the firm is: max $p(X)X - c(X)$ s.t. $[x(X)/X] - np(X) > 0$, where X is firm output, $p(X)$ is an inverse demand function, $c(X)$ is the firm's cost function and $n \in [0,1]$ is a parameter set by the state.

Under central planning, variable costs are determined essentially by the level of labor employed, there being no charge for capital. Following economic reform, capital charges are introduced but the continued intervention of the state in the capital market suggests that labor costs continue to dominate $c(X)$. Under these circumstances, labor becomes the focus of the regulatory constraint, and the firm is led to choose a higher labor-capital ratio than would be the case without regulation. On the other hand, to the extent that the government continues to provide cheap capital, firms are led to demand inefficiently high levels of capital. The resulting equilibrium capital-output mix cannot be predicted in general, but its coincidence with the efficient mix is unlikely.

While the net direction of factor-bias may be unpredictable, it is clear that the firm has an incentive to inflate its costs. As Daughety (1984) has shown, the optimal level of waste or rent dissipation may be derived from the above problem, the solution to which requires that the firm maximize $(1-n)$ times revenue subject to the regulatory constraint. Figure 1 shows the equilibrium price-output combination (p^*, X^*) for the case of linear demand and $c(X) = (c+w)X$, where w is waste. Revenue, and thus profit, is maximized at output X^*. The unregulated monopolist produces X^u and charges p^u whilst the regulated firm which produces efficiently will be at (p^R, X^R). OX^* is less than the competitive output, OX^C, but greater than

---

[2] In the case of a monopoly, this is equivalent to an operating cost constraint. Daughtey analyses such regulation in the context of a capitalist market economy.

unregulated output, OX^u, hence there are welfare gains from regulation. But this is to take the unregulated monopoly in a capitalist market economy as the point of reference for welfare comparisons.

Our concern is with the welfare implications of a transition from centrally-planned enterprise to regulated monopoly. It is evident that the consequences of the reform depend upon the centrally-planned price-output combination. Suppose the social cost of production before and after the reform to be given by $c(X)=c+w$ and ignore second-best effects. In Figure 2, the efficiency loss owing to a regulated monopoly is the area AFGEB. Under central planning, any price-quantity combination is possible. Thus, there may be excess demand, excess supply or the market may be in equilibrium. The comparison in the latter case is straightforward: welfare is improved after the reform if the centrally-planned quantity is less than OX^*, it is reduced for quantities between OX^* and OX^C, unaffected for quantity OX^*, and the outcome of the comparison is ambiguous for planned output greater than OX^C.

Where central planning leads to excess demand in the product market, there are two possibilities: (1) Planners opt for a price-quantity combination within the area OX^*GH. Thus, there is excess demand, and costly rationing mechanisms such as queuing and black market pricing come into play. Further, the consumer is provided with less of the good than OX^* and hence there are unambiguous gains from reform. (2) The planned price-output combination lies within the area X^*GEX^C. Here also there is excess demand, but the two factors noted under (1) work in opposite directions. Welfare is increased relative to the regulated monopoly by the provision of a quantity between OX^* and OX^C, but rationing costs remain. The welfare effect of the reform is thus ambiguous.

The case of excess supply is somewhat more complicated. One plausible example will suffice to indicate the nature of the problem.

Suppose the planned price-output combination is given by (p^P,X^P). This is point J in Figure 2. Thus, there is excess supply of X^QX^P. This quantity has been produced at cost KLX^PX^Q which may be considered pure waste since future plans take no necessary account of its existence and price cannot fall below p^P.[3] Since consumers receive only OX^Q rather than the efficient quantity, there are additional costs given by the triangle MNE and the area AKNB, the latter owing to inefficient production of OX^Q. On the benefit side, consumers under central planning gain the surplus p^*GMp^P in excess of that available to them in the regulated monopoly case. However, of this, area p^*GFA is a pure transfer unless there is waste owing to

---

[3] I assume that none of this output finds its way via theft onto the black market at a lower price and assume zero storage costs for the surplus.

Figure 1

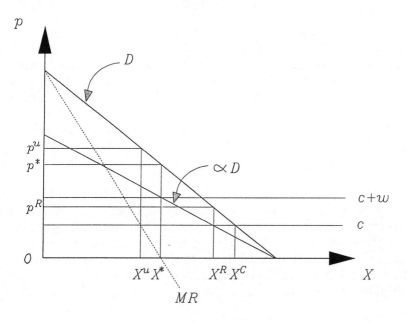

Figure 2

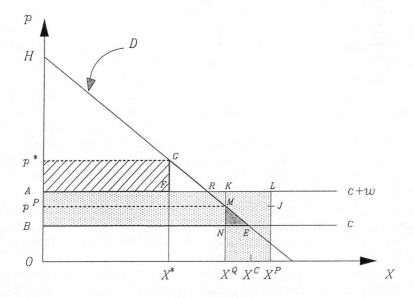

rent-seeking activity following the reform. If this possibility is ignored, a reform leads to an increase in welfare if KLX^PX^Q + MNE + AKNB > AFGEB + AFGMp^P.

The above analysis reveals the ambiguity in measuring the welfare implications of the transition from central planning to socialism in less than one country. This ambiguity arises on account of the arbitrary nature of central planning. Suppose now that the regulated monopoly both faces a soft budget constraint and has a maximand other than profit. Given the imperfection of factor markets and the different ownership structures prevalent under socialism in less than one country, this is a more realistic description. Now, also the price-quantity combination chosen by the regulated monopoly is arbitrary and generalized comparisons become impossible.

Hence a post-reform economy in which regulated monopoly typifies production agents will have inefficient product markets. Further, the outcome of a welfare comparison between the pre- and post-reform situations is ambiguous. If socialism in less than one country represents a transitory stage in the move from central planning to a competitive economy, this may be of little consequence. There may, however, exist a transition trap which calls into question the gain from the original reform.

IV. REFORM OF SOCIALISM

If the goals of the original reform of a centrally-planned economy are to be achieved, the transitory economic system described in the previous sections must itself be the subject of a further market-oriented reform. In principle, this may proceed in one of two ways: either incentives of economic agents are such that reform is the outcome of an endogenous process -- that is, the economic system is unstable -- or, external pressure for further reform from, say, international financial institutions places such reform on the political agenda and the government is able to design an incentive-compatible reform package. I consider these possibilities in turn.

Economic system stability is determined, in the final resort, by the potential gainers and losers from economic reform and their capacity to mobilize political support either for or against such reform. In principle, it is possible to conceive of reform of socialism in less than one country in either of two directions; a centralization of economic decision-making via, for instance, the reintroduction of central planning, or a decentralization of economic decision-making in conjunction with an extension of private property rights within the economy. I begin with a consideration of market-oriented reform.

Neither private enterprise owners nor managers stand to gain from such a reform. In the absence of market competition, rents accrue to the enterprise, and whereas the price of inputs would fall after a reform, the soft budget constraints diminishes the importance of this consideration.

The likelihood of increased levels of unemployment following the move to a capitalist market economy implies that workers who feel their jobs are threatened will not support reform. On the other hand, in their capacity as consumers, workers would be the major beneficiaries of system change. Ideological considerations aside, state functionaries will not favor any reform which removes the soft budget constraint on account of the considerable rents that would be lost thereby. Opposition to reform from the state bureaucracy is also to be expected owing to the considerable loss of power implied by increased reliance on market rather than political allocation.

Thus, the only certain gainers from reform are the consumers. Being the largest groups in society, free riding hinders lobbying for reform. Hence, socialism in one country represents a stable economic system with respect to significant further market-oriented reform.

The peaceful revolution, whereby several communist governments collapsed in Eastern Europe in 1989-90, was a popular quest for greater freedom.[4] The new political parties formed in the wake of a transition to democracy all declared themselves in favor of a decentralizing reform. Further, the extra economic freedom granted enterprise managers and state bureaucrats under socialism in less than one country renders a return to central planning -- at least in its original form -- infeasible. Thus, socialism in less than one country is a stable economic system.

This means that further reform requires some form of exogenous intervention. The difficulties that capitalised rents pose for reform have been noted by Tullock (1980) and impediments to reform of rent-seeking societies have been pointed out by Buchanan (1980), who models the problem as a prisoner's dilemma with asymmetric payoffs. A cooperative agreement to move to the efficient outcome requires side payments to be made to the potential losers from the reform. However, the agreement to such side payments by consumers, in the case of socialism in less than one country, would involve a tacit acknowledgement that those earning rents in the present system are "entitled" to them. Buchanan argues that resistance to such side payments will be intense if the current losers "think that the winners rigged the game from the outset."

It is interesting to note that most reform packages suggested or implemented in the Soviet Union and Eastern Europe have involved purportedly short-run reductions in the welfare of the working population. Popular resistance to these packages may be explained in terms of

---

[4] See Schnytzer (1990).

Buchanan's model. Given the more or less democratic framework within which reform discussions take place, thereby precluding economic reform by force, socialism in less than one country represents a transition trap.

V. CONCLUSIONS

I have proposed an economic system that is a logical consequence of incomplete reform of a socialist centrally-planned economy. Basic elements of the system were present in the country with the longest history of reform, Hungary. The system represents a transitional stage between central planning and a western market economy. There is however no theoretical basis upon which to establish in general whether the system is more or less efficient than a centrally-planned economy. But such an economic system has properties that render it stable.

References

Boardman A.E. and A.R. Vining, 1989. "Ownership and Performance in Competitive Environments: A Comparison of the Performance of Private, Mixed and State-Owned Enterprises", *Journal of Law and Economics*, 32, 1-33.

Bornstein, M., 1985. *Comparative Economic Systems*, 5th Edition, Irwin.

Buchanan, J.M., 1980. "Reform in the Rent-Seeking Society", in J.M. Buchanan, R.D. Tollison and G. Tullock, editors, *Toward a Theory of the Rent-Seeking Society*, College Station.

Daughety, A.F., 1984. "Regulation and Industrial Organization", *Journal of Political Economy*, 92, 932-953.

Eckel, C.C. and A.R. Vining, 1985. "Elements of a Theory of Mixed Enterprise", *Scottish Journal of Political Economy*, 32, 82-94.

Hillman A.L. and A. Schnytzer, 1986. "Illegal Activities and Purges in a Soviet-type Economy", *International Review of Law and Economics*, 6, 87-99.

Schnytzer, A. 1990. "An Economic Model of Regime Change: Freedom as a Collective Good", presented at the meetings of the *European Public Choice Society*, Meersburg.

Tullock, G., 1980. "The Transitional Gains Trap", in J.M. Buchanan, R.D. Tollison and G. Tullock, editors, *Toward a Theory of the Rent Seeking Society*, Texas A. and M. Press.

Chapter 9

RESTORING PROPERTY RIGHTS

Marton Tardos

Property rights designation is a central issue in the economic problems that confront socialist economies in transition. After diverse experiences ranging from China to the Soviet Union, we all understand the inadequacies of central planning which was established through the abolition of private property, and we are aware of the functional deficiencies of an economy which is hierarchically organized and is subordinated to mandatory plans. Under socialism, neither the workers in the nationalized firms nor the members of the cooperatives and collective farms had property rights that permitted them to become real owners of the enterprises. They rather remained wage laborers and were obliged to work for or within the collective institutions, the socialist enterprises and the cooperatives that were assigned property rights. The incomes that were thereby earned minimally sustained the workers and their families.

We also are obliged to acknowledge that the transition from planned to market socialism as in the reform models of Yugoslavia which has experimented the most, and in Hungary, have not been successful. These "market socialist" systems purported to combine the preexisting power structure and macroeconomic regulation with the market, but could not substantially modify the inefficiencies that were the consequence of central planning. The systems which sought to combine markets with the socialist ownership structure did not succeed in providing the necessary prerequisites for efficient resource allocation and economic growth.

The shortcomings of the market-socialist reforms were due to the ambiguous intentions of the authorities, who did not fully commit themselves to economic change. The maintained one-party political system did not permit the realization of the essential prerequisite for a market economy -- the separation of the responsibilities of the factors of production, labor and capital. From hindsight, it is evident that it was the absence of private ownership that underlay the economic stagnation experienced under market socialism. An end to stagnation would require that enterprises be assigned owners who do not have an incentive to dissipate the enterprise's capital.

I. PAST OWNERSHIP AND INCENTIVES

The problem of ownership and incentives is difficult to solve under a market-socialist system. First, the objective of increasing the value of capital as the self-contained and pivotal task of the enterprise is contrary to socialist principles. Second, the assignment of nationalized capital to owners who are detached from the state and seek efficiency objectives substantially diminishes the power of the centralized Party and State.

The first of these two difficulties is ideological in kind. Political decision-makers who are indifferent to ideology would ignore the counter-arguments. And if one also considers the economic costs and the constraints on development that are due to the absence of independent ownership interests, then one could certainly conclude that economic stagnation is an unacceptable price of adherence to socialist ideology.

Past reforms in Hungary have included the substantial concession to socialist ideology of transferring state enterprises into the hands of self-management boards composed of enterprise councils and assemblies. The creation in 1984-1985 of council or assembly managed enterprise forms in Hungary was a necessary response to the impasses that derived from the prior practices of macroeconomic and enterprise management. The political leadership in all likelihood chose self-management rather than other advocated property forms, because it believed that the employees of the enterprises would support this solution to the property-rights problem. Also, the new self-management enterprise forms did not infringe upon the political monopoly of the single Party.

Were owners to have been designated who were assigned discretion independent of the state, the situation would have been different. The central authorities would then have had reason to fear the introduction of enterprise self-management that effectively transferred the state's property to the enterprise councils. Only an acute social crisis and social consensus of the highest degree could have warranted such a radical change before the elimination of political monopoly of the Party.

The attitude of society toward denationalization is also problematical. It is improper to ask questions such as: who used to applaud nationalization and the collectivization "in those days"? How many supported these policies? Or how many people are now satisfied with the existing economic order? Rather, the objective is to seek solutions that impress upon the greater part of society the benefits of the elimination of the economic hardships that have been the consequence of the ownership structure. One would suppose that the majority of society sympathizes with the idea of denationalization, or at least, does not object. An important exception is, however, enterprise managers who claim that they themselves, in addition to their management function, are well able to function as owners of the enterprises. Their claim is that the sole reason for their inadequate past economic performance has been the relentless central intervention. Afterwards, as the story goes, managers were hampered by the enterprise councils and assemblies that were imposed upon them.

Such claims by enterprise managers cannot be substantiated. The sole maintainable part of the claim is that an economy in order to grow requires independent and vigorous managers. The touchstone of good management is the efficiency that is associated with profit maximization. The freedom of managers can be defined only in terms of the freedom to maximize profits. If the capital administered by the manager yields an adequate rate of return, managerial performance is adequate. However, management must be professionally monitored, and this the self-managing enterprise councils and the state administrators cannot themselves do. Ultimate owners or residual claimants on the other hand have the incentive to maximize the present value of the enterprise.

I shall propose that the problem of Eastern European property reforms requires a pragmatic answer that combines solutions that are imperfect because of politico-social constraints. To substantiate this position, I shall draw attention to difficulties associated with large scale property-rights reform, and then review the positive and negative attributes of the various approaches to property-rights assignment in socialist economies in transition.

II. DIFFICULTIES IN TRANSITION

Attention can be drawn to three aspects of the transition from socialism. First, some countries having completed so-called socialist nationalization began to institute markets. Here the Marxian thesis about socialist revolutions, which holds that this all-embracing social change differs substantially from all others, is verified in a peculiar way. According to Marx, all earlier changes in social formations were built upon the foundations present in a new system that had evolved from the old, whereas the "socialist relations of production" were not developed in capitalism. This implies that the almost exterminated institutions of the market must be recreated from first principles, if the achievements of the socialist transformation, which are nationalization through the liquidation of the market and collectivization, have been unsatisfactory.

Yet, as the Eastern European reform experiences demonstrate, markets cannot function adequately without private capital and capitalist institutions. Private capital cannot however instantaneously become the dominant influence in an economy and society that has undergone large-scale nationalization. There is no precedent for rapid transition from socialism to private ownership on the scale that is required. In those Western industrial countries where privatization followed nationalization, the experience is instructive with respect to the means and techniques employed. But privatization was there the solution to a different problem. For even in the heyday of nationalization, private capital remained dominant, and subsequent privatization meant changes in degree, not in kind.

A second issue is evaluation of the performance potential of a capitalist market economy. The centrally planned economy has revealed itself to be neither capable of satisfying human needs nor efficient in utilizing resources; but this does not imply that the theoretical model of the indisputably more efficient capitalist market economy provides an unambiguously preferable solution to all economic problems. Nor does the efficiency of the capitalist market economy justify various unfavorable aspects of capitalist development, such as impoverished lower strata of society. The capitalist market emphasizes efficiency rather than social justice. Potential inequities that are moderated in contemporary developed market economies are prevalent in many developing countries. These less desirable features of capitalist development provide a basis for a motive in principle to combine markets with social justice.

How the transition from market socialism to a more efficient economic system should take place has not been rigorously specified. The transitional structure could be described by the following maxim. During the process of formation of the new market-oriented East-Central European society, there will be conflicts of private interest; during this phase, the deficiencies of the capitalist market economies must be also kept in sight, with an awareness that solutions to the problems associated with these deficiencies will need to be deferred, as part of the cost of transition from market socialism to a superior economic system.

Although it is in the national interest to institute market-oriented reform, individual citizens will maintain different attitudes toward change. Individuals may be unable to judge their particular benefits and sacrifices, but also individual benefits and costs associated with change will vary. The transformation of the economic system and property-rights reform must therefore be organized in a way which evokes minimal resistance on the part of the people. This is intrinsically difficult, because property-rights reform -- although motivated by efficiency considerations -- has fundamental effects on income distribution. What is "fair and just" is more difficult to determine than what is "efficient".

III. SELF-MANAGEMENT

One of the paths of transition, and the simplest from the point of view of socialist ideology, is the full-fledged implementation of the prior self-management of enterprises instituted under market socialism (Soos, 1989). This means of privatization is administratively easy to institute. Also, this solution is not a large deviation from socialism, since property rights are assigned to the working collective. The limited Yugoslav (1948, 1965), then later Polish (1982) and Hungarian (1967) variants of this solution have, however, not proven successful. The reason for the failure lies in the limitations on the property-rights entitlement of the enterprise collective. The collective is given the right to manage and to use the enterprise's assets, even formally. This discretion, which was extended in the case of plants to decision-making regarding production schedules and product development, was frequently manipulated by managers and regional authorities. Statutes and decrees limited opportunities to take advantage of benefits that would derive from maximizing the value of the enterprise's assets. Nor did the workers in any meaningful sense become owners of the enterprises.

No practical program has been proposed whereby self-management would entail a complete grant of all rights concerning enterprise capital to managers. It may not be incidental that this solution has been proposed and experimented with only in the theoretical models of Ward (1958), Vanek (1970), and others concerned with the behavior of the labor-managed firm.

All workers could be assigned equal shares of their enterprise's capital, or perhaps shares proportional to a measure of work achievement. Workers could then freely dispose of their assets. Is it however acceptable that the workers of an enterprise be instantaneously assigned ownership in the introduction of property-rights reform? Such property-rights assignment is socially unjust, because of the randomness of employment locations. The infrastructural sector is not suitable for profit-oriented management of capital, and hence there are restrictions on the rights of workers to claim ownership in the public sector or non-market sectors. The assignment of capital to workers who happen to be in the market sectors would thus be arbitrary and unjust. Workers in relatively capital-intensive enterprises would reap large gains, relative to workers employed in labor-intensive enterprises. Complexities also arise regarding allocation of property to new employees after shares in an enterprise have been assigned to current workers.

Thus this model of transition from socialism to private property has limitations.

The above form of property rights reassignment is also inappropriate for cooperatives. In some countries, cooperatives are able to compete successfully with private enterprises. However, this does not support an argument that an economy-wide system based upon such collectivism would also be successful. In a mixed market economy, the achievements of cooperatives reflect their ability to adapt to the conditions of market competition. However, we have no evidence that an economy composed of cooperatives based on limited property rights is capable of generating the competitive conditions necessary for efficiency.

IV. PERSONAL SOCIAL PROPERTY

In Hungary, some economists have favored the superliberal and, at the same time, supersocialist conception of Tibor Liska (1988), which is called personal social property. This doctrine attempts to revitalize the controlling and regulating role of property rights in a way which would neutralize the limiting exclusive characteristics of private property for those who are deprived of the possession of it. The principle is: "Those who guarantee the most benefits, can manage social property".

This conception combines competitive bidding with utopian ideas. The "Plan and Market Cashier", who is indifferent to economic institutions and is guided only by social interest, is central to the logic of the system. He disposes of social property and hands it over to that person or group that is prepared to pay the most. Those that are prepared to pay the most will use the property most efficiently. After an auction, there is nothing to prevent others from entering new bids to secure the property from the present owners. Takeovers can therefore occur.

The model provides a counter to property-based monopoly, and thus is more liberal than a market based on capitalist private property. This does not mean, however, that the scheme is feasible. The benevolent operation of an organization (the Plan and Market Cashier) with great decision-making power and which is indifferent to institutions contradicts any prior social experience. It is unlikely that the scheme would be able to allocate social property appropriately via bidding mechanisms, because of financing constraints. Nor is it likely that the bidding technique would enable the Cashier to reallocate the rights and duties of previously successful bidders without constraining the working of the system. In a non-competitive market, the scheme assigns monopoly power, although with competitive bidding the monopoly rents are appropriated.

There is also a limitation of the system which derives from the aspirations to interpret it as a social ideal. Society cannot consist of entrepreneurs only. There will be those who do not wish to be entrepreneurs, and who will seek security in riskless income.

All this is not really a counter-argument against the Personal Social Property conception. The conception is however utopian. The founding of a society that is more just and at the same time more efficient than any previous society is improbable.

V. DISTRIBUTION OF STATE CAPITAL TO CITIZENS

At the first sight, the most ethical solution to the problem of conversion of nationalized state capital to private ownership is distribution among the citizens (Bertalan Diczhaki, 1988). This would be possible, of course, only after the assessment of the value of the property concerned and its transformation into equal stock-holdings.

Yet, as soon as we seek to translate this conception into practice, we meet difficulties.

The value of the property (the discounted present value of the profit yielded by it) is unknown and estimates can be very inaccurate. Injustice could therefore arise. Citizen A might receive a share worth one unit of capital from the assets of enterprise X, and citizen B would obtain the same from the assets of enterprise Y. Even after purchase and sale of the shares, *ex-post* one individual could gain considerably more wealth than another.

Inequality could be avoided *ex-ante* by assigning all citizens shares in a national mutual fund encompassing all assets. But, then, more difficult to resolve is the question, who should be treated as a citizen? Those who are currently alive? Those with many descendants alive, and so with large expected bequests, would be advantaged, while families who are soon going to multiply would lose.

The difficulty with these various means of privatization is the quest for social consensus. Similar difficulties are associated with the assignment of property rights to workers.

A wave of envy resulting from inequities associated with administrative reprivatization could be socially destabilizing. The long-run benefits of the transition from socialism to private property might therefore be compromised.

VI. GRADUAL REPRIVATIZATION

The most radical proponents of the market would eliminate the state from ownership, and would reallocate all nationalized assets to the private sector. If foreign investors were not prepared to buy shares, and if domestic private accumulation and purchasing propensity were insufficient to facilitate a rapid transformation of ownership, these proponents accept that substantial time may be required to complete the process of privatization, perhaps 15 to 20 years. Smaller firms and commercial and service units could be more readily privatized, since in these cases one can more readily ensure that the value of the capital invested (and thus ventured) by the new owner reflects the value of the enterprise. Those state enterprises which are not capable of rapid privatization would be transformed by the state to business corporations, gradually or in one step, and be sold thereafter, according to demand. There are different conceptions of this process, all of which include artificial measures:

A. The state signs over its property rights in an enterprise to new owners, when the latter have bought more than 20% of the capital of the company, and the state further specifies how the remaining part of the capital may be sold (Kovalez, 1989).

B. The state participates in the management of the gradually privatized enterprise as a co-partner, and creates business institutions to support this activity (Kotz, 1986).

C. The state offers special shares to ultimate owners, who pay off the value of the assets from the dividends of the shares they bought on trust. They become unlimited owners after the full amortization of the debt. This solution might be accompanied by active or passive participation of state business representatives (Asztalos, 1988).

The proponents of these various recommendations have the objective of accelerating private capital accumulation and investment. The principal advantage of these types of solutions is the direct transformation of state capital into private assets, with attendant private risk bearing. Ultimately these methods of privatization must necessarily be used. They are gradual, however, and hence the issue of the combination of these methods with other supplementary ones arises.

VII. DEPOSIT OF STATE CAPITAL INTO INVESTMENT TRUSTS

Management of state business capital could remain the task of the government or specific state investment funds could be set up (Matolcsy, 1988). The latter could be directed for example by a board of trustees elected by Parliament. Finding ultimate owners (private entrepreneurs or foundation owners) for state property would be a duty of the state administration. The investment fund would be responsible for profit-oriented management of state business capital, transitionally and also in the long-run.

In the fields of primary production and more competitive activities, investment trusts can be responsible for state capital. These trusts would manage the state-owned part of the enterprise and corporate capital in the non-infrastructural sectors. Every legal state and private enterprise would prepare for the function of an investment trust, not only institutions organized for this purpose. All these would take over shares or packages of shares from the investment fund and other legal corporations by auction.

The main advantage of this type of solution is speed and simplicity. Weaknesses are that the political manipulation of the investment fund and of the state investment trusts cannot be ruled out, which threatens the system with management contradictory to attitudes of private owners. Therefore, this type of solution can only be considered transitional.

VIII. TRANSFER OF STATE CAPITAL TO FOUNDATIONS, INSURANCE COMPANIES AND PENSION FUNDS

In the Western capitalist countries, substantial holdings of capital are owned by foundations, associations, villages, cities, and self-managed social-security organizations. These institutions exist in Hungary as well. Their activities are not well managed and they lack capital. The institutions suffered because of socialist nationalization. After appropriate decentralization, state business capital could be transferred to them. This would provide a foundation for their independent activities and facilitate trade in assets in the whole economy.

However, this scheme, on which I have elaborated (Tardos, 1988), also has inadequacies. The institutions tend to be risk-averse and hence are limited in the risk that they are prepared to bear. In liberal market economies, similar institutions are regulated in the scope of investment possibilities. Nevertheless, two-thirds of the shares listed on the New York Stock Exchange are institutionally owned.

IX. CONCLUSIONS

Each of the schemes considered in this paper for reassignment of property rights in the transition from socialism evokes some or other objection. The difficulty is that the transition from socialism while sought for efficiency purposes has profound effects on the domestic distribution of income. Consensus can be established on criteria for efficiency and the need for private property rights to facilitate the efficient functioning of markets, but consensus with regard to income distribution is inherently more difficult.

References

Asztalos, L. Gy., 1988. Pislogó sárga fény az alagútban (Blinking yellow light in the tunnel), *Biztosító Kutató Csoport*.

Bertalan Diczhazi A., 1988. Népi szocializmus vázlata (A sketch of peoples socialism), *Figyelő*.

Kotz, L., 1986. Változatok a részvényre (Variations on stocks), *Tervgazdasági Fórum*.

Kovalez, S., 1989. Draft program for privatization of the Polish Economy, *Central School of Planning*.

Liska, T., 1988. Ökonosztát, Közgazdasági és Jogi, *Könyvkiadó*.

Matolcsy, Gy., 1988. Vazlatok a tulajdonreformra (Sketches for a reform of ownership), *Gazdaság*.

Soós, K.A., 1989. Privatizálás dogmáktól mentes önigazgatás, tulajdonreform, (Privatization, self management free from dogmas, and reform of ownership), *Közgazdasági Szemle*, 7-8.

Tardos, M., 1988. Gazdasági szervezetek és tulajdon. (Economic organizations and ownership), *Gazdaság*.

Vanek, Y., 1970. *The General Theory of Labor Managed Economies*, Ithica, NY, Cornell University Press.

Ward, B., 1958. The firm in Illiria: Market Syndicalism, *American Economic Review*, 48, 566-89.

Chapter 10

LIBERALIZATION DILEMMAS

Arye L. Hillman[1]

In Western market economies gainers and losers from international trade policies are identified by claims to the returns from private factor ownership. The identification of gainers and losers permits the formulation of a theory of endogenous policy determination that explains why protectionist policies are chosen in the face of the Pareto-efficiency of free trade.[2] The theory indicates how asymmetric distributions of the claims to an economy's factor endowments underlie departures from free trade: should factor claims be symmetric, so that all individuals have claims in the same proportion as the economy's aggregate factor endowments, individuals' utilities and aggregate national income are maximized by free trade. Protectionist policies in a capitalist economy thus reflect different policy interests that derive from diverse private factor claims.[3]

Socialism subsumes or moderates these different interests, insofar as

[1] I thank my colleague Adi Schnytzer for many and long discussions on the topic of this paper. Previous versions of the paper were presented at the (then) Karl Marx University of the Economic Sciences, Budapest, the Bar-Ilan Conference on Markets and Politicians, the Research Department Seminar of the Bank of Israel, and at the Hebrew University of Jerusalem. I thank participants for helpful comments.
[2] In the presence of intersectorally immobile factors, owners of capital specific to import-competing industries benefit from protectionist trade policies, while owners of capital specific to export industries lose. If all factors are intersectorally mobile, the Stolper-Samuelson Theorem sets the interests of the owners of capital against wage earners. For a review of the literature on the political economy of protection, set in a market-capitalist economy, see my 1989 survey.
[3] On the relation between individual and aggregate factor endowments and the determination of international trade policy, see Mayer (1984).

physical (if not human) capital is collectively rather than privately owned. Diversity in the returns to human capital is also moderated by egalitarian income-distribution principles that are associated with socialism. Neo-classical international theory therefore suggests that an economy with substantial socialist industry should, ceteris paribus, be more open than a private-property-rights capitalist counterpart.

The *planned* socialist economy has however motives for not permitting free trade, since unregulated market-determined trade would disrupt domestic production plans. The international trade of the planned socialist economies was accordingly coordinated within CMEA (the Council for Mutual Economic Assistance). Planned international trade does not imply an absence of trade.[4] However, in contrast with Western market economies, enterprises in the centrally planned economy do not confront unregulated import competition.

There is a substantial literature on the international trade of the planned socialist economy.[5] The broad purpose of this paper is to consider the influences underlying the determination of international trade policy in an economic system that combines markets with socialist industry. The particular focus is however on past protectionist policies and liberalization attempts in Israel, wherein markets have coexisted with a significant sector composed of the workers' enterprises.

The explanation that I shall proposed for the past combination of protectionist policies and liberalization intentions is a social contract that facilitated a market-based development process while maintaining consistency with the principle of protection of workers' job security. The contract designates reciprocal responsibilities to the enterprise and the state: the enterprise assures the employment security of workers, and is assigned "responsibility to supply" in the domestic market; the state for its part ensures that the enterprise's supply responsibilities are not compromised by socially less conscious competitors who might, as the consequence of lower social awareness of the needs of maintained job security, have lower costs. The social contract assures full employment in the presence of markets.

In Israel the social contract transcended ownership characteristics of industry. The contract was adhered to not only by the workers-collective enterprises, but also by private enterprise, which was assigned the "responsibility to supply" particular goods, and in return exhibited the

---

[4] Ideology has however influenced the planned economies' international trade policies. Stalinist systems in particular have an autarkic bias: see Schnytzer (1982).
[5] See Wiles (1968), Holzman (1974), and the survey by Wolf (1988).

requisite social awareness regarding workers' job security.[6]

I. COMPARATIVE OBSERVATIONS

The preeminence assigned to workers' job security in the conduct of economic policy has not been unique to Israel. Comparisons with regard to the objective of job security could be made with a number of countries. In this paper, I shall make some comparative references to Hungary, which in 1968 formally abandoned central planning in favor of decentralized markets but maintained a socialist ownership structure for industry. Under the system of Hungarian "market socialism", a social contract similar to that which is attributable to Israel can be interpreted to have served in place of the direct assurance of workers' job security that had previously been provided by the plan under Hungarian planned socialism.

It is the common attribute of the social contract directed at ensuring workers' job security in a market economy and the Hungarian response when the planner was eliminated that provide the basis for any comparative observations that follow. *It is inappropriate to generalize to infer necessary correspondences beyond this.* Comparisons between the means whereby similar social contracts have applied in Israel and under Hungarian "market socialism" require due recognition of the profound institutional distinctions and differences in geopolitical characteristics and circumstances. Hungary was in particular a member of the CMEA (or Soviet block)[7], Israel a pro-western democracy. Also, whereas the state in Hungary exercised the formal collective claim to the capital of industrial enterprises, in Israel there was not state socialism; although there are state enterprises, workers' collective ownership of industry has been under the independent auspices of The General Organization of Workers (the Histadrut) which predated the reestablishment of Israel as an independent state.[8] As well, in Hungary socialism was an all-embracing imposed economic system of the Marxist-Leninist type, whereas in Israel *voluntary* collectivism left significant scope for private enterprise. In development performance, Israel achieved

---

[6] For further elaboration on how privately owned enterprises cooperated in the pursuit of social and development objectives, see my 1988 paper.

[7] On geopolitical aspects of economic organization in Hungary, see Kornai (1988).

[8] The Histadrut was founded in 1920, the modern state of Israel achieved independence in 1948. In 1988 the Histadrut in Israel accounted for some 25 percent of GNP, state enterprises for some 20 percent, and the private sector for the remaining 55 percent. In Hungary there have been wide ranges in the informal estimates (5 to 20 percent) of the shares during different times in the 1980s of second-sector and informal (non-reported) private enterprise in national income.

higher growth rates and higher income levels.[9]

I do not wish to downplay these very significant differences. My emphasis here however is on the commonality of workers-collective or socialist industry in a market setting. Enterprise managers in Histadrut enterprises in Israel have not been subject to central planning directives, just as under Hungarian "market socialism", there was formally no central planner to direct enterprise managers. In both economies, socialist or workers-collective industry was prominent (virtually all-encompassing in Hungary), and paternalism was manifested in assured job security in a market economy without the guiding hand of a central planner. I turn now to the questions regarding liberalization that arise in such circumstances.

II. THE QUESTIONS

As I have observed, because of absence or moderation of policy conflicts based on diversity of individuals' claims to capital ownership, neo-classical international trade theory would predict socialism to be conducive to liberal international trade policies. Yet in Israel, and also under Hungarian market-socialism, when markets have been combined with workers-collective or socialist industry, revealed trade policies have been highly protectionist. The questions which are raised and which subsequent sections of this paper address are: Why did the significant presence of workers-collective or socialist industry not introduce the predicted neo-classical tendency towards Pareto-efficient free-trade policies that would maximize aggregate income? In the light of the highly protectionist outcomes, did the presence of socialist industry in a market setting enhance protectionist tendencies? And if so, what amendments are required to the neo-classical model of international trade to provide a theory of endogenous policy determination that encompasses the failure of collective claims to capital when markets are combined with socialist industry to yield the predicted bias towards liberal trade policies?

III. SOCIALISM AND COMPETITION

It is instructive in seeking answers to these questions to begin with some empirical regularities concerning industry concentration in socialist economies. Empirical evidence associates planned socialist economies with

---

[9] World Bank statistics which use exchange rates for conversion to US dollars show 1986 per capita incomes of $6210 and $2020 respectively for Israel and Hungary. However, a comparison that uses purchasing power parity prices (Summers and Heston, 1988) to compute per capita incomes reveals a considerably smaller difference: for Israel 1985 per capita GNP (at 1980 prices) was $6280, for Hungary 1980 per capita GDP (at 1980 prices) was $5765.

high concentration of industry. In a comprehensive study, Eva Ehrlich (1985) compared the concentration of labor employment in the period from 1900 to 1970 in small capitalist, large capitalist, and socialist economies. She concluded that although the European socialist economies were small with respect to area, population, and national markets, their establishment sizes were somewhat, and enterprise sizes many times, larger than those of the large capitalist countries'. Ehrlich hypothesized that enterprise size would vary positively with domestic market size. This was confirmed by the data for capitalist economies: the large capitalist economies were characterized by larger enterprise size. However, enterprise size was larger yet in the small planned socialist economies than in the large market capitalist economies. On average, the size of enterprises in the small socialist economies was three to four times larger than in capitalist economies.

The results reported by Ehrlich may have been due to either the attribute of planning or that of socialism of the planned socialist economy - - or perhaps some interactive components. There are in particular however a number of characteristics of centrally planned systems that underlie high industry concentration: (i) Stalinist development strategy emphasized heavy industry, with scale economies. Also, in the earlier stages of Stalinist systems, scarcity of managerial inputs limited the number of independent enterprises.[10] (ii) In a centrally planned system, a small number of enterprises enhances informational efficiency via a smaller communications network for implementing planning directives. (iii) Expansion of output in a planned socialist system characteristically entails an increase in the target output set for an incumbent enterprise; there is no counterpart in the course of planned socialist development to entry by fringe competitors who might over time expand to challenge a dominant incumbent. (iv) Since markets have no allocative role, market power is of no consequence for the planned economy.

Now consider the experience of Hungary as background for the question: Will concentration of industry fall in an economy that makes the transition from planned to market socialism? In Hungary the elimination of central planning and formal delegation of decision making to enterprise managers did not result over time in a reduction in the high level of industry concentration associated with planning. Although various policies were introduced with the intention of reducing concentration and increasing competition, the large socialist enterprises retained dominance in their respective industries. A second sector that arose in the 1980s based on free

---

[10] Scarcity derived in part from political criteria for appointment of management. The quality of managerial competence was thereby also compromised.

enterprise introduced many thousands of small new enterprises into the economic system. However, the new enterprises were legally constrained in size and scope of activities and, despite the large numbers of new firms and free entry and exit, were not a source of competition for the large state enterprises.[11] Overall, although some limited instances of decomposition occurred, the large enterprises maintained their number and dominant industry status during the 1980s. During the same period there was consistent full employment of labor.

Sustained full employment and concentrated industry structure in a market system with socialist industry characterized the economy of Israel. In Israel the economy was never centrally planned. Socialism (not of the Marxist variant, but of a voluntary character) was however the dominant organizational principle underlying the preindependence economic system and the economic structure of the post-1948 modern state.[12] The socialist organizational structure was conspicuously (and popularly) expressed in agriculture in the kibbutz. However, the socialist or Histadrut sector of the economy was also dominant in industry, and in service sectors. A significant part of the economy has as a consequence been composed of a market-socialist subsector.[13]

The association observed by Ehrlich to exist between industry concentration and socialist industry has been reflected in the structure of the Histadrut subsector.[14] High concentration has however also been a characteristic of industries where private enterprise is dominant.[15] Where a number of enterprises were present, formal or informal cooperative agreements could encompass enterprises independently of ownership. The Restrictive Trade Practices Act did not specify monopolization of a market to be illegal or socially undesirable, and some provisions of the Act can be viewed to have facilitated rather than hindered cooperation among enterprises.[16] High concentration was thus not exclusively associated with industries where the workers' collective enterprises were dominant; and the collectivist

---

[11] The second sector did provide opportunities for workers in socialist industry to supplement their incomes. On the second sector, see Bauer (1988), Tardos (1983), Gabor and Horvath (1987).

[12] See Shapiro (1976). There was a pragmatic basis for collectivism. Low reservation wages could be avoided, and local defense facilitated.

[13] This has led Adi Schnytzer (1989) to describe the economic system as "socialism in less than one country".

[14] See my 1988 paper.

[15] For a study of concentration of industry in Israel, see Bregman (1986). In my 1988 paper dominant firms are distinguished according to Histadrut affiliation and private ownership.

[16] See my 1988 paper.

subsector itself had no precedent of past planning to provide foundations for its highly concentrated industrial structure.

IV. THE SOCIAL CONTRACT

I turn now to the explanation for the concentrated industrial structure that persisted after the cessation of central planning in the market-socialist system of Hungary, and which in the absence of central planning has characterized both the Histadrut and private sectors of the economy of Israel. Two explanations that I wish to discount are prominence of natural monopoly,[17] and an intrinsic interest of the state in the creation and maintenance of monopolies and cartels. High concentration and non-competitive markets were a consequence of the economic system, not an objective of policy. The model of policy determination that I propose is based on the response to the problem of maintaining workers' employment security in the absence of central planning.

Socialism assigns preeminence to domestic employment stability. In distinction, market capitalism is consistent with significant numbers of workers remaining unemployed for extended periods of time. "Socialist" industry or "socialist" markets would differ little from capitalist industry and markets, if workers were subject to the instability of a business cycle, and were assigned in part to a pool of unemployed workers who bear the cost of fluctuations in economic activity. Under planned socialism, the planner avoids such instability by directly assigning labor to employment. The placement of socialist industry in a market setting introduces decentralized decision making and potential market fluctuations in demand for labor. The market-socialist social contract between the enterprise and the state provides for job security, notwithstanding the market.

In Hungary "responsibility to supply" under market socialism replaced the legal obligation of the enterprise to supply under planned socialism. The large state enterprises and cooperatives maintained their designated supply and employment responsibilities after the elimination of central planning in 1968. The responsibilities of incumbent enterprises precluded the need for alternative sources of supply; and in the event that the designated enterprises found themselves confronting difficulties in meeting employment and supply responsibilities, the state provided supplementary assistance to ensure that employment responsibilities could be satisfied.[18]

---

[17] This is not to deny that the small domestic market of Israel does not give rise to instances of natural monopoly.

[18] Marton Tardos (1983) provides evidence on how the large socialist enterprises in Hungary fared subsequent to the introduction of the New Economic Policy in 1968: he reports that after a short vacillation large enterprises further strengthened their positions; with the same implication, Janos Kornai (1983) presents data

In Israel, the economy was subject to various international economic boycotts (or refusal to supply). As a consequence, the fostering of special relationships abroad was often necessary to ensure supply of raw materials and intermediate goods. Foreign private investment was often inhibited by the precariousness with which continued viability of Jewish settlement in the land of Israel was perceived by outside investors. In a spirit of cooperative endeavor, enterprises in the socialist sector, or private enterprise where willing (and not duplicative of established facilities), were assigned responsibilities for the provision of different needs. Associated with supply responsibilities were employment responsibilities, often in designated locations to achieve population dispersion objectives. Development was achieved not by the directives of a planner, but by cooperation and voluntariness in the framework of a decentralized market economy with assigned responsibilities.

When the limits to extensive development were achieved and intensive development would have proceeded by competitive entry, the conjunction of the enterprise's "responsibility to supply" and the state's "responsibility to protect" the enterprise from less socially conscious competitors established the enterprise's right to supply.

V. INTERNATIONAL TRADE

The "right to supply" provides the link to international trade policy.

The case for free trade as optimal for a small market economy is independent of the identification of the claimants to the returns from capital. The potential gains from free trade are moreover greater in a non-competitive economy, because of the competitive discipline of import competition.

Under market socialism, trade liberalization is however inconsistent with the contract between enterprise and state. The contract precludes market-determined competitive imports. The criterion regarding the permissibility of imports will be whether there is a "need" for imports of a particular good, as reflected in the ability of the domestic enterprise with "responsibility to supply" to provide a close substitute for the proposed imported good.[19]

The social contract will also be reflected in policies towards foreign investment. The contract accommodates foreign investment that does not

---

showing that taxes and subsidies were used to compensate the enterprises for changes in profits due the 1980 price revision. Government subsidies persisted throughout the 1980s in Hungary, to facilitate the enterprises meeting their supply and employment responsibilities.

[19] On application of this criterion in Israel, see my 1988 paper.

contradict established supply responsibilities. There is thus a predisposition towards joint ventures with domestic controlling interests.

Again Hungarian market-socialism is illustrative. International trade within the CMEA was planned in advance via bilateral negotiations conducted at the national level. Hungary as a market socialist economy continued to participate in planned CMEA exchange. Since CMEA trading partners precommitted to receive Hungarian goods as part of their national plans, CMEA exports provided Hungarian industry with assured markets that ensured employment stability. Demand for the output of the socialist (but decentralized) enterprises was thereby guaranteed. CMEA imports were likewise anticipated and planned in advance, and therefore did not compromise domestic responsibility to supply.[20] The market-socialist social contract was also reflected in the manner of conduct of international trade with the West. The contract requires that market (as opposed to planned) imports be regulated, to forestall competitive imports that are inconsistent with designated domestic supply responsibilities. Consistently, Western imports were directly controlled by various means.[21]

There is of course no shortage of examples of countries that have pursued highly protectionist international trade policies. However, although protectionist policies have been widely prevalent under different economic systems, it is the paternalistic motive reflected in commitment to workers' job security via the assignment of responsibility to supply that is the key element in the formulation of protectionist policies in market-socialist systems. The parallels to protectionist motives in Israel are not to be sought in the import substitution policies that have been prevalent in the developing (or less-developed) economies, nor in the domestic income-distribution motives in the Western market economies, but in the international trade policies associated with "socialist markets". As in CMEA trade, imports in Israel have as a general rule been non-competitive with domestic output, and have been directly regulated by exchange controls and import licensing, and import licenses have in general been denied if imports would compromise a domestic enterprise's responsibility to supply. On the other hand, licenses have been granted if requested by the domestic enterprise which itself has the responsibility to supply. Imported consumer

---

[20] For elaboration on the CMEA trading relationship, see Hillman and Schnytzer (1990).

[21] These means included foreign exchange controls, import licensing, import duties, and a global quota on hard currency allocation for consumer goods' imports. The high absolute cost (in many instances higher quality) of foreign goods also inhibited substitution of Western imports for domestically produced output. See Gacs (1986, 1989), Oblath (1989).

goods have been available, but where consumers have wished to purchase a foreign good that has a close domestic substitute, the payment of a substantial premium has been required. "Responsibility to supply" has encompassed imports, via the designation of "exclusive authorized importers". In accord with the principle of designated "responsibility to supply", the exclusive importers have in various instances themselves been domestic import-competing producers.[22]

There has also been a revealed preference that direct foreign investment take the form of joint ventures. The holding company of the workers' enterprises exhibited a preference to secure controlling interests or outright ownership in enterprises that had been established as the consequence of foreign investment. The appropriate social consciousness of the enterprise could thereby be assured. At the time, enterprises that were profitable under private foreign ownership or as joint ventures became losing ventures as workers-collective enterprises.

VI. RENTS AND SELF-INTEREST

I have thus far sought to explain protectionist motives when markets coexist with socialist industry with reference to a social objective, achieved by a social contract that ensures worker's job security in the presence of markets that are potential sources of employment and income instability. "Market socialism" is however not devoid of self-interest.

The theory of endogenous protection as set in market-capitalist economies bases explanations for departures from free trade on economic rents associated with private factor ownership. The predictions of the theory regarding protectionist self-interest are readily applicable to a private enterprise that has been designated "responsibility to supply": the private residual claimants are the beneficiaries of rents that derive from the state's "responsibility to protect". There is an evident common interest between the enterprises' workers and private residual claimants in ensuring persistence of the social contract.

The prediction that the presence of socialist industry in a market economy moderates protectionist demands rests on the presumption that legal claims to factor ownership determine the assignment of rents. Where responsibility to supply is assigned to a collective workers' enterprise, there are in principle no private residual claimants to the enterprise's profits.[23] Yet because of monitoring (or principal-agent) problems, rents need not

---

[22] For elaboration see my 1988 paper.

[23] Bonuses may be paid to enterprise managers and workers. However, such bonuses are not specific to market socialism, and as well characterize planned socialist and market-capitalist systems.

accrue to legal residual claimants. Or there may simply be ambiguities in defining de jure ownership. In seeking to establish the basis for protectionist interests in a market socialist system, we are therefore obliged to identify de facto rather than de jure residual claimants.

Peter Wiles has suggested that market socialism is a system of "private profit and public ownership".[24] The inference is that the principal-agent problem is particularly severe under market socialism. In a planned socialist system, enterprise managers are accountable to planners, and can be penalized for failing to meet the requirements of the plan.[25] In a market-capitalist system, managers are themselves residual claimants or are accountable to private owners, who have incentives to monitor managers.[26] Management is also subject to the discipline of a market in the assets of the enterprise.[27] Managers of a workers' collective enterprise in a market economy are accountable to neither a planner nor a private owner, and are not subject to the discipline of potential acquisition.

The absence of monitoring by either the planner or a private owner facilitates discretionary expenditures that are a source of rents. Part of these rents are dissipated via hidden or on-the-job unemployment. Another component accrues to managers. The gains to management from discretionary expenditures are enhanced in an economic system that stresses formal egalitarianism in official incomes, but accommodates discretionary managerial expenditures as part of the costs of production.[28] Strategic interaction between the state and the enterprise endogenizes the value of rents; since protectionist rents can be supplemented by direct subsidies that are strategically evoked by the enterprise managers' awareness of the preeminence assigned by the government to worker's

---

[24] Wiles (1977), p.36.

[25] On the rents that nonetheless arise in the planned economy, see Hillman and Schnytzer (1986).

[26] See Demsetz and Lehn (1985).

[27] See Morck, Schleiffer, and Vishney (1989).

[28] For observations on Hungary, see Salgo (1986) who points to the relation between the interests of management of state enterprises and the interests of the state agencies that have sustained the large enterprises with subsidies and sheltered them from competition. Comparative observations with regard to Israel (see Mandelbaum, 1988) likewise point to the presence of rents in enterprises with responsibility to supply. Because of selection procedures and flexibility in the imposition of financial discipline, enterprise managers and other employees can earn in excess of the income available in their best market alternative. The economic rents thus earned would be diminished or eliminated by liberalization. Bregman (1987) provides evidence indicating a negative relationship between enterprise size and profitability.

employment security, and by enterprises' monopoly power that, as the converse of responsibility to supply, facilitates the ability to withhold supply.[29]

Hence, the social contract is also a basis for private gain. The gain derives from the state's inability to credibly precommit not to assist, in the event that the enterprise confronts difficulties in meeting its employment responsibilities. Enterprise managers are presented with opportunities to engage in activities that have been termed "rent seeking" in the Western literature,[30] or which in the terminology of market socialism are associated with the conception of a "soft" budget.[31]

VII. NEO-MERCANTILIST OBJECTIVES

Where efficiency objectives have preeminence, high concentration of industry and domestic market power are not valued consequences of "responsibility to supply". However, these same attributes further the pursuit of neo-mercantilist objectives. Of particular importance is the switch in the direction of trade that can be achieved by protection when an enterprise can exercise domestic market power. The transformation from import competition to exports allows foreign currency outlays to be replaced by earnings of foreign exchange, while at the same time both eliminating competition from socially less conscious enterprises abroad and increasing the rents accruing to the domestic enterprise.[32]

Figure 1 provides a demonstration: D depicts the domestic demand function confronting the enterprise (or the cartel) which has the domestic responsibility to supply, MR is domestic marginal revenue, and MC is marginal cost. P is a given world-market price.[33] In a regime of free trade, the enterprise could not exercise domestic price discretion and would produce output q_2. Domestic consumption would be q_4, composed of the enterprise's output plus imports which are given by ($q_4 - q_2$). But let the enterprise have "responsibility to supply". Successive increases in an import duty away from free trade lead the enterprise to respond as would a competitive industry by expanding output towards q_3, at which point domestic consumption is entirely satisfied by domestic output. Protection

---

[29] See Hillman, Katz, and Rosenberg (1987), Schaffer (1989).

[30] See for example Hillman and Riley (1989).

[31] See Kornai (1986).

[32] Helpman (1988) has pointed to another advantage of domestic monopoly in the context of macroeconomic stabilization policy. High concentration and domestic market power facilitated price stabilization in 1985 in Israel without the appearance of excess demand in domestic markets.

[33] It is assumed that quality is not an absolute impediment to foreign sales.

Figure 1

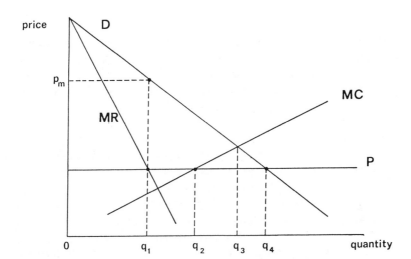

which facilitates a further increase in domestic price has no effect when the domestic industry is competitive.[34] However, an enterprise with domestic market power responds to further protection by contracting output from q_3. Output contraction ceases at q_2, the original free trade output. A further increase in protection evokes exports, and the enterprise continues to substitute exports for domestic supply until the price P_m is attained and the output $(q_2 - q_1)$ is exported. A protective tariff or foreign exchange controls and import licensing can sustain this equilibrium. Independently of the protectionist means adopted, the domestic enterprise's responsibility to supply not only "saves" foreign exchange by eliminating imports, but contributes to foreign exchange earnings. A competitive domestic industry could at best be induced by protectionist policies to expand output to eliminate imports without exports.[35] Although protection increases the enterprise's profits, rents can be altogether dissipated by discretionary managerial expenditures and hidden unemployment. The enterprise notwithstanding its domestic market power may therefore be observed to be

---

[34] Competitive price adjustment maintains the stable domestic market- clearing autarkic price.

[35] Exports by the competitive industry would require an export subsidy.

incurring a financial loss, and to require direct subsidies that supplement the indirect subsidies secured via protection. This is again the manifestation of the soft budget.

VIII. POLICY DILEMMAS

Consider now a government intent on liberalization. Commitment to liberalization can be demonstrated by free-trade agreements such as Israel has entered into with the European Community and the United States. When the time comes for protectionist barriers to be removed, the inconsistency between "responsibility to supply" and trade liberalization gives rises to a policy dilemma, since liberalization contradicts the social contract. T h e domestic pressure to continue to honor the contract is broadly based. Where an enterprise is privately owned, the private residual claimants have an incentive to hold the state to its "responsibility to protect". The argument will be made in terms of the precedent of the enterprise's "responsibility to supply" and the obligations which the enterprise has with regard to workers' employment and income security. In a collective workers' enterprise, the same incentives reside with managers as de facto residual claimants. In neither case do workers whose job security is sustained by designated "responsibilities to supply" have an interest in abrogation of the social contract. The basic premise is that a socially conscious enterprise cannot fairly be expected to confront import competition from profit-maximizing foreign producers. Confronted with such competition, the domestic enterprise can only respond by dispensing with excess labor or the hidden unemployment within the enterprise; but this the government will find unappealing if committed to ensured job security.

The manner of Israel's response to the implementation of the free-trade agreements with the U.S. and EEC reflects the liberalization dilemma. Means were sought of reconciling the social contract with the commitments to liberalize imports. Responses to the dilemma included supplementary duties that were protective tariffs in all but name[36], discriminatory methods of valuation of imported intermediate goods that advantaged domestic enterprises, and arbitrary impediments to import competition set by the Standards Institute. There are evident similarities with the non-tariff barriers that in the western market economies substituted for the tariff reductions negotiated under the various rounds of GATT negotiations. However, again, the appropriate comparison is with the international trade policy attendant upon Hungarian market socialism. Hungary's acceptance

---

[36] Pelzman (1989) investigates the duties known by the acronym "tama". For a catalogue of restrictive devices, see Hillman (1988).

of the GATT regulations and its official position regarding trade liberalization with the west were contradicted by the protectionism that sustained the large socialist enterprises which had the social responsibility in the absence of a planner to protect the job security of the workers.

Problems of communication and understanding can readily arise between national negotiators when the contradictions associated with the liberalization dilemma became evident. The western foreign trading partners themselves extensively use protectionist means, in particular non-tariff barriers and administrative anti-dumping and escape-clause procedures, to assist domestic industries.[37] However, the economic systems of the EEC and the US exhibit a greater tolerance for unemployment than allowed by the social contract that governs the relation between enterprise and state under market socialism, since "socialist" markets encompass a paternalism that is inconsistent with market-determined competitive imports that threaten workers' job security.

IX. CONCLUDING REMARKS

The broad objective of this paper has been to consider why economies with significant collective ownership of industry have not pursued the liberal trade policies that neo-classical theory associates with symmetric domestic factor claims. I have focused on Israel, and for comparison have made reference to the paternalistic protection of workers' job security that characterized Hungarian market socialism.

Protectionist policies have been linked to a social contract that in the absence of central planning permits the functioning of markets without subjecting workers to the employment fluctuations and income insecurity associated with capitalist-market systems. The enterprise's "responsibility to supply" that ensures domestic employment stability is sustained by the state's "responsibility to protect". The latter responsibility derives from the higher costs of production imposed on the domestic enterprise relative to socially less conscious enterprises that pursue cost minimization objectives without regard for the social obligations of workers' employment security.

Although founded in paternalistic motives, there are rents and rent dissipation associated with the social contract. The contract gives rise to or sustains high concentration of industry because of domestic barriers to entry. The entry barriers preempt a functioning capital market that might direct investments into activities that conflict with established supply respon-

---

[37] See for example Baldwin (1985) on the U.S. and Verreydt and Waelbroeck (1982) on the EEC. Hillman and Ursprung (1988) provide a formalization of Western protectionist policies that circumvent GATT.

sibilities. The consequence is the absence of effective anti-trust laws and monopolies and cartels that are protected from foreign competition. Market-capitalist or neo-classical conceptions would suggest other motives for the same phenomena.

Postscript

In the latter part of the 1980s, elements of the social contract were abrogated in Israel. Labor unemployment in 1989 reached the neighborhood of 10%. The value of output produced increased, indicating previous hidden unemployment. Because of accumulated losses, the Histadrut industrial conglomerate was obliged to contract and consolidate.[38] The kibbutz and moshav sectors also required restructuring and rescheduling of debt. At the same time impediments to liberalization via difficulties in adherence to the free-trade agreements diminished.

Hungary, which I have used for comparative reference as a "market socialist" system, began on its road to market-oriented reform with the elimination of central planning in 1968. However, soft budget constraints, concentrated industry, and hidden unemployment remained characteristics of Hungarian industry after more than two decades of market socialism. Political reforms that began in 1989 moved Hungary to a multiparty democratic system, and liberalizing economic reforms expanded organizational possibilities in the private sector as Hungary sought to begin to move away from "socialist" markets to an economic system that encompasses the presence of factor markets and factor-market allocation mechanisms.

Potential broader relevance for the market-socialist social contract is reflected in proposals in other economies undertaking the transition from socialism, that means be sought of combining socialism with liberal democracy in a market system.

---

[38] A source of difficulty was that permission had been given in 1986 to borrow from foreign banks whose conception of soft budgets differed from that of the domestic banks.

References

Baldwin, Robert, 1985. *The Political Economy of U.S. Import Policy*, M.I.T. Press, Cambridge.

Bauer, Tamas, 1988. "Economic reforms within and beyond the state sector," *American Economic Review, Papers and Proceedings*, 78, 452-460.

Bregman, Arie, 1986. *Industry and Industrialization Policy in Israel*, Bank of Israel, Jerusalem.

Bregman, Arie, 1987. "Government intervention in industry: The case of Israel," *Journal of Development Economics*, 25, 353-367.

Demsetz, Harold and Ken Lehn, 1985. "The ownership structure of corporations: Causes and consequences," *Journal of Political Economy*, 93, 1155-1177.

Ehrlich, Eva, 1985. "The size and structure of manufacturing establishments and enterprises: An international comparison," *Journal of Comparative Economics*, 9, 267-295.

Gacs, Janos, 1986. "The conditions, chances and predictable consequences of implementing step-by-step liberalization of imports in the Hungarian economy," *Acta Oeconomica*, 36, 231-250.

Gacs, Janos, 1989. "The progress of liberalization of foreign trade in Hungary," presented at Conference on *Attempts at Liberalization*, Budapest, November.

Gabor, Istvan and Tamas Horvath, 1987. "Failure and retreat in the Hungarian private small-scale industry," *Acta Oeconomica*, 38, 133-153.

Helpman, Elhanan, 1988. "Macroeconomic effects of price controls: The role of market structure," *Economic Journal*, 98, 340-354.

Hillman, Arye L., 1988. "Impediments to a competitive environment in Israel," *Symposium on American-Israeli Economic Relations to Mark the 40th Anniversary of the State of Israel*, New York.

Hillman, Arye L., 1989. *The Political Economy of Protection*, Harwood Academic Publishers, London and New York.

Hillman, Arye L., Eliakim Katz, and Jacob Rosenberg, 1987. "Workers as insurance," *Oxford Economic Papers*, 39, 813-820.

Hillman, Arye L. and Heinrich Ursprung, 1988. "Domestic politics, foreign interests, and international trade policy," *American Economic Review*, 78, 729-745.

Hillman, Arye L. and John Riley, 1989. "Politically contestable rents and transfers," *Economics and Politics*, 1, 17-39.

206   Markets and Politicians

Hillman, Arye L. and Adi Schnytzer, 1986. "Illegal activities and purges in a Soviet-type economy: A rent-seeking perspective," *International Review of Law and Economics*, 6, 87-99.

Hillman, Arye L. and Adi Schnytzer, 1990. "Creating the reform-resistant dependent economy: An analysis of the CMEA international trading relationship," Working Paper, *Socialist Economics Reform Unit, The World Bank*.

Holzman, Franklyn D., 1974. *Foreign Trade under Central Planning*, Harvard University Press, Cambridge, MA.

Kornai, Janos, 1980. "Hard and soft budget constraint," *Acta Oeconomica*, 25, 231-245, reprinted in Janos Kornai, *Contradictions and Dilemmas*, Corvina: Budapest, 1985, 33-51.

Kornai, Janos, 1983. "Comments on the present state and the prospects of the Hungarian economic reform," *Journal of Comparative Economics*, 7, 225-252, reprinted in Janos Kornai, *Contradictions and Dilemmas*, Corvina, Budapest, 1985, 81-123.

Kornai, Janos, 1988. "Individual freedom and reform of the socialist economy," *European Economic Review*, 32, 233-267.

Mandelbaum, Moshe, 1988. "The politization of economic activity in Israel," *Symposium on American-Israeli Economic Relations to Mark the 40th Anniversary of the State of Israel*, New York.

Mayer, Wolfgang, 1984. "Endogenous tariff formation," *American Economic Review*, 74, 970-985.

Morck, Randall, Andrei Schleiffer, and Robert Vishny, 1989. "Alternative mechanisms for corporate control," *American Economic Review*, 79, 842-852.

Oblath, Gabor, 1989. "Opening up in Hungary: The relevance of international experiences and some peculiarities," presented at Conference on *Attempts at Liberalization*, Budapest, November.

Pelzman, Joseph, 1989. "Are tama rates an import-restricting device?", presented at *Israel Economic Association* Conference, Jerusalem.

Salgo, Istvan, 1986. "Economic mechanism and foreign trade organization in Hungary," *Acta Oeconomica*, 36, 271-287.

Schaffer, Mark E., 1989. "The credible commitment problem in the center-enterprise relationship," *Journal of Comparative Economics*, 13, 359-382.

Schnytzer, Adi, 1982. *Stalinist Development Strategy and Practice*, Oxford University Press.

Schnytzer, Adi, 1988. "The Israeli economic system: Overview and comparative analysis," *Symposium on American-Israeli Economic Relations to Mark the 40th Anniversary of the State of Israel*, New York.

Shapiro, Yonathan, 1976. *The Formative Years of the Israeli Labor Party*, Sage Publications.

Summers, Robert, and Alan Heston, 1988. "A new set of international comparisons of real product sand price level estimates for 130 countries, 1950-1985," *Review of Income and Wealth*, 1-25.

Tardos, Marton, 1983. "The increasing role and ambivalent reception of small enterprises in Hungary," *Journal of Comparative Economics*, 7, 277-287.

Verreydy, Eric and Jean Waelbroeck, 1982. "European Community protection against manufacturing imports from developing countries: A case study in the political economy of protection," in Jagdish Bhagwati, editor, *Import Competition and Response*, University of Chicago Press for National Bureau of Economic Research, 369-393.

Wiles, Peter J.D., 1968. *Communist International Economics*, Blackwell, Oxford.

Wiles, Peter J.D., 1977. *Economic Institutions Compared*, Blackwell, Oxford.

Wolf, Thomas A., 1988. *Foreign Trade in a Centrally Planned Economy*, Harwood Academic Publishers, London and New York.

Chapter 11

THE FAILURE OF RECENTRALIZATION IN CHINA:
INTERPLAYS AMONG ENTERPRISES, LOCAL GOVERNMENTS
AND THE CENTER

Kang Chen

Decentralization entails a shift of decision-making power from the top toward the bottom of the hierarchy. Centralization or recentralization is, naturally, defined by the reverse process. In a three-level hierarchy, the outcomes of decentralization or recentralization can be complicated by the presence of the intermediatory levels. Such has been the case in China where economic and social change in the 1980s involved three hierarchical levels: enterprises, local governments, and the central government. The interactions among these parties and the associated problems merit study, not only for their immediate relevance to China's economic reform, but also for their relevance to the Soviet Union, Yugoslavia, and the Czech and Slovak Federal Republic, since reforms in these countries are also characterized by shifts of power among multi-level hierarchies.

After a decade of economic reform, the Chinese economy evolved away from a centrally planned economy. The scope of central planning was reduced substantially. The industrial products covered by the state mandatory plan fell from about 40% of the industrial gross output value in 1984 to 17% in 1989. The variety of producer-goods distribution under the state's monopoly was reduced from 256 in 1984 to 17 in 1989.[1] The number of agricultural products and consumer goods controlled by the Ministry of Commerce fell from 188 in 1979 to 23 in 1989. In 1988 and early 1989 there were even discussions about altogether abolishing the mandatory plan within three years.

The reforms decentralized much decision-making to the firm and the local government levels. Enterprise autonomy was expanded. Firms could

---

[1] *Economic Daily* (Jingji Ribao), October 16, 1989.

independently make decisions to change output quantity and variety, production technology, the time of production, and to some degree output prices. To improve incentives, they were allowed to retain a large fraction of profits. A survey of 403 state-owned enterprises in 1988 (Du, 1990) revealed that, among the sampled firms, in 1987 the average share of outside-plan production was 55.9 percent, and the average profit retention rate was 34.2 percent.

However, decentralizing economic reforms did not bring about a straightforward transfer of decision-making from the central government to economic agents. Local governments "captured" and expanded control over enterprises through a variety of informal mechanisms, and as well as through control over geographically immobile factors and resources (Wong, 1987). The China Enterprise Management Association at a meeting in 1988 pointed to "three pests" harassing enterprise managers. Each stemmed from interference with enterprise operations by local governments (Hartland-Thunberg, 1989). Local authorities have been extremely inventive in finding new means of retaining power. Progress toward the objective of increasing enterprise autonomy would therefore entail diminution of the scope of authority of local governments. For while the decision-making power of the central government has been greatly reduced, much of the discretion has been shifted to local governments rather than transferred to enterprises as originally intended by the center.[2]

How does one characterize China's economic system, given the changes in decision-making structure? This question has invited many answers. Some describe China as "a federation without a federal constitution" (Zhao, 1990). Others propose an "aristocratic economy" ruled by "dukes" and "princes" (Shen and Dai, 1990). Whatever terminology is used, local governments are indicated to be playing an increasingly important role. To understand the Chinese economy, it is therefore important to acknowledge the relationships between the center and local governments, and to take into account the evolving roles of Chinese local governments in the process of economic reform.

This paper is intended to enhance understanding of the interplays among the hierarchical levels of government and the enterprises. The following section will discuss how the Chinese local governments expanded their power in the decentralization process and how much power they actually gained. Their behavior in the reform process and impacts on macroeconomic policies will be described in Section II, which will also answer the seemingly paradoxical question: Why have local governments

---

[2] Thus, China's decentralization in 1980s is the least thorough one by Neuberger's (1979) classification.

come to be regarded as anti-reform forces, and yet at the same time also as "pro-reform forces" working against recentralization? Section III will discuss the dilemma facing the Chinese central government in dealing with local authorities. Are the central officials capable of enforcing their demands and taking power away from the local governments as they have done many times in the past? What are the constraints on recentralization? Concluding remarks will be presented in Section IV.

I. ADMINISTRATIVE DECENTRALIZATION

Economic reforms in the 1980s have devolved control over resources and decision-making power to provincial and local governments, as well as to enterprises. Indeed, decentralization and reform have become closely associated in economic discussions in China. Because of the sheer size of the country and the numbers of people involved, administrative decentralization has been viewed as an important goal of economic reforms. It was seen as a means of using locally available information more effectively, of allowing local preferences greater influence over local spending decisions, and of providing material incentives to local governments and enterprises to pursue growth objectives, as they would be the main beneficiaries of increased incomes.

The administrative decentralization started in 1980 with the introduction of the *Center-Local Revenue Sharing System*, under which the local governments were given specific shares of financial revenues, and were made responsible for meeting revenue targets and for their budgets. Since the center had different interests and objectives from those of local governments, there was intense bargaining on sharing ratios. In fact, the essence of central-local relations has been a complex bargaining relationship that revolves around finances, the budgetary process and the national banking system.[3]

The revenue sharing system gave local governments incentives to increase budgetary revenues. In many areas local officials responded to the new incentives in a surprisingly entrepreneurial fashion.[4] They found out very soon, however, that their autonomy was constrained by limited discretion with respect to production, investment, and bank loans. With constant bargaining, various "contract responsibility systems" were established for material allocation, investment, bank loans, and foreign trade. "Baogan", a contractual responsibility system which balances power between the center and local governments, has taken shape. "Baogan" of budget, material allocation, investment, and bank loans has given local

---

[3] See Lieberthal and Oksenberg (1988).
[4] See Susan Shirk (1989), p.358.

governments substantial power in four areas.

1. Tax Policy and Administration

China's current tax system originated from the old profit-remittance system and inherited from it two important features. First is the sharing of responsibilities between the center and the provinces for tax policy and administration, and the sharing of taxes collected. China differs from many other countries in that the central government collects very few of its own taxes. Reliance is placed on local governments for the collection of all revenues other than customs duties and selected excises.

The second feature of the current tax system is the disparity in tax treatment stemming from the negotiated nature of taxes under the contract responsibility system. Various taxes are used to adjust for price distortions, and to equalize profitability, both within and across industrial sectors. For example, rates of product tax ranged in 1986 from 3% to 66%, and there were some 400 different commodity groups subject to tax at different rates.[5] Furthermore, enterprises were sometimes granted exemptions on taxes if in financial difficulty. Conversely, large increases in profits associated with successful management tended to be taxed away through the adjustment tax. The tailoring of taxes to specific enterprise circumstances was a manifestation of the soft budget constraint in China.

The enterprise-specific tax policy was thus designed for income redistribution, not for macroeconomic management. The administration of revenue collection has been almost entirely in the hands of local governments, because they monitor the enterprises within "the management contract responsibility system." Therefore, most of the tax leverage comes from industrial bureaus at the provincial level and from provincial authorities responsible for tax administration. The central authorities play a limited role in directing resources through taxation. In fact, as a result of revenue-sharing, the center's influence reflected in its share of total revenue has been declining in recent years.[6] Table 1 shows that the center's share fell from 52.9 percent in 1981 to 43.9 percent in 1985.

2. Material Allocation and Production Plans

The material supply system used to be an important element of central planning. All projects included in the state plan received allocations of key raw materials through the material supply system. This role has diminished since the economic reforms began. After the introduction of the two-tier pricing system, the scope of market regulation of capital goods continued

---

[5] See World Bank (1988), p.402.
[6] *Economic Daily* (Jingji Ribao), October 14, 1989.

to expand, decreasing the proportion of production material distributed according to the state mandatory plan to less than 20 percent.[7]

While the central government voluntarily reduced its direct involvement in economic activities in order to give enterprises more autonomy, local governments took the opportunity to expand their own power. For instance, although the number of industrial products under the state mandatory plan has fallen from 120 in 1984 to about 60 in 1989, local governments have increased the number of products subject to the control of *local* mandatory plans. As a result, some enterprises have all their products tied up in the state or local plans, leaving no scope for the play of market forces. In 1988, only 18 percent of Shanghai's gross industrial output fell under the state mandatory plan; however, in many industrial sectors, especially in metallurgy, textiles, and some machine-building enterprises, production was almost 100 percent planned. Even above-quota output was subject to local mandatory plans (Dong, 1988). As a result of decentralization, local governments secured greater power than the center in making production decisions.

Table 1

Division of Revenues between Central and Local Governments
(in percentage)

	1981	1982	1983	1984	1985	1986 --- 1989
Center	52.9	48.6	48.0	46.2	43.9	N/A
Local	47.1	51.4	52.0	53.8	56.1	N/A

Source: *Statistical Yearbook of China 1988*, p.681.
Note: Although data are not available on the division of revenues between local and central governments, local government expenditure can be taken as a proxy for local revenues on the assumption that local governments do not incur ex-post deficits. The estimates of local and center shares of revenues given in this table are calculated based on this assumption.

---

3. Investment Decisions

In 1979, most of fixed asset investment was still firmly under the control of the central government. Subsequently the influence of the central government declined, and that of local governments and enterprises

---

[7] See Hua et.al. (1988).

increased. In the spirit of decentralization, provincial authorities were granted powers to approve investment projects locally, subject to limits on total investment.[8] Provincial governments extended this "free limit" to prefectures, cities, and counties, which were given their own individual free limits. For example, some provinces were granted power to approve investment projects up to 200 million yuan, some counties up to 30 million yuan.[9] This significantly reduced the central government's control over investments. The impact is even greater when local governments and enterprises break up large investment projects into smaller projects to evade the project selection and approval process of the state planning commission. Table 2 shows the sources of finance for fixed asset investment. Investment funded by the state budget has declined from 28% in 1981 to 13% in 1987.

Table 2

Sources of Finance for Fixed Asset Investment

	1981	1982	1983	1984	1985	1986	1987
Value (Billion Yuan)	96.1	123.0	143.0	183.3	254.3	302.0	364.1
Source of Finance (%)							
Total	100.0	100.0	100.0	100.0	100.0	100.0	100.0
State Budget	28.1	22.7	23.8	23.0	16.0	14.6	13.1
Domestic Loans	12.7	14.3	12.3	14.1	20.1	21.1	23.0
Foreign Investment	3.8	4.9	4.7	3.9	3.6	4.4	4.8
Self-raised Fund and Other	55.5	58.1	59.3	59.1	60.3	60.0	59.2

Source: *Statistical Yearbook of China 1988*, p.559.

4. Control of Financial Resources

From Table 2, it is clear that a larger share of investment was being financed through bank loans rather than through government budgets. This, however, should not be viewed as evidence of true financial autonomy. The increasing share of investment financed by bank loans reflects the increasing influence of local governments on investment decisions.

In the past, the government budget was the principal instrument for

---

[8] The World Bank (1988), ibid.
[9] *Economic Daily* (Jingji Ribao), October 10, 1989.

mobilizing savings and for directing investment. These responsibilities have come to rest more heavily on the household and enterprise sectors, with a major intermediation role played by the financial sector. Enterprise reform has allowed profits to be retained by enterprises and surpluses to be accumulated in bank accounts. Banks were to intermediate these funds, and to channel them into profitable investments. *Duocun Duodai*, a policy which allows bank branches that succeed in attracting more deposits to extend more credit rather than having to remit these funds to a higher level of the banks, has been implemented. Since a large proportion of any credit expansion would return to the same branch in the form of increased deposits, the new arrangements made it possible for bank branches to create a multiple expansion of credit on the basis of an initial increase in deposits.

Under close supervision of local governments, however, banks have had limited scope for independent decisions and have contributed little to capital mobility. Because the real rate of interest charged on bank loans is negative, credit is rationed. More credit extension means more subsidies from the central government. Local governments do not like to see local banks remit excess reserves to the next level in the hierarchy, or to see banks lend excess reserves to banks in other localities --- even to branches of the same bank. Since local governments effectively control local banks, and often the careers of bank directors and their families, banks are careful to heed local government priorities; acting in the "interest of the region" is more important than profits. Thus, local extra-budgetary investments have become a major force of expansion drive, and the center has little control over these investments. Indeed, giving banks autonomy actually means giving control of financial resources to local governments.

In sum, local governments have expanded their economic authority. They are sometimes called "dukes" or "princes", because they virtually have the same power as historically the aristocracies had. The situation varies, however, from region to region. Some dukes are more powerful than others. The provinces favored appear to be those in a position to withhold remittances to the central government, as compared to those provinces that receive transfers.

II. BEHAVIOR OF LOCAL GOVERNMENTS IN THE REFORM PROCESS

Given the expansion of power, the revenue-sharing system, and the still very much distorted price structure, the behavior of local governments is quite "rational." Their objective is: *to maximize local budgetary revenues subject to the constraints of protecting and improving the economic welfare of regional residents, especially the urban residents* (Hua et.al., 1988). First, they disguise their real revenues, since in the absence of estimates of taxable capacity the center has no way of knowing how a province's collection relates to its taxable capacity. Many provincial governments keep two accounts, one for the auditors of the central government, the other for their own use. In this way, they can retain more revenues before engaging in negotiations with the center with respect to the sharing ratios. Second, local governments divert resources into production of processing goods, prices of which are unreasonably high relative to energy and raw materials. By so doing, it is easier to balance budgets. Last, they protect their regional interest by limiting the interregional mobility of resources which can be used to generate local budgetary revenues.

I shall now consider the behavior of local governments from regional and sectoral perspectives, the consequences for macroeconomic control and industrial policies, and behavior in the context of the relationships among enterprises, local governments, and the center.

1. Regional Protectionism

Local protectionism has been frequent, and has resulted in fragmented domestic product markets that prevent product and regional specialization. It seems that all levels of local officials -- from province to town -- can impose barriers that prevent or impede access to their local market.

In regions well endowed with raw materials, the local authorities have an incentive to establish their own regional processing industry, since this is more profitable than selling the raw materials to other regions. Hence, interregional sales of raw materials are restricted. However, local suppliers of raw materials are willing to sell to regions which have well established processing industries, since with advanced technology and more efficient production, the latter can pay higher prices. Local governments have to intervene to forcibly stop these transactions. Some local authorities even sent "Minbing", which is China's army reserve, to set up check points on the highways and to patrol the borders. Newspapers have reported news of "Silkworm War", "Wool War", "Tea War", "Tobacco War", "Coal war", "Cotton War", and wars with respect to other raw materials. Some guerrilla tactics were used in these wars (Li, 1989). The wars have been extended to daily-use articles and light industrial products.[10] In order to protect local industry, some local governments restrict the import of goods from other areas. Some force stores in their regions to purchase local substandard products.

Regions specialized to the processing industry have sought to block the interregional transfer of technology, to prevent resource-endowed regions from producing processed goods. However, this has proved more difficult

---

[10] *China Daily*, June 19, 1990.

than blocking the physical movement of goods. All provincial governments have been quite successful in establishing production capacity in processing sectors.

2. Sectoral Dimension

The behavior of local governments in the sectoral dimension is summarized by the following two features.

(1) *Shoot Set Projects*: "Shoot Set" is a term from volleyball. It is a ball quickly set with a short and flat trajectory. "Shoot set projects" refer to investments that yield quick financial profits in the short run. In recent years, local governments and enterprises have concentrated investments on a few consumer goods and household electrical appliances in light industry while knowing that markets for these products would saturate very soon. Availability of inexpensive capital and a soft budget constraint combined with decentralized investment decisions and bureaucratic intervention in local bank lending make these duplicate investments financially feasible.

(2) *Antique Reproduction*: Because of the protectionism exercised by the local governments, there has been a move from specialization toward self-sufficiency. Duplicate investments, reproduction of obsolete equipment and technology, have become common practice. An example is the demand structure in the capital equipment market in 1985. Demand for large scale, high-tech, precision, and special-purpose equipment was low. On the other hand, small scale, low-grade, and general-purpose equipment was in great demand. More than one thousand old style blast furnaces have been built in Shanxi province since 1984 (Deng and Luo, 1987). "Antique reproduction" has been common for many kinds of equipment in many places.

Severe structural imbalance has resulted from excess investment in processing industries and the machine-building industry, and under-investment in bottleneck sectors such as energy, transportation and basic raw materials. This has created a dilemma for the central government, which has had to find ways of funding needed investments in infrastructure and basic industry, while facing the reality of both a declining influence over such investments and a declining capacity to fund them.

3. Impacts on Macroeconomic Control

Kornai (1980) has characterized managers of enterprises in centrally planned economies as having a tendency to engage in "expansion drives" that lead to "investment hunger." Despite recent modifications in the investment allocation system and management reforms, the budgetary constraints of Chinese state-owned enterprises have remained "soft", long-term commitments are still inconsistent with abilities, and growth is still independent of economic performance. Chinese organizations still have incentives to overinvest. However, the center of expansion has shifted from budgetary projects initiated by the ambitious central planners to extrabudgetary projects initiated by equally ambitious local officials. The difference between the central and local officials is that there is a self-constrained mechanism for the center, whereas the constraint is not present at the local level. The central planners can initiate expansion drives of the scale of the "great leap forward" in 1958, but have to bear the consequences, and have the inescapable task of stabilizing the economy and the currency. Local government officials also have the power to launch expansions under the "Baogan" system, but need not concern themselves with macroeconomic stability, since that is the responsibility of the central government. Their sole constraint is orders of retrenchment from the center. Therefore, the key issue of macroeconomic policy is how to control the expansion drives of local governments, when the success of macro-economic policy depends totally on the cooperation of local authorities.

Local officials oppose tight monetary and fiscal policies, because such policies hinder the growth of local budgetary revenues, the growth of industry and employment, and achievements in their term of office. Hence the local officials undermine or counteract the center's policies by skillful manipulations. The phrase "the center has policy, the local has strategy", is used to describe the game between the central and local governments.

Since local officials control tax collection and local banks, they have the upper hand in this game. In 1989, the central government adopted an austerity program to curtail inflation. The center's plan was to cut fixed asset investments by 90 billion yuan relative to 1988. This plan encountered strong resistance from the local governments. In the first half of 1989, fixed investments were only cut by 8.1 billion yuan.[11] With more effort from the center, by the end of 1989, fixed investments were decreased by about 50 billion yuan from the previous year, which is only 55.6 percent of the original specified target.[12] This is representative of the diminished effectiveness of the center in implementing its sought-after macroeconomic policy objectives.

4. Impacts on Industrial Policy
Because of the different interests of the central and local governments, the effects of industrial policy can differ from original objectives. For example, high taxes on tobacco and alcoholic beverages were intended to

---

[11] *Economic Daily* (Jingji Ribao), October 10, 1989.
[12] See State Statistical Bureau of the PRC, 1990. "*Communique on the Statistics of 1989 Economic and Social Development,*" February 20, 1990.

discourage the production and consumption of these goods. However, tax sharing and the high profitability of these goods simply implied very good sources of income for local governments. Cigarette factories, distilleries, and breweries have mushroomed over the country.

At times, it is even impossible to implement policy in response to the deterioration of structural balance. The central government sought to allocate increased resources to bottleneck sectors such as energy, transportation, and basic raw materials. However, since local governments were increasing investment in the processing industries, the imbalance deteriorated. Since the center has failed to make local governments adjust their investment allocations, it has become a race of investments, with local authorities' increasing investment in processing sectors to generate more budgetary revenues, and the central government seeking to invest in basic industries to maintain structural balance (Research Group of Macroeconomic Management, 1987). The race seems to be even. Data on changes in shares of gross output value, employment, and investment in China's industrial sectors reveal a remarkable stability over time (see Table 3).

Table 3

Shares by Industrial Sectors
(in percentage)

	Gross Output			Employment			Investment		
	1981	1984	1987	1981	1984	1987	1981	1984	1987
Metallurgy	8.8	8.2	8.0	6.4	6.3	6.3	11.5	11.9	12.2
Power	3.8	3.4	3.1	1.8	1.8	2.0	12.0	12.9	15.3
Coal and Coke	2.8	2.6	2.2	8.2	8.2	7.4	10.3	12.5	7.2
Petroleum	5.4	4.8	4.2	1.0	1.1	1.3	14.3	15.0	12.5
Chemical	11.4	11.8	11.8	8.8	8.8	9.1	9.7	10.6	12.0
Machinery	20.9	25.0	28.0	30.0	29.0	27.2	13.3	12.8	13.5
Building Materials	3.8	4.1	4.5	9.0	9.6	10.9	3.9	4.9	5.8
Forest	2.0	1.8	1.5	3.9	3.7	3.5	2.6	2.0	1.2
Food	13.3	12.3	11.1	6.2	6.5	6.8	5.7	5.3	7.2
Textile, Clothing and Leather	20.5	18.8	18.0	16.0	16.2	17.3	12.2	8.0	8.6
Paper-making and Cultural Articles	3.7	3.5	4.0	5.1	4.9	5.7	2.1	1.5	2.0
Others	3.6	3.7	3.6	3.7	4.0	2.6	2.3	2.6	2.5

Sources: 1) Shares of gross outputs are from: *Industrial Statistical Yearbook of China 1988*, pp. 54-57. 2) Shares of employment and investment are estimated by the author based on data from *Statistical Yearbook of China*, various years.

Statistical evidence reveals that sectoral investment has been allocated on the basis of fixed relative shares, with few criteria other than the previous year's investment allocations; coal and forest sectors are exceptions, since here the relationship has been affected by investment from village enterprises. Such investment behavior has been described as *plane expansion* and *plane contraction* (Deng and Luo, 1987). In an expansion period, every sector is investing, regardless of whether the investment is worthwhile according to economic criteria. In a period of austerity, every sector has to cut back, including those sectors with worthwhile investment projects. This again can be explained by the influence of local governments and is related to income distribution. Capital is very difficult to transfer between sectors or enterprises. The immobility of capital leaves the task of structural adjustment to new investment. After the investment-system reform, different profit rates among different industrial sectors have become signals and incentives for structural adjustment. On the other hand, uneven profit rates have led to unequal income distribution, which is not permitted to persist for long. Governments at all levels come under pressure to intervene and even out profits before any significant change in sectoral structure can take place. The base for a "just" distribution of profits is the existing capital-stock, as revealed by the data. Hence, the allocation of new investment is constrained by the existing structure of the capital stock (Wang, 1987).

5. Contradictions in Local Governments' Behavior

Local governments are usually regarded as anti-reform forces, because they are aware that their economic power will be eroded in the process of market-oriented reforms (Milanović, 1989). Hence, local governments intercept the power that the center intended to pass to enterprises, and they have considerable latitude in deciding how to carry out the policy directives from the center, if at all.

It is clear that local officials are the major obstacles when the central government is pushing forward reforms. After the June incident of 1989, however, local governments have come to be viewed as "pro-reform forces" which counteract the reversal of reforms at the center (Jiang, 1990). Local governments have frustrated the attempts to close semi-private rural enterprises and to blunt the exertions of recentralization of financial revenues and material allocation, and have kept reform initiatives alive.[13]

The answer to the question, are local authorities anti-reform forces or pro-reform forces, is not simply positive or negative, because of contradictions in local governments' behavior. When confronted with

---

[13] *Oxford Analytica*, May 22, 1990.

enterprise managers, local officials oppose reform measures which give managers more autonomy or give markets more latitude, since these reduce their power. On the other hand, they support decentralization because of the benefit they have derived, and hence they wish to preserve the *status quo*. The *status quo* includes all the power described in Section I. It also includes the privilege of accessing material supply channels for their personal interests, and the privileges associated with "privatized" state assets under their supervision. They oppose recentralization, since this would take away such power and privileges. Moreover, officials from different regions may have different positions. For example, the officials from inland provinces may support some recentralization measures for reasons of regional equity, because the open-door policy and fiscal decentralization have in the past benefited the coastal provinces more than the inland provinces.

The behavior of local governments is rational, yet it has created economic and social problems. The problems with the "Baogan" system were anticipated in its early stage of implementation (Shi and Liu, 1989). Almost all problems associated with economic development and reform can be traced to the "Baogan" system dictating the conduct of local governments (Shen and Dai, 1990). The consequence is a dilemma for Chinese leaders.

III. DILEMMA OF DEALING WITH "DUKES" AND "PRINCES"

Neither a reform-minded center nor a center favoring central planning has been able to control the "Baogan" system. If prices can adjust freely to reflect scarcity, regions endowed with natural resources will be able to benefit from their comparative advantage. If property rights to enterprises are clarified, interests of local governments and enterprises will be separated, thus reducing the incentives for local government protectionism. However, the Chinese reformers have not been able to implement such changes. Another option is recentralization. The constraints on recentralization are illustrated by the unsuccessful attempt to increase direct central control over the economy in 1989.

During the history of the People's Republic, there have been repeated cycles of decentralization and recentralization (Zhao, 1990). However, the situation has changed since the economic reforms in 1980s, with profound impacts on the Chinese economy and society. Recentralization is hindered by constraints on unemployment and enterprise efficiency.

(1) Unemployment

Providing jobs for China's labor force is a major objective of Chinese policy makers. The problem is especially severe in the rural areas. With the implementation of the *Household Production Responsibility System*, there has been a great improvement in agricultural productivity. However, the disguised unemployment under the commune system surfaced after the decollectivization. As a result, there were about 80 million rural surplus laborers looking for jobs.[14] There is insufficient land for them to farm in the countryside, and there are not enough jobs for them to work in the cities. In the 1980s, the development of rural township and village enterprises (TVE's), which are collective and private entities, absorbed 67 million of them.[15] Rural TVE's have become the major source of rural employment. For several years, rural industries have produced approximately a third of China's industrial output, and have become one of the major sources of revenues for local governments. The growth of rural TVE's has substantially increased the income of rural residents. Strong ties, such as income and employment linkages, fiscal linkages, and various rewards for local government officials, have been established between TVE's and the local economy (Byrd and Gelb, 1990).

The development of rural TVE's has depended upon the new product markets. Without the *Two-Tier Pricing System*, the rural TVE's would not have been able to gain access to capital goods through markets, and would no longer exist. Recentralization, however, would harm the growth environment of rural TVE's. Increased central control of material and credit allocation would reduce the scope of the market that has facilitated the growth of rural TVE's. The ability of rural TVE's to absorb surplus labor would then be reduced. The rural labor force has been growing by 10 million persons per year, and unemployment would cause social problems that no government could ignore.

(2) Enterprise Efficiency

Because of the vaguely specified property rights associated with the state-owned enterprises, budget constraints have been "soft", and enterprise managers have had little incentive to use resources efficiently. Table 4 shows China's industrial labor productivity by different types of enterprise ownership. The average annual growth rate of labor productivity in 1980-1987 was about 5.2% for the state-owned enterprises, relative to 12.3% for urban collectives, and 18% for rural TVE's.

One of the major goals of reform is to improve enterprise efficiency. At the beginning, state-owned enterprises were given more autonomy with respect to decisions affecting production, investment, and workers' income.

---

[14] *China Daily*, October 28, 1989. Estimates for the size of surplus rural work force vary from 70 million to 156 million, depending on the methods of estimation. See Jefferey Taylor (1988).

[15] *Economic Daily* (Jingji Ribao), October 24, 1989.

Table 4

Indexes of Industrial Output, Labor, and Labor Productivity

Year	Total Output	Total Labor	O/L	State-owned Output	State-owned Labor	O/L
1980	100.00	100.00	100.00	100.00	100.00	100.00
1981	104.31	104.02	100.28	102.50	104.62	97.97
1982	112.46	108.39	103.76	109.73	107.44	102.13
1983	125.04	111.53	112.12	120.03	108.94	110.18
1984	145.40	119.39	121.79	130.73	110.05	118.80
1985	176.95	125.09	141.46	147.65	114.43	129.03
1986	196.17	134.64	145.70	156.78	118.63	132.16
1987	230.55	140.09	164.57	174.49	122.56	142.38

Year	Urban Collectively Owned Output	Labor	O/L	Rural TVE's Output	Labor	O/L
1980	100.00	100.00	100.00	100.00	100.00	100.00
1981	108.97	104.69	104.08	109.05	102.01	106.90
1982	119.20	107.35	111.04	119.57	106.75	112.01
1983	133.84	110.15	121.50	143.17	111.64	128.25
1984	173.41	114.92	150.90	202.08	131.26	153.96
1985	221.72	119.40	185.70	308.97	141.14	218.90
1986	239.74	124.72	192.23	405.06	161.64	250.60
1987	288.72	128.01	225.54	539.17	169.77	317.58

Source: *Statistical Yearbook of China*, various year.

Since there were "carrots" but no "sticks", wages in the state-owned enterprises "swallowed" profits (Dai and Li, 1988). An attempt in 1984 to impose uniform tax rates as "sticks" and to ensure budgetary revenues failed, because it required significant redistribution, and the losers from the redistribution were strong enough to stop this plan (Hua et.al., 1988). In the end, the *Management Contract Responsibility System*, which had been experimented with earlier and spread to the whole country in 1987, was imposed as an option that increased the accountability of state-owned enterprises on the one hand, and protected the state's interest on the other. Under this system, enterprise managers would sign contracts with their supervisory authorities, which were usually local governments, fixing the terms of taxes, profit remittances, and sometimes increases in fixed assets.

New problems stemmed from this system (Du, 1987). However, it has been judged acceptable given the ownership framework (Study Group in Institute of Economics, 1989).

The center cannot communicate directly with the nation's 800 thousand state-owned enterprises, and hence has to rely on local governments to administer the contracts. The *revenue-sharing* and the "Baogan" system have served as a means of stimulating the initiative of local officials, to make them effective monitors of state-owned enterprises. Recentralization of administrative control over enterprises would damage this incentive scheme and the monitoring system, and thereby would decrease enterprise efficiency. As a result, enterprise budgets would be softer, with more lost-making units emerging. The burden of the state budget would increase, and inflationary pressure would be higher. Such conditions permit local officials to turn their pivotal positions into a source of influence and constraint on the center.

These two constraints underlie the unsuccessful attempt of the Chinese center to recentralize authority in 1989 and 1990. After the June incident of 1989, it became totally unclear in China as to what was an attribute of "bourgeois liberalism" and what belonged to "perfection of the socialist system." In an attempt to clear the confusion and to assert the platform of the new leadership, *Economic Daily* carried a series of interviews in October 1989 with officials from the Ministry of Finance, the State Planning Commission, the Chinese Academy of Social Sciences, the State Administration of Industry and Commerce, the State System Reform Commission, the Ministry of Agriculture, the Ministry of Material Supply, and the Ministry of Commerce.[16] The major policy assertions were the following.

A. Plan and Market: The *Bird Cage* theory about the plan-market relationship was correct,[17] and the market-oriented reform was a mistake. The bird (the market) was flying too freely, and it was time to make the cage (the state plan) smaller and tighter. The State Planning Commission wanted to expand the scope of the mandatory plan and reduce outside-plan investments. The Ministry of Commerce wanted to increase the number of consumer goods and agricultural products under its control, and give state commercial firms preferential treatment. The Ministry of Material Supply wanted to increase the share of capital goods under its distribution, and to

---

[16] *Economic Daily* (Jingji Ribao), October 14, 16, 17, 18, 19, 23, 24, 25, 1989.
[17] The *Bird Cage* theory was developed by Chen Yun during the 1950s. The theory described the state plan as a cage, and the market as a bird inside the cage. The bird should be allowed to fly provided it remains inside the cage.

restrict the entry of the non-public sector into wholesale business for major producer goods.

B. Center and Local Relations: The *Center-Local Revenue Sharing System* was also a mistake. The need for strengthening of the central authority should be emphasized. The Ministry of Finance stressed the significance of raising the "two ratios", i.e. the ratio of fiscal revenue to the national income, and the ratio of central government revenue to local revenue.

C. State and Nonstate Sectors: As the backbone of the socialist economy, large and medium sized state-owned enterprises should be given preferential treatment in loans, supply of energy and raw materials, transportation, and foreign exchange allocation. The nonstate sector is only supplementary to the state sector. More restrictions should be applied to individual and private sector activities. The Administration of Industry and Commerce prepared an industry/product list specifying where individual or private businesses were allowed to operate. Private businessmen were to be barred from operations related to "important" producer goods, some staple foods, and long distance wholesale trade. This was a major policy change from that advocated by the ousted leader Zhao Ziyang. Zhao's policy was to let the nonstate sector outgrow the state sector (Shirk, 1989).

D. Coast and Inland: The former regionally oriented development policy should be replaced by a sector-oriented policy that would favor trans-regional or trans-sectoral industrial cooperation. The new policy deemphasized coastal development and the development of the Special Economic Zones (SEZ's). This was another major policy change. Under Zhao, the coastal provinces were allowed to take advantage of their natural strengths, their industrial plant and skilled manpower, port facilities, and ties to overseas Chinese capitalists, who prefer to invest in their home regions. Zhao's idea was to let coastal regions develop first, and then to let the impact spread into inland regions.

E. Two-tier Pricing System: The two-tier pricing system had caused corruption and economic disorder. It should be eliminated and a single-track pricing structure should prevail over a period of time.

F. Management Contract Responsibility System: The *Management Contract responsibility System* should be honored and the terms of contracts extended "to set people's mind at rest."

G. Rural Policies: The *Rural Household Production Responsibility System* should remain the basic management pattern of China's agricultural production for quite a long time to come. The rural policy should be kept stabilized since any disruption in grain production would be a disaster to national stability. The growth of rural TVE's should be kept under control. They should make structural adjustments, and should not be allowed to compete with state-owned enterprises for energy and raw materials. No new loans were to be extended to them, and the total lending should have zero growth.[18]

Most of these policies were adopted by the Fifth Plenum of the Thirteenth Communist Party's Central Committee.[19] However, the viability of the policies was challenged immediately by the problems that were created. As a result of the discriminatory credit policy toward the rural TVE's, more than 800 thousand rural enterprises went out of business in 1989.[20] The industrial output of rural TVE's increased 12.7%, which is a substantial slowdown when compared with the 33% growth rate in the 1984-1988 period. The rural TVE's provided 50% less jobs in 1989 than in 1988, thereby increasing rural unemployment by at least five million.[21]

The central government's policies caused a great debate. In the face of the challenges from local governments and the mounting problems of unemployment, the center was compelled to change its policies. In March 1990, the State Planning Commission announced that the state would continue policies favorable to rural industry such as tax cuts and access to bank loans.[22] The Commission even gave an "instructive plan target" of 15% growth for the rural industries. Officials from the Commission were quoted as saying that: "We ourselves are not sure we have fully understood the importance of rural industries." This was a very significant policy change. It meant that the product market could not be closed, and that the recentralization of material and credit control could not proceed very far.

Deterioration of enterprise efficiency was another source of major concern for the central government. Overall industrial labor productivity increased by only 1.6% in 1989. Profits and taxes per 100 yuan of fixed assets dropped from 21.99 yuan in 1988 to 19.41 yuan in 1989,[23] thereby contributing to a budgetary deficit of 9.2 billion yuan, which was 1.8

---

[18] *Economic Daily* (Jingji Ribao), November 6, 1989.
[19] See David L. Shambaugh (1989).
[20] *Oxford Analytica*, May 22, 1990.
[21] *China Daily*, October 28, 1989.
[22] *China Daily*, March 17, 1990.
[23] See State Statistical Bureau of the PRC (1990), ibid.

billion higher than planned.[24]

The budgetary deficit would have been greater, had fiscal revenues not been protected by the *Management Contract Responsibility System*. The central government understood the merits of this system, and swiftly extended contracts that expired in 1989. By June 1990, more than 77% of industrial enterprises had had their contracts extended.[25]

Because the *Management Contract Responsibility System* remained in place, the center could not abandon the "Baogan" system. The planned recentralization of financial revenues was not achieved, and the central government's allocation of materials increased only slightly. One by one, the center abandoned the policies directed at recentralizing economic authority.[26]

IV. CONCLUDING REMARKS

China's reforms in the course of the 1980s were characterized by rural decollectivization and administrative decentralization. These two changes reinforced one another in a manner that inhibited both subsequent recentralization and further reform. Local governments became the major barrier standing in the way of either moving backward or going forward. They were a liberalizing influence in sustaining past policies and resisting recentralization, but the very authority and means that permitted this also gave rise to local protectionism that was contrary to domestic rationalization of resource and commodity flows.

---

[24] *People's Daily* (Renmin Ribao), overseas edition, June 26, 1990.
[25] *People's Daily* (Renmin Ribao), overseas edition, July 14, 1990.
[26] *Oxford Analytica*, ibid.

References

Byrd, William A., and Alan Gelb, 1990. "Why industrialize? The incentives for rural community governments", in William A. Byrd and Lin Qingsong, editors, *China's Rural Industry: Structure, Development, and Reform*, Oxford University Press, Oxford, 358-87.

Dai Y., and H. Li, 1988. "Wage swallowing up profit --- a hidden danger in the reform of China's economic system", *Economic Research* (Jingji Yanjiu), No. 6.

Deng, Yingtao, and Xiaopeng, Luo, 1987. "On the limitation of total quantity analysis and policy in China's economic theory and practice," *Economic Research* (Jingji Yanjiu), No. 6.

Dong, Furen, 1988. "The reform of economic mechanism and the reform of ownership", *Economic Research* (Jingji Yanjiu), No. 7.

Du, Haiyan, 1987. "The contractual system: an initial choice in reforming the state owned enterprises", *Economic Research* (Jingji Yanjiu), No. 10.

Du, Haiyan, et.al., 1990. "Autonomous rights of state-owned enterprises, market structure and incentive systems - investigation and analysis of 403 state enterprises", *Economic Research* (Jingji Yanjiu), No. 1.

Hartland-Thunberg, Penelope, 1989. *A Decade of China's Economic Reform: Challenges for the Future*, The Center for Strategic and International Studies, Washington, D.C.

Hua, Sheng, Zhang, Xuejun, and Luo, Xiaopeng, 1988. "Ten years in China's reform: looking back, reflection and prospect", *Economic Research* (Jingji Yanjiu), No. 9, No. 11, and No. 12.

Jiang, Fan, 1990. "Economic conditions of China's regional pluralism", in Jia Hao, editor, *The Democracy Movement of 1989 and China's Future*, The Washington Center for China Studies, Washington, D.C., 218-33.

Kornai, Janos, 1980. *Economics of Shortage*, North-Holland, Amsterdam.

Li, Zuoyan, 1989. "On silkworm war", *Cost and Price References* (Chengban Yu Jiage Ziliao), 62, 32-36.

Lieberthal, Kenneth, and Michel Oksenberg, 1988. *Policy Making in China*, Princeton University Press, New Jersey.

Milanovič, Branko, 1989. *Liberalization and Entrepreneurship: Dynamic of Reform in Socialism and Capitalism*, M. E. Sharpe, New York.

Neuberger, Egon, 1979, "Classifying economic systems", in Morris Bornstein, editor, *Comparative Economic Systems: Models and Cases*, Fourth Edition, Richard D. Irwin, Illinois, 19-27.

Research Group of Macroeconomic Management, Economic Institute, Chinese Academy of Social Sciences, 1987. "Review and reflection of investment system reforms", *Economic Research* (Jingji Yanjiu), No. 5.

Shambaugh, David L., 1989. "The fourth and fifth plenary sessions of the 13th CCP Central Committee", *The China Quarterly*, 120, 859-62.

Shen, L. and Y. Dai, 1990. "Formation, defect and origin of the economy divided by dukes or princes under emperor in China," *Economic Research* (Jingji Yanjiu), No. 3.

Shi, X., and J. Liu, 1989. "Economist must primarily esteem history and fact: review on ten Years in China's reform", *Economic Research* (Jingji Yanjiu), No. 2.

Shirk, Susan, 1989. "The political economy of Chinese industrial reform", in Victor Nee and David Stark, editors, *Remaking the Economic Institutions of Socialism*, Stanford University Press, California, 328-62.

Study Group in Institute of Economics, CASS, 1989. "Reflections on the reform theory of socialist economic system", *Economic Research* (Jingji Yanjiu), No. 10.

Taylor, Jefferey R., 1988. "Rural employment trends and the legacy of surplus labour, 1978-86", *The China Quarterly*, 116, 736-66.

Wang, Zhigang, 1987. "Symposium on fundamental theory and methodology of China's contemporary macroeconomic research convened by our editorial office", *Economic Research* (Jingji Yanjiu), No. 7.

Wong, Christine P.W., 1987, "Between plan and market: The role of the local sector in post-Mao China", *Journal of Comparative Economics*, 11, 385-398.

World Bank, 1988. *China: Finance and Investment.*

Zhao, Suisheng, 1990. "On the failure of economic reform in China", *Chinese Intellectual*, Vol.5, Spring.

Chapter 12

MARKET-ORIENTED REFORM AND FISCAL POLICY

Mario I. Blejer and György Szapáry[1]

One of the most prominent economic developments of this decade--a development with perhaps a modest immediate impact on the world economy but with the potential to have a substantial impact in the future--is the spreading and deepening of market-oriented economic reforms in centrally planned economies (CPEs). Initiated in Yugoslavia and Hungary, boldly pursued in China, and now also being experimented within the Soviet Union, Poland, and elsewhere, these reforms carry the potential to dramatically increase the efficiency of these economies and expand their role in the global economy.[2] Recognizing that the rigidities inherent in central planning have seriously inhibited the efficient allocation and use of resources and have not provided adequate incentives for productivity gains, CPEs have moved to enhance freedom of choice for economic agents in the decision-making process and strengthen the role of market forces through the gradual removal of administrative controls and the fostering of competition. Even when basic structures, such as widespread state ownership of productive factors, have not been radically changed, reforms

---

[1] The authors are grateful for comments and suggestions from Bela Balassa, Gerard Belanger, David Burton, Steven Dunaway, Martin Fetherston, Stanley Fischer, Peter Heller, Shogo Ishii, Mohsin Khan, Linda Koenig, George Kopits, Mihaly Kupa, Piroska Nagy, Barry Naughton, Gur Ofer, Dwight Perkins, Louis Putterman, Douglas Scott, Vito Tanzi, Gene Tidrick, Christine Wallich, and Shahid Yusuf. The usual disclaimer applies.
[2] On the Hungarian reforms, see, for example, Kornai (1980a and 1986), de Fontenay et al. (1982), Marer (1986), and Brada and Dobozi(1988). On the reforms in the U.S.S.R, see Hough (1986) and Goldman (1987); the latter includes a chapter on the Chinese reform and its relevance for Soviet economic reforms. On the general subject of reforms in CPEs, see U.S. Congress Joint Economic Committee (1986), Dembinski (1988), Hardt and McMillan (1988), Littlejohn (1988), and Winiecki (1988).

have aimed at introducing elements that replicate free-market conditions, inducing economic agents to behave and react as they would in a competitive environment. As a result, the role of central planning has diminished and, in the design of economic policy, more emphasis is being given to the use of indirect levers of macroeconomic management to regulate the behavior of increasingly autonomous economic agents. These systemic changes have altered the functions and objectives of macroeconomic policy instruments, requiring their adaptation to the changing needs.

I. THE REFORM PROCESS

Although the reform process has affected the whole range of policy implementation, the evolution has been particularly marked in the case of fiscal policy. Under strict central planning, the limited objective of fiscal policy is to administratively allocate resources by directly regulating the rate of capital accumulation and by maintaining household incomes at a level consistent with the availability of consumer goods.[3] Tax policy as such does not fulfill a major function, since the private sector plays only a minor role in the production process and state enterprises are required to remit all their surplus funds to the government. Thus, the primary instrument of fiscal policy under central planning is government expenditure. Government funds are channeled back to enterprises through the financing of investment and working capital and in the form of subsidies. Therefore, in addition to its overall allocative function, the budget plays an important redistributive role by shifting resources among industries, sectors, and geographic regions. The level of expenditure is essentially determined by the quantitative output and investment targets set out in the plan and, during periods of overheating, cutbacks in expenditure are used to reduce inflationary and balance of payments pressures.

Within the reform process, as economic agents are increasingly guided by market signals, macroeconomic management requires the use of indirect levers and thus a consistent set of new policy instruments is needed. Fiscal policy becomes a central component of such a set, with its macroeconomic role therefore enhanced. Despite the rapid growth of literature dealing with the reform process, relatively little attention has been paid to the changing role of fiscal policy and to other fiscal aspects of the reforms. This is so, perhaps, because the focus has been on agricultural and enterprise reforms--the two cardinal elements of economic transformation in CPEs.

---

[3] See Fetherston (1983) for a discussion of fiscal policy and Wanless (1985) for a discussion of taxation in CPEs; both provide a description of selected country cases.

However, the recent bouts of inflation in China, Hungary, and Poland--with the latter two also experiencing external problems--have highlighted the importance as well as the difficulties in maintaining macroeconomic stability as the reforms proceed. Given the important role that fiscal policy should play within this context, its evolving functions in CPEs deserve to be carefully analyzed, particularly with a view to assessing the extent to which fiscal policy may contribute to the cause and/or to the cure of internal and external imbalances during the reform process. This paper attempts to undertake such an analysis by examining the case of China.

In the new system of economic management emerging in China, the main macroeconomic function of budgetary policies is to provide the Government with an effective policy tool to manage aggregate demand. To achieve this task, it is clear that fiscal instruments should be flexible and, at the same time, provide policymakers with a fair degree of control and with predictable options and results. Flexibility, however, does not imply that policy regulations have to be loose but that the central authorities have to possess the ability to adapt and change the rules, which have to be precise and transparent, in a timely manner in response to evolving circumstances. How well can fiscal policy in China fulfill this role under present circumstances? To answer this question, it is necessary to consider the characteristics of the existing policy instruments, as currently designed and applied, and assess how suitable they are to serve as efficient tools for short-term macroeconomic management. A second important question regarding the capacity of fiscal policy to fulfill its macroeconomic task relates to whether there are built-in elements in the reform process that tend to create fiscal imbalances. To evaluate this aspect, it is necessary to assess the ability of the emerging system to avoid a deterioration of public finances without implementing policies that negate the basic intent of the reforms. To this end, a review of recent fiscal trends and an analysis of the underlying forces behind those trends are needed.

The purpose of this paper is to provide some answers to these questions and to draw a number of general implications from the Chinese experience. Although it focuses mainly on the analysis of the revenue side, where the nature of the reforms is more unique and their policy implications more complex, it also addresses some expenditure issues, principally in the context of their consistency with the need to maintain macroeconomic balance.

The paper is organized as follows: Section II provides a brief background description of the nature and achievements of the reforms in China. Section III briefly reviews budgetary developments from the beginning of the reforms, also providing some perspective on the structure of China's public finances relative to the revenue and expenditure structure of other countries. Section IV then analyzes, from a forward-looking perspective, the impact of reforms on government finances. Finally, Section V presents some concluding remarks.

II. ECONOMIC REFORMS IN CHINA

For the last ten years, China's economy has been undergoing a profound transformation associated with wide-ranging reforms aimed at decentralizing the decision-making process; increasing reliance on market forces in the goods, capital, and exchange markets; and opening up China's economy to the outside world. The economic, institutional, and sociopolitical characteristics of CPEs are, of course, not uniform, nor have been the approaches to reforms. China has many characteristics that set it apart from most other CPEs, such as its large size and population, its relatively low level of economic development, the relative importance of the rural sector, and the strong tradition of regional autonomy. These factors have exerted considerable influence on China's approach to reform, but there are indeed lessons that can be generalized from the Chinese experience and that are relevant for other CPEs as they, too, proceed with their reforms.

A description of the process of reform in China is beyond the scope of this paper and is, in any case, the subject of an extensive literature of its own.[4] Some background, however, is necessary to understand the economic and institutional setting within which fiscal policy has evolved in China.

The reforms started in the rural areas with the introduction of the household responsibility system, which gave farmers increased autonomy in deciding the price and product composition of their output. At the same time, measures were taken to allow and legalize the transfer of land use rights -- steps meant to encourage investment by farmers in agriculture.[5] From 1984, the focus shifted to urban areas, with policies to increase autonomy of state enterprises. The objective was to find ways that, while

---

[4] See, in particular, Perkins (1988), Harding (1987), and Riskin (1987); all three contain good bibliographies of the recent literature on China's economic reforms. See also Chow (1985), Perry and Wong (1985), Wong (1985), World Bank (1985), U.S. Congress Joint Economic Committee (May 1986), Perkins (1986), Balassa (1987), Rabushka (1987), Reynolds (1987a and 1987b), Bettelheim (1988), and Burki (1988).

[5] The nontransferability of land use rights has inhibited investment in agriculture. For a discussion of agricultural reforms in China, see, for example, Lardy (1983 and 1986), Griffin (1984), Perkins and Yusuf (1984), Walker (1984), Putterman (1985), and Wiens (1987).

preserving the basic framework of state ownership, could allow the separation of management from ownership. To this end, the authorities moved toward various forms of management contracts, called the contract responsibility system, under which the management of the enterprise undertakes certain contractual obligations vis-a-vis the government--typically involving minimum output and profit targets--in exchange for greater freedom over investment decisions, price and wage policy, etc.[6] A further aspect of reforms was the development of nonstate activities, allowing collectives and individuals to own and operate enterprises. By 1987, nonstate enterprises accounted for approximately 40 percent of industrial production.[7] Parallel to these measures, associated reforms were initiated in prices, taxes, the financial structure, and the foreign trade and exchange systems. The reforms have contributed to impressive economic growth: real GNP grew by an average of almost 10 percent per annum during 1979-88, compared with about 4 percent during the preceding two decades. Living standards have increased substantially in both rural and urban areas. Exports have diversified and grown rapidly, more than doubling their share in GNP (to over 13 percent).[8] The rapid growth in incomes has been accompanied by a substantial increase in household savings, allowing a high rate of investment without excessive reliance on foreign borrowing. However, the reforms have also created new problems for macroeconomic management, as decentralization unleashed productive forces that have at times led to expansionary pressures that the Government was not able to immediately control.[9] Most recently, these pressures have led to a surge in inflation to the highest level experienced in China since 1949.[10]

---

[6] For a discussion of industrial reforms in China, see, for example, Byrd (1982), Field (1984), and Tidrick and Chen (1987).

[7] Nonstate enterprises include collective, household, and individual enterprises. Collective enterprises account for most of the nonstate enterprises. The degree of autonomy of collective enterprises vis-a-vis local authorities varies, but generally these enterprises have much greater freedom in decision making, operate in a more competitive market environment, and face harder budget constraints than state enterprises. See World Bank (1989b).

[8] For a discussion of China's expanding role in world trade, see, for example, Lardy (1987).

[9] Carver (1986) and Naughton (1987 and 1988) discuss issues of macroeconomic disequilibrium and management in China under reforms. The evolving role of monetary policy in China is examined in De Wulf and Goldsbrough (1986), and Szapary (1989). Wolf (1985) discusses the general framework within which macroeconomic disequilibrium and stabilization can be analyzed in CPEs.

[10] The process of inflation in China is examined in Feltenstein and Farhadian (1987), and Feltenstein and Ha (1988).

The Chinese economy is characterized by a mixed structure, under which the role of central planning has been substantially reduced, while that of market mechanisms has been expanded. This structure is still evolving and a distinctive feature of the present stage is a "two-track" price system associated with extensive use of bargaining mechanisms. Typically, the producer, that is, the farmer or the enterprise, negotiates with the Government a production quota that has to be sold at regulated prices, but output in excess of the quota can be sold at market prices or at prices negotiated between buyers and sellers within government-guided limits.[11] In this system, production decisions at the margin are influenced by market signals, even though a substantial proportion of transactions still takes place at regulated prices.[12] Similarly, China maintains a dual exchange rate system, under which a proportion of foreign trade is transacted at a floating rate that is substantially more depreciated than the officially administered exchange rate.

The two-track system has tended to reduce price distortions and increase competition and efficiency. However, it has also constrained the efficient use of macroeconomic policy instruments, because the Government has had to deal with situations where different producers face different input and output prices for the production of the same goods, making it difficult to evaluate gains in efficiency and to predict with some degree of certainty the impact of specific policy measures. The situation is further complicated by the substantial autonomy local governments have in regulating prices, setting production quotas, and controlling interregional and foreign trade.[13]

China's leaders have been aware of these difficulties and reforms were envisaged as a transition to a system under which most prices were to be determined by market forces. The challenge was to adapt and develop the appropriate macroeconomic instruments, such as fiscal policy, needed to govern the allocation of resources and manage the economy under China's evolving economic structure.

---

[11] A characteristic of this system is the bargaining for low output quotas and high, administratively priced, input quotas.

[12] Currently, approximately 30-40 percent of retail sales takes place at market prices and a similar proportion of sales is subject to state-fixed prices. The rest is subject to "guided" prices; these prices typically move closely in line with market prices. The dual-price system in China's industrial sector is discussed in Byrd (1987) and Wu and Zhao (1987).

[13] There is a good discussion of the role of local governments in China's economic development in Shirk (1985) and Wong (1985a and 1987).

III. BUDGETARY DEVELOPMENTS WITHIN THE REFORM PROCESS

The budgetary developments described here refer to the state budget that consolidates the financial operations of the central and local governments. Local governments are all those below the national level; thus, the budgets of provinces, counties, municipalities, and townships are included.[14]

A. Tax Reforms and Trends in Revenue

Reform of the tax system has been an important part of China's economic reforms. Prior to 1979, enterprises remitted all their surplus funds to the budget and, in turn, the Government undertook to provide finance for their investment and working capital requirements. Enterprises faced a set of administratively determined input and output prices and were not held responsible for their financial results; instead, their main responsibility was to fulfill quantitative output targets established under the plan. Enterprises, therefore, had little incentive to improve efficiency and productivity, or to pursue profits and avoid losses that were covered by the Government.

The enterprise reforms aimed, as discussed above, at increasing productivity by enhancing the enterprises' decision making autonomy and by making them responsible for their financial results. To attain this objective, it was necessary to allow enterprises to retain a portion of their profits that could be used for investment and for incentive payments to management and labor in the form of bonuses. Therefore, the Chinese authorities began in 1978 to experiment with profit retention schemes and profit taxation for selected enterprises. In light of these experiences, in 1983 the authorities initiated a changeover for all enterprises from profit transfers to income taxation. By 1986, almost all enterprise profits were subject to taxation rather than being fully remitted to the Government.

Profit taxation has undergone several changes since its institution. One

---

[14] The presentation of budgetary data follows the format of the International Monetary Fund's Manual on Government Finance Statistics and therefore differs from that in national sources. The main differences involve (1) the treatment of foreign and domestic nonbank borrowing that in the national presentation is treated as revenue, while in the Government Financial Statistics format it is considered as financing; (2) the treatment of certain subsidies that are deducted from revenue in the national presentation rather than added to expenditure; and (3) the inclusion of off-budget construction expenditures that are excluded from the national budget presentation.

of the distinctive features of the current system is the lack of uniformity and the much larger degree of discretion it exhibits compared with the tax systems of market economies. China has a 55 percent income tax rate for medium-sized and large-sized state-owned enterprises and a number of different rates for small, collective, and household enterprises.[15] However, on top of the regular income tax, an adjustment tax has been applied to compensate for differential profitability due to factors external to the enterprise, such as the structure of administered output prices in relation to the evolution of input costs, particularly raw materials. Since the adjustment tax is designed to serve as an equalizer, it is applied at different rates that vary, sometimes significantly, from case to case, depending on the particular circumstances of the enterprise. A further large element of discretion was introduced into the tax system in 1984 with the inauguration of the enterprises contract responsibility system; under this system the entire tax liability of an enterprise is negotiated on a case-by-case basis.[16]

Another aspect of tax reform was the introduction, in 1984, of four separate indirect taxes to replace the previous consolidated industrial and commercial tax.[17] In China, indirect taxes are directly collected from enterprises and, unlike in market economies, they can rarely be shifted forward because of price controls. They are used, in addition to their revenue-generating potential, to compensate for perceived variations in enterprise profitability arising from the incomplete nature of price reforms. Since potential profitability is difficult to evaluate objectively, indirect taxes contain a discretionary component that translates into a wide range of rates.[18] In fact, since many prices are still regulated, the applicable rates of the indirect taxes are determined jointly with the price of the taxable product, with one of the objectives of the tax-cum-price mix being the

---

[15] Mining enterprises involved in oil, natural gas, coal, and mineral production are subject to a progressive resource tax on profits. Collective enterprises are subject to a special profit tax enacted in 1985 levied at rates based on a eight-grade progressive scale, ranging from 10 to 55 percent. The tax is collected by, and the revenue from it fully accrues to, the county-level authorities. Many new collective enterprises are exempted from the tax for an initial period that ranges from two to five years.

[16] A detailed description of China's tax system is provided in World Bank (1989a). See also Easson and Jinyan (1987) and World Bank (1988a).

[17] The four indirect taxes are the product tax, the value-added tax, the business tax, and the urban maintenance and construction tax. The coverage of some of these taxes has been changed over the years, partly with a view to broadening the tax base.

[18] See World Bank (1989a).

Table 1 China: Government Revenue, 1978-1988 1/
(In percent of GNP)

	1978	1979-81	1982-84	1985-87	1988 2/
Total revenue	34.0	30.8	27.8	25.5	19.0
Revenue from enterprises	20.4	17.5	12.9	8.1	5.0
Of which: Profit remittances	(18.9)	(16.5)	(11.8)	(0.8)	(0.3)
Profit tax	(1.5)	(1.0)	(1.1)	(7.3)	(4.7)
Taxes on:					
Income and profits 3/	21.2	18.3	13.8	7.7	5.3
Goods and services 4/	11.2	10.8	10.4	10.9	8.7
International trade	0.8	0.9	1.1	1.8	1.0
Other taxes	--	--	1.5	3.6	2.7
Nontax revenue 5/	0.8	0.8	1.0	1.4	1.3

Source: China, Ministry of Finance.

1/ Total revenue includes nontax revenue.
2/ Calculated by using the original budget estimates and a GNP estimate based on
a rate of growth of 11 percent of real GNP and 20 percent in prices.
3/ Including profit remittances.
4/ Includes product, value added, and business taxes.
5/ Excluding profit remittances.

equalization of profits.[19] One of the most salient features of the evolution of government revenue since the beginning of the reforms has been the continuous decline of total revenue as a ratio of GNP, from 34 percent in 1978 to less than 20 percent estimated in the 1988 budget (Table 1). The main reason for this trend has been the steady fall in revenue from the enterprise sector (direct taxation plus remittances). Although part of this fall has been the intended and desirable outcome of the decentralization process, the declining trend also reflects, as discussed in the next section, the unintended tax consequences of the reforms.

Compared with other countries, the level of revenue relative to national income is still somewhat higher in China than in countries with comparable per capita income, although the difference has narrowed considerably since the late 1970s (Table 2). On the other hand, compared to other CPEs, China's revenue level is substantially lower. This reflects, in part, the absence of social security contributions to the budget in China, where

---

[19] Note that this practice runs counter to the objective of letting profits serve as a guide to resource allocation. Their cascading nature, however, makes an accurate tailoring of these taxes difficult to achieve.

Table 2. International Comparison of Revenue 1/

Country Group	Per Capita Income 2/ (U.S. dollars)	Revenue as a percent of GNP/GDP	Individual Income Tax	Corporate Profit Tax	Taxes on Goods and Services	Taxes on International Trade	Social Security Contributions
			(In percent of total revenue)				
China							
1978	215	34.0	--	60.0 3/	32.9	2.4	--
1988	300 2/	19.0	--	26.2 3/	45.6	5.5	--
Low-income countries	265	16.7	8.3	9.6	26.3	32.6	2.2
Middle-income countries	1,720	25.0	9.7	17.8	24.5	17.8	6.7
Industrial market economies	11,210	33.9	26.6	7.6	25.2	2.1	24.8
Centrally planned economies	...	50-80 4/	1.0-8.0	30-64 3/	13-30	...	0.5-12.5
Hungary	2,020	60.7	1.4	18.0	27.6	5.4	20.1

Sources: International Monetary Fund, Government Financial Statistics Yearbook, 1987; World Bank, World Development Report 1988; and Wanless (1985).

1/ The country composition of the low-income and middle-income countries and industrial market economies is that found in the World Bank's World Development Report 1988; the revenue data for these countries have been derived from statistics in the International Monetary Fund's Government Financial Statistics Yearbook, 1987. These data do not necessarily refer to the same year for all countries; the years range from 1980 to 1986 (depending on the availability of data), but for the bulk of the countries the data refer to 1985-86. The data for centrally planned economies are taken from Wanless (1985) and refer to 1981 or 1982; the countries included are Czechoslovakia, the German Democratic Republic, Poland, Romania, and the U.S.S.R. The data for Hungary have been derived from national sources and refer to 1984-86.

2/ Refers to 1986.
3/ Includes profit remittances.
4/ As a percent of net material product.

retirement benefits--as well as other welfare benefits such as education and health care--are still largely the responsibility of the enterprise sector. Despite the changes brought about by the reforms, China's tax structure still has more in common with the tax structure of CPEs than with that of other countries. Profit taxes still make up a relatively large part of revenue--a characteristic of CPEs where a substantial portion of revenue comes from the socialized enterprise sector. Other characteristics that China shares with CPEs are the very low level--in fact, in the case of China, the virtual absence--of individual income taxation and the low level of taxes on foreign trade.[20] In addition, China relies relatively more heavily on domestic indirect taxes than any of the other groups of countries. However, since indirect taxes in China often cannot be shifted through price changes because of price controls, these taxes become akin to a profit tax as their incidence falls fully on the enterprise.

B. Trends in Public Expenditure

The reforms also had a profound impact on public expenditure which, as a ratio of GNP, fell from 34 percent in 1978 to an estimated 21 percent in the 1988 budget (Table 3). Most of the reduction took place in capital outlays. The decentralization of the decision-making process and the larger profit retention by the enterprises have naturally meant a reduction in the Government's role in financing investment. Consequently, capital expenditure relative to GNP more than halved over the last decade. Concurrently, a growing proportion of investment by enterprises has been financed by self-owned funds and bank loans. Within current expenditure, the level of defense spending has fallen the most as the Government demobilized about one million persons.[21]

Subsidies, after rising substantially in the early years of the reforms, remained broadly unchanged at approximately 6 percent of GNP. There are two types of subsidies provided through the budget in China--consumption and enterprise subsidies. Initially, consumption subsidies rose sharply as the Government provided compensation to urban consumers for price increases arising from the agricultural reforms and the liberalization of agri-

---

[20] It should be noted, however, that efforts have been made to tax individual incomes which have increased substantially as a consequence of the reforms. As a result, receipts from personal income taxes, while still very low, increased in importance in 1988.

[21] Simultaneously, a considerable number of military plants were converted to civilian use. Many of these factories, which were typically located in remote areas in the interior of the country ("third front" factories) for security reasons, were encouraged to relocate to the cities and coastal areas. See Naughton (1988a).

Table 3 China: Government Expenditure, 1978-1988
(in percent of GNP)

	1978	1979-81	1982-84	1985-87	1988 1/
Total expenditure	33.8	34.1	29.4	27.1	21.1
Current expenditure	19.1	22.6	21.8	19.6	15.7
Of which:					
Defense	4.6	4.6	3.1	2.1	1.5
Economic services	4.9	4.2	3.2	2.6	1.9
Subsidies	3.2	6.4	7.0	6.1	5.3
To enterprises	(1.0)	(0.9)	(1.4)	(3.0)	(2.8)
Other 2/	(2.2)	(5.5)	(5.6)	(3.1)	(2.5)
Capital expenditure	14.7	11.5	7.6	7.5	5.4

Source: China, Ministry of Finance.

1/ See footnote 2 to Table 1.
2/ Includes price subsidies on consumption goods (daily necessities) and subsidies to agricultural inputs.

cultural price controls. Subsequently, these subsidies declined as a ratio of GNP, in line with the policy of relying on increases in productivity and wages rather than on subsidies to maintain and enhance living standards. On the other hand, subsidies to cover enterprise losses have increased steadily. Essentially, higher enterprise losses have arisen from the rigidity of administered prices in the face of increasing costs.

In China, as in other CPEs, the level of government expenditure is not a very good indicator of the role of the state in the economy, since the Government, as owner of enterprises, has many other means of command over resources, which is not typically the case in market economies. Nevertheless, some perspective might be gained from an international comparison. As shown in Table 4, the level of expenditure in China is slightly lower than in low-income countries and substantially lower than in middle-income and industrial countries. It is only about one third of the level of expenditure in Hungary, another CPE undergoing important reforms. The difference vis-a-vis the countries other than Hungary is due essentially to the virtual absence of social security and welfare payments from the government budget in China. Compared to Hungary, a further major source of difference is that subsidies and transfers are much higher in Hungary, owing mainly to substantial subsidies to exports to COMECON

Table 4. International Comparison of Expenditure 1/

Country Group	Per Capita Income 2/ (U.S. dollar)	Expenditure as a Percent of GNP/GDP	Capital	Current	Social Security and Welfare	Interest Payments	Subsidies and Current Transfers
				(As percent of total expenditure)			
China							
1978	215	33.8	43.5	56.5	--	n.a.	9.3
1988	300 2/	21.1	25.6	74.4	--	1.1	25.1
Low-income countries	265	22.8	21.7	78.3	4.4	8.4	14.0
Middle-income countries	1,720	29.5	21.0	79.0	10.3	11.5	16.4
Industrial market economies	11,210	37.5	6.5	93.5	36.6	11.7	35.5
Hungary	2,020	62.7	14.8	85.2	20.0	1.1	38.9

Sources: See Table 2.

1/ See footnote 1 to Table 2.
2/ Refers to 1986.

countries, as well as higher consumer, agricultural, and housing subsidies. In China, however, there are substantial hidden subsidies, for example, in the form of artificially low interest rates and an overvalued administered exchange rate, which are not reflected in the budget.

C. Fiscal Policy Stance

Prior to the reforms, balanced budgets were emphasized and the government budget recorded small surpluses almost every year for three decades. In the initial years of the reforms, the budget was characterized by large deficits, averaging over 3 percent of GNP per annum (Table 5). Beginning in 1981, the Government felt it should shift emphasis of macroeconomic policies toward stabilization and that budgetary deficits should be controlled. Reflecting this policy, the deficit, while fluctuating from one year to another, fell to as low as 0.5 percent in 1985. However, since 1985, the deficit has been rising again, as there has been a renewed tendency for revenue to fall faster than expenditure as a ratio of GNP.

In the early years of the reforms, more than 80 percent of the deficits were financed by the People's Bank of China, the central bank. In 1981, the Government began issuing bonds and, since then, such bonds have financed an increasing proportion of the deficit. Foreign borrowing has also become a growing source of finance, averaging over 25 percent per annum of the total financing of the deficit during 1986-88. Until recently, government borrowing from the central bank had not significantly contributed to monetary expansion. That has changed since 1987, however, with such borrowing contributing importantly to reserve money growth. When seen against the increase in inflationary pressure,[22] the fiscal deficit and its financing become factors in the inflationary process, bringing the budget into the center of macroeconomic management. This is more significantly so in view of the accommodating stance of credit policy toward enterprises and given the obstacles to implementing restrictive monetary policies.[23]

IV. THE FISCAL IMPACT OF ECONOMIC REFORMS
A. Analytical Considerations

Against the background of the previous description, one can now

---

[22] Since 1986, the rate of inflation has risen substantially, with the increase in the retail price index, including both controlled and market prices, reaching approximately 26 percent during the 12 months ended in January 1989. The increase in market prices was even higher.

[23] On the constraints on monetary policy in the context of China's reforms, see Szapary (1989).

Table 5 China: Budget Deficit and Financing, 1979-1988

	1979	1980	1981	1982	1983	1984	1985	1986	1987	1988 1/
					(In percent of GNP)					
Budget deficit	-5.2	-3.3	-1.3	-1.4	-1.7	-1.6	-0.5	-2.0	-2.4	-2.1
Financing	5.2	3.3	1.3	1.4	1.7	1.6	0.5	2.0	2.4	2.1
Domestic	4.3	2.9	0.6	1.5	1.5	1.3	0.5	1.4	1.8	1.5
People's Bank of China	(4.3)	(2.9)	(-0.5)	(0.6)	(0.8)	(0.7)	(-0.2)	(0.7)	(1.3)	(--)
Nonbank	(--)	(--)	(1.1)	(0.9)	(0.7)	(0.6)	(0.7)	(0.7)	(0.5)	(1.5)
Foreign	0.9	0.4	0.7	-0.1	0.2	0.3	0.1	0.6	0.6	0.6
					(As percent of total deficit)					
Domestic	82.5	84.9	44.8	102.8	88.5	82.9	97.6	71.7	76.5	72.9
People's Bank of China	(82.5)	(84.9)	(-39.7)	(40.8)	(44.8)	(42.9)	(-51.2)	(38.0)	(56.4)	(--)
Nonbank	(--)	(--)	(84.5)	(62.0)	(43.8)	(40.0)	(148.8)	(33.7)	(20.1)	(72.9)
Foreign	17.5	15.1	55.2	-2.8	11.5	17.1	2.4	28.3	23.5	27.1

Source: China, Ministry of Finance.

1/ See footnote 2 to Table 1.

analyze the impact that the reforms have had on China's public finances, and assess, with a particular focus on revenue, the potential policy implications of the deepening of the reform process.

Four aspects of the reform's fiscal consequences are discussed in this section. In the area of government revenue, the issues that need examination relate to the factors behind the very slow growth of receipts from the enterprise profit tax and the consequent steady decline in total revenue as a share of national income. The reform, by allowing enterprises to retain a significant proportion of their profits and giving them greater freedom of decision over the use of these profits, necessarily reduces the intermediation role of the budget. Therefore, the decline in revenue relative to GNP has been, to a large extent, intended and has been a natural consequence of the reform process. However, beyond this policy objective, there are additional consequences arising from the reform process that are contributing toward a continuous and unintended reduction in the level of government revenue.

The ways in which the reforms have been implemented seem to have led to the emergence of a long-term elasticity of tax revenue significantly below unity and an erosion of the corporate tax base itself (e.g., the taxable profits of the enterprises). Moreover, the way in which another integral part of the reforms, the growing decentralization of fiscal authority to lower levels of government has been implemented, has tended to reduce the revenue that is transferred to the central government, a development that also has potential implications for macroeconomic management. These three aspects of revenue developments are discussed here in detail. In addition, some expenditure issues associated with reforms are also discussed. A reduction in the intermediation role of the budget necessitates a cut in government spending commensurate with the decline in resources transferred to the budget. The concern in this area is that the use of resources through the budget is being reduced at a slower pace than government revenue and that a possible consequence of the deepening of reforms may be an intensification of this trend.

An important factor in the reduced income elasticity of revenue is the contract responsibility system that, in most cases, has introduced a degree of regressivity into the enterprise income tax. As noted, the contract responsibility system for state enterprises was introduced in 1984 to increase efficiency by providing greater decision-making autonomy to enterprise managers. The system, which has been extended to most state-owned enterprises since 1987, involves a contractual agreement between the management of the enterprise and its owner--that is, the central or local government.[24] The management contracts typically cover a period ranging from three to five years and stipulate a minimum amount of profit to be realized and/or tax to be paid to the Government each year; profits above the contracted amount--which usually is either the amount of profit realized in the year prior to the signing of the contract or some fixed rate of increase over that amount--are fully retained by the enterprise or taxed at a lower rate. Firms that fail to meet their minimum profit objective must, in principle, pay their minimum tax obligation from self-owned funds. Currently, about 90 percent of medium-sized and large-sized state enterprises operate under the contract responsibility system.

From the fiscal point of view, the expectation was that the contract system would expand the tax base in the longer run through improving enterprise performance. However, the intended results are weakened by the way the tax obligations are set in the contracts. Since below-quota profits are subject to a flat tax and above-quota profits are taxed at a lower (or zero) rate, enterprises retain an increasingly larger portion of their total profits as output and profits expand, resulting, in this manner, in an elasticity of less than unity for the enterprise profit tax.[25] The relationship between average, marginal, and statutory rates implied by this characteristic example is depicted in Figure 1. Note that if contracts are strictly enforced, the elasticity of the profit tax actually increases from zero to 0.5 at the quota level; but, although continuing to rise as profit increase above the quota, it remains consistently below unity.[26]

---

[24] The central government owns many of the largest state enterprises, but most of the state enterprises are owned by local governments at the provincial, municipal, and county levels.

[25] The tax/contract relationship can be formalized to illustrate the type of problems posed by the contract system and the factors affecting the elasticity of revenue. An example could be useful to illustrate the point. A typical contract embodying the type of continuously decreasing average tax rate and the below-unity elasticity implied by the system is provided in the case of the Beijing Broadcast Equipment Industrial Corporation. The 1987 contract stipulates that a minimum of Y 10.6 billion in profits should be realized, which, regardless of the actual result achieved, will be taxed at the statutory 55 percent enterprise income tax rate. This guarantees to the Government an income tax revenue of Y 5.8 billion. Any excess of profit over Y 10.6 billion would be taxed at the rate of 27.5 percent, therefore reducing the average tax rate below the statutory rate. For other examples, see World Bank (1989a).

[26] Clearly, if the contracts are nonenforceable downward--that is, if profits below the quota are only taxed at the statutory rate on realized profits rather than on the quota amount (a practice that seems to take place in some instances)--the elasticity falls from unity below the quota to 0.5 at the quota level.

As currently implemented, the contract system not only works toward reducing the tax/GNP ratio--a problem in itself if the level of expenditure is not falling commensurately--but also limits the flexibility in using tax policy for macroeconomic management. Although it could be argued that long-term contracts are beneficial in encouraging efficiency improvements, by fixing contracts for several years, the system has constrained the ability of the central government to introduce new revenue measures in a timely manner, or to alter current ones, in order to meet changing economic circumstances. The loss of flexibility is all the more serious as the decreasing average tax rate embodied in most contracts tends to reduce built-in stabilizers and to introduce a procyclical aggregate demand element into the tax system.

B. Erosion of Profits

The second reason for the declining trend in revenue from the profit tax--and to some extent from indirect taxes--is related to factors that have had a negative effect on the tax base itself, namely, taxable enterprise profits. While aggregate data on enterprise profits are not available, data on profits of state-owned enterprises with independent accounting, which account for over half of industrial output, declined from 13.5 percent of GNP in 1980 to about 7 percent in 1987.[27] This trend is confirmed by estimates that show that enterprise savings declined from about 19 percent of GNP during 1979-81 to 15 percent during 1985-87;[28] given the generally regressive taxation of profits, the decline in savings points to a fall in profits. Note that, in the context of the contract system, if taxable profits fall as a proportion of GNP, the tax/income ratio will tend to decline at a compounded exponential rate.

One of the most important factors contributing to the decline in taxable profits is the continuous presence of price controls at the final product level, which has prevented many enterprises from shifting increased costs to prices. These increased costs have arisen from a variety of sources.

---

[27] Source: Statistical Yearbook of China, various issues. A survey of 17 enterprises in three cities (Beijing, Chengdu, Guangzhou) also shows that in 11 of these enterprises, gross profits declined relative to the value of output between 1983 and 1987 (information obtained by the authors on visits to these enterprises).
[28] Calculated as a residual after deducting from gross domestic saving, state budget and household savings. Gross domestic saving is calculated as gross domestic investment plus or minus the external current account balance. This estimate of savings, however, includes the extrabudgetary surpluses of local governments and is, therefore, not a fully accurate measurement of enterprise savings. (Source: Statistical Yearbook of China, various issues).

Figure 1
Tax Rates Within the Contract System

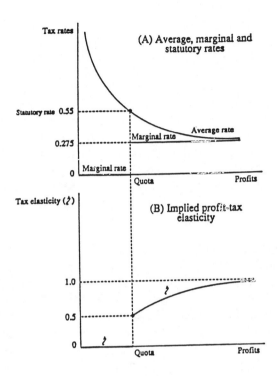

Note on Figure 1

Since at profit levels below the established quota, the tax liability is constant (and is equal to the statutory rate times the quota), the marginal tax rate is zero over that range, while the average rate falls as profits rise. Given the implied zero marginal tax rate, the resulting tax elasticity also equals zero. At the quota level, statutory and average rates coincide and, for profits beyond the quota, the marginal rate rises to 27.5 percent. Since the marginal rate then remains constant at the 27.5 percent rate, which is lower than the statutory 55 percent rate on quota profits, the average rate continues to fall, converging asymptotically toward the marginal level. Given the one-step increase in the marginal rate, the tax elasticity exhibits a jump from zero to 0.5 at the quota level and rises monotonically thereafter, although it remains always below unity since the marginal rate never exceeds the average.

most importantly from higher input prices (particularly certain types of raw materials whose prices are not tightly controlled), higher depreciation rates arising from a changeover to more realistic accounting practices, increased burden of higher indirect taxes, and a depreciation of the exchange rate.[29] In addition, the increased autonomy of enterprises in the use of their financial resources, coupled with an accommodating credit policy, has led to a relatively rapid increase in wages and benefit payments, which also has tended to dampen profits.[30] Finally, China has allowed many enterprises to deduct from pre-tax profits not only the payment of interest on loans but also the repayment of loan principal. This policy has been intended to be a transitory arrangement to put on an even footing enterprises that have to rely on bank loans and those that continue to benefit from budgetary grants to finance investment. The practice has had the effect of reducing the taxable income of enterprises, as reliance on loans to finance investment has increased under the reforms and a growing number of loans have become due.

C. Regional Decentralization

In a country of China's size, regional decentralization is dictated by efficiency considerations and the Chinese authorities have viewed the regional decentralization of fiscal powers as an integral part of the reform process. However, the direction in which such decentralization is moving affects the buoyancy of tax revenue and tends to erode the amount of revenue transferred to the central government. In China, local governments, mostly provincial and city governments, are responsible for the collection of virtually all major taxes. The revenue thus collected is shared upward with the next level of government.[31] This process of

---

[29] The nominal effective exchange rate depreciated by about 45 percent between the third quarter of 1983 and the third quarter of 1988. Furthermore, since 1987, an increasing proportion of the transactions has been carried out at foreign exchange transaction centers where the rate, which is more freely affected by market forces, is much more depreciated than the administered rate (in November 1988, the rate at the adjustment centers was about Y 7 per U.S. dollar, compared with the administered rate of Y 3.72 per U.S. dollar).

[30] Real unit labor costs in industrial enterprises rose by close to 13 percent during 1983-87 (Source: Statistical Yearbook of China).

[31] Typically, cities share with the provincial government and the latter shares with the central government. However, some cities, for example, Chongqing, Shanghai, and Tianjin, share all or part of their revenue directly with the central government. The sharing arrangements are not uniform; they are subject to negotiation and may vary from one case to another. Over the years, the revenue-sharing arrangements have undergone many changes, but, since the inception of the reforms in the late

regional decentralization has tended to depress revenue collection, particularly after the introduction of the contract responsibility system for enterprises. Although tax policy and statutory tax rates are nominally set at the national level by the central government, local governments are responsible for the negotiation of management contracts with the enterprises they own. Within the framework of these contract negotiations, local authorities have the power to set effective tax rates through the establishment of quota profits and the rate of taxation of above-quota profits. Furthermore, given the sharing rules, local authorities have a clear stake in keeping as much financial resources as possible within their territory to finance their own preferred projects and are not keen on sharing revenue with the higher levels of government. This objective is often pursued through generous tax treatment granted within the framework of management contracts. In this way resources remain within the local government's jurisprudence and local authorities can then tap these resources through "voluntary" contributions from enterprises to local projects--contributions which, of course, are not shared with the central government. Thus, while the effective "tax burden" of the enterprises is not reduced and may, in effect, be significantly higher than implied by its tax obligations, explicit tax revenue, and particularly the budgetary revenue of the central government, is eroding.

To address this problem and to provide incentives for local governments to collect and remit taxes, recent revenue-sharing arrangements, introduced mostly since 1988, are based on contracts that feature a quota arrangement, somewhat akin to the system of management contracts with enterprises. Under this system, local governments contract to remit to the higher level of government a predetermined amount of revenue and retain all or part of the revenue above the quota. Typically, as with enterprises, the quota is calculated as the revenue remitted in the year prior to the signing of the contract plus a fixed increment.[32] In some cases, the revenue to be transmitted is fixed in nominal terms for a number of years, as in the case of Shanghai. The new revenue-sharing contracts between the central and local governments further weaken the center's control over, and flexibility in, the use of fiscal policy for macroeconomic

---

1970s, the trend has been toward granting local governments a greater degree of fiscal authority and allowing them to retain more revenue. On the evolution of fiscal relations between the center and the provinces, see Donnithorne (1983), Ferdinand (1987), and Oksenberg and Tong (1987).

[32] For instance, the contract with Guangdong Province sets the amount of revenue to be transmitted to the central government during 1988-90 as the revenue transmitted in 1987 augmented by 9 percent each year.

purposes. This is so for two main reasons. First, the relatively low level of incremental revenue transfer that these contracts appear to set leaves increased amounts of resources in the hands of local governments, thereby compounding, as far as central government revenue is concerned, the revenue-depressing effects of the enterprise contract responsibility system.[33] Second, the fixed increment featured in the quota arrangement implies that the revenue transmitted to the central government is not influenced by the underlying economic conditions, which affect only the revenue accruing to the local governments. The latter do not see themselves as having overall demand management responsibilities.[34] The establishment of enterprises shielded from nation-wide competition is possible because local governments maintain power to restrict the inflow of goods from other provinces and they can also preempt the use of inputs produced in their own province.[35]

---

[33] Since the national budget consolidates all levels of government, taxes collected by local governments, but not remitted to the center, boost overall budgetary revenue. However, local governments do not tend to maintain budgetary surpluses (among other reasons, to avoid worsening their future bargaining position with the central government) and, therefore, increases in retained revenue, particularly if they arise after the budget has been approved, tend to generate higher local expenditure (which is difficult to control at the central level) and do not contribute to the improvement of the consolidated balance.

[34] The behavior of local governments is motivated primarily by local interests and not necessarily by macroeconomic considerations at the national level. Local governments see themselves as being able to influence the level of economic activity in their province but not the general level of prices in the country or the overall balance of payments. The quota arrangement tends to impart a procyclical bias to the fiscal system, a bias that, again, is compounded by the declining average tax rate on enterprise profits under the contract management system. Local governments can also expand their revenue base by setting up locally owned enterprises. When local governments are allowed to remain a higher proportion of the revenue they collect, there is added incentive for them to set up enterprises even if, from a global point of view, the creation of such enterprises may represent a misallocation of resources. Shirk (1985) and Naughton (1988c) make the same point.

[35] There is a discussion of the considerable barriers to entry in China in Naughton (1988d). This, of course, creates serious distortions in the allocation of resources from a national perspective. Finally, the quota arrangement could exacerbate the differences between poor and rich provinces, putting pressure on the central government to transfer more resources to less advanced provinces even as its own revenue base is eroding.

D. Expenditure Issues

Although the decline in government expenditure as a proportion of national income has been significant, viewed against the built-in factors that depress the elasticity of government revenue, there is a question whether the pace of spending reduction is consistent with future macroeconomic balance. The decline in the level of government expenditure has been constrained by three factors:(1) the incomplete nature of price reforms, which has resulted in increased enterprise losses financed through budgetary subsidies; (2) a perceived need to increase consumer subsidies as a way to compensate urban dwellers for the price hikes resulting from agricultural reforms and to avoid, in this manner, the strengthening of a constituency against the continuation of the reforms; and (3) the limited success of the Government in transferring investment responsibilities to enterprises in proportion to the increase in their retained earnings.

In addition to addressing these issues, the probable expenditure consequences of further reforms also need to be considered against the forces that work toward reducing the buoyancy of tax revenue. Despite the temporary halt in the pace of price reform announced in late 1988, the progressive liberalization of the goods markets--so that the bulk of transactions will be carried out at market prices--remains the core objective of the reform drive. Given a generalized downward stickiness of prices, exacerbated by the current state of excess demand, the readjustment of relative prices following any significant price liberalization is likely to result in an increase in the price level.[36] Such an increase could affect budgetary expenditure in several ways. First, higher commodity prices will raise government expenditure on goods and services, as well as capital spending, which will be affected by higher input prices. Second, price reform is likely to be accompanied by wage reform, which will increase the Government's wage bill. Third, the demand for consumer subsidies will probably rise in order to mitigate the impact of the price increases.[37] Finally, the price reform may also have an effect on subsidies to

---

[36] In the presence of a dual-track price system, the impact of price liberalization on the general level of prices depends on certain characteristics of the markets. For a theoretical discussion of these issues, see Roemer (1986).

[37] These two issues should, however, be qualified. The principal purpose of wage reform in an ongoing process of economic reform is to bring market forces to bear on the labor market and on production efficiency. Under these circumstances, a wage reform, though expenditure augmenting for the budget in the short run, enhances productivity and hence is likely to have a positive impact on revenue in the long run. Moreover, a wage reform should, eventually, result in a reduction of consumption subsidies as real wages rise.

loss-making enterprises, although the balance of this effect cannot be assessed a priori; while the freeing of prices will allow many enterprises affected by price controls to become profitable, higher input prices and wages are likely to aggravate the situation of others, increasing pressures for higher subsidies. All told, while the liberalization of prices is expected to raise efficiency and hence should contribute to a strengthening of public finances in the long run, in the short to medium term it is likely to intensify the upward pressures on expenditure. In addition to price reforms, further enterprise and welfare reforms are under way encompassing mainly housing, unemployment compensation, and pensions. Although it is difficult to estimate precisely their budgetary impact, it is safe to predict that they will tend to put additional pressure on government expenditure. Further pressure on expenditure will come from the need to increase capital spending to relieve major bottlenecks in transportation, energy, and agriculture. Against these prospects, streamlining the tax system and the revenue-sharing arrangements to enhance the elasticity of revenue becomes crucial to prevent the emergence of serious fiscal imbalances that could undermine continuation of the reforms.

V. CONCLUDING REMARKS

The central elements of economic reforms in CPEs have been the granting of greater decision-making powers to enterprises and individuals and the enhancement of the role played by market forces within the basic framework of socialist ownership. These changes impose on the policymaker the need to develop adequate instruments of indirect control over the behavior of increasingly autonomous economic agents. Among these instruments, fiscal policy plays a vital role, given its power both to control aggregate demand and to affect resource allocation. To fulfill its role within the new environment, fiscal policy needs to be refashioned as it becomes an indirect lever of economic management rather than merely a tool for the administrative allocation of resources. As in market economies, fiscal policy now has a major role to play in managing aggregate demand, especially to avoid imbalances that could derail the reform process.

In this paper, we have analyzed the evolution of fiscal policy in China with the objective of trying to answer two questions: how well can fiscal policy fulfill its new macroeconomic role, and whether there are built-in elements in the reform process that tend to create fiscal imbalances. With respect to the first question, it is clear that fiscal instruments, particularly on the revenue side, have been transformed pari passu with the changes in the economic system. However, serious conflicts are still present, particularly with regard to the revenue impact of the enterprise contract responsibility system and the revenue-sharing system set up between the center and China's provinces. Both systems are, in themselves, valuable reform instruments that have infused the Chinese economy with a dynamism often lacking in other CPEs. However, the ways in which these systems have been put into practice have weakened the ability of the central government to use fiscal policy for macroeconomic management purposes.

Problems with the current practices arise largely from the high degree of discretion they entail. As the experience with the contract responsibility system has shown, the centerpiece of the system is the case-by-case negotiation of taxes between the Government and the enterprises. This is likely to lead to taxation rules that vary from one enterprise to another and which may be very costly to change once the long-term contracts are signed. The regional revenue-sharing arrangements, by leaving increased resources in the hands of local governments and by increasing their powers to effectively set tax rates, have eroded the command of the center over the mobilization of resources and have reduced its capacity to predict the outcome of policy measures. In short, the predominance of bargaining that leads to discretionary tax policies and the way in which decentralization of fiscal authority has been implemented have reduced the flexibility of the system and weakened the effectiveness of taxation as a macroeconomic policy instrument.

Bargaining has been the means by which compromises have been reached between the need to introduce new policy instruments and the impact of these instruments on conflicting regional, sectoral, and enterprise interests. However, the discretion entailed in the bargaining process detracts from the benefits of the reforms because it makes fiscal policy less predictable and less effective. Also, discretion in the form of case-by-case negotiation of taxation tends to validate distortions that could ultimately negate the benefits of reforms. Moreover, granting greater decision-making powers to enterprises and strengthening market forces will not lead to more efficient allocation of resources if decisions at the level of the firm continue to be made in an environment of soft budget constraints. Since discretion is bound to soften the budget constraint, it works against allocative efficiency.

With respect to the second question, that is, the impact of reforms on the evolution of fiscal accounts, the Government is confronted with a policy conflict. The objective of allowing enterprises to retain and freely dispose of a larger portion of their earnings has meant, necessarily, less fiscal revenue for the Government. While the appropriate level of government revenue is difficult to assess in an economy undergoing profound trans-formation, the success of the reforms necessitates the maintenance of macroeconomic stability, which requires a degree of stability between revenue and expenditure. The need to maintain such fiscal discipline sets the broad framework within which the financial consequences of reform must be fitted. The Government needs, therefore, to either divest itself further of spending responsibilities or redress the erosion of revenue elasticity that has arisen from the manner in which the reforms are being implemented.

While there is still scope for the Government to relinquish spending responsibilities, there is increasingly limited room to reduce the level of expenditure further. Ways must therefore be found to enhance the elasticity of government revenue.

It will be difficult, however, for the Chinese authorities to prevent the continuous decline in the revenue/GNP ratio within a system in which a large portion of incomes--that is, individual incomes in both rural and urban areas--is only lightly taxed or not subject to taxation at all, while the effective tax rate on those incomes that are taxed is subject to case-by-case bargaining. One way to reverse this trend would be to increase the tax burden of enterprises across the board. Such a measure, however, is not in the spirit of the reforms, since enterprises already carry a major portion of the country's tax burden.[38] An alternative response, which would be more consistent with the objectives of the reforms, is to reduce the discretionary elements of tax policy. This could be achieved by subjecting all enterprises to a flat uniform income tax rate and by allowing only after-tax profits to be subject to negotiation and contracting between state enterprises and their owners. Such contracted "tax" liability would be similar to the payment of dividends to shareholders, in this case the Government. As long as the contracting system is in use, another approach could be to rebase the quota, that is, to adjust each year the quota profit to reflect the previous year's realized profit. If such an adjustment were made, the decrease in the tax revenue/GNP ratio implied by the current practice of fixing a constant quota profit for several years could be avoided. Another response would be to broaden the tax base by finding alternative revenue sources, such as taxation of those sectors--like agriculture and households--that have gained from recent policies. Raising indirect taxes does not offer an alternative solution so long as the incidence of these taxes cannot be shifted owing to price controls.

As regards the revenue-sharing arrangements between the center and provinces, one problem is that they rely excessively on bargaining which

---

[38] In addition, there has been a tendency for a "clawback" of enterprise profits through surcharges on "extra" profits and taxes on extrabudgetary receipts. Such surcharges and ad-hoc taxes are, of course, inimical to the spirit of the contract system.

leads to a large degree of nonuniformity of treatment. A more important issue, however, is that the system, by leaving more resources in the hands of local governments, may encourage local authorities to use their power to restrict competition and thus lead to the establishment of noneconomic industries. The obvious solution here lies in reducing trade and entry barriers to increase competition. An issue often debated in China is the appropriate level of fiscal balance during the reform process. As mentioned before, prior to the reforms, balanced budgets were emphasized. However, the level of tolerable fiscal imbalance during and after the reforms is not necessarily the same as the level prevailing in the pre-reform system. Indeed, at least in the early stages of the reforms, the negative macroeconomic consequences of deficits might be offset by changes in the behavior of households, which are themselves reacting to the change in incentives. Before the reforms, household income grew relatively slowly; income has grown faster under the reforms, however, and the Government has been willing to give greater freedom in its disposition. This has resulted in a voluntary decision on the part of households to save a greater proportion of their income.[39] In fact, the sharp rise in the household demand for money in recent years, which partly reflects increases in voluntary savings, has allowed the Government to reap the benefits of seigniorage and finance a higher budget deficit than it would otherwise have been able to do without putting additional pressure on aggregate demand. However, the appropriateness of the fiscal balance cannot be abstracted from the stance of overall demand management policies. Clearly, if credit policy toward enterprises remains as accommodative as it has been in recent years, the room for financing budget deficits is reduced. In this context, it is necessary to mention a factor that presently works toward widening the budget deficit. There is a built-in asymmetry in the current system, in that enterprises that have benefited from reforms and have seen their profits rise are taxed less and less as a result of the declining average tax rates implied under the management contracts, while enterprises incurring losses because of price controls or other reasons have their losses covered by the budget. In other words, the budget seems to lose out on account of both profitable and nonprofitable state-owned enterprises.

Systemic reforms in CPEs involve a delicate balancing of conflicting goals where considerations of economic efficiency, social equity, ideology, and political interests are bound together in a complex relationship. A

---

[39] Household savings have grown rapidly since the start of the reforms. Qian (1988) has found that in rural areas, where welfare benefits are lacking and there are greater opportunities to invest, such as in housing, the savings rate is much higher than in urban areas.

central issue to which no satisfactory solution has yet been found in practice is how to eliminate the soft budget constraint for enterprises that now operate with greater autonomy but within the basic framework of state ownership. Fiscal policy can and must play a crucial role in hardening the budget constraint, but for this a compromise has to be found to solve the conflict between decentralization of decision making for efficiency purposes and maintenance of macroeconomic control and flexibility. Clearly, decentralization of decision making does not mean decentralization of macroeconomic instruments, which have to remain under the control of the central authorities. The need to adopt more transparent fiscal rules, while also keeping degrees of freedom to accommodate changing developments, seems to be the evident lesson to learn from the Chinese experience as other centrally planned economies also undertake market- oriented economic reforms.

References

Balassa, Bela, 1987. "China's Economic Reforms in a Comparative Perspective," *Journal of Comparative Economics*, 410-26.

Bettelheim, Charles, 1988. "Economic Reform in China," *Journal of Development Studies*, 15-49.

Brada, Josef C. and Istvan Dobozi, editor, 1988. *The Hungarian Economy in the 1980s*, Greenwich, Connecticut: Jai Press.

Burki, Shahid J., 1988. "Reform and Growth in China," *Finance and Development*, International Monetary Fund and World Bank, Washington, D.C., 46-49.

Byrd, William, 1984. "Recent Chinese Economic Reforms: Studies of Two Industrial Enterprises," *World Bank Staff Working Papers*, no. 652, Washington, D.C.: The World Bank.

Byrd, William, 1987. "The Impact of the Two-Tier Plan/Market System in China's Industry," *Journal of Comparative Economics*, 295-308.

Carver, Dean, 1986. "China's Experiment With Fiscal and Monetary Policy" in *China's Economy Looks Toward the Year 2000*, U.S. Congress, Joint Economic Committee, 1, 110-31, Washington, D.C.: Government Printing Office.

Chow, Gregory C., 1985. *The Chinese Economy*, New York: Harper and Row.

de Fontenay, Patrick, et al., 1982. *Hungary: An Economic Survey*, Occasional Paper no. 15, Washington, D.C.: International Monetary Fund.

Dembinski, Pawel H., 1988. *Les economies planifiees*, Paris: Editions du Seuil.

De Wulf, Luc and David Goldsbrough, 1986. "The Evolving Role of Monetary Policy in China," *Staff Papers, International Monetary Fund*, 209-42.

Donnithorne, Audrey, 1983. "New Light on Central-Provincial Relations," *Australian Journal of Chinese Affairs*, 97-104.

Easson, A.J. and L. Jinyan, 1987. "The Evolution of the Tax System in the People's Republic of China," *Stanford Journal of International Law*, 399-447.

Feltenstein, Andrew and Ziba Farhadian, 1987. "Fiscal Policy, Monetary Targets, and the Price Level in a Centrally Planned Economy: An Application to the Case of China," *Journal of Money, Credit, and Banking*, 137-55.

Feltenstein, Andrew and Jimin Ha, 1988. "Measurement of Repressed Inflation in China: The Lack of Coordination Between Monetary Policy and Price Controls," paper prepared for the *World Bank*.

Ferdinand, Peter, 1987. "Centre-Provincial Relations in the People's Republic of China Since the Death of Mao: Financial and Political Dimensions," *University of Warwick*, working paper no. 47.

Fetherston, Martin J., 1983. "Fiscal Developments and Issues in Selected Centrally Planned Economies," Departmental Memorandum, DM/83/72, Washington, D.C.: International Monetary Fund.

Field, Robert Michael, 1984. "Changes in Chinese Industry Since 1978," *The China Quarterly*, 742-61.

Goldman, Marshall, I., 1987. *Gorbachev's Challenge: Economic Reform in the Age of High Technology*, New York: W.W. Norton.

Griffin, Keith, editor, 1984. *Institutional Reform and Economic Development in the Chinese Countryside*, New York: M.E. Sharpe.

Harding, Harry, 1987. *China's Second Revolution: Reform After Mao*, Washington, D.C.: Brookings Institution.

Hardt, J. and C. McMillan, 1988. *Planned Economies: Confronting the Challenges of the 1980s*, Cambridge, Cambridge University Press.

Hough, J., 1986. *Opening Up the Soviet Economy*, Washington, D.C.: Brookings Institution.

Kornai, Janos, 1980a. "The Dilemmas of a Socialist Economy: The Hungarian Experience," *Cambridge Journal of Economics*, 147-57.

Kornai, Janos, 1980b. *Economics of Shortage*, Amsterdam: North-Holland.

Kornai, Janos, 1986a. "The Hungarian Reform Process: Visions, Hopes and Reality," *Journal of Economic Literature*, 1687-1737.

Kornai, Janos, 1986b. *Contradictions and Dilemmas*, Cambridge, Massachusetts: MIT Press.

Kornai, Janos, 1986c. "The Soft Budget Constraint," *Kyklos*, 3-30.

Lardy, Nicholas R., 1983. *Agriculture in China's Modern Economic Development*, Cambridge: Cambridge University Press.

Lardy, Nicholas R., 1986. "Agricultural Reform," *Journal of International Affairs*, 39, 91-104.

Lardy, Nicholas R. 1987. *China's Entry into the World Economy: Implications for Northeast Asia and the United States*, Lanham, Maryland: University Press of America.

Littlejohn, Gary, 1988. "Central Planning and Market Relations in Socialist Societies," *Journal of Development Studies*, 75-101.

Marer, Paul, 1986. "Economic Reforms in Hungary: From Central Planning to Regulated Market," in *U.S. Congress, Joint Economic Committee*, Washington, D.C.: Government Printing Office, 3, 223-97.

Naughton, Barry, 1985. "False Starts and Second Wind: Financial Reforms in China's Industrial System", in *The Political Economy of Reform in Post-Mao China*, edited by Elizabeth J. Perry and Christine Wong, Cambridge, Massachusetts: Harvard University Press, 223-52.

Naughton, Barry, 1986. "Finance and Planning Reforms in Industry," in *China's Economy Looks Toward the Year 2000*, *U.S. Congress, Joint Economic Committee*, Washington, D.C.: Government Printing Office, 1, 604-29.

Naughton, Barry, 1988a. "The Third Front: Defense Industrialization in the Chinese Interior," *The China Quarterly*, 351-86.

Naughton, Barry, 1988b. "Macroeconomic Management and System Reform in China," paper prepared for the conference on *The Chinese Developmental State: Change and Continuum*, University of Sussex.

Naughton, Barry, 1988c. "Industrial Decision Making in China," paper prepared for the *World Bank*.

Naughton, Barry, 1988d. "The Chinese Industrial Enterprise: Structure and Capabilities," paper prepared for the *World Bank*.

Naughton, Barry, 1987. "Macroeconomic Policy and Response in the Chinese Economy: The Impact of the Reform Process," *Journal of Comparative Economics*, 334-53.

Oksenberg, Michel and James Tong, 1987. "The Evolution of Central Provincial Fiscal Relations in China, 1950-83: The Formal System," University of Michigan.

Perkins, Dwight H. and Shahid Yusuf, 1984. *Rural Development in China*, Baltimore: Johns Hopkins University Press.

Perkins, Dwight H., 1986. *China: Asia's Next Economic Giant*, Seattle: University of Washington Press.

Perkins, Dwight H., 1988. "Reforming China's Economic System," *Journal of Economic Literature*, 601-45.

Perry, Elizabeth J. and Christine Wong, editors, 1985. *The Political Economy of Reform in Post-Mao China*, Cambridge, Massachusetts: Harvard University Press.

Putterman, Louis, 1985. "The Restoration of the Peasant Household as Farm Production Unit in China: Some Incentive Theoretic Analysis," in *The Political Economy of Reform in Post-Mao China*, edited by Elizabeth J. Perry and Christine Wong, Cambridge, Massachusetts: Harvard University Press, 63-82.

Qian, Yingyi, 1988. "Urban and Rural Household Saving in China," *Staff Papers, International Monetary Fund*, 592-627.

Rabushka, Alvin, 1987. *The New China: Comparative Economic Development in Mainland China, Taiwan, and Hong Kong*, Boulder, Colorado: Westview Press.

Reynolds, Bruce L., editor, 1987a. *Reform in China: Challenges and Choices*, New York: M.E. Sharpe.

Reynolds, Bruce, editor, 1987b. "Chinese Economic Reform: How Far, How Fast?" *Journal of Comparative Economics*, special issue.

Riskin, Carl, 1987. *China's Political Economy: The Quest for Development Since 1949*, Oxford University Press.

Roemer, Michael, 1986. "Simple Analysis of Segmented Markets: What Case for Liberalization?" *World Development*, 429-39.

Shirk, Susan L., 1985. "The Politics of Industrial Reform" in *The Political Economy of Reform in Post-Mao China*, edited by Elizabeth J. Perry and Christine Wong, Cambridge, Massachusetts: Harvard University Press, 195-221.

State Statistical Bureau, *People's Republic of China*, Statistical Yearbook of China (various issues).

Symposium on Enterprise Reforms in China, 1987. Diaoyutai Guest House, Beijing, October 4-10.

Szapary, Gyorgy, 1989. "Monetary Policy and System Reforms in China".

Tidrick, Gene and Jiyuan Chen, 1987. *China's Industrial Reforms*, Oxford University Press.

U.S. Congress, Joint Economic Committee, 1986. *China's Economy Looks Toward the Year 2000*, Washington, D.C.: Government Printing Office.

U.S. Congress, Joint Economic Committee, 1986. *East European Economics: Slow Growth in the 1980s*, Washington, D.C.: Government Printing Office.

Walker, Kenneth R., 1984. "Chinese Agriculture During the Period of the Readjustment, 1978-83," *The China Quarterly*, 783-812.

Wanless, P.T., 1985. *Taxation in Centrally Planned Economies*, London: Croom Helm.

Wiens, Thomas B., 1987. "Issues in the Structural Reform of Chinese Agriculture," *Journal of Comparative Economics*, 372-84.

Winiecki, J., 1988. *The Distorted World of Soviet-Type Economies*, Pittsburgh: University of Pittsburgh Press.

Wolf, Thomas A., 1985. Economic Stabilization in a Planned Economy: Towards an Analytical Framework, *Staff Papers, International Monetary Fund*, 78-131.

Wong, Christine, 1985a. "Material Allocation and Decentralization Impact of the Local Sector on Industrial Reform" in *The Political Economy of Reform in Post-Mao China*, edited by Elizabeth J. Perry and Christine Wong, Cambridge, Massachusetts: Harvard University Press.

Wong, Christine, 1985b. "The Second Phase of Economic Reforms in China," *Current History*, 260-63.

Wong, Christine, 1987. "Between Plan and Market: The Role of the Local Sector in Post-Mao China," *Journal of Comparative Economics*, 385-98.

World Bank, 1985. *China: Long-Term Development Issues and Options*, Baltimore: Johns Hopkins University Press.

World Bank, 1988. *China: Finance and Investment*, Washington, D.C.

World Bank, 1988b. *World Development Report*, Washington, D.C.

World Bank, 1989a. *China: Revenue Mobilization and Tax Policy:Issues and Options*, Washington, D.C.

World Bank, 1989b. *China: Rural Industry: Overview, Issues, and Prospects*, Washington, D.C.

World Bank, 1989c. *Enterprise Management Reforms: Issues and Options*, Washington, D.C.

Wu, Jinglian and Renwei Zhao, 1987. "The Dual Pricing System in China's Industry," *Journal of Comparative Economics*, 309-18.

Chapter 13

THE POLITICAL-ECONOMY PERSPECTIVE ON
TRADE POLICY

Robert E. Baldwin

Both economists and political scientists are engaged in developing the
theoretical structure of political economy, especially as it applies to
international relations.[1] The motivation for political scientists is their
recognition of the importance of economic factors in shaping domestic and
international political relationships in today's interdependent world. When
focussing on the goals of the political and economic actors, they define
political economy as the dynamic interactions in international relations
arising from the pursuit of power and wealth (Knorr 1973, Gilpin 1975,
Keohane, 1984). Alternatively, when focussing on the organizational
structure in which the political and economic actors operate, they define the
subject as the study of the interaction of the state and the market (Gilpin,
1988).

Many economists are also dissatisfied with the traditional confines of
their discipline. As economic analysis demonstrated the need for government intervention to overcome the failure of the market mechanism to
achieve welfare-maximizing allocations of economic resources in some
circumstances, economists began to inquire whether the political process
would function in a manner to bring about the adoption of the required
policies. This, in turn, stimulated interest in applying economic tools and
methods in analyzing the political processes by which public policy choices
are determined, and political economy is defined by some economists in
these terms. Other economists view political economy simply as the study

---

[1] Discussions of recent approaches to international political economy by political
scientists are included in Gilpin (1988) and Keohane (1984), while summaries of
recent contributions in this field by economists are presented in Frey (1984) and
Hillman (1989).

of the manner in which economic and political factors interact in the determination of public policies.

This paper examines the different approaches of economists and political scientists toward the subject with the aim of determining if integrating these approaches can provide a better framework for analyzing international economic and political relations than either discipline by itself. The political economy of nations' trade policies will be used to illustrate the explanatory methods of the two disciplines and the possibilities of a broadened analytical framework based on both.

I. CONTRASTS IN APPROACHES OF THE TWO DISCIPLINES
A. The Economist's Framework for Political Economy

In analyzing the public choice process in political markets, most economists use the same neoclassical framework that they employ in investigating the decision making process in economic markets. Households are assumed to be rational in the sense of being able to order the set of economic and social choices available to them in a consistent manner, and their preferences for these goods and services are assumed to depend only on their own consumption of these items. Each household maximizes its welfare subject to such constraints as the size of its budget and its voting power. Firms are assumed to maximize profits subject to the same types of constraints.

On the basis of this self-interest framework, economists view the public choice process as one in which households and firms are the demanders of particular public policies, while public officials are the suppliers of public policies. The nature of the policies sought by households and firms depends on the effect of the policies on their economic welfare. For example, in the simple two-good, two-factor (capital and labor) Heckscher-Ohlin model of international trade, workers in a capital-abundant country that is exporting the capital-intensive good will favor protectionist policies, since these policies will raise the price of the labor-intensive import good and thereby increase labor's real income. Capitalists will favor free trade for the opposite reason. In contrast, with a specific-factors model where capital is immobile between the two sectors and labor possesses industry-specific skills, both workers and capitalists in the import-competing industry will benefit from protection. Public officials, who also act out of economic self interest, seek to be reelected and, therefore, respond to the policy demands of those who provide the votes and campaign funds needed for reelection.

A variety of formal models have been developed to explain the determination of public policies within this self-interest framework.[2] For example, Mayer (1984), using a framework in which citizens vote directly on trade policy, shows that a country's trade policy depends on the relationship between the country's aggregate endowment ratio and the median voter's factor endowments. Stigler (1971), Peltzman (1976), and Hillman (1982) view the government as maximizing a political-support function by balancing the marginal gain in political support from those who benefit from domestic or international regulatory measures against the marginal loss in support from those who lose. Brock and Magee (1978), Findlay and Wellisz (1982) and others analyze the protection-setting process in game theoretic terms where private groups with opposing economic interests lobby public officials for government assistance. Feenstra and Bhagwati (1982) make the government itself a part of the domestic bargaining process. Hillman and Ursprung (1988) and Das (1986) are among those who include foreign private interests and governments as participants in the political process by which a country's trade policy is determined.

In such economic self-interest models, the free-rider problem is used to explain why consumers do not organize and lobby against protection, although their losses from protection often exceed the gains of producers. Trade policy has the characteristic of a public good in the sense that a beneficiary from a policy such as free trade cannot be excluded from its benefits, even if the person does not contribute to the costs of obtaining the policy. Consequently, the individual consumer, whose economic stake in whether a particular industry is protected is usually quite small, has the incentive not to reveal his or her true preferences in the hope that others will contribute to the costs of lobbying for free trade. In contrast, those import-competing producers who have a significant economic interest in the protection versus free trade decision because of their high market shares in an industry are likely to lobby actively for protection. Consequently, the protectionist option may be selected in the political market. As Olson (1965) argues, the free-rider problem may also prevent import-competing industries in which there are a large number of small firms or the concentration ratio is low from organizing into effective pro-protection lobbying groups.

Although political economy models involving a balancing of political

---

[2] These models represent examples of positive political economy. However, another important part of the field is concerned with the welfare implications of particular policy outcomes, taking into account the resources used in achieving the policy and in competing for the rents created by the policy. The papers by Krueger (1974) and Bhagwati (1980) illustrate this branch of the subject.

pressures are the most popular in economics, some economists have pursued alternative approaches. One (Staiger and Tabellini, 1987) emphasizes the time-inconsistency problem associated with discretionary policies such as tariffs. To illustrate this point, suppose that workers who move out of an industry in response to a decline in the price of the industry's output caused by increased imports must begin at a lower wage in the industry to which they move than those already there, because they do not possess the necessary industry-specific skills needed to earn a higher wage. If the country is small so that free trade is the Pareto optimal policy, the government will have an incentive to announce a policy of free trade to achieve the optimal allocation of labor but then surprise the workers with a tariff that improves the distribution of income by raising wages in the import-injured industry.[3] The free-trade policy is, therefore, time-inconsistent. However, workers will come to expect the tariff and fewer will leave the first industry after a price decline. Yet the tariff is still needed on income-distribution grounds to prevent wages in the industry from falling even below the level that could be earned as unskilled labor in other industries. The final outcome is a distribution of income that is no better than would be achieved under free trade but a lower social welfare level due to the production and consumption distortions associated with protection. Thus, the reason for protection, according to Staiger and Tabellini, is the inability to precommit to a liberal trade policy.

Explaining protection as a form of social insurance for risk-averse individuals in an uncertain trading environment is another approach, as such authors as Eaton and Grossman (1985), Dixit (1986, 1987a, 1987b) and Hillman (1989, ch. 9) point out. If market failure prevents private insurance markets from functioning, risk-averse individuals may increase their expected utilities by achieving reductions in price variability through protectionist policies. However, there is some controversy over just what causes of market failure justify a protectionist social-insurance response. Feenstra (1987) extends the uncertainty framework across countries to show that tariffs and export subsidies can be welfare increasing if markets for claims to future output are imperfect or missing.

The above approaches all utilize the usual self-interest assumption of economic models. However, another approach emphasizes the social concerns of voters and public officials in the policy formation process. A

---

[3] Initially the price must decline enough in the industry so that it is advantageous for some workers to move even if they must accept a lower wage. After the tariff is imposed, the workers who had moved to another industry will not return to the industry of their initial employment because it is assumed they would have lost their sector-specific skills and thus will have to start again as unskilled workers.

good example is Corden's (1974, p. 107) concept of the conservative social welfare function. This concept assumes that governments have an income distribution target such that "any significant absolute reductions in real incomes of any significant section of the community should be avoided." As Corden states, this means that increases in income are given relatively low welfare weights by governments and decreases very high welfare weights. He maintains that this particular set of social values is important in explaining the income maintenance purpose of the temporary protection often granted industries seriously injured by rapid increases in imports. In a simple model with uncertainty, Deardorff (1987) also shows that the conservative social welfare function can be used to explain the preference of governments for quotas instead of tariffs.

All of the models described above are concerned with domestic political economy, that is, they aim at explaining how domestic and, in some cases, international pressures influence governments' international economic policies. They do not deal with international political economy, namely, the interactions among governments on economic policy issues. There is, however, a rapidly growing body of economic literature that does concern itself with this issue. It takes governments or government agencies as the basic decision making unit and utilizes game theory to analyze the interactions among states on such matters as monetary, fiscal, exchange-rate and trade policies. Hamada (1976) is generally given credit for being the pioneer in this field. The models developed thus far for analyzing the problems of international economic coordination have not, however, been linked to the models of domestic political economy described above.

B. The Political Scientist's Approach to Political Economy

As in their study of international relations in general, political scientists make the state the central actor in their models of international political economy. The state is viewed as an autonomous, rational actor primarily concerned with increasing its political and economic power relative to other nations. In carrying out its role, the state both influences and is influenced by other states and its own citizens. The structure of the international economic and political system as well as the nature of existing institutions also plays a major role in shaping behavior in the models of political scientists.

The best-known modern theory relating political factors and international economic policies, the theory of hegemonic stability, maintains that the existence of an liberal international economic regime depends on a particular structure of the international system. Specifically, this theory holds that strong liberal international economic regimes are most likely when a hegemonic state, which itself is committed to a liberal ideology, dominates the international economy (see Gilpin, 1987, pp. 72-80 and Keohane, 1984). The hegemon is so large that the costs of free-riding on the part of small states, who take advantage of the export opportunities created by the dominant country but do not liberalize themselves, are small compared to its gains. Proponents of this theory point to the dominant trading positions of Great Britain in the nineteenth century and the United States in the immediate post-World War II period to account for the creation of open trading regimes in these periods. However, they also predict the disintegration of such regimes as the power of the hegemon declines through the normal process of uneven economic growth in the world economy.

The continued openness of the international economy in the 1970s and 1980s, despite the decline in the power of the United States, has led to the development of several variations on the hegemonic model. Some scholars, for example, Keohane (1984) and Lipson (1982), argue that institutions established during a hegemonic interval, such as the GATT, continue to exist after the decline of the dominant power and act as a brake on the disintegration of the liberal trading order.[4]   Others, for example, Pastor (1980), point to the durability of the changes in the nature of domestic policymaking that occurred during the hegemonic period. According to Milner (1988), the existence of a greater degree of openness than expected under the hegemonic stability theory is attributable to changes in firms' attitudes toward an open trading system that are related to increased international economic interdependence.

C. Critique of the Two Approaches

As the preceding outline of political economy models indicates, economists and political scientists come to the study of the subject with very different perspectives. Economists adopt a microeconomic viewpoint with households, managers of profit-maximizing firms, and public officials as the basic building blocks for their models. In contrast, political scientists usually view the subject in macropolitical terms with the state as the basic decision making unit.

One of the merits of economists' political economy models is that they rest on a well-defined behavior theory. This economic self-interest framework has significantly improved our understanding of why actual policy outcomes diverge from those that would maximize national economic welfare. In the trade- policy field, for example, one can better appreciate why an industry such as textiles and apparel with its large number of

---

[4] The following discussion of these variations relies heavily on Milner's (pp. 12-14, 1988) analysis of this matter.

workers located in many states is able to secure high rates of protection or why such industries as steel and oil, which are able to raise large sums for lobbying purposes, are also very successful in gaining protection. In contrast, such sectors as footwear and ceramics, which are smaller and less wealthy, are much less successful in their efforts to restrict imports.

There are, however, some features of trade policy that are not easily explainable by these models. It is difficult, for example, to explain on lobbying grounds alone the price preference given to small and minority businesses over both foreign and domestic suppliers under the federal government's procurement procedures. Such groups are not very effective in organizing and bringing political pressure on public officials. The tendency for tariffs to be high and duty cuts low in industries where wages are low is also difficult to explain with economic self-interest models (Baldwin, 1985). A framework that includes the broad social concerns of voters seems to be needed to explain such behavior. Furthermore, one of the key variables that supposedly influences an industry's lobbying ability, namely, the concentration ratio in the industry, turns out to be statistically insignificant in most empirical studies and often has the wrong sign (Anderson and Baldwin, 1987). There is also considerable experimental evidence and an abundance of directly observed behavior indicating that free-riding, the phenomenon on which the conclusion that the concentration ratio will be significant rests, is much less extensive than political economists have assumed (Johansen, 1977 and Andreoni, forthcoming).

Public policies in certain other economic areas are even more difficult to explain on the basis of these models. One is a government's aid to developing countries, which is often not tied to specific industries or even countries. The numerous domestic programs that exist to aid groups whose lobbying power is weak fall into the same category. In contrast, in some instances we observe highly successful lobbies being formed by groups not only composed of large numbers of small decisionmakers but by individuals who are not directly affected economically by the policy outcome. On environmental issues, for example, some of these groups have been highly successful in opposing business groups whose economic stakes in the outcome are high. Lobbying and political-support models also seem inadequate for explaining the decisionmaking process on issues relating to the international monetary system and exchange rates.

Models emphasizing such concepts as uncertainty, imperfect information, and the inability to commit to credible policies are leading to new insights into policymaking, but they are still in an early stage of development. They also seem more promising in explaining general policies such as overall levels of tariff protection rather than accounting for protection differentials among industries. Similarly, broadening the self-interest model to include government behavior based on altruistic motives, as the social concerns model does, makes some observed policy behavior more understandable. However, the microfoundations of this model have not been spelled out in sufficient detail.

None of the economic models focussing on domestic political economy is linked very well with models of international political economy. For example, models analyzing negotiations among countries with different trade-policy objectives, e.g., Baldwin and Clarke, 1987, are not integrated with models explaining how these different policy objectives are influenced by domestic economic and political factors. Similarly, existing models of international macroeconomic cooperation do not attempt to explain the domestic foundations of the divergent policy goals of the countries involved.

Still another drawback of the political economy models developed by economists is their failure to analyze the interaction between international economic and political policies. But, as we have seen in the post-World War II period, international security objectives can have a major impact on international economic policies (and vice versa). Consider the liberal trade and generous foreign aid policies pursued by the United States in the late 1940s and the 1950s. A major reason why they were introduced was the hope on the part of U.S. political leaders that they would help strengthen the so-called free world's resistance to communist expansion. Yet the typical economist's model of political economy does not include such political factors. Thus, as the Cold War eased, the lessening of pressure for trade liberalization by public officials charged with maintaining international security may be a more important factor in accounting for the increase in U.S. protectionism than lobbying pressures from industries injured by increased imports.

As noted before, most political economy models developed by political scientists make the state the key decisionmaking unit. The state is viewed as seeking to maximize its influence or power in order to carry out its well-defined political and economic goals, which usually are related to national security. However, it is also recognized that elected or appointed individuals are the ones who actually make the decisions being analyzed. If these individuals and those they represent have identical preference patterns for the choices they face, it is perfectly legitimate to treat the state as the decision making unit. But if those making political decisions have different preferences among themselves or are responsive to political pressures from common-interest groups with differing preferences, it is technically incorrect to treat the state as a rational decisionmaker.

Suppose an investigator observes many instances in which the state always chooses alternative A (some international economic or political option) to alternative B and also many cases in which the state always chooses alternative B over alternative C. Say a new situation develops in which the choice faced by the government is between C and A. If the observer assumes that the state acts rationally, he or she will predict that the state prefers A over C, since rationality requires the ranking of pairs of alternatives to be consistent with each other, that is, if A is preferred to B and B is preferred to C, then A is preferred to C. However, if decisions by the state are the result of political actions by citizens, for example, through a majority voting process, then the state's preferences need not be consistent with each other.[5]

This is simply one of the consequences of the impossibility theorem proved by Kenneth Arrow (1963). Arrow showed that it is impossible to derive a social welfare function, that is, society's ordering of all social states based an its members' individual ordering of all social states, that satisfies certain apparently reasonable conditions. These include a positive association of social and individual values, the independence of irrelevant alternatives, ruling out the imposition of social preference for some alternative regardless of the preferences of individuals, and the exclusion of a dictatorial social welfare function, that is, one that is based solely on the preference of one person.

While many government policy decisions (even in the executive branch) are based on voting by divergent interest groups, many decisions are also made by an individual, e.g., the president, who is behaving in an optimizing manner. The objective of a political leader charged with formulating national and international policies seems best described as attempting to maximize national welfare rather than as maximizing power or influence and wealth. These latter goals seem unduly limiting in describing the behavior of modern national leaders. However, a national political leader, like other actors in the political and economic system, faces a constrained maximization problem. In attempting to maximize national welfare as he or she sees it, the president, for example, is constrained by such factors as the desire to get reelected (or to elect a new president of the

---

[5] Assume that there are three individuals, each with consistent but different preferences, and that decisions are reached by the majority voting rule. Suppose individual 1 prefers A to B and B to C and, therefore, A to C; that individual 2 prefers B to C and C to A and, therefore, B to A: and that individual 3 prefers C to A and A to B and, therefore, C to B. In a choice between A and B, A will be selected, since two individuals prefer this order, while only one prefers B to A. For the same reason, in a choice between B and C, alternative B will be selected. Moreover, in a choice between C and A, C will be selected rather than A, since both individuals 2 and 3 prefer this order.

same party), and the need to follow constitutional procedures, abide by various treaties, and accept certain traditions.

What might seem to be inconsistent behavior on the surface, because, for example, the president at one time grants a country's request for military assistance or an industry's petition for protection but at another time rejects requests that seem identical, may be easily explainable by changed domestic political or economic conditions coupled with the president's desire to be reelected. The requests for military assistance may not differ in security terms, but in one case there may be a significant group of U.S. citizens who have relatives in one of the countries, while the requests for protection may differ in that one comes during a recession and the other during a period of high inflation. Paying attention to such microfoundations of policy determination is essential, if political economy is to develop as a field in which general behavioral principles can be established that are useful in predicting policy action under specified conditions.

The general dissatisfaction with the theory of hegemonic stability seems due in large part to its failure to provide an adequate micro-foundation for explaining the behavior of states. In the absence of a framework for explaining the manner in which the policy preferences of individual voters are combined through various political and economic pressure groups with those of others to influence the behavior of government officials, political scientists have been unable to agree on why the liberal international regime did not completely collapsed as the United States lost its dominant position.

II. ELEMENTS IN A MICRO-POLITICAL ECONOMY MODEL
A. The Basic Framework

In beginning at the micro-level to develop a political economy model that is useful for analyzing the issues of interest to political scientists as well as economists, it is necessary to adopt a broader view of an individual's preferences than economists' usually do. The social states that individuals are assumed to be able to rank in a rational manner must describe all the conditions that are relevant for an individual's economic and political behavior. A particular social state should describe such economic features as the amounts of each private and public good in the hands of each individual and country, and such political characteristics as citizens' voting and property rights, the degree of freedom of speech and religion in one's own country and in other countries, the institutional structure of governments, and the nature of the political relationships among countries. The preferences of an individual involve economic trade-offs such as less of one good for more of another, or a lower income for the individual in return for higher income levels for others, political trade-offs such as restrictions on the right to own firearms for greater public safety, and economic/political trade-offs such as a lower personal income for greater political freedom or a different form of government within one's own country or in another nation. Individuals register their preferences for private economic goods by purchasing the utility-maximizing combination in economic markets with the incomes they earn. However, they register their preferences for economic goods and political conditions that are determined through collective action by voting and by supplying funds or labor aimed at influencing the preference patterns of others.

A second feature of the basic model is that individuals do not possess complete knowledge about all social states. Acquiring knowledge is costly in terms of the direct outlay of resources required and the alternative activities foregone because of the time needed to absorb knowledge. Individuals practice a form of "rational ignorance" in spending time and funds in gaining knowledge only about economic and political matters that they believe have a significant impact on their social welfare. However, this still leaves individuals facing many choice situations in which they do not know where their economic or political self-interests lie. Individuals also acquire a considerable amount of their knowledge as a by-product of the activity of implementing their preferences. For example, they acquire new information about a product or a political candidate from advertisements seen in driving to work or in watching a favorite television program.

It also seems reasonable to put certain restrictions on the nature of a typical individual's preferences. For example, the prospect theory of Kahneman and Tversky (1979, 1984) relating to the manner in which individuals view gains versus loses is accepted. There is empirical support, these psychologists find, for the view that individuals place a greater welfare weight on the loss of a given amount of income than on an income gain of the same amount. It will be assumed that individuals view changes in the income levels of others in this manner too.

This relationship is important for explaining why government assistance is usually provided only for industries that are declining in relative terms. Consider an import-competing industry in which profit and wage levels, as well as its growth rate, are comparable with most other sectors of the economy. The marginal cost of gaining a higher level of protection through lobbying efforts will generally be higher than the marginal benefits from protection because the public and the government view an improvement in the industry's relative economic position as being undeserved. Due to the relatively low weights attached by the industry's employees to income increases, the free-rider problem may also make it difficult to raise funds voluntarily for lobbying purposes. In contrast, if output, profit and employment levels decline in this industry as a consequence of increased import competition, the marginal cost of increasing protection through lobbying will decline as the public views an expansion of domestic production in more favorable terms and the free-rider problem is easier to overcome, since employees place a higher valuation on an income loss than an income gain. However, the influence of public attitudes toward increased protection will usually be such that the any increase in protection still leaves output and employment in the industry at lower levels than initially.

It is further assumed individuals value certain economic and political conditions so highly that they are unwilling to forego these in return for greater amounts of most other economic goods or political conditions. For example, while most individuals are willing to accept a small temporary decrease in real income to help workers in another industry adjust to significantly greater import competition or to help citizens of a very poor country accelerate their development rate, they are not prepared do so when their own jobs are threatened for some reason and they are seeking government assistance themselves. Similarly, they are unwilling to accept limits on such political conditions as the freedom of speech and religion in return for a higher economic income. An important implication of these relationships is that individuals do not attempt to free-ride on the activities of others when facing choices involving these strong preferences. For many people, this is the situation when the choices involve taking political action on such matters as environmental issues that significantly affect the quality of life or voting in a presidential election. In these cases, individuals believe the personal stakes for them are so high that they cannot risk free-riding, even though they are only one of many individuals involved in the decisionmaking process.

Imperfect competition in political markets as well as economic markets is another basic assumption. The view is rejected that elected officials have no independent control over public policies because, if they do act independently, they will be displaced by other officials who maximize voting support by following the preferences of voters and pressure groups. Instead, in keeping with what seems to be the actual situation, it is assumed that incumbents have considerable latitude in supporting particular policies on which their constituents are indifferent or may not share the views of the elected officials. Elected officials are also assumed to be active players in the efforts to alter voter preferences by providing information favorable to their positions.

B. A Trade-Policy Application

The manner in which public policies are shaped by various economic and political factors can be illustrated by considering the case of an initially unprotected industry seeking import relief through the political route on the grounds of import injury. There are essentially three ways by which the industry can bring political pressure on those who can supply protection: by using their voting power, by providing government officials and opinion-makers in the private sector with information favorable to their position, and by contributing to the campaign funds of key elected officials in the hope that this will make them more sympathetic to the industry's position. In Figure 1 let the curve, OB, indicate the revenues in excess of variable production costs received by firms in the industry at different specific duty levels.[6] Furthermore, let the curve, OC, depict the costs of lobbying (using the optimum combinations of the three methods mentioned above) at the different tariff levels.[7] It is assumed that the marginal cost of increasing the level of protection a certain amount increases as the tariff level rises. The profit-maximizing tariff level, Ot, is where the slopes of the two curves are equal and the expenditures on lobbying needed to obtain this tariff level are OL.

Consider the kinds of factors that influence the shape of the lobbying-cost curve. If the president regards the openness of U.S. markets as an important element in some foreign policy initiative he or she is pursuing or believes anti-inflationary policies are an important part of his or her current policy agenda, the curve is likely to be so steep that lobbying will not be profitable for the industry. The president's ability to command wide media coverage when lobbying for his or her own position can be very effective in raising the lobbying costs for private industries. In contrast, if the industry's efforts to gain increased protection happens to coincide with a tight presidential election, a period of high unemployment or a large balance-of-trade deficit, the costs of lobbying will tend to be lower for the industry.

In many instances, whether protection is granted may not be a matter of importance to the president. In this situation, the president may grant protection only after being convinced that doing so would not be regarded

---

[6] The net revenue curve levels off when the prohibitive tariff level is reached.

[7] There has not been much consideration given to the optimum combination of lobbying methods for a particular industry. However, industries consisting of large numbers of employees and many small firms located in many states, such as the textiles and apparel industries, appear to find that using their voting strength to influence legislators directly is the most efficient method of lobbying. In contrast, industries that have a comparatively small number of employees and are not widely dispersed across states but who are organized in a oligopolistic manner, such as the oil industry, seem to rely more extensively on providing campaign funds to elected officials as well as disseminating favorable information to the public and elected officials.

Figure 1

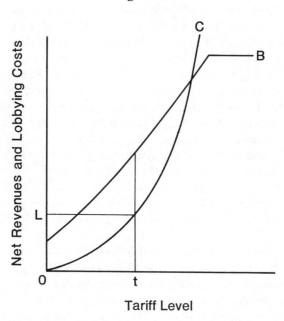

by the general public as providing special favors to the industry or by foreign governments as unduly protectionist. Consequently, it is up to the industry to convince the public and members of Congress through lobbying efforts that the industry deserves protection. Industries that are small in employment and financial terms have little chance of gaining protection through the political route under these conditions. The public's willingness to accept protection for the industry is influenced by such factors as the income levels of the workers in the industry and the degree of injury suffered by the industry, the reason for the increase in imports (was it due to unfair foreign trade practices?, for example), the extent to which the public understands the welfare effects of protection, and the national security, environmental, and health implications of increased production in the industry.

The industry's lobbying costs are also affected by the anti-protectionist lobbying efforts of other domestic industries using the product as an intermediate input into their production process, multinational firms with foreign operations who fear retaliatory action, importers of the good, and foreign governments and foreign firms. Obviously, the more economically important the product is for these groups and the larger they are in voting and in financial terms, the more extensive will be their counter-lobbying activities.

In addition, the form of protection being sought by an industry has an important bearing on the costs of lobbying. For example, country-selective voluntary export agreements (VEAs), in which only the countries responsible for most of the increase in imports limit their exports, are favored by governments because they minimize the objections of foreign governments to restrictions on their exports. Not having to compensate other countries by reducing protection levels on other products also prevents domestic opposition from other import-competing industries who fear their products will be selected in the compensation process. Even the countries whose exports are limited often will not complain too strongly, since they capture the windfall gains associated with the quantitative restriction of imports.[8]

In stating that the equilibrium level of protection in the situation portrayed in Figure 1 will be Ot, it is assumed that the firms in the industry are organized so as to maximize their profit prospects at the industry level. However, suppose that, instead of acting in a cooperative manner, each firm views the situation in terms of the profits it will receive under the alternative scenarios of being the only one to spend on lobbying or being the only one not to incur lobbying expenditures. If each firm is one of many small production units, it is unlikely to contribute to lobbying activities under either scenario, and the free-rider problem may prevent the industry from receiving any protection. As mentioned earlier, however, when the livelihood of most individuals in an industry is endangered, the free-rider problem is likely to be overcome, at least in part.

C. The Role of Institutions, Economic Structures, and Ideas

At a more fundamental level, the prospects for liberal versus protect-ionist trade policies are influenced by such considerations as the institutional structure of the government, the nature of the international trading regime, the distribution of economic resources among countries, the dominant ideology regarding the effects of protection, and the traditions of the government in dealing with requests for protection. For example, the willingness of the Congress since 1934 to allow the executive branch to

---

[8] Providing import protection to the injured industry is generally preferred by the public to providing domestic subsidies, since consumers who benefit from the lower price of imports bear the costs of assisting the industry. Providing a subsidy financed by domestic taxes is likely to alter the domestic distribution of income more significantly.

handle most modifications of individual tariffs has played an important role in reducing protection over the years, since the president tends to be more liberal on trade-policy matters than the Congress. At the same time, the fact that the U.S. Constitution gives Congress the right to regulate foreign trade helps to explain why Congress plays a more important role in determining trade policy than, for example, in setting exchange-rate policy. Whether a protectionist petition follows an administrative route, such as the International Trade Commission (ITC) provides in import-injury cases, or goes directly to the Office of the U.S. Trade Representative (USTR), as in Section 301 cases, has an important bearing on the likelihood that an industry will gain protection. Industries that are small in terms of voting and financial power will favor the ITC route, while large, politically powerful industries will prefer the direct route through USTR. Similarly, whether there is an international organization, such as the GATT, with a set of international trading rules and a well-established dispute-settlement process is important for shaping the extent of protectionism in the world. Again, small countries will prefer strong international organizations, while large countries will try to prevent such organizations from gaining too much power and thereby constraining the actions of the large countries.

The influence of the international distribution of factor endowments and technological knowledge on trade policy is illustrated by the change in U.S. trade policy since the late 1960s. As other nations have caught up with the United States technologically and in labor skills and capital stock, cases of injury due to increased imports have increased significantly and raised the pressures for protection. The importance of ideas can be illustrated by the increased influence of the "new" international trade theory, in which increasing returns and imperfect competition are emphasized. The case for free trade is not as strong when viewed within this framework.

The relative importance of the above factors in shaping government economic policies varies greatly with the policy issues under consideration. For example, political pressures from private interest groups influence government decisions on trade policy much more than on exchange-rate policy. While trade policy can be targeted to particular industries, changes in exchange rates affect all industries. Consequently, the free-rider problem is more serious for such issues as exchange-rate policy, and it is not surprising that the private political pressures for policy change that do develop in this field usually come from broad coalitions of businesses such as the National Association of Manufacturers rather than from individual industries. There is also less expertise in the private business sector on the effects of exchange-rate changes than in the case of import protection, partly because of the collective nature of these changes and because of the greater complexity of the economic impact of exchange-rate changes. A need for secrecy to minimize speculation also reduces the role for the private sector. As Destler and Henning (forthcoming) point out, U.S. exchange-rate policy is determined mainly by Treasury and Federal Reserve officials. However, political pressures from foreign countries also play a significant role in shaping exchange-rate decisions, since exchange-rate changes are equivalent to general taxes and subsidies on exports and imports.

Relatively small groups of government officials in the executive and legislative branches also make most decisions on national security matters. Again, the collective impact of national security decisions, the need to prevent knowledge about certain decisions from getting into the hands of potential adversaries, and the highly technical nature of the issues involved tend to limit public debates on national security matters to the broad outlines of these policies. However, as the Vietnam War demonstrated, political pressures from private citizen groups can sometimes play a crucial role in this field too.

An obvious drawback of the broad analytical framework set forth in Part III is its lack of simplicity. Yet, while, *ceteris paribus*, a simple theory is to be preferred to a complex one, a simple theory that fails to explain adequately political-economic behavior in many trade or other economic policy situations is inferior to a complex but general theory. Fortunately, in many situations, certain elements of a broad theory can be taken as "givens". For example, in trying to explain differences in political behavior in two policy situations, it may not be necessary to consider explicitly the nature of the existing institutions, economic structure, and prevailing ideology, since they may be the same in both situations and do not play an independent role in accounting for the differences in policy outcomes. Similarly, it may be evident in some cases that the personal economic stakes of the major participants are so strong that a narrow economic self-interest model is the appropriate analytical framework. But, to avoid ignoring important political-economic determinants of policy outcomes, these simplications should be the result from an evaluation of the problem that begins with the type of broad framework outlined here.

References

Anderson, Kym and Robert E. Baldwin, 1987. "The Political Market for Protection in Industrial Countries," in Ali M. El-Agraa, editor, *Protection, Cooperation, Integration and Development: Essays in Honour of Professor Hiroshi Kitamura*, London: Macmillan Press.

Andreoni, James, forthcoming. "Why Free Ride? Strategies and Learning in Public Goods Experiments", *Journal of Public Economics*.

Arrow, Kenneth J., 1963. *Social Choice and Individual Value*, Second Edition, New York: John Wiley and Sons.

Baldwin, Robert E., 1985. *The Political Economy of U.S. Import Policy*, Cambridge: MIT Press.

Baldwin, Robert E. and Richard N. Clark, 1987. "Game-Modeling Multilateral Trade Negotiations", *Journal of Political Modeling*, 9, 257-284.

Bhagwati, Jagdish N., 1980. "Lobbying and Welfare," *Journal of Public Economics*, 14, 355-363.

Brock, William A. and Stephen P. Magee, 1978. "The Economics of Special Interests: The Case of the Tariff", *American Economic Review*, 68, 246-250.

Corden, W. Max, 1974. *Trade Policy and Economic Welfare*, Oxford: Clarendon Press.

Das, Satya P., 1986. "Foreign Lobbying and the Political Economy of Protection," Department of Economics, University of Wisconsin-Milwaukee.

Deardorff, Allan V., 1987. "Safeguards Policy and the Conservative Social Welfare Function", in Henryk Kierkowski, editor, *Protection and Competition in International Trade*, Oxford: Basil Blackwell.

Destler, I.M. and C. Randall Henning, forthcoming. *Exchange Rate Policymaking in the United States*, Washington, D.C.: Institute for International Economics.

Dixit, Avinash, 1986. "Trade and Insurance with Moral Hazard," Princeton University.

Dixit, Avinash, 1987a. "Trade and Insurance with Adverse Selection," Princeton University.

Dixit, Avinash, 1987b. Trade and Insurance with Imperfectly Observed Outcomes," Princeton University.

Eaton, Jonathan and Gene Grossman, 1985. "Tariffs as Insurance: Optimal Commercial Policy When Domestic Markets Are Incomplete," *Canadian Journal of Economics*, 18, 258-272.

Feenstra, Robert C. and Jagdish S. Bhagwati, 1982. "Tariff Seeking and the Efficient Tariff", in Jagdish Bhagwati, editor, *Import Competition and Response*, Chicago: University of Chicago Press and National Bureau of Economics.

Feenstra, Robert C., 1987. "Incentive Compatible Trade Policies," *Scandinavian Journal of Economics*, 89, 373-387.

Findlay, Ronald and Stanislaw Wellisz, 1982. "Endogenous Tariffs, the Political Economy of Trade Restrictions, and Welfare," in Jagdish Bhagwati editor, *Import Competition and Response*, Chicago: University of Chicago Press and National Bureau of Economics.

Destler, I.M. and C. Randall Henning, forthcoming. *Exchange Rate Policymaking in the United States*, Institute for International Economics.

Frey, Bruno S., 1984. *International Political Economy*, Oxford: Basil Blackwell.

Gilpin, Robert, 1975. *U.S. Power and the Multinational Corporation: The Political Economy of Foreign Direct Investment*, New York: Basic Books.

Gilpin, Robert, 1988. *The Political Economy of International Relations*, Princeton: Princeton University Press.

Hamada, Koichi, 1976. "A Strategic Analysis of Monetary Interdependence," *Journal of Political Economy*, 84, 77-99.

Hillman, Arye L., 1982. "Declining Industries and Political-Support Protectionist Motives," *American Economic Review*, 72, 1180-1187.

Hillman, Arye L., 1989. *The Political Economy of Protection*, New York: Harwood Academic Publishers.

Hillman, Arye L. and Heinrich W. Ursprung, 1988. "Domestic Politics, Foreign Interests, and International Trade Policy," *American Economic Review*, 78, 729-745.

Johansen, Leif, 1977. "The Theory of Public Goods: Misplaced Emphasis?", *Journal of Public Economics*, 7, 147-152.

Kahneman, Daniel and Amos Tversky, 1979. "Prospect Theory: An Analysis of Decision Under Risk," *Econometrica*, 47, 263-291.

Kahneman, Daniel and Amos Tversky, 1984. "Choices, Values, and Frames," *American Psychologist*, 39, 341-350.

Keohane, Robert O., 1984. *After Hegemony: Cooperation or Discord in World Political Economy*, Princeton: Princeton University Press.

Knorr, Klaus, 1973. *Power and Wealth: The Political Economy of International Power*, New York: Basic Books.

Krueger, Anne O., 1974. "The Political Economy of the Rent-Seeking Society," *American Economic Review*, 64, 291-303.

Lipson, Charles, 1982. "The Transformation of Trade," *International Organization*, 36, 417-456.

Mayer, Wolfgang, 1984. "Endogenous Tariff Formation," *American Economic Review*, 74, 970-985.

Milner, Helen V., 1988. *Resisting Protectionism*, Princeton: Princeton University Press.

Olson, Mancur, 1965. *The Logic of Collective Action*, Cambridge: Harvard University Press.

Pastor, Robert, 1980. *Congress and the Politics of U.S. Foreign Economic Policy*, Berkeley: University of California Press.

Peltzman, Sam, 1976. "Toward a More General Theory of Regulation," *Journal of Law and Economics*, 19, 211-240.

Staiger, Robert and Guido Tabellini, 1987. "Discretionary Trade Policy and Excessive Protection," *American Economic Review*, 77, 340-348.

Stigler, George, 1971. "The Theory of Economic Regulation," *Bell Journal of Economics*, 2, 3-21.

Chapter 14

THE ECONOMICS AND POLITICAL ECONOMY OF MANAGED TRADE

Wilfred J. Ethier*

Even as the virtues of the free market are extolled daily, trade between national markets becomes increasingly managed. Such management has long been commonplace in international primary-product markets and in the trade of the now-unfashionable centrally-planned economies. But recent decades have seen the proliferation of management of the trade of manufactures between industrial (and newly industrializing) economies.

The instrument of such management is the voluntary export restraint. This is an arrangement whereby a government (or firms) protects an industry by persuading the authorities (or firms) in a trading partner to restrict exports. Such protection allows the country to avoid violating existing international agreements (such as the General Agreement on Tariffs and Trade)[1], and sometimes its own trade laws as well, and also to avoid the danger of retaliation posed by unilateral action, all at the cost of forfeiting the revenues that would be raised were tariffs, say, employed instead.

---

* The research for this paper was supported by a grant from the Bank of Sweden Tercentenary Foundation. I am grateful for comments received during the Conference on Markets and Politicians at Bar-Ilan University and during seminars at the Institute for Advanced Studies in Jerusalem, at Tel-Aviv University and at the University of Western Ontario.
[1] More accurately, it is unclear whether such restraints do in fact violate the GATT or not, especially when governments play no official formal role in the restraint agreement itself. But there is no interested party to object: the importing and exporting governments accept the agreement and other interested governments, who compete with the restrained exporters, see themselves as beneficiaries.

During the most recent two decades these arrangements have become the most prominent means by which protectionist initiatives have been implemented in the industrial world. Over one hundred agreements now manage upwards of ten percent of world trade, and in some sectors such arrangements are far more prominent than this summary statistic would indicate. The lion's share of world trade in textiles and apparel is now covered, as is over one third of Japan's export of manufactures to other industrial countries.

These arrangements are invariably sector-specific, though within various frameworks that can vary sector by sector. The arrangement usually limits (or otherwise influences) trade in one direction between two countries, but sometimes two-way trade is addressed (semiconductor trade between the United States and Japan). The framework might be multilateral (the Multifiber Arrangement in textiles) or isolated and bilateral (Canadian lumber exports to the United States). There might be a series of independent arrangements linking a single exporter to diverse importers (Japanese automobile exports), a single importer to several exporters (United States imports of machine tools), or several exporters to several importers (steel). But regardless of the framework, the key negotiations and agreements are bilateral. Thus the evolution of the trade policies of industrial countries toward manufactures has displayed a basic tension, between the spread of bilateral, sector-specific restrictions and the continuing multilateral effort to fashion a liberal trade order (the GATT and its negotiating rounds).

Managed trade is restricted trade. Thus the basic conclusions of the traditional theory of protection remain relevant, indeed they remain centrally relevant. But contemporary efforts to manage trade also share characteristics quite distinct from those addressed by the traditional theory, as, for example, in the archetypal analysis of the effects of a tariff. This paper attempts to identify these characteristics and to address their implications.

I. DISTINCTIVE FEATURES OF MANAGED TRADE

Trade in manufactures among the industrial countries is managed, when it is, through a series of bilateral, sector-specific, voluntary export restraints (VERs).[2] The following features distinguish such arrangements from standard tariffs.

(a) The restrictions are quantitative. That is, the trade is subject to quota rather than tax, though taxes may be present as well.

---

[2] See Kostecki (1987) for a description of actual VERs and Pomfret (1989) for a survey of their theory.

(b) The restrictions are voluntary on both sides of the market. This is essential, because a primary reason to resort to such measures is to circumvent the spirit of the GATT in specific areas, without bringing down the entire GATT structure, by ensuring that no nation involved has a motive to complain. This need not require industry interests in both countries to welcome the arrangement: it will be negotiated, at least to a significant degree, by government officials who may be willing to sacrifice something in one sector for a *quid pro quo* elsewhere, or even without a *quid pro quo*, in order to preserve a relationship that is in the national interest overall.[3] This should be kept in mind. Nevertheless, there must be a strong presumption that industry interests are not hurt, or at least not hurt too much: these agreements are typically negotiated in a politically-charged atmosphere that draws the attention of the interests concerned and that induces them to exert themselves to the utmost politically.[4] And of course the negotiations are sector-specific.

(c) The restrictions are temporary (at least in original intent) responses to established import positions that have harmed import-competing interests. It is true that management arrangements often seem to linger for quite a while, and in textiles and apparel, at least, they have acquired the status of a permanent fixture. But actual agreements are invariably for quite short periods and usually the original intent is not to renew them many times. The original agreement itself is almost always the response to a large, established import presence (usually a recently established or recently enlarged one), not to the prospect that such a presence may come about.[5] No doubt this is partly a matter of political economy: being able to point to a recently large volume of imports makes it easier to enlist the sympathy of fellow citizens for restrictions. But it is also a reflection of the voluntary element in these arrangements: for us to offer importers significant rents from their share of our market they must have a significant share of that market. Finally, there must be a significant import-competing interest adversely affected by the imports. This interest is, of course, the source of the political pressure to manage trade.

---

[3] This is clearly a possibility in the case of orderly marketing arrangements, which involve explicit agreements between the two governments involved. But governments also usually play a central role in the formation of other restraints in which they take no formal part.

[4] It is also sometimes the case, though, that one purpose of the negotiations is to prevent the atmosphere from becoming even more politically charged.

[5] Of course there may well be the prospect that the import presence might become much larger yet in the absence of an agreement to prevent that.

All this indicates the presence of an implicit social commitment to grant import-competing sectors the possibility of temporary relief from trade-related difficulties. In a deeper sense it is this implicit commitment itself that is the true instrument of protection, analogous to the permanent tariff addressed by traditional theory. Actual temporary trade arrangements are merely incidents in the operation of the permanent protection afforded by the commitment. Thus the implicit commitment may affect industries with significant import potential that are not currently managed.

(d) The restrictions are discriminatory. This is a major way in which managed trade violates the spirit of the GATT. It implies that an analysis of such trade should consider the roles played by at least three distinct groups of firms: import-competitors, restrained exporters and unrestrained exporters. As noted above, unrestrained exporters can usually be expected to benefit from a VER and so do not pressure their government to protest its formation. The activities of such firms have been central to how many such agreements have in fact functioned, and in some industries they have played a dominant role in the evolution of trade management (e.g., textiles, steel). Discrimination is thus a vital property of managed trade.

Discrimination also implies a fourth potential group of firms: import-competitors that are not part of the arrangement. In reasonably competitive markets characterized by constant costs these firms are unlikely to be affected very much by trade management in which they do not participate. But significant economies of scale raise the possibility that restrained exporters may divert production from the newly restricted markets to compete in countries not within the arrangement. For example, the negotiation of the VER on Japanese automobiles sold in the United States aroused fears in some countries that the Japanese would be induced by the agreement to compete more fiercely in those countries in order to maintain production levels. Thus there is a part of the global industry that is threatened by such arrangements, and this holds the potential for defeat of the basic goal of bypassing the GATT by ensuring that no one will file a protest. But this does not happen. Perhaps unprotected import-competitors require significant diversion, and not just the threat of such diversion, to be roused to effective action. Probably more important is a desire on their part to acquire managed trade of their own, regardless of whether diversion takes place or not. They would then not be likely to agitate for legal challenges to a VER, as that would make it more difficult for them to acquire a VER of their own. The response by other importers of Japanese cars to the VER on Japanese exports to the United States was not to challenge that agreement formally; it was to negotiate VERs of their own with Japan.

The situation is more complex if trade management involves two-way trade, that is, the exporting country that restrains (in some way) its exporters also establishes a floor for (or otherwise encourages) imports from its partner. In this case third-country firms are threatened both with diversion and with the loss of an established or potential export market. It is interesting that the U.S.-Japanese semiconductor agreement, involving two-way trade management, did induce the formation of a GATT dispute panel.

The rest of this paper is concerned with an analysis of the circumstances under which trade management might arise and the implications thereof. To limit the scope of the paper, I ignore two potentially interesting features mentioned above. First, I will not consider cases where one party to an arrangement is induced to participate by a concession in some other industry or by some other aspect of its international position. Thus I consider only cases where the agreement is detrimental to none of the interests involved in its implementation. As argued above, this is likely in practice to be at least approximately correct, and, in any event, I have elsewhere analyzed to some extent the case of trade-offs.[6] Second, I shall not enquire into implications of the apparent implicit social commitment to import-competing interests. Again, I have discussed this elsewhere.[7]

II. MANAGEMENT IN COMPETITIVE MARKETS

Consider first the possibility of managed trade emerging when markets are competitive. Figure 1 shows a free-trade equilibrium at E, the intersection of the home (H) and foreign (F) offer curves. The home economy imports the quantity OC of good A in exchange for the quantity CE of good B, implying an international price of A in terms of B of CE/OC. Consider the possibility of a VER on foreign exports of A.

The negotiation and implementation of such an agreement almost always involves the two governments and the two national A industries. We are interested in arrangements that are truly voluntary, that is, that all four of these agents are willing to accept. The two A industries are presumably concerned with the incomes accruing to them,[8] but the interests of the governments depend upon the political economy. The interesting polar cases are where the government is simply an agent of the industry,

---

[6] See Ethier (1989).

[7] See Ethier and Fischer (1987) and Ethier (1989). Also relevant are Dean and Gangopadhyay (1989) and Yano (1989).

[8] The industry pressure groups presumably include factors specific to the industry. In a Heckscher-Ohlin-Samuelson context, where there are no specific factors, it presumably includes the factor employed intensively in the A sector.

Figure 1

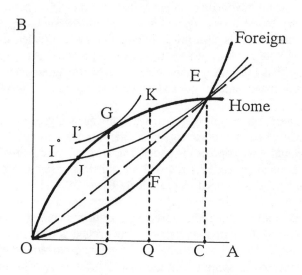

and so not an additional agent in its own right, and where the government is concerned with national welfare, represented , say, by a system of trade indifference curves. In general, the government can be thought of as wishing to maximize some weighted average of A-industry welfare and national welfare, with the weights depending upon the underlying political economy.

To see what this implies, consider how the four agents would be affected by a VER of OQ in Figure 1. Home residents import OQ and pay KQ for it, of which KF constitutes rent accruing to holders of the quota rights. $I°$ denotes the foreign trade-indifference curve corresponding to free trade. Exclusive of the quota rents, the foreign economy trades at F and so experiences a decline in welfare as a result of the restraint. Also at F the foreign relative price of A is lower than at E, so the foreign A industry is also worse off. This illustrates the key role of the quota rents: without them neither foreign agent would accept the restraint, regardless of the foreign political economy.

So assume that the rents are given to the foreign A industry, as is in fact nearly always the case. Then the foreign economy will trade at K and experience higher welfare than at free trade, provided the quota is not large enough to place K at or to the left of J. The foreign government would desire such an arrangement as long as it attaches sufficient weight to national welfare. If it is concerned only with national welfare, the government would prefer a quota of OD, which corresponds to the optimum export tax, but it would be willing to accept any quota leading to trade between E and J.

The effect of the restraint on the foreign A industry is ambiguous: the industry loses because of the lower foreign price of A, but it gains the rent. Whether the industry gains over all depends on the size of the rent, and that depends upon the home offer curve not being too elastic.[9] At J the foreign economy has the same welfare as in free trade, but its B sector is better off. Thus the foreign A sector must be worse off, even with the full quota rent; the range of restrained trades that the sector will accept is some proper subset of the range from E to J. At G, a small increase in a quota will leave foreign welfare unchanged but make the B sector better off. Thus the A sector is made worse off, that is, it is beyond its most desired point, which therefore must lie to the right of G (and could simply be E). Suppose that this is K. Then between E and K both the foreign industry and the foreign government would favor a more restrictive restraint. Between K and G the industry would want a less restrictive restraint while a government seeking to maximize foreign welfare would want a more restrictive one. Between G and J both would want the restraint to be less restrictive. A welfare maximizing government would accept no restraint more restrictive than J, and the industry would wish to cast its veto before getting that far.

The situation is simpler at home. Any restraint moves the home economy to a lower trade-indifference curve (not shown) and so would be unacceptable to a welfare maximizing government. The home A industry, on the other hand, wants as restrictive an arrangement as possible. Thus the key is the home political economy, the extent to which the home government wishes to maximize the welfare of its A industry. Since the point is easily understood, we may as well assume that the government is simply the agent of the industry. Then there are three independent agents: the home A industry, the foreign A industry and the foreign government. A VER will be negotiated if it is in the interest of each of these agents.

In the present case this means that there will be a VER leading to trade in a proper subset of the interval from K to J, at a particular point depending on details of the bargaining process between the three agents. All three desire a restraint more binding than any that would produce trade between E and K. Between K and G the key bargaining is within the

---

[9] If the home offer curve is perfectly elastic, so that E, G and J coincide, a small quota will have a negative second-order effect on foreign welfare and a positive first-order effect on the welfare of the foreign B industry. Thus it must have a negative first-order effect on the A industry.

foreign economy, as the foreign A-sector wants a less restrictive agreement and a welfare-maximizing government a more restrictive one. Between G and J the key bargaining is international: the home agents want a more restrictive agreement and the foreign agents a less restrictive one.

In sum, two conditions are necessary for a VER in a competitive context. The home political economy must be such that the home government attaches sufficient weight to the interests of the home industry, and the home offer curve must be sufficiently inelastic to generate rents sufficient to allow a restraint to benefit the foreign industry.[10]

The competitive model has been the traditional framework for the study of trade restraints, and has also been the basis (implicit or explicit) for most empirical work. But in the remainder of this paper I consider imperfectly competitive markets. There are several reasons for this. First, the competitive analysis is large and well-known, while the imperfectly competitive work is more recent and still being developed. Second, imperfect competition is in fact prevalent in many industries where trade has been managed. Finally, several of the features discussed in Section I become interesting or significant only in an imperfectly competitive context.

III. THE BASIC IMPERFECTLY COMPETITIVE MODEL

Consider an imperfectly competitive domestic market in which n home firms and n* foreign firms sell a homogeneous product. Furthermore, I assume that n and n* are each at least as large as two, so that each firm faces competition from firms in both countries.

Assume the following profit functions for the representative foreign and home firms:

$$\pi^*(x;y) = p(z)x - F^* - c^*x$$

$$\pi(y;x) = p(z)y - F - cy$$

where y denotes sales by each home firm and x the sales of each foreign firm, $z = ny + n^*x$ and p(z) is the inverse demand function. F and c denote the constant fixed and marginal costs faced by each home firm and F* and c* those faced by each foreign firm.

---

[10] An alternative to the second condition would be for the foreign government to compensate the foreign industry even beyond the quota rents, or simply to coerce it into acceptance. Note that this implies an international asymmetry in political economy: in one country the industry controls the government while in the other it is the reverse.

I shall focus exclusively on Cournot-Nash equilibria. The first-order condition for foreign-firm profit maximization is:

$$(FFE) \qquad p = \frac{c^*}{1 - (1-\theta)/n^*\epsilon}$$

where $\epsilon = -zp'/p$ and $\theta = ny/z$, the share of the home market supplied by home firms. Note that, while ϵ is the *market* elasticity of demand, the Cournot-Nash equilibrium description implies that the elasticity relevant to the foreign *firm* is $n^*\epsilon/(1-\theta)$. Assuming for simplicity that the elasticity ϵ is constant and exceeds unity, *FFE* gives a negative relation between p and θ, and this is shown in Figure 2 below.

Also, profit maximization by home firms requires:

$$(HFE) \qquad p = \frac{c}{1 - \theta/n\epsilon}$$

HFE gives a positive relation between p and θ that is also shown in Figure 2. The intersection of *FFE* and *HFE* determines the equilibrium price and home-firm share of the home market. Figure 2 shows an equilibrium with domestic production ($\theta > 0$). The case where domestic firms are driven out of business by foreign competition may also arise if *HFE* lies entirely above *FFE*, and, of course, *HFE* may alternatively lie entirely below *FFE*, so that no trade takes place.

This model differs from the previous competitive one in that there are three -- not four -- relevant groups of agents: foreign firms, who care about foreign profits; home firms, who care about their own profits; the home government, who cares about either home welfare or home profit, or some combination of the two. Of course the foreign government is still also relevant, but the foreign economy is affected only by the profits earned by foreign firms. Thus the interest of the foreign government is identical to that of the foreign firms.

It will prove convenient to see how contours corresponding to particular values of the variables of concern to each of the agents appear in the p-θ plane. I start with home welfare.

(a) Home welfare contours. A change in domestic welfare u can result from an income effect of an alteration in the cost of the country's import bundle, or from a change in production acting on the wedge p-c between the country's valuation of production and its cost. Thus the welfare change can be expressed as follows.

Figure 2

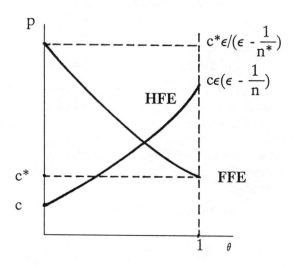

$$du = -Mdp + n(p-c)dy = -z\,dp + n\,d\pi.$$

Here M denotes total imports. Substitution produces the second equality. Under this interpretation, an increase in p lowers welfare because it decreases consumer surplus in the distorted z market. An increase in π, at given p, increases welfare because it means that the source of supply of z is shifted from foreign firms to domestic firms, saving p-c in resources. Home welfare contours are depicted in Figure 3(a). Note that the indifference contours have "reverse curvature", giving preference to autarky and to extensive dependence on imports rather than to moderate dependence. This will be important for what follows. It arises because an increase in p lowers welfare by reducing consumers' surplus, while an increase in θ substitutes domestic production for imports, thereby saving p - c per unit, and this saving becomes more and more pronounced as p becomes larger.

When $\theta = 0$, HFE is steeper than the welfare contour passing through it. But a tedious calculation reveals that some welfare contour has the same slope as HFE at some critical value θ°. Furthermore, this contour lies entirely above HFE, and another critical market share $\theta' < \theta^\circ$ yields the same welfare as does autarky ($\theta = 1$). Thus international trade is necessarily *beneficial* if FFE intersects HFE below the critical level θ'. But above the critical level international trade is *harmful*. In general, trade allows the economy to increase its consumer surplus at the cost of buying the goods at a greater price (p) than the social cost (c) of producing them

Figure 3

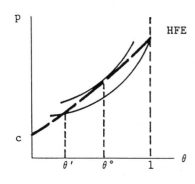

(a) Home welfare contours

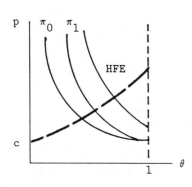

(b) Home profit contours

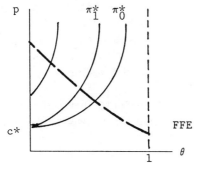

(c) Foreign profit contours

at home. The latter effect dominates if p - c becomes too large.

(b) Home profit contours. Now consider how the profits of home firms relate to the equilibrium values of p and θ. Along the p axis, and when p = c, π = -F and du = -z dp. In the interior of the p-θ plane:

$$\pi = (p-c)y - F = (p-c)(\theta z/n) - F$$

implies[11]

$$d\pi = (\theta z/n)[(p-c)\hat{\theta} + (c\epsilon - p[\epsilon-1])\hat{p}].$$

Therefore π contours are negatively sloped and convex to the origin as long as p lies between c and cϵ/(ϵ-1), which include all points of interest. Profit contours are shown in Figure 3(b). Movements up and to the right along *HFE* always result in successively higher home profit contours.

(c) Foreign profit contours. The properties of foreign-firm profit contours can be derived in an exactly analogous fashion, so I omit the details. Figure 3(c) shows the results. Movements upward and to the left along *FFE* bring successively higher foreign profit levels.

IV. A VER IN THE BASIC MODEL

Now consider a voluntary export restraint. First I describe how this would alter the above equilibrium, and then I enquire into when such a VER can be expected to emerge.[12]

(a) Equilibrium effects of a VER. I suppose that a VER establishes an exogenous upper bound on the exports of *each* foreign firm. If in equilibrium x was less than or equal to this constraint it obviously has no effect, as long as we continue to look at Cournot-Nash equilibria. If the constraint is binding, foreign firms will find themselves off *FFE*, exporting the constrained amount, and each would be able to raise its own profit if it could export more, given the sales of all n + n* - 1 rivals. Home firms, however, will still be on *HFE*, because here each home firm maximizes profit given the sales of its rivals, *regardless* of what determines those sales. Thus in this model a binding VER can be described as simply a movement up and to the right along *HFE*.

(b) A profit-seeking home government.[13] Suppose first that the home government acts as the agent of the home industry, whose profit it wishes

---

[11] A circumflex denotes logarithmic differentiation.

[12] This section borrows heavily from Ethier (1989).

[13] This subsection may be thought of as offering a formal analysis of one of the possibilities raised in Hillman (1990).

to maximize. Since these profits are always increased by an upward movement along *HFE*, the home government will always wish to negotiate as stringent a restraint as possible. But if the agreement is truly voluntary, the foreign government will accept it only if foreign profit is not affected adversely. To see when this will be the case, we must superimpose foreign profit contours onto *HFE*. This is done in Figure 4.

Panel (a) shows the case where all foreign profit contours cut *HFE* from below. Straightforward algebraic manipulation reveals that this will happen if $c > c^* > c[1 - 1/\epsilon(n+1)]$ or if $c[1 - 1/\epsilon] > c^*$. In this situation upward movements along *HFE* necessarily lower foreign profit. Thus a VER cannot emerge in this case.[14]

In panel (b) $c^* > c$. Here -- or if $c[1 - 1/\epsilon(n+1)] > c^* > c[1 - 1/\epsilon]$ --there must exist a critical market share θ_v where foreign profit is maximized. If the free trade θ exceeds this critical value, the foreign government will again refuse to accept any binding VER. But when $\theta < \theta_v$ it will find a trade restriction to be in its own interest. I will refer to the situation of $c^* > c$, or of $c[1 - 1/\epsilon(n+1)] > c^* > c[1 - 1/\epsilon]$, and $\theta < \theta_v$ as the *HK* or Harris-Krishna case (not to be confused with *Hare-Krishna*) since it corresponds to the possibilities uncovered by Harris (1985) and Krishna (1989). Of course these particular conditions are determined by this model structure.[15] But the circumstances have intuitive appeal: if the foreign firms have a cost advantage they may want to be free to compete with home firms; if they are at a disadvantage, they may be willing to strike a deal. In the latter case they are more likely to want to deal the smaller is the market share they have been able to establish[16].

Suppose, then, that we are in the *HK* case. Then there must exist a market share $\theta^*(\theta)$ that exceeds θ_v and that yields foreign firms the same profit as does θ. Both governments desire an agreement at least restrictive enough to leave θ no less than θ_v. The home government wants as restrictive an agreement as possible. The foreign government would prefer θ_v, but will not lose with any agreement implying a home share in the interval $[\theta_v, \theta^*(\theta)]$. The latter is thus the core, and the two governments

---

[14] This is also trivially true if $c^* > c/(1 - 1/n\epsilon)$, since then **HFE** will lie entirely below all contours corresponding to nonnegative foreign profit, so there will be no active foreign firms.

[15] Harris and Krishna use different models than I and so obtain different conditions, but they were concerned with the same basic phenomena. See also Eichenberger and Harper (1987) and Hillman and Ursprung (1988).

[16] If $c = c^*$, the *HK* case cannot emerge in this model unless there are more foreign firms than domestic ones, if $n = n^*$, the *HK* case cannot emerge unless foreign firms are at a cost disadvantage.

Figure 4

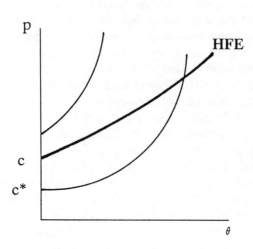

(a) No Agreement

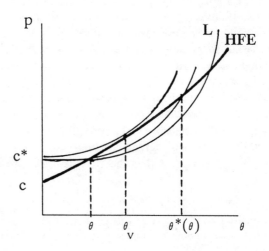

(b) *HK* Case

will agree to establish a VER that results in being in the interval, at a position determined by the actual bargaining process.

That it may be possible to establish a VER that benefits both home and foreign firms is the basic Harris-Krishna conclusion. A little thought reveals that it might be possible to raise both countries' welfare as well. To investigate this, alter the home government's assumed objective.

(c) A welfare-seeking home government. Suppose now that the home government wishes to maximize national welfare. There are now three distinct agents, and I suppose again that a VER can be established only if all three agree. As before, home firms always want a restraint and the foreign government will accept one only in the HK case. So consider the latter and ask whether the home government will want a restraint. This requires an examination of home welfare contours. This is provided in Figure 5.

Clearly, if the free trade θ is less than θ' no binding constraint will be in the home interest. Thus both sides will desire a VER only if $\theta' < \theta_v$ and if the free trade θ lies between the two. It also matters whether θ exceeds $\theta°$ or not.

Suppose first that it does. Then, just as when profit was its only concern, the home government wants as restrictive an agreement as it can get. Again, the foreign government will not accept anything outside of $[\theta_v, \theta^*(\theta)]$. Thus they will agree on a VER that puts θ somewhere in this interval. This is shown in Figure 5(a).

Suppose next that θ is less than $\theta°$, as in Figure 5(b) and 5(c). Let $\theta'(\theta)$ denote that home market share that exceeds $\theta°$ and yields the same level of home welfare as does θ. The home government will accept no VER that does not increase the home share to at least $\theta'(\theta)$, and the foreign government will not allow it to increase to more than $\theta^*(\theta)$. Thus no VER will emerge if $\theta^*(\theta) < \theta'(\theta)$, as in Figure 5(b). But if $\theta^*(\theta) > \theta'(\theta)$, the core will be $[\theta'(\theta), \theta^*(\theta)]$ or $[\theta_v, \theta^*(\theta)]$, whichever is smaller, and a VER will be negotiated leading to a home market share somewhere in the relevant interval. Figure 5(c) depicts this possibility.

Thus a VER may be useful even when both governments conscientiously try to raise national welfare. But the conditions for this are restrictive. They include: (i) the HK case; (ii) $\theta \geq \theta'$; (iii) either $\theta \geq \theta°$ or $\theta^*(\theta) > \theta'(\theta)$. How are such Pareto-improving restraints on trade possible? One of the consequences of trade management is production shifting. If production is shifted from a location where marginal costs are high to one where marginal costs are low, the benefit could be large enough to generate a welfare improvement overall. The condition $c \leq c^*$ is not necessary for the HK case, but it is necessary for a Pareto-improvement.

Figure 5

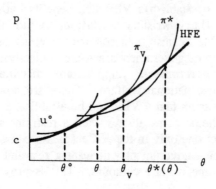

(a) VER

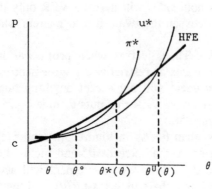

(b) no VER

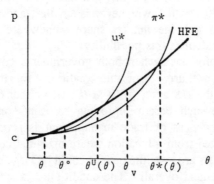

(c) VER

At this point probably most of us would respond by suggesting that VERs do not in fact often emerge when the import-competing firms are the low-cost producers. This apparently implies that actual arrangements are not Pareto-improving, and that government policy is motivated by some sacrifice of national welfare for sectoral interests. I think there is considerable merit to such a view. But I also think that it is easy to accord it too much emphasis. This is because central features of managed trade, not included in the basic model of this section, cast different light on that view. This will become clear below.

V. ENTRY IN THE IMPERFECTLY COMPETITIVE MODEL

Thus far we have taken n and n* as given. But a central feature of trade management in an imperfectly competitive context is its relation to entry and exit. Suppose now that foreign firms can be expected to enter the market until the profit of the typical foreign firm falls to some long run level. The contour labeled L in Figure 4(b) corresponds to that level of profit, presumably lower than what foreign firms are earning now. This is not the long-run profit contour, where n* is endogenous; that would be a horizontal line at the height corresponding to long-run average revenue. Rather it is the contour, *given the present configuration of firms*, that corresponds to the long run-profit level. As foreign firms enter and n* increases, profit contours shift.

Note first that entry of foreign firms cannot transform a situation like Figure 4(a) into one like Figure 4(b), since n* plays no role in the conditions that distinguish the two. Thus if marginal costs and the number of home firms preclude the HK case, foreign entry will not alter this fact.

Suppose, then, that foreign profit contours do cut HFE from above, for a while, so that the HK case is conceivable. Then, if foreign firms focus only on the long run, they would welcome any VER that precluded entry (by giving all quota allowances to existing firms), provided that the resulting θ left them on a profit contour above L. Thus any point on HFE lying above L is acceptable. Clearly this must enlarge the range of acceptable agreements (relative to those that are preferable to the existing short run value of θ), and it could introduce the HK case into a situation from which it would otherwise be absent because the present θ exceeds θ_v.

Of course, foreign firms care about present profit as well as future profit. Thus only a subset of that part of HFE above L would presumably be acceptable, the size of that subset depending upon the speed of industry adjustment that would occur without an arrangement and the existing firms' rate of time preference. But it is clear that the entry of foreign firms increases the likelihood of the HK case and increases the range of acceptable quotas. This is the first basic implication of entry.

Existing foreign firms presumably care only about their own future profit and not that of potential rivals. But a foreign government that values foreign national welfare would be concerned about total profit extracted from the domestic market by foreign firms, and not about the distribution of that profit among older foreign firms and newer entrants. Thus the prospect of entry might make the foreign government either more willing or less willing to enter into a VER, depending upon the likely effect of such entry on total profit. Also a foreign government that values foreign welfare may be less willing than existing foreign firms would like to use the quota mechanism to restrict entry. But the basic point is that the prospect of entry means that the profit of existing foreign firms no longer coincides with the effect on foreign welfare, so the foreign government once again becomes a separate agent from foreign firms.

These considerations seem to be quite important in practice in at least some industries. A major implication of the restraints on Japanese automobile exports to the United States, where quotas were allotted in proportion to past sales, was that firms with established positions, such as Toyota and Nissan, were shielded from increased competition by firms, such as Toyo Kogyo and Isuzu, that had not yet built up market share.

We have considered entry of foreign firms. The potential entry of domestic firms is less interesting. First, entry of import-competing firms does not in practice appear to be relevant in industries where trade management does occur, although the possible role of such management in retarding exit might be. Second, existing firms want as restrictive an agreement as they can get in any case, and the prospect of entry or exit does not change this, even if it does change the value an existing firm would attach to such an agreement.[17]

A third possible type of entry would be that of foreign firms who can bring their technology into the domestic market and produce there. If these firms are also subject to management, no new element is added, because our earlier discussion is not sensitive to where production actually takes place. The United States automobile industry, for example, has in the past argued that American production of Japanese firms should be included in the quotas, and the issue has arisen in a third country context with the European proposal to include American production in future European

---

[17] Exit of domestic firms might have some influence on the willingness of *foreign* firms to deal, however. As we have seen, one of the conditions allowing for the emergence of the HK case is $c[1 - 1/\epsilon(n+1)] > c^* > c[1 - 1/\epsilon]$. If exit takes place it will reduce n, thereby lowering the left-most term and so reducing the range of possible values of c^*. In this sense exit can reduce the probability of the HK case emerging.

restraints on imports of Japanese automobiles. Nevertheless, common practice has been not to include such production in the arrangement. Foreign firms producing in the home market are not part of the domestic industry interest group, and their profits are not part of domestic welfare.[18] In effect, these firms play the same role as unrestrained exporters: the fact that their production takes place in the domestic economy does not matter. Thus the basic issue raised is that of discrimination. The next section addresses that explicitly.

VI. THE DISCRIMINATORY EFFECT OF MANAGED TRADE

The fact that managed trade is essentially discriminatory can have a profound effect on the implications of such management for economic welfare, especially for that of importing countries.[19] A frequent situation where discrimination arises is when a VER is established with a group of exporters who have large established positions in the domestic market, but not with another group of exporters, newer producers, who do not yet have established positions but who have lower costs. This is consistent with our earlier discussion: with lower costs they are unlikely to be in an *HK* situation; without an established base it would be difficult for home interests to rouse resentment against them.

Suppose, then, that in addition to the home (H) and foreign (F) firms as above, there is also a low-cost group L of foreign firms with marginal cost $c_L < c, c^*$. They have their own Cournot-Nash equilibrium condition:

$$(LFE) \qquad p = \frac{c_L}{1 - \mu/n_L \epsilon}$$

where n_L is the number of L firms and their market share is $\mu = n_L x_L/z$. Here x_L denotes the sales of the typical L firm and now $z = ny + n^*x + n_L x_L$. The equilibrium condition for H firms continues to be *HFE*, but that for F firms must be rewritten:

---

[18] Both statements need to be qualified to the extent that these firms increase the rents of domestically-owned specific factors that they employ.

[19] But this aspect has not received much attention in the literature. Indeed Pomfret (1989, p 204) states, "The most surprising feature of economists' analysis of VERs is the lack of attention given to their discriminatory nature." But the issue is addressed empirically in Dinopoulos and Kreinen (1988) and theoretically in Dean and Gangopadhyay (1989).

$$(FFE°) \qquad p = \frac{c^*}{1 - (1-\theta°)/n^*\epsilon}$$

where $\theta° = \theta + \mu$. *HFE*, *FFE°* and *LFE* jointly determine equilibrium p, θ and μ.

Point E in Figure 6(a) depicts an equilibrium between H and F firms, before the L firms enter the market. In the case shown, $c^* < c$ and all F profit contours cut *HFE* from below. Thus the *HK* case is not possible and trade management cannot be negotiated, even though H firms desire a VER and it may also be possible to enhance H welfare in this way (H welfare contours are not shown).

Now allow the L firms to enter. Since *FFE* has the same functional form as *FFE°*, the latter can be depicted by the same curve in Figure 6(a), if the horizontal axis is also used to measure $\theta°$. F profit contours are also drawn the same as before. Substitute *LFE* into *HFE* to obtain, after some manipulation:

$$(HFE°) \qquad p = \frac{c°}{1 - \theta°/n°\epsilon}$$

where $n° = n + n_L$ and $c° = (n/n°)c + (n_L/n°)c_L$. Clearly $n° > n$, $c° < c$ and $n°c° > nc$. Thus *HFE°* lies below *HFE*, and, at each value of p, has a smaller slope $dp/d\theta$.

Equilibrium is determined by the intersection of *HFE°* and *FFE°* at E´ in Figure 6(a). This point shows equilibrium p and $\theta°$; θ is determined by the corresponding point H´ on *HFE*, and therefore μ equals the distance H´E´. Entry of the L firms lowers the market price and reduces the shares of both H and F firms.

There are also additional possibilities for trade management. We must consider a possible restraint on only F exports, a restraint on only L exports, and a restraint on both F and L exports. H firms, of course, want as binding a restraint as possible on as many firms as possible. Our earlier discussion suggests that the L firms, as the least-cost producers, would be the least likely to wish to have their exports restrained, so assume that they would not in fact agree to a VER on themselves alone.

A VER that restrains only F firms can be depicted as a movement upwards and to the right along *HFE°*. In the situation depicted in Figure 6(a) F firms are willing to negotiate a VER involving themselves alone. At first blush it would seem paradoxical that F firms, originally unwilling to restrain their exports, should be made willing to do so by the advent of lower-cost competitors who would remain unrestrained. The reason is that

Figure 6

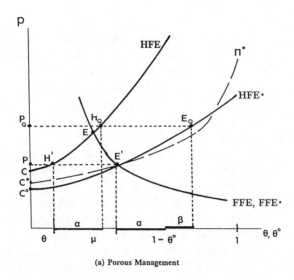

(a) Porous Management

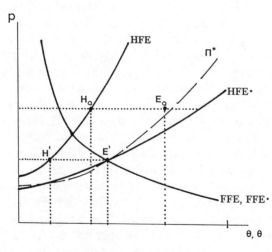

(b) Comprehensive Management

the loss of the status of least-cost producers reduces the attraction of unrestrained competition to the F firms relative to that of implicit collusion, even if only among themselves.

Consider a VER that moves equilibrium from E′ to E_Q. H firm equilibrium moves from H′ to H_Q. Both H firms and L firms experience increased market shares with a higher price, so their profits rise a result of the management. F firms experience the price rise while losing market share, but since they move to a higher profit contour they also benefit. Depending on circumstances, H welfare might even rise. The possibility of a Pareto improvement arises because of the production switching brought about by the arrangement. In the figure, α represents a switch of market share from F firms to H firms; with c > c*, as in this case, this switch reduces global production efficiency. But β represents a switch from F firms to L firms, and this is globally beneficial.

Figure 6(b) shows another possibility. Here the F iso-profit contour at E′ cuts $HFE°$ from below. Thus a movement up along the latter reduces profit for the F firms, and they will not agree to a VER limited to themselves alone. But if the profit contour possesses a sufficiently gentle slope, a VER restraining both F and L firms can be negotiated that benefits all firms. Consider a restriction that moves H firms from H′ to H_Q in Figure 6(b). Suppose quotas are set so that E_Q determines the division between μ and $\theta°$. If the profit contour at E′ is less steep than HFE at H′, as in the figure, it is possible to find an E_Q that both raises μ and is on a higher F profit contour than that through E′. Thus the arrangement brings all firms an increase in profits. Again, both harmful and beneficial production switching occurs, and this may or may not increase global production efficiency. Note that in Figure 6(b) all firms are included in the arrangement, but it is still discriminatory in the sense that it reallocates production among the restrained firms. Note also that in this case all restrained firms have lower marginal costs than H firms, but a Pareto improvement is still possible because of this internal reallocation.

The critical importance of the discrimination inherent to managed trade should now be apparent. That the deflection of output to low-cost outsiders could add a welfare-enhancing aspect to such arrangements should come as no surprise. More surprising is the possibility that the existence of such firms might facilitate the commencement of such management, even if they themselves decline to participate. The "porous" nature of VERs, where outsiders replace restrained imports at least in part, is often observed in practice. Import-competing firms would like to minimize this by including as many foreign sources in the arrangement as possible. As we have seen, under some circumstances a VER must indeed be comprehensive to be feasible, but under other circumstances just the reverse is true.

Section IV implied that relatively high foreign marginal costs were important in inducing voluntary foreign participation and, especially, in allowing for welfare-enhancing trade management. The observation that import-competing firms are in practice least anxious to press for management when they have a cost advantage therefore causes the theory to generate scepticism about the voluntary nature of participation and about the possibility of welfare-enhancing (or, at least, cushioned welfare-reducing) management. But consideration of discrimination changes this outlook radically because it shifts attention to the role of relative cost differences *between* foreign firms.

Time and time again we have in practice witnessed trade management implemented by restraints on the exports of foreign firms with established positions while leaving unrestrained the exports of newer, lower-cost producers. Presumably this is because their lower costs make them less likely to agree to participate and because their lack of established market share makes it difficult both for import-competing firms to marshall domestic political support for their inclusion and for the importing country to offer them rents as compensation. Typically these firms increase their exports as a result of the management. Sometimes this results in the successive expansion of management to include most of the world's producers (e.g., textiles and apparel), sometimes it causes the management to collapse (e.g., shoes), and sometimes it results in the continued restraint of only some firms (e.g., automobiles). But the concerns emphasized in this section seem to be of central importance in any case.

VII. CONCLUDING REMARKS

This paper has sorted out the circumstances under which managed trade might be expected to emerge and has investigated the implications of a policy environment in which it is an endogenous possibility. Two features that appear to be crucial are the allocation of rents and the discrimination inherent in such management.

A major result is the conclusion that trade management might in fact prove useful even if policy is directed toward enhancing national welfare. A countervailing implication is the complex sensitivity of welfare consequences upon exogenous parameters. In addition, the models I have considered are very special. I have used an informal and geometric exposition to avoid investing specific conditions with excessive dignity. More important are the possibilities (or "parables") that the analysis suggests and explains.

References

Arad, R. and A. L. Hillman, 1979. "Embargo threat, learning and departure from comparative advantage," *Journal of International Economics*, 9, 265-276.

Dean, J. and S. Gangopadhyay, 1989. "Strategic trade practices in the presence of a VER," unpublished manuscript.

Dinopoulos, E. and M. E. Kreinen, 1988. "Effects of the U.S.-Japan auto VER on European prices and on U.S. welfare," *Review of Economics and Statistics*, 70, 484-491.

Eichenberger, J. and I. Harper, 1987. "Price and quantity controls as facilitating devices," *Economics Letters*, 23, 223-228.

Ethier, W. J., 1988. "Antidumping," unpublished manuscript, International Economics Research Center, University of Pennsylvania.

Ethier, W. J., 1989. "Voluntary export restraints," unpublished manuscript, International Economics Research Center, University of Pennsylvania. Forthcoming in: Takayama, A., H. Ohta and M. Ohyama, editors, *Trade, Policy, and International Adjustments*, Academic Press.

Ethier, W. J. and R. Fischer, 1987. "The new protectionism," *Journal of International Economic Integration*, 2, 1-11.

Fischer, R., 1986. *Essays in Game Theory and International Economics*, Ph. D. dissertation, University of Pennsylvania.

Harris, R., 1985. "Why voluntary export restraints are 'voluntary'," *Canadian Journal of Economics*, 18, 799-809.

Hillman, A. L., 1990. "Protectionist policies as the regulation of international industry," *Public Choice*, forthcoming.

Hillman, A. L. and H. Ursprung, 1988. "Domestic politics, foreign interests, and international trade policy," *American Economic Review*, 78, 729-745.

Kostecki, M., 1987. "Export-restraint arrangements and trade liberalization," *The World Economy*, 10, 442-450.

Krishna, K., 1989. "Trade restrictions as facilitating practices," *Journal of International Economics*, 26, 251-270.

Pomfret, R., 1989. "The economics of voluntary export restraint agreements," *Journal of Economic Surveys*, 3, 199-211.

Yano, M., 1989. "Voluntary export restraints and expectations: An analysis of export quotas in oligopolistic markets," *International Economic Review*, 30, 707-723.

Chapter 15

CHANGES IN TRADE-POLICY REGIMES

James H. Cassing

One of the curiosities of trade policy regimes is that policies spawned
in response to large but temporary external shocks seem to persist long after
the shock has subsided. Thus protection frequently appears in an industry
in response to sudden, adverse terms of trade shocks and then lives on even
after relative prices have returned to "normal." Political scientists attribute
this to an increased commonality of interests during cyclical troughs which
may facilitate overcoming fixed costs of putting a lobby organization in
place. The lobby, it must be argued, is then maintained even when
"normality" returns to the markets so long as the maintenance costs are less
than the perceived benefits secured through the political process. Similarly,
free trade is commonly imposed on just the same industries when they
experience large favorable terms of trade shocks and then *this* regime seems
to displace the protectionist one when prices return to normal. This is the
clear impression from recent studies such as Hufbauer *et.al.*(1986) wherein
industries in the U.S., such as ball bearings, simply do not petition to retain
special protection when prices are especially firm even though they lose
their protected status for the future. What seems curious is not so much
that large shocks engender regime changes, but that the regime thus
enfranchised then seems to win the day after the shock has disappeared and
to persist in the very same economic environment that had previously
supported an alternative policy regime. Certainly that trade protection
regimes shift over time and then the new regime becomes a bit entrenched
is one possible interpretation of the pattern of tariff regimes reported in
Gardner and Kimbrough (1989). While political economy explanations of
regime changes are legion (see the survey by Hillman, 1989), models of
regime persistence are harder to find, especially in the economics literature.
This paper aims to provide such a model of "policy hysteresis" which is at
least consistent with the stylized facts.

The basic version of the model is presented in the next section and extended in subsequent sections. While the context is very different, the formal structure of the basic model draws upon the recent work on "hysteresis" and the first of two main theorems really owes to Baldwin (1988) and to Baldwin and Krugman (1986). Dixit (1989) provides a framework that could free the model from some of the more restrictive assumptions and Rust (1987) provides a guide for formal empirical investigation.

I. THE BASIC MODEL

Consider a small open economy comprised of an exporting sector and an import-competing sector. While we do not formally model the supply of protection until later, we will suppose that protection delivered is responsive to "lobbying" and that the policy-making process is biased in favor of the special producer interests in the import-competing sector. In particular, we will assume that the policy-maker may impose a predetermined import quota, $\overline{Q}$, or not. Import-competing firms receive the quota protection initially if they "lobby" with sunk cost N, N > 0, and continue to receive the quota protection if they maintain their lobby at maintenance cost M, M ≥ 0. As in all such hysteretic models, a crucial assumption is N > M. Each "firm" is assumed to consist in part of some industry specific factor in fixed supply which represents the lobby's interests. The magnitudes of N and M should be taken to reflect not just the costs of advocating protection, but the costs of prevailing or not over any anti-protectionist sentiment or coalition as well.

While the results are robust to a wide variety of market structures, the lobbying story makes the most sense and the exposition is the cleanest when the industry behaves as a domestic single price monopoly subjected to the discipline of a competitive world market. Thus, there is no free-rider problem in organizing the lobby and the imposition of a quota allows the import-competing sector to extract monopoly profits on the residual domestic demand. We will assume that any quota rents are of no consequence to the lobby and that selling to the world market as a discriminating monopolist is prohibited. (The appendix shows that both of these assumptions are only for convenience.)

The model is a dynamic discrete time one wherein external terms of trade are stochastic and identically independently distributed in each period. Uncertainty is resolved at the beginning of each period at which time the monopolist must make output and lobbying decisions. Inventories are not allowed. In order to make this concrete, denote:

   t,   time subscript
   p_t,   world price

q_t,   output
$c(q_t)$,   total cost; $c' > 0$

$Y(p_t)$,   profit maximum given no quota when p_t obtains
($= p_t q_t - c(q_t)$, i.e. rent accruing to the industry
specific factor); $Y' > 0$
$Y(\overline{Q})$, profit maximum given the quota $\overline{Q}$ but gross of N or M.
Now, in any period t, the net profit, R_t, is given by:

$$R_t = \begin{cases} Y(p_t) & \text{if no lobby} \\ Y(\overline{Q}) - N & \text{if initiate lobby} \\ Y(\overline{Q}) - M & \text{if maintain lobby} \end{cases}$$

Risk neutral producers--the monopolist in this case--now solve the stochastic dynamic programing problem

$$\max E \sum_{t=0}^{\infty} R_t \, \delta^t$$

where E is the mathematical expectations operator and δ is a deterministic discount factor assumed constant with $\delta \in (0,1)$ for any t. Recall that p_t is i.i.d.

II. THE MAIN RESULTS

We now set out to derive the two main results in the prototype model, namely, the *possibility* and the *likelihood* of policy hysteresis. First, we will establish the existence of a non-degenerate interval $[p_{lt}, p_{nt}]$ where, in period t, p_{lt} denotes the world price below which the producer when unprotected will initiate a lobby, thereby acquiring quota protection, and p_{nt} denotes the world price above which the protected producer will cease to maintain the lobby, thereby losing the quota protection. The point is that for $p_t \in [p_{lt}, p_{nt}]$, the existing policy regime will not change. But a draw of an outlier, $p_t < p_{lt}$ or $p_t > p_{nt}$, can change the policy regime from free trade to protection or *vice-versa*. And, once changed, the new regime will persist until another outlier in the opposite direction obtains. Second, we will show that there is some presumption that regimes really do persist in the sense that under reasonable assumptions, the values p_{lt} and p_{nt} are determined endogenously in such a way that the expected value of p_t is in that interval, i.e. $Ep_t \in [p_{lt}, p_{nt}]$. Thus, it really is only "outliers" or "shocks" that alter the current policy regime to a new regime which itself then endures, at least expectationally. While the validity of this model of regime changes is in the end an empirical issue, the results do suggest a certain efficiency argument for safeguard-clause-like protection which prevents large, temporary adverse terms of trade shocks that might otherwise shift the trade regime to one of longer term, more entrenched protection.

A. The Possibility of Policy Hysteresis

Given our notation, the first result, albeit in a totally different context, owes to Baldwin and Krugman (1986) and here appears formally as:

Proposition 1

(A technical assumption is that for some external price sufficiently low, it pays to lobby, i.e., to use the notation introduced below, there exists a p_t' such that $Y(p_t') + \delta v_{nt} < Y(\overline{Q}) - N + v_{lt}$.)

Suppose that p_t is i.i.d.

Then, there exists a non-degenerate interval $[p_{lt}, p_{nt}]$ such that for $p_t \in [p_{lt}, p_{nt}]$ there is no regime change. Furthermore, when the regime is free trade (protection), there is a regime change to protection (free trade) whenever $p_t < p_{lt}$ ($p_t > p_{nt}$) obtains.

Proof:

The proof focusses on regime changes. A firm can lobby or not. If the firm lobbied last period, it will continue to lobby and have DPV of $Y(\overline{Q})-M+\delta v_{lt}$ so long as

$$Y(\overline{Q})-M+\delta v_{lt} > Y(p_t) + \delta v_{nt}$$

where δ is the discount factor and v_{lt}, v_{nt} are the values of a firm beyond period t that now chooses the strategy l (lobby) or n (no lobby), respectively. Since v_{lt}, v_{nt} are fixed and $Y' > 0$, a firm will cease to maintain its lobby and choose the strategy n for any $p_t > p_{nt}$ where p_{nt} solves

(1) $Y(\overline{Q})-M+\delta v_{lt} = Y(p_{nt}) + \delta v_{nt}$

Similarly, if the firm is not currently lobbying, it will initiate a lobby and have DPV of $Y(\overline{Q})-N+Ptv_{lt}$ so long as

$$Y(\overline{Q})-N+\delta v_{lt} > Y(p_t) + \delta v_{nt}$$

Since v_{lt}, v_{nt} are fixed and $Y' > 0$, a firm will initiate a lobby and choose strategy l for any $p_t < p_{lt}$, where p_{lt} solves

(2) $Y(\overline{Q})-N+\delta v_{lt} = Y(p_{lt}) + \delta V_{nt}$

Subtracting equation (2) from equation (1) yields $Y(p_{nt}) - Y(p_{lt}) = N - M > 0$.

Since $Y' > 0$, $p_{nt} > p_{lt}$.   q.e.d.

The result is illustrated in Figure 1 which relates the random variable p_t to the level of quota restriction. For exposition, we measure vertically the quota-equivalent tariff as the measure of protection. In the basic model so far there are only two policy regimes, free trade and the quota $\overline{Q}$. Once on the free trade locus $[p_{lt}, \infty)$, free trade will be the policy until $p_t < p_{lt}$ is drawn. However, once the policy regime jumps to the protection locus

Figure 1

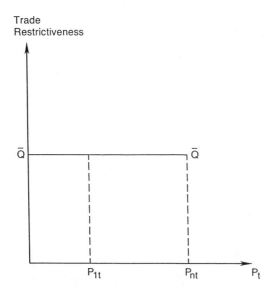

$\overline{QQ}$, this regime will displace free trade for any $p_t < p_{nt}$ and, in particular, now persist in the interval $[p_{lt}, p_{nt}]$ where free trade was previously sustained. The next section aims to show that this hysteresis may be more than an unlikely curiosity in the sense that "usually" the p_t drawn will be in the interval $[p_{lt}, p_{nt}]$ if policy is geared, as it seems to be, toward responding to "market disruption."

B. The Likelihood of Policy Hysteresis

Suppose that the p.d.f. of p in any period t--we drop the t subscript since p is i.i.d.--was as in Figure 2. Then there would be a sense in which policy hysteresis might be likely because most of the probability mass of the random variable p is in the interval where the policy maintained depends on the most recent outlier drawn. At first face, this would look like a mere coincidence. However, the endpoints of the interval are determined endogenously as the solution to a stochastic dynamic programming problem which itself involves properties of the p.d.f. of p.

In order to solve for p_{lt} and p_{nt}, we must use equations (1) and (2), not just their difference as in proposition 1. Consequently it is necessary to "model" the $\overline{Q}$ that policy-makers are willing to grant if lobbied. In the U.S. and some other countries there appears currently to be a preoccupation with "fairness" defined in terms of normality. Drawing upon this sylized fact, and still within the context of the basic domestic monopoly model,

Figure 2

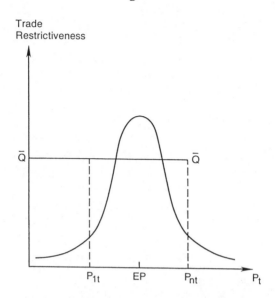

suppose that the policy-maker stands ready through quotas to guarantee "normal prices" defined as the expected value Ep if lobbied. (This is in fact a remedy in some escape clause, unfair trade practices, and countervailing duty investigations. Probably expected profits, EY(p), are not used due to information revelation difficulties and moral hazard problems.) In this model we can then pin down $Y(\overline{Q}) = Y(Ep)$.

We now set out to find some properties of p_{nt} and p_{lt} which relate these prices to Ep. The idea is to exploit equations (1)-(2) and our knowledge from proposition 1 that $p_{lt} < p_{nt}$.

From equation (2), p_{lt} solves

$$Y(p_{lt}) = Y(\overline{Q}) - N + \delta(v_{lt} - v_{nt})$$

$$= Y(\overline{Q}) - N + \delta[\int_{o}^{p_{lt+1}} (N-M)f(p)dp$$

$$+ \int_{p_{lt+1}}^{p_{nt+1}} (Y(\overline{Q})-M-Y(p)+\pi)f(p)dp]$$

where p_{lt+1} is p_l in period $t+1$ and similarly for P_{nt+1}. Intuitively, the LHS represents profits today in the absence of a lobby. The RHS is comprised of profits today with a lobby and the discounted difference between the future value of adopting today the strategy "lobby" over "not lobby." This term is itself decomposed in the bracketed term as two integrals. The first integral shows the difference between the two strategies if in $t+1$ it pays to lobby and there is not a lobby in place, N-M, weighted by the probability that $p_{t+1} < p_{lt+1}$ so that the lobby strategy is adopted.

The second integral represents the probability weighted future difference between the two strategies when p_{t+1} happens to fall in the hysteresis interval $[p_{lt+1}, p_{nt+1}]$ where it does not pay to switch strategies. (Of course, beyond P_{nt+1} there is no difference since free trade reigns and the lobby is simply not maintained.) The term $Y(\overline{Q})-M-Y(p)$ is the payoff difference in period $t+1$ and π is the discounted future value of the difference beyond $t+1$. Note that this second integral term is (weakly) between M and N. This is because the terms without the probability weights are simply the difference between the strategies "maintain a lobby" and "not lobby." In the interval of hysteresis it pays to continue whichever strategy is in place. Therefore, the gain must be less than N, or else it would pay to drop free trade, and yet greater than M, or else it would pay to not maintain the lobby. Now, since the first integral term is itself less than N, and since together the terms in the brackets are probability weighted from zero to p_{nt+1}, we have a useful result.

Lemma 1

$$0 < \delta \left[\int_{0}^{p_{lt+1}} (N-M)f(p)dp \right.$$

$$\left. + \int_{p_{lt+1}}^{p_{nt+1}} (Y(\overline{Q}) - M - Y(p) + \pi)f(p)dp \right] < N-M$$

Proof: The proof is one by contradiction. In the interval $[P_{lt+1}, P_{nt+1}]$, nondegenerate by Thm.1, we know that there is no change in the strategy -- lobby or not lobby.

Therefore, lobby at t implies
$$Y(\overline{Q}) - M + \delta v_{lt+1} > Y(P) + \delta v_{nt+1}$$
That is, it pays to continue the lobby in the hysteresis interval. So,
$$Y(\overline{Q}) - M - Y(P) + \pi > 0 \qquad (1)$$
Similarly, not lobby at t implies
$$Y(P) + \delta v_{nt+1} > Y(\overline{Q}) - N + \delta v_{lt+1}$$
So,

$$Y(\overline{Q}) - N - Y(P) + \pi < 0 \qquad (2)$$

From (1) and (2)

$$0 < Y(\overline{Q}) - M - Y(P) + \pi < N - M \qquad q.e.d$$

Call this term H, for hysteresis, so that $O < H < N\text{-}M$. Using the above notation, and following the same discussion for equation (1) as for equation (2), we can rewrite these equations as

(1´) $Y(p_{nt}) = Y(\overline{Q}) - M + H$

(2´) $Y(p_{lt}) = Y(\overline{Q}) - N + H$

We are now in a position to discuss the "likelihood" of hysteresis being important. The result requires that M, the lobby maintenance cost, not be "too high." Formally, we state:

Proposition 2

Suppose $Y(\overline{Q}) = Y(Ep)$ and, $M < H$. Then $p_{lt} < Ep < p_{nt}$.
Proof:
From (1´) $Y(P_{nt}) > Y(Ep)$.
Since $Y´ > 0$, we have $p_{nt} > Ep$.
From (2´) and Lemma 1,
    $Y(p_{lt}) < Y(Ep)$
Since $Y´ > 0$, we have $p_{lt} < Ep$.   q.e.d.

The importance of the proposition resides in the demonstration that under relatively unrestrictive conditions, but within the context of the model, there is a presumption of hysteresis. Obviously, a special case would be that of zero maintenance cost of the lobby, $M=0$, since we know $H > 0$. If we relax the assumption that $M < H$, then the proposition is weakened to $p_{lt} < Ep$, which might be read as a presumption of free trade. Finally, if the profit function is concave in p, we can recast the proposition in terms of a guaranteed expected profits government policy, $Y(\overline{Q}) = EY(p)$, to establish that $p_{lt} < Ep$ since then we would have $Y(P_{lt}) < EY(p) < Y(Ep)$. In order to get $E(p) < p_{nt}$, however, we need an assumption such as $(Y(Ep) - EY(p)) < H\text{-}M$.

We next discuss variations on the prototype model and, among other things, argue that the possibility and presumption of policy hysteresis are quite robust propositions.

III. EXTENSIONS

The model has a particular structure in terms of the market organization, the lobby organization, and the political response assumption. Since all of these components are reflected in the key equations -- (1) and (2) -- there are some obvious extensions. The discussion below addresses some of the possibilities with particular reference to modifications in the interval of hysteresis and the "likelihood" argument.

A. Domestic Competition

The assumption of a domestically monopolized import-competing industry is not forceful to the economics of the model. So long as there is an industry specific factor, the owners of that factor have an interest in any protection that will then increase rents. This is, in fact, the usual model in rent-seeking and politics of protection analysis (see for example Bhagwati, 1982, and the papers therein). Thus, we can interpret $Y(\overline{Q})$ as the profit, or return to the industry-specific factor, that a quota $\overline{Q}$ would confer on the industry. Propositions (1) and (2) remain unchanged. (An appendix shows this for the case of "water-in-the-quota" -- non-binding -- as well.)

The politics of the model are now less straight-forward, however, since a share of increased industry profits accrues to firms whether or not they participate in the lobby. Nonetheless, to the extent that free-riding can be overcome, the analysis goes through. If free-riding cannot be overcome completely, then the output prices needed to induce or maintain a lobby would be lower and so the interval $[P_{lt}, P_{nt}]$ would shift leftward. Given proposition 2, this would, not surprisingly, impart a free trade bias.

B. Lobby Organization

While there is no explicit model of the actual pressure group organization, the implication is that policy-makers can be "educated" if the appropriate level of resources is expended. Political scientists and some economists have suggested that this requisite level of expenditure depends on how long the lobby has been entrenched or how long ago it was disbanded (for a review, see Cassing, McKeown, and Ochs, 1986). In terms of the prototype model, this would be captured by positing M to be a decreasing function of the lobby's lifespan and N to be an increasing function of a free trade regime's lifespan.

In equations (1) and (2), the history would enter to alter the critical values p_{lt} and p_{nt}. The maintenance cost M_t falling through time would work to increase p_{nt} and the organizational cost N_t rising over time would work to lower p_{lt}. While the terms v_{lt} and v_{nt} complicate matters, they drop out of the difference between equations (1) and (2) that fixes the hysteresis interval. Thus, during the free trade regime, p_{lt} falls so that the exogenous terms of trade deterioration in any period t necessary to engender protection must be progressively more severe. Similarly, during the quota regime, p_{nt} rises so that the favorable terms of trade shock necessary to cause the lobby's demise must be progressively more favorable. Thus, in light of proposition 2, which continues to hold, there is a sense in which the persistence of a particular policy regime is self-reinforcing.

C. Political Response

The prototype model is not explicit about the underpinnings of the political response to the lobby. The policy-makers either confer on the industry quota protection of $\overline{Q}$ or nothing at all. The literature on the political economy of protection, however, typically endogenizes both the level of protection and, more recently, the choice of policy tools (see for a discussion Cassing and Hillman, 1985, 1986) and Kaempfer (forthcoming). In this spirit, the policy response could be endogenized by assuming that N_t and M_t are choice variables of the industry and that the quota response depends on the levels, $Q_t = g(N_t, M_t)$. It can be shown in some rather specific cases -- e.g., a three period model -- that the propositions (1) and (2) continue to hold. The conjecture is that this will be a general result. Of more interest, but beyond the scope of this discussion, is the dynamic path of protection during the quota regime and the dynamics of p_{lt} and p_{nt}.

IV. CONCLUSION

Large, but temporary, economic shocks seem to engender changes in trade policy regimes which persist long after the shock has subsided. One explanation of this is that pressure groups are activated by large shocks such as terms of trade changes, which are necessary to overcome a sunk cost of organizing, and then the regime is not displaced when the shock terminates because the costs of maintaining a policy once enacted are below the initial organization costs. Political scientists often speak in these terms, but the model focusses our attention on what is needed in terms of structure. While the possibility of policy hysteresis is of interest, the "likelihood" of it seems most important and worth pursuing.

Appendix 1. Discriminating Monopoly

Suppose that the domestic monopolist can sell with a quota domestically at p (or max p, p_t) and internationally at p_t.

Claim: Proposition 1 carries through.

Proof:

Write, $S(p_t)$ as the producer surplus generated from sales abroad by the discriminating monopolist. The conditions become:

Initiate a lobby if

(1) $Y(\overline{Q}) + S(p_t) - N + \delta v_1 > Y(p_t) + \delta v_n$

Since $S' > 0$, $Y' > o$, and $S' < Y'$, $\exists$ a critical p_1 such that lobby if $p_t < p$ where p_1 solves (1) as an equality.

And, cease to lobby if

(2) $Y(Q) + S(p_t) - M + \delta v_1 < Y(p_t) + \delta v_n$

As above, $\exists$ a critical p_n such that lobbying ceases if $p_n < p_t$ where p_n solves (2) as an equality.

Subtracting (1) from (2) yields

$S(p_n) - S(p_1) + N\text{-}M = Y(p_n) - Y(p_1)$

or,

$G(p_n) - G(p_1) = N\text{-}M > 0$

where $G(p) = Y(p) - S(p)$

Since $G' > 0$, we have $p_n > p_1$ q.e.d.

Appendix 2. Competition with the Possibility of "Water in the Quota"

Denote by $Y(\overline{p})$ profits (producers' surplus) with the quota guaranteed price.

Claim: Proposition 1 carries through.
Proof:

The conditions are now:
Cease lobbying if
(1) $Y(p_t) + \delta v_n > \max(Y(\overline{p}), Y(p_t)) - M + \delta v_1$

Assuming that for some sufficiently low p_t, RHS < LHS, and that for some higher p_t, RHS > LHS, $\exists$ a critical p_n such that a lobby ceases if $p_t < p_1$ where p_1 solves (1) as an equality.

And, initiate a lobby if
(2) $Y(p_t) + \delta v_n < \max(Y(\overline{p}), Y(p_t)) - N + \delta v_1$

As above, there exists a critical p_1 such that a lobby is initiated if $p_t < p_1$ where p_1 solves (2) as an equality.

Subtracting (2) from (1) yields

$R(p_n) - R(p_1) = N - M > 0$

where

$R(p) = Y(p) - \max(Y(\overline{p}), Y(p))$

Since $G' \geq Y'$, using $G' > 0$ when $p \leq \overline{p}$

and $G' = 0$ when $p > \overline{p}$, we have $p_n > p_1$. q.e.d.

References

Baldwin, Richard, 1988. "Hysteresis in import prices: The beachhead effect," *American Economic Review*, 78, 773-85.

Baldwin, Richard, and Paul Krugman, 1986. "Persistent trade effects of large exchange rate shocks," *NBER Working Paper* No. 2017.

Bhagwati, Jagdish N., 1982. Editor, *Import Competition and Response*, University of Chicago Press for NBER.

Cassing, James H. and Arye L. Hillman, 1985. "Political influence motives and the choice between tariffs and quotas," *Journal of International Economics*, 19, 279-90.

Cassing, James H. and Arye L. Hillman, 1986. "Shifting comparative advantage and senescent industry collapse," *American Economic Review*, 76, 516-23.

Cassing, James H., Timothy McKeown, and Jack Ochs. 1986. "The political economy of the tariff cycle," *American Political Science Review*, 80, 843-62.

Dixit, Avinash, 1989. "Hysteresis, import penetration, and exchange rate pass-through," *Quarterly Journal of Economics*, 104, 205-28.

Gardner, Grant W. and Kent P. Kimbrough, 1989. "The behavior of U.S. tariff rates," *American Economic Review*, 79, 211-18.

Hillman, Arye L., 1989. *The Political Economy of Protection*, New York: Harwood Academic Publishers.

Hufbauer, Gary C., Diane T. Berliner, and Kimberly A. Elliott, 1986. *Trade Protection in the United States: 31 Case Studies*. Washington, DC: Institute for International Economics.

Kaempfer, William H. Forthcoming. "Explaining the modes of protection: A public choice perspective," in Odell, John, and Willett, Thomas D., editors, *Blending Political Science and Economic Approaches to Trade Policy*, (forthcoming).

Rust, John. 1987. "Optimal replacement of GMC bus engines," *Econometrica*, 55, 999-1034.

Chapter 16

FOREIGN-EXCHANGE MARKETS AND CENTRAL-BANK INTERVENTION

Manfred Gärtner[1]

Experience shows that, even under systems of flexible exchange rates central banks usually have been unable to withstand the temptation to intervene in foreign exchange markets. Empirical investigations into the motives behind such intervention began with Wonnacott's (1965) analysis of the float of the Canadian dollar in the 1950s. Subsequently, there has been scrutiny of the more recent experience with floating currency prices after the collapse of the Bretton Woods system.

This paper begins by summarizing the present state of empirical research on the motives for central bank intervention, and then moves on to its central theme, which is to propose and analyze a political-self-interest model of central bank intervention behavior. Central bankers are assumed to intervene in the foreign exchange markets in order to minimize the loss which results on the one hand from not complying with the demands of agents in the domestic economy, and on the other hand from violating guidelines established by international organizations such as the International Monetary Fund. The propositions which derive from the model are compared with the interventionist policies that have been pursued by the monetary authorities of Canada, the Federal Republic of Germany, Japan, the United Kingdom, and Switzerland.

[1] I should like to thank Carsten Detken for research assistance. An earlier version of this paper was presented at the Bar-Ilan Conference on Markets and Politicians; thanks go to the discussants, Martin Paldam and Avi Weiss, for a host of constructive comments.

I. CAUSES OF CENTRAL BANK INTERVENTIONS: A SUMMARY OF RECENT RESULTS

Empirical work on the motives for central bank intervention has generally been rather heuristic. There has been a lack of serious attempts to derive intervention-response functions from a well formulated theoretical model. The general type of empirical intervention equation employed in the literature (see Table 1 below) may be derived by postulating loss-minimizing behavior on the part of the central bank.

Assume the quadratic loss function to be minimized is

$$(1) \qquad L_t = \Theta_1(e_t^* - e_t^*)^2 + \Theta_2(I_t - I_t^*)^2,$$

where e is the logarithm of the real exchange rate, and I is central bank intervention. An asterisk characterizes target levels of the respective variable. L denotes total central bank loss which may result either from deviations of the real exchange rate from its target value or from undesired currency reserve changes.

Assuming that intervention works, we may substitute into (1)

$$(2) \qquad e_t = \pi I_t + \phi(Z),$$

where Z is a vector of unspecified variables affecting the real exchange rate. Minimizing L with respect to I yields the first order condition

$$(3) \qquad \delta L_t / \delta I_t = 2\Theta_1[\pi I_t + \phi(Z_t) - e_t^*]\pi + 2\Theta_2(I_t - I_t^*) = 0$$

which may be solved for the optimal intervention to yield

$$(4) \qquad I_t = I_t^* - \frac{\Theta_1 \pi}{\Theta_2}(e_t - e_t^*).$$

Since $\delta^2 L / \delta I^2 = 2(\Theta_1 \pi^2 + \Theta_2) > 0$, the intervention rule (4) is confirmed to minimize central bank loss.

Equation 1 describes a series of ellipse-shaped iso-loss curves as shown in Figure 1. Given the options described by equation 2 and represented by a straight line, current loss is minimized at point M. Of course, if intervention were *not* effective, equation 2 would be a vertical line, and central bank loss would always be minimized on the abscissa in a point such as M', i.e. without intervention.

The model consisting of (1) and (2) is a simplification in two respects. First, (1) implies that central banks are completely myopic, being concerned only with today's loss and discounting future losses completely. Second, equation 2 is a rather crude representation of what in the ideal

Figure 1

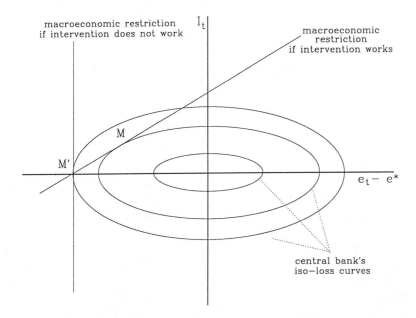

case should be a complete macroeconomic model. In defense of settling for (2), one may argue that probably no two economists and most likely no two central banks would agree on the same macro model. Hence, using (2) implies the basic consensus that intervention works. To specify whether this holds only in the short or medium run or in general is not vital, as long as central banks focus on minimizing today's loss and discount the future to some degree.

While the role of the intervention target I* is usually assumed to be captured by some constant or some simple autoregressive representation in I, two alternative hypotheses regarding e* dominate the literature. The first is *leaning against the wind* and postulates

(5) $\quad e_t^* = e_{t-1}.$

The second is *exchange-rate targeting* and sets the target equal to purchasing power parity e_{PPP}:

(6) $\quad e_t^* = e_{PPP}.$

Recent research on the empirical determinants of central bank intervention is cast in terms of a dichotomy between these two targets. The first postulates that intervention responds to $e_t - e_{t-1}$ and thus is designed to reduce volatility. The second implies that central bank intervention responds to $e_t - e_{PPP}$ and thus is aimed at maintaining the country's competitive position.

Including both targets (5) and (6) simultaneously in (4), and assuming $I_t^* = \gamma + \beta I_{t-1}$, we arrive at

$$(7) \qquad I_t = \gamma + \beta I_{t-1} - \frac{\Theta'_1 \pi}{\Theta_2} (e_t - e_{t-1}) - \frac{\Theta''_1 \pi}{\Theta_2} (e_t - e_{PPP}).$$

Table 1 presents intervention functions from eleven studies, all of which are more or less based on a structural equation such as (7). The results are in each case representative of the respective author's work, though with augmented specifications or for certain subperiods results may have occasionally differed.

Moving down the columns below $\dot{e}_t \equiv e_t - e_{t-1}$ and below $e_t - e_{PPP}$ and checking estimation coefficients and t-values, it becomes evident that there is overwhelming evidence in favor of the leaning against the wind hypothesis. Only Artus' estimate of German interventions for a very early post-Bretton-Woods period and my own work for Switzerland appear to provide evidence of a significant role for exchange rate targets.

Since estimation periods and the specification of estimation equations and variables differ between the studies listed in Table 1, Table 2 provides estimates of equation 7 for each country covered in Table 1 with an estimation period from January 1974 up to the most recent available data.[2] The results are more or less in harmony with the general message of Table 1: For each country the evidence is more supportive of leaning against the wind than of exchange rate targeting. The only country for which the null hypothesis of no exchange rate targeting can be discarded on the basis of these estimates is Japan.

II. A PUZZLE, A PROPOSED EXPLANATION, AND SOME TESTS
A. A Puzzle

A decade and a half of experience with flexible exchange rates has demonstrated that market-determined currency prices are characterized by unexpectedly high day to day or month to month volatility and also by large and lasting changes in the purchasing power of currencies in international goods markets. The two intervention strategies addressed in

---

[2] UK data are up until June 1988, Canadian data until September 1988, Japanese and Swiss data until November 1988, and German data until December 1988.

Table 1

FOREIGN EXCHANGE MARKET INTERVENTION AFTER BRETTON WOODS

Country	Time period	Explanatory variables				Statistics		Source	Measurement of	
		Constant	I_{t-1}	$\dot{e}_t$	$e-e_{PPP}$	$\bar{R}^2$	DW(h)		e	I
Germany	1973(4)-1975(7)	—	—	0.359 (6.30)	0.463 (4.98)	0.80	2.08	Artus[a] (1977)	$/DM	bill.DM at const. parity
Germany	1974(2)-1979(12)	-0.037 (0.12)	—	-0.773 (5.18)	—	0.24	2.07	König/Gaab (1982)	DM/$	bill.DM
Germany	1973(3)-1979(12)	-41.2 (0.1)	—	115.4 (5.1)	—	0.25	2.00	Argy (1982)	Index/DM	bill.$
Germany	1974(3)-1977(8)	0.122 (1.74)	—	0.074 (7.40)	0.005 (n.s.)	0.52	1.91	Neumann[b] 1984)	$/DM	bill.DM
Germany	1973(3)-1979(4)	0.96 (22.4)	—	0.003 (3.99)	—	0.54	2.00	Dornbusch[c] (1980)	$/DM	$(%)
United Kingdom	1972(3)-1977(10)	112.8 (1.4)	0.62 (5.3)	163.1 (3.6)	—	0.53	(0.00)	Argy (1982)	Index/£	bill.$
United Kingdom	1977(11)-1980(2)	-67.95 (0.81)	—	311.95 (2.80)	-52.29 (1.80)	0.62	2.03	Hacche Townend[d] (1981)	Index/£	not indicated
United Kingdom	1973(2)-1982(4)	-425.10 (0.97)	0.39 (2.55)	-53.81 (2.48)	-1826.18 (1.27)	0.35	1.85	Kearney McDonald (1986)	£/$	not indicated
Japan	1973(3)-1976(10)	-1.395 (3.9)	0.224 (1.9)	8.4 (3.0)	—	0.51	(3.47)	Quirk[e] (1977)	$/yen	$
Japan	1973(3)-1979(4)	0.97 (50.5)	—	0.004 (4.41)	—	0.44	1.94	Dornbusch[f] (1980)	$/yen	$(%)

Table 1 continued

Country	Period					$\bar{R}^2$		Author (year)	Units
Japan	1973(3)–1979(12)	11.2 (0.1)	0.16 (1.5)	210.5 (3.7)	—	0.24	(-0.03)	Argy (1982)	Index/yen bill.$
Canada	1970(7)–1977(12)	-1.46 (7.29)	—	-145.4 (6.97)	—	0.83	1.50	Longworth[g] (1980)	Can.$/$ mill.$
Canada	1964(II)–1977(III)	—	—	1.339 (6.61)	0.057 (0.44)	0.76	—	Knight Mathieson[h] (1983)	Can.$/ ·Index $
Switzer-land	1974(1)–1984(6)	-8.25 (5.20)	-0.14 (1.62)	-0.28 (1.57)	-0.10 (2.28)	0.76	-2.16	Gärtner[i] (1987)	Francs/$ (real) mill.$
Group	1973(2)–1979(4)	1.01 (103.8)	—	0.003 (3.25)	—	0.31	2.01	Dornbusch[j] (1980)	Index/$ $(%)

Notes: Absolute t-values are given in parentheses; n.s.= not significant (t-value not given); I_{t-1} = lagged intervention; $\dot{e}$ = percentage rate of change of the exchange rate; e − e_{PP} = deviation of exchange rate from purchasing power parity. Methods to establish e_{PP} level differ between authors. $\bar{R}^2$ is the coefficient of determination adjusted for degrees of freedom; DW and h are the Durbin-Watson and the Durbin-h test statistics for autocorrelation among residuals respectively. For more details consult the indicated sources. All authors except Knight and Mathieson use monthly data.

Comments:
a) e_{PP} is estimated; DW is given after correction for first-order autocorrelation of residuals
b) linear approximation of nonlinear model; variables are divided by var(exchange rate); ė = spot rate minus forward rate
c) ė is unanticipated depreciation; further regressors are inflation and unemployment rates
d) additional regressors are money growth and a money market pressure proxy; functional form is nonlinear
e) additional regressor: volume of spot transactions in Tokyo during previous month
f) ė is unanticipated depreciation
g) 1976(12) excluded (elections in Quebec)
h) FIML estimate of intervention function as part of full macro-model; real exchange rate regressor operational only during period of float; six additional dummies relate to institutional arrangements during period of fixed exchange rates.
i) additional regressors are seasonal dummy variables
j) ė is unanticipated depreciation; group consists of Canada, France, Germany, Japan and the UK

Table 2

LEANING AGAINST THE WIND VS EXCHANGE RATE TARGETING IN FIVE COUNTRIES

Country	Constant	I_{t-1}	I_{t-2}	I_{t-3}	$\dot{e}_t$	$(e_t - e_{PPP})$	$\bar{R}^2$	h(DW)	SER
Canada	0.014 (1.06)	-0.35 (5.54)	-0.15 (2.38)	—	-7.49 (8.28)	-0.003 (0.015)	0.37	-0.545	0.17
Germany	0.005 (1.60)	0.14 (2.02)	-0.09 (1.33)	—	-0.57 (6.94)	-0.03 (1.88)	0.24	-3.065	0.04
Japan	0.008 (2.55)	0.31 (4.55)	—	—	-0.41 (4.49)	-0.06 (2.39)	0.24	-3.239	0.04
United Kingdom	0.009 (1.17)	—	0.17 (2.48)	-0.10 (1.43)	-1.05 (4.77)	-0.01 (0.11)	0.17	(2.06)	0.09
Switzer-land	-0.05 (3.84)	-0.17 (2.20)	-0.11 (1.63)	0.18 (2.83)	-0.28 (2.22)	-0.05 (1.86)	0.74	(2.09)	0.06

Notes: The endogenous variable is the percentage rate of change in the foreign exchange holdings of the country's central bank, expressed in US dollars. The estimated equations for Switzerland and the United Kingdom include a set of dummy variables capturing quarterly and annual seasonality, respectively. These results are suppressed. Where applicable, the notes of Table 1 apply. SER is the standard error of the regression.

the work cited above, leaning against the wind and exchange rate targeting,directly address these empirical characteristics, the first being designed to reduce volatility, and the second seeking to keep exchange rates in line with purchasing power parity.

The puzzle with regard to the basic conclusion derived from Tables 1 and 2 is, however, that central banks focus their interventionist efforts on a problem which the market has already taken care of, but ignore the much more serious problem of exchange rate misalignments. Financial markets offer ample facilities for hedging against exchange rate volatility. In contrast, there is no straightforward way whereby firms undertaking international transactions can hedge against large and persistent medium-term movements of real exchange rates.

B. A Political Self-interest Model of Central Bank Interventions

The explanation which I propose for this puzzle takes the view that central banks are also political entities which, to varying degrees, respond to political demands and strive for support from those groups or actors which are considered relevant. The institutional framework which defines and controls the role of the central bank differs among the countries considered here. Each country accordingly merits its own analysis. However, here I focus on those factors which may be considered common to all central banks, notwithstanding individual differences.

The point of departure is the hypothesis that *central banks maximize political support*, which stems from two sources. The first source is *domestic support*, which reflects the interests of the exporting and import competing industries, and of consumers and voters in general. I postulate that domestic support is maximized by stabilizing the country's competitive position, which is achieved by keeping the exchange rate at PPP level

In an open economy under the present international monetary order, the action and success of central banks is subject not only to scrutiny at home. Central bank officers are involved in a network of international contracts and organizations. Their *rating of performance abroad* reflects the degree to which policies comply with the recommendations or guidelines formulated by international institutions. With regard to exchange rate policy, exchange rate targeting is viewed as a beggar-my-neighbor policy, and is thereby stigmatized by international organizations. The International Monetary Fund's guidelines on exchange rate policies of 1973 and of 1977 limit permissable active intervention strategies to smoothing of short-run fluctuations.[3] Hence, to the extent that IMF approval matters, a central bank maximizing political support at home and from abroad must seek a compromise between the two objectives of exchange rate targeting and leaning against the wind, that is, between following equation 5 or 6.

It should be noted that the two exchange rate objectives are special cases of the general formulation

$$(8) \qquad e_t^* = e_{PPP} + \alpha^i \sum_{i=1}^{n} (e_{t-i} - e_{t-i-1}).$$

Here n-1 denotes the time which has passed since the exchange rate was last at PPP, i.e. $e_{t-n-1} = e_{PPP}$. If $\alpha = 0$, then $e_t^* = e_{PPP}$, and the interventionist strategy is exchange rate targeting. If, at the other extreme, $\alpha = 1$, then $e_t^* = e_{t-1}$, which corresponds to leaning against the wind. Domestic support is maximized by $\alpha = 0$, and compliance with international guidelines is maximized by $\alpha = 1$. The trade off is reflected in the quadratic political support function

$$(9) \qquad S = \beta_D \alpha^2 + \beta_I (1-\alpha)^2, \qquad \beta_D, \ \beta_I < 0.$$

The first order condition yields the solution $\alpha^* = \beta_I/(\beta_D + \beta_I)$ where α^* is between 0 and 1. Thus, a central bank which trades off domestic and international support will typically neither be actively engaged in pursuing a fixed target rate such as e_{PPP}, nor be satisfied with smoothing activities only. In terms of (8) one expects the pursued exchange rate target to follow the actual exchange rate with some lag. It is of course not necessary, for the coefficients revealed in empirical studies to follow the exact order postulated in equation 8. The assumption of a geometrically distributed lag has been made for expository convenience only.

C. Estimates Based on the Political Self-interest Model

Table 3 reports results of tests of the hypothesis that central bank intervention is directed at maximizing political support. Open lag distributions for exchange rate changes were estimated which place no

---

[3] Of course, non-active intervention strategies such as complete abstention or intervention for reasons not related to the exchange rate, such as providing domestic money growth, are at last equally well received by the IMF as leaning against the wind. Also, leaning <u>with</u> the wind is completely ruled out by the IMF guidelines. While these options are not covered by equation 8, and need not to be in the present context, I will return to them in connection with the political self-interest model to be presented below.

Table 3

FLEXIBLE EXCHANGE RATE TARGETS IN FIVE COUNTRIES

Country	Constant	I_{t-1}	I_{t-2}	I_{t-3}	$e_t - e_{PPP}$	$\dot{e}_t$	$\dot{e}_{t-1}$	$\dot{e}_{t-2}$	$\dot{e}_{t-3}$	$\bar{R}^2$	h(DW)	SER
Canada	0.014 (1.07)	-0.35 (5.56)	-0.15 (2.39)	—	—	-0.749 (8.32)	—	—	—	0.38	-0.542	0.170
	0.011 (0.73)	-0.33 (4.48)	-0.23 (3.14)	—	—	-1.51** (3.42)	—	—	—	0.20	(1.94)	0.195
Germany	0.006 (2.03)	—	-0.12 (1.70)	—	-0.03 (1.91)	-0.55 (6.84)	-0.31 (3.90)	-0.15 (1.72)	—	0.29	(1.97)	0.036
	0.005 (1.83)	—	-0.14 (1.70)	—	-0.04 (2.18)	-0.23** (2.67)	-0.31 (3.48)	-0.22 (2.18)	—	0.13	(2.05)	0.040
Japan	0.009 (2.77)	0.24 (3.61)	—	—	-0.05 (2.23)	-0.44 (5.02)	-0.34 (3.71)	—	—	0.29	-1.2	0.041
	0.009 (2.82)	0.24 (3.42)	—	—	-0.06 (2.64)	-0.30* (3.17)	-0.28 (2.97)	—	—	0.23	-0.765	0.042
United Kingdom	0.009 (1.17)	—	0.16 (2.32)	-0.09 (1.37)	—	-1.00 (4.68)	-0.50 (2.28)	—	—	0.20	2.07	0.093
	0.01 (1.23)	—	0.15 (2.15)	-0.10 (1.36)	—	-0.68** (3.28)	-0.57 (2.52)	—	—	0.15	1.98	0.095
Switzerland	-0.042 (3.24)	-0.26 (3.37)	-0.15 (2.22)	0.18 (2.80)	—	-0.23 (1.89)	-0.33 (2.69)	-0.43 (3.42)	-0.16 (1.21)	0.77	(2.06)	0.061
	-0.043 (3.33)	-0.26 (3.47)	-0.16 (2.37)	0.17 (2.75)	—	-0.34* (2.50)	-0.32 (2.68)	-0.42 (3.37)	-0.16 (1.26)	0.77	(2.03)	0.061

Notes: An asterisk on a coefficient indicates, that the DM/$ rate has been used as an instrument for current devaluations. Two asterisks indicate that the yen/$ rate has been used for the same purpose. Where applicable, the notes of Table 1 and 2 apply.

restrictions on the coefficients.[4] Again, desired intervention is represented by an autoregressive process in actual intervention.[5]

All results but those obtained for Canada acccord with the view that central bank intervention balances exchange rate targeting and leaning against the wind; since, in addition to the current rate of devaluation, either lagged exchange rate changes and/or exchange rate undervaluation appear as significant regressors. The positive coefficients for lagged intervention which appear, may also capture lagged intervention responses to other predetermined variables via a Koyck transformation.

The fit levels of the estimated equations are very low. This is a cause of concern, but comfort may be derived from the fact that the basic message of the estimates is rather robust, showing up in instrumental variable estimates as well as when different subsamples are analyzed.

While the obtained results are in accord with the political self-interest model, the results presented in Table 3 are open to other interpretations. In order to arrive at hypotheses with more discriminatory power, I now examine more closely the political self-interest interpretation of foreign exchange market intervention.

Table 4, which serves as background for the following discussion, demonstrates the four stylized constellations that may occur between the polar strategies of leaning against the wind and exchange rate targeting. The first relates to the present *movement* of the exchange rate and calls for an accumulation or decumulation of reserves, depending on whether the home currency appreciates or depreciates. The second adresses the current *level* of the exchange rate and specifies an accumulation or decumulation of reserves, depending on whether the home currency is overvalued or undervalued.

Obviously, there are constellations under which both strategies require intervention in the same direction. This holds for the elements on the main diagonal. In these cases, the requests of the domestic economy can be addressed by policies that are acceptable to the international community. The extent to which such cases arise is determined by the moving exchange rate target, defined above as a weighted average of present and past exchange rate changes.

---

[4] A similar statistical specification is used in Gärtner (1987) and Honegger (1989). These studies do not provide a behavioral model, though, but basically settle for measurement without explicit theory.

[5] This may appear inadequate in times of money growth targets. However, attempts to take into account that money is simply the sum of domestic credit and international reserves by including domestic credit among the regressors have been completely unsuccessful.

Table 4: Matrix of conflicts between two intervention strategies

		CENTRAL BANK STRATEGY: EXCHANGE RATE TARGETING	
		Home currency overvalued	Home currency undervalued
		Accumulation of reserves	Decumulation of reserves
Home currency appreciates — Accumulation of reserves		(1.1) No Conflict $[\dot{e}_t(e_t^- e_{PPP}) > 0]$	(1.2) Conflict $[\dot{e}_t(e_t^- e_{PPP}) < 0]$
Home currency depreciates — Decumulation of reserves		(2.1) Conflict $[\dot{e}_t(e_t^- e_{PPP}) < 0]$	(2.2) No Conflict $[\dot{e}_t(e_t^- e_{PPP}) > 0]$

CENTRAL BANK STRATEGY: LEANING AGAINST THE WIND

The elements *off* the main diagonal characterize constellations of conflict between the two interventionist strategies, with one requiring an accumulation of reserves, the other one a decumulation.

Two considerations determine how the central bank will behave in this situation of conflict. The first is that requirements of domestic and international objectives address variables on different levels: The domestic economy is interested in ends, not means, i.e. that the exchange rate is at or moves close to its PPP target, with *how* this is achieved being of secondary importance. By contrast, the international community provides guidelines on *policies*, and is concerned with the means whereby ends are achieved or sought. The second consideration is that the characterization of the support of the International Monetary Fund as dependent on the weight parameter α is not quite appropriate for the off-main-diagonal scenarios. For the latter scenarios, a policy of complete non-intervention is at least as tolerable as leaning against the wind. This provides an additional relevant policy option in cases of conflict. The market is moving the exchange rate towards PPP, and leaning against the wind--which blows towards PPP--rather than not intervening gives rise to an exchange rate which is inferior for the domestic economy, with no offsetting support from the IMF. Hence, the central bank maximizes support in cases of conflict by not interfering in the foreign exchange market at all.

Table 5 presents tests of the hypothesis that central bank intervention behavior differs between situations of conflict and situations of harmony in the way described above. The results are mixed: The political support model seems to work very well for Japan and for Switzerland, where we find strong evidence that the monetary authorities only lean against destabilizing wind which threatens to worsen exchange rate misalignments, but leave it up to the market when the wind is blowing towards PPP. For Japan there is a statistically significant response both to current and lagged devaluations when there is no conflict between exchange rate targeting and leaning against the wind, but no response in the cases of conflict. The same holds for Switzerland, where all six estimated responses to exchange rate changes exactly fit into the proposed pattern.

German intervention supports a more moderate version of the model, since the Bundesbank apparently does not cease to intervene in situations of conflict, but obviously does intervene more forcefully in situations of no conflict. This unexpected behavior in off-diagonal situations may be a technical implication of the European Monetary System, though, which does not necessarily reflect the preferences of the Bundesbank.

Canadian and British foreign exchange market interventions do not appear to be governed by the motives postulated by the political support model, since estimation coefficients do not differ between cases of conflict and no-conflict by conventional standards.

D. Do Exchange Rate Disequilibria Affect Domestic Support Symmetrically?

Equation 1 implies that deviations of the exchange rate from its target value affect central bank loss symmetrically, i.e. independently of their direction. In terms of Table 4 this meant that cases in the northwest and southeast elements on the main diagonal could be put in one category, cases in the southwest and northeast elements off the main diagonal in the other. If we now allow for the possibility that undervaluation might be considered a smaller problem than overvaluation, specifications must allow coefficients to differ between all four quadrants of Table 4. Tables 6-10 present the results of such estimates.

As has already been suggested by the results presented in Table 5, Canadian intervention does not really reflect whether a situation of conflict exists between exchange rate targeting and leaning against the wind, or a state of harmony. If anything, Canadian authorities appear to respond more forcefully to appreciations of the Canadian dollar than to depreciations. However, this is only a partial result, since responses to lagged *interventions* also differ between scenarios. For example, in element (1,2)

Table 5

ARE INTERVENTIONS MAXIMIZING POLITICAL SUPPORT?

Country	Constant	I_{t-1}	I_{t-2}	I_{t-3}	$\dot{D}e_t$	$(1-D)\dot{e}_t$	$\dot{D}e_{t-1}$	$(1-D)\dot{e}_{t-1}$	$\dot{D}e_{t-2}$	$(1-D)\dot{e}_{t-2}$	$\bar{R}^2$	h(DW)	SER
Canada	0.014 (1.05)	-0.35 (5.54)	-0.15 (2.38)	—	-7.49 (5.85)	-7.49 (5.86)	—	—	—	—	0.37	-0.547	0.171
Germany	0.003 (1.07)	—	—	—	-0.58 (5.37)	-0.25 (2.59)	-0.31 (2.74)	-0.33 (2.64)	—	—	0.21	(2.07)	0.038
Japan	0.008 (2.71)	0.25 (3.72)	—	—	-0.74 (6.35)	-0.11 (0.82)	-0.42 (3.57)	-0.17 (1.3)	—	—	0.32	-1.69	0.039
United Kingdom	0.008 (1.01)	—	0.16 (2.36)	-0.11 (1.55)	-1.22 (3.86)	-0.89 (3.00)	-0.21 (0.74)	-0.87 (2.49)	—	—	0.24	(2.10)	0.093
Switzerland	-0.051 (4.02)	-0.26 (3.65)	-0.16 (2.52)	0.17 (2.98)	-0.73 (4.03)	0.23 (1.15)	-0.31 (2.18)	-0.36 (1.88)	-0.52 (3.38)	-0.11 (0.61)	0.79	-1.85	0.061

Notes: D = 1 if there is a situation of no conflict, which corresponds to elements on the main diagonal in Table 4. Otherwise D = 0. For Germany and Switzerland the other country's dollar rate is used as an instrument. Where applicable the notes of the above tables apply.

Table 6

Asymmetric Intervention in Canada

CENTRAL BANK STRATEGY: EXCHANGE RATE
TARGETING

		Home currency overvalued	Home currency undervalued
		Accumulation of reserves	Decumulation of reserves
	Home currency appreciates	(1.1) 42 cases $\dot{e}_t$ -8.68(-3.59)	(1.2) 54 cases $\dot{e}_t$ -11.93(-5.63)
	Accumulation of reserves	I_{t-1} 0.02(0.09) I_{t-2} -0.34(-1.34)	I_{t-1} -0.59(-5.81) I_{t-2} -0.22(-2.33)
CENTRAL BANK STRATEGY: LEANING AGAINST THE WIND	Home currency depreciates	(2.1) 34 cases $\dot{e}_t$ -3.37(-1.78)	(2.2) 59 cases $\dot{e}_t$ -6.18(-3.50)
	Decumulation of reserves	I_{t-1} 0.21(0.53) I_{t-2} -0.11(-0.45)	I_{t-1} -0.23(-2.60) I_{t-2} -0.07(-0.80)

$$\bar{R}^2 = 0.42$$

Table 7

Asymmetric Intervention in Germany

CENTRAL BANK STRATEGY: EXCHANGE RATE
TARGETING

		Home currency overvalued	Home currency undervalued
		Accumulation of reserves	Decumulation of reserves
	Home currency appreciates	(1.1) 66 cases $\dot{e}_t$ -0.74(-5.09)	(1.2) 28 cases $\dot{e}_t$ -0.22(-1.39)
	Accumulation of reserves	$\dot{e}_{t-1}$ -0.44(-3.05)	$\dot{e}_{t-1}$ 0.02(0.12)
CENTRAL BANK STRATEGY: LEANING AGAINST THE WIND	Home currency depreciates	(2.1) 59 cases $\dot{e}_t$ -0.31(-2.18)	(2.2) 39 cases $\dot{e}_t$ -0.29(-1.40)
	Decumulation of reserves	$\dot{e}_{t-1}$ -0.56(-3.51)	$\dot{e}_{t-1}$ -0.15(-0.86)

$$\bar{R}^2 = 0.24$$

Table 8

Asymmetric Intervention in Japan

CENTRAL BANK STRATEGY: EXCHANGE RATE TARGETING

	Home currency overvalued	Home currency undervalued
	Accumulation of reserves	Decumulation of reserves
Home currency appreciates — Accumulation of reserves	(1.1) 46 cases $\dot{e}_t$ $-0.66(-4.26)$ $\dot{e}_{t-1}$ $-0.48(-3.16)$ I_{t-1} $0.39(3.06)$	(1.2) 44 cases $\dot{e}_t$ $0.06(0.29)$ $\dot{e}_{t-1}$ $-0.09(-0.39)$ I_{t-1} $0.08(0.50)$
Home currency depreciates — Decumulation of reserves	(2.1) 41 cases $\dot{e}_t$ $-0.23(-1.04)$ $\dot{e}_{t-1}$ $-0.33(-1.94)$ I_{t-1} $0.14(1.50)$	(2.2) 60 cases $\dot{e}_t$ $-0.83(-3.09)$ $\dot{e}_{t-1}$ $-0.15(-0.78)$ I_{t-1} $0.79(3.12)$

CENTRAL BANK STRATEGY: LEANING AGAINST THE WIND

$$\bar{R}^2 = 0.33$$

Table 9

Asymmetric Intervention in United Kingdom

CENTRAL BANK STRATEGY: EXCHANGE RATE TARGETING

	Home currency overvalued	Home currency undervalued
	Accumulation of reserves	Decumulation of reserves
Home currency appreciates — Accumulation of reserves	(1.1) 53 cases $\dot{e}_t$ $-0.95(-1.9)$ $\dot{e}_{t-1}$ $-0.23(-0.61)$ I_{t-2} $0.32(3.43)$ I_{t-3} $-0.06(-0.69)$	(1.2) 43 cases $\dot{e}_t$ $-1.05(-2.28)$ $\dot{e}_{t-1}$ $-0.91(1.99)$ I_{t-2} $0.38(1.23)$ I_{t-3} $-0.31(-1.00)$
Home currency depreciates — Decumulation of reserves	(2.1) 36 cases $\dot{e}_t$ $-0.61(-1.13)$ $\dot{e}_{t-1}$ $-0.68(-1.30)$ I_{t-2} $0.38(1.23)$ I_{t-3} $-0.31(-1.00)$	(2.2) 54 cases $\dot{e}_t$ $-1.37(-2.13)$ $\dot{e}_{t-1}$ $-0.61(-1.23)$ I_{t-2} $-0.27(-1.71)$ I_{t-3} $-0.22(-1.34)$

CENTRAL BANK STRATEGY: LEANING AGAINST THE WIND

$$\bar{R}^2 = 0.22$$

Table 10

Asymmetric Intervention in Switzerland

		CENTRAL BANK STRATEGY: EXCHANGE RATE TARGETING	
		Home currency overvalued	Home currency undervalued
		Accumulation of reserves	Decumulation of reserves
CENTRAL BANK STRATEGY: LEANING AGAINST THE WIND	Home currency appreciates / Accumulation of reserves	(1.1) 61 cases $\dot{e}_t$ -0.93(-3.36) $\dot{e}_{t-1}$ -0.21(-1.16) $\dot{e}_{t-2}$ -0.70(-3.47) I_{t-1} -0.39(-3.51) I_{t-2} -0.26(-2.69) I_{t-3} 0.11(1.31)	(1.2) 29 cases $\dot{e}_t$ -0.004(-0.01) $\dot{e}_{t-1}$ -0.08(-0.26) $\dot{e}_{t-2}$ -0.29(-0.88) I_{t-1} -0.45(-2.65) I_{t-2} -0.31(-1.68) I_{t-3} 0.03(0.18)
	Home currency depreciates / Decumulation of reserves	(2.1) 53 cases $\dot{e}_t$ 0.33(1.05) $\dot{e}_{t-1}$ -0.33(-1.15) $\dot{e}_{t-2}$ -0.14(-0.56) I_{t-1} -0.16(-1.75) I_{t-2} -0.15(-1.37) I_{t-3} 0.24(2.59)	(2.2) 48 cases $\dot{e}_t$ -0.51(-1.68) $\dot{e}_{t-1}$ -0.60(-2.34) $\dot{e}_{t-2}$ -0.25(-0.95) I_{t-1} -0.41(-3.16) I_{t-2} -0.26(-2.19) I_{t-3} 0.07(0.66)

$$\bar{R}^2 = 0.78$$

the massive interventionist response to appreciations is partly offset within the next two months.

The German Bundesbank obviously only intervenes in the foreign exchange market when the mark is overvalued relative to the dollar. Somewhat strangely, though, it seems to resist further appreciations just as well as movements towards PPP. It could be, however, that this is just a quirk resulting from the established rules of the European Monetary System and the role of the Bundesbank within that system.

The picture obtained for Japan is well in line with the hypotheses of the political self-interest model. In addition, there is some asymmetry between elements (1,1) and (2,2), not only, because coefficients and t-values obtained for e_t and e_{t-1} are somewhat larger in (1,1), but also because we estimate a significant positive coefficient for I_{t-1}, which reinforces and prolongs the primary response.

The results obtained for the United Kingdom do not give a clear picture, though there are some hints that the Treasury has been more concerned with undervaluation of the pound and the accompanying problem of imported inflation than with overvaluation.

Finally, the Swiss results correspond well with the political support model, since no significant coefficients for present or lagged exchange rate changes are found off the main diagonal. Also, there is evidence for an asymmetry in the intervention rule followed by the Swiss National Bank, since leaning against increasing overvaluation appears to be done with more determination than leaning against increasing undervaluation.

III. SUMMARY AND CONCLUSIONS

This paper has presented a model of central bank behavior based on the supposition that central bankers have optimizing objectives, which entail trading off domestic support for compliance with guidelines set by the IMF. The international objective is attained by behaving in a manner that the IMF would find satisfactory. The attainment of the domestic objective entails achieving an exchange rate that is stable at purchasing power parity. The implications are:

(1) except for corner solutions that might arise--central banks adopt an exchange rate target which is more flexible than purchasing power parity, but do not discount past exchange rate movements as heavily as the strategy of leaning against the wind would imply;

(2) central bank political support is maximized by adopting a flexible intervention strategy that actively pursues the above flexible target when the exchange rate is moving away from purchasing power parity, but entails non-intervention when market forces are moving the exchange rate towards purchasing power parity.

An empirical analysis of interventionist behavior reveals that the political self-interest model is well supported by Japanese, Swiss, and to a lesser extent, by German data, but not in the cases of Canada and the United Kingdom.

DATA APPENDIX

The common source for the data employed is the International Monetary Fund's *International Financial Statistics*, computer tapes. All variables are in natural logarithms:

e =   real exchange rate domestic currency per US dollar ($\equiv w + p^* - p$)

w =   exchange rate domestic currency per US dollar, end of period (source: line ae)

p*=   US wholesale prices: industrial goods, 1980 = 100, period average (source: line 63a)

p =   Domestic prices, 1980 = 100, period average

Canada:	aggregate industrial selling price (source: line 63)
Germany:	wholesale prices: industrial goods (source: line 63)
Japan:	wholesale prices: (source: line 63)

Switzerland: wholesale prices: home goods (source: line 63a)
United
Kingdom: industrial output prices (source: line 63)

I_t = $r_t - r_{t-1}$

r =   foreign exchange of respective National Bank, millions of US dollars, end of period (source: line 1d.d)

e_{PPP} =   average real exchange rate domestic currency per US dollar during the period 1973(1) - the most recent observation available on tape, which varies between 1988(6) and 1988   (12).

Dots over variables indicate first differences (i.e. percentage rates of change of the original variable)

The following set of dummy variables captures rigid quarterly and annual patterns:

D_1 =   1 for months of February, May, August and November; 0 otherwise

D_2 =   1 for months of March, June, September and December; 0 otherwise

D_3 =   1 for month of December: 0 otherwise

D_4 =   1 for month of January: 0 otherwise

D_1 - D_4 are used for Switzerland, D_3 and D_4 for the United Kingdom. The dummy variables are suppressed in Tables 2-5.

References

Argy, Victor, 1982. "Exchange-rate management in theory and practice", *Princeton Studies in International Finance*, No. 50, Princeton University Press.

Artus, Jaques R., 1977. "Exchange rate stability and managed floating: the experience of the Federal Republic of Germany", *IMF Staff Papers*, 23, 312-33.

Dornbusch, Rudiger, 1980. "Exchange rate economics: where do we stand?", *Brookings Papers on Economic Activity*, 143-85.

Gärtner, Manfred, 1987. "Intervention policy under floating exchange rates: an analysis of the Swiss case", *Economica*, 54, 439-53.

Hacche, Graham and J. Townend, 1981. "Exchange rates and monetary policy: modelling sterling's effective exchange rate, 1972-80", in W.A. Eltis and P.J.N. Sinclair, editors, *The Money Supply and the Exchange Rate*, Oxford: Oxford University Press, 201-47.

Honegger, Ralph, 1989. "Currency intervention: empirical findings from Switzerland, Germany and Britain", *Economic and Financial Prospects*, June/July, 1-4.

Kearney, C. and Ronald MacDonald, 1986. "Intervention and sterilization under floating exchange rates: the UK 1973-1983", *European Economic Review*, 30, 345-64.

Knight, M.D. and Donald J. Mathieson, 1983. "Economic change and policy response in Canada under fixed and flexible exchange rates", in J.S. Bhandari and B.H. Putnam, editors, *Economic Interdependence and Flexible Exchange Rates*, Cambridge, Mass: MIT Press.

König, Heinz and Werner Gaab, 1982. "Smoothing exchange rates by central bank interventions?", in *Experiences and Problems of the International Monetary System*, Economic Notes, Siena: Monte dei Paschi di Siena.

Neumann, Manfred J.M., 1984. "Auf der Suche nach der Interventionsfunktion der Deutschen Bundesbank", in W. Ehrlicher and H. Richter, editors, *Devisenmarktinterventionen der Zentralbanken. Schriften des Vereins für Socialpolitik*, NF volume 139, Berlin: Duncker und Humblot.

Longworth, D. 1980. "Canadian intervention in the foreign exchange market: a note", *Review of Economics and Statistics*, 66, 284-7.

Quirk, Peter J. 1977. "Exchange rate policy in Japan: leaning against the wind", *IMF Staff Papers*, 24, 642-64.

Wonnacott, Paul 1965. *The Canadian Dollar*, Toronto: Toronto University Press.

Chapter 17

THE POLITICAL ECONOMY OF THE
INTERNATIONAL DEBT CRISIS[*]

Ngo Van Long

The international debt crisis has for the most part been viewed in the literature as a macroeconomic phenomenon.[1] The "crisis" has however involved interplay among private banks, debtor country governments, creditor country governments, international institutions, and interest groups in the countries concerned. This paper models the "crisis" from a perspective that takes account of individual behavioral incentives[2] and shows how debt negotiations (with diverse features such as conditionality provisions,[3] swap programs with side payments in kind,[4] etc.), the

---

[*] An earlier version of this paper was presented at the Conference on Markets and Politicians at Bar-Ilan University, Israel, and at seminars at the University of Guelph and the Kiel Institute of World Economics. I thank Gordon Tullock for helpful comments.
[1] Krugman (1988), Helpman (1988), Froot (1989), Sachs (1988a, 1988b), among others, studied the benefits of voluntary debt reduction; Kenen (1989), Eaton and Gersovitz (1981) examined the incentive for debt repudiation; Bulow and Rogoff (1989), Gale and Hellwig (1989) developed game-theoretic models of renegotiation.
[2] Anna Schwartz (1989) drew attention to the role of individuals' self-interest motives (p. 8), and hinted at empire-building motives of those who run international institutions (p. 13). The lack of attention to the political-economy element has for example been acknowledged by Helpman (1988, p. 1): "In order to rigorously deal with policy responses it is necessary to employ an explicit model of government behaviour. But no accepted model is available for this purpose. For this reason I focus instead on market outcomes and investment-driven adjustments".
[3] For example, in return for an IMF loan of $3.6 billion in 1982, Mexico had to agree to cut its budget deficit and increase its trade surplus. Nigeria was reportedly asked to privatize ninety-six government controlled enterprises and to devalue its currency when it approached the IMF for a loan of $540 million. Dozens of

involvement of the World Bank and the International Monetary Fund, the active role played by the U.S. Treasury, can be given coherent microfoundations based on self-interest.

A number of aspects of behavior that appear puzzling when viewed from a macroeconomic perspective are addressed and explained. Was it rational for private banks to provide, as they did, additional loans to troubled debtor countries when every dollar of additional lending was immediately discounted by the market? Why did creditor country governments intervene in the negotiations? Why did the IMF and the World Bank seek an expansion of their scope of activities and require countries to adopt economic reforms as a condition for financial aid? Why was there strong resistance to policy reforms on the part of key actors within debtor country governments?

In the game-theoretic model that is to be presented, a coalition encompassing the private banks, the creditor country governments and the international institutions negotiates with each debtor country government that itself reacts to pressure groups within the country. The outcome of the game is shown to depend on the rates of time preferences of various actors, the extent to which actions of individual players can be monitored, and the historical distribution of rents within the debtor country. Higher concentration of rents tends to reduce and lower rates of time preference increase, the likelihood of a settlement involving new lending.

The basic model is presented in Section I, where the preferences and the opportunity sets of the participants in the game are described. The equilibrium outcome of the game is discussed in Section II. A summary and final comments are provided in Section III.

I. THE MODEL
A. The Basic Setting

I focus on a single debtor country. Let B denote its outstanding debt, borrowed at the beginning of period one.[5] The country was obligated to pay rB at the end of period one and $(1+r)B$ at the end of period two.

---

countries were asked to reform their internal economic policies.

[4] According to the Bank of International Settlements (BIS), U.S. regulators allowed banks that took part in the Mexican swap scheme not to show other claims on Mexico at a lower value. See BIS (1988, p. 137).

[5] Thus we assume that all debts are incurred by the public sector. This is an abstraction from reality. According to Sachs and Huizinga (1987, pp. 565-566), in the 1979-1982 period, lending to the LDC's public sectors was about two-fifths greater than to the private sectors. In the 1982-1986 period, lending was more predominantly to the public sectors.

Investment took place in period one from the proceeds of the investment, but the investment yielded no return.[6] I assume that rB has been paid and that there is no prospect that (1+r)B will be paid in period two. In the absence of active intervention from international institutions and creditor country governments, one expects a negotiated settlement. Complete default is undesirable for the debtor, for two reasons. Firstly, the debtor country may wish to maintain a good reputation, to borrow in the future.[7] A second reason for the debtor country to make a partial repayment is that legal remedies are available to creditors.[8] Bulow and Rogoff (1989, p. 161) have argued that debtor countries would not unilaterally cancel the debts, because ... "the nuisance value (to the defaulting debtor country) of having its goods and trading accounts tied up in legal actions may be quite high". Private banks, on the other hand, may want to adopt a "partial forgiveness" policy, because a lower debt overhang may increase investment incentives in the debtor country. Krugman (1989) proposes that the debt may be so high that countries are on the wrong side of the "debt-relief Laffer curve".[9] I presume that a negotiated settlement to the "crisis" would obtain, and that such an outcome would be Pareto-optimal, if banks acted cooperatively and overcame the free-rider problem.[10]

I proceed by first examining the problem facing the banks, on the assumption that they have perceived that the existing debts cannot be repaid in full. I then consider the role of the international institutions. This is followed by an analysis of the internal politics of the debtor-country and the creditor-country governments.

---

[6] In fact, it has been argued that a large part of the funds borrowed before 1982 by the troubled Latin American debtor countries . . . "went to finance consumption, including oil and other consumer goods, not to mention extravagant living by corrupt officials. Some funds were invested in inefficient unprofitable state-owned enterprises producing products at marginal costs in excess of competitive world prices" (Schwartz (1989, p. 4)).

[7] The theoretical argument that "reputation matters" has been advanced by Eaton and Gersovitz (1981) and has been disputed by Bulow and Rogoff (1989).

[8] See Kaletsky (1985), Alexander (1987) and Bulow and Rogoff (1989, Appendix) for details.

[9] This argument was also made by Sachs (1988a, 1988b). See also Froot (1989).

[10] Each bank, in providing some debt relief, is also helping other banks. Thus debt reduction is a public good, and private provision of public goods is likely to be insufficient. See Cornes and Sandler (1986) on voluntary contribution to public goods and also Guttman (chapter 2, this volume). For discussion of the free-rider problem in the context of debt crisis, see Helpman (1988, p. 38).

B. The Banks

In what follows, unless otherwise stated, I abstract from the free-rider problem by assuming that banks form a syndicate in their dealing with the troubled debtor country. The negotiated outcome is either voluntary debt relief (the debtor country is to pay the banks, at the end of period two, an amount bB where b $< 1+r$) or there is new lending.[11]

Assume that, with debt relief, the creditors can be certain that bB will be paid. Consider the case where L dollars are needed to complete a project, and that the resulting output of the project is given by:

$$Q = \theta F(L) \tag{1}$$

where θ is a random variable, $0 < \theta_1 \leq \theta \leq \theta_2$, with cumulative probability distribution $G(\theta, R)$ where R denotes the extent of economic reforms to be undertaken by the debtor-country government. By definition,

$$G(\theta', R) = \text{Prob}(\theta \leq \theta' \mid R). \tag{2}$$

Assume that $G(\theta, R) > 0$ for $\theta > \theta_1$, and

$$G_R < 0 \text{ for } \theta_1 < \theta < \theta_2 \tag{3a}$$
$$G_R = 0 \text{ for } \theta = \theta_i \ (i = 1,2). \tag{3b}$$

Assumptions (3a) and (3b) imply that the probability that output exceeds a given number is an increasing function of the level of reform. Technically, a distribution with a higher R represents a first order stochastic dominance over distributions with lower R.

Given L, the implicit contractual payment to the banks, P, is specified as follows :

$$P = (1+r)B + (1+r)L \text{ if } \theta \geq \theta_c \tag{4}$$
$$P = \theta F(L) \text{ if } \theta < \theta_c \tag{5}$$

where θ_c is defined by:

$$\theta_c F(L) = (1+r)B + (1+r)L. \tag{6}$$

This means that if θ exceeds θ_c then the banks can receive back principal and interest of both the old and the new loans, otherwise all the output will be paid to the banks.

Let s represent the banks' opportunity cost of funds, where b $<$ $(1+s) < (1+r)$. Clearly, as long as

$$EP \geq (1+s)L + bB \tag{7}$$

(that is, expected payment exceeds the cost of the new loan and the amount the banks would receive if they would not advance the new loan), the banks will find new lending preferable to voluntary debt relief. If (7) holds with equality, the banks will be indifferent between the two alternatives, and in this case,

$$[(EP)(1+s)^{-1}] / [L + (bB)(1+s)^{-1}] = 1 \tag{8}$$

---

[11] This is only to simplify matters, and there are no reasons why a combination of the two is not possible.

Let V denote the value (in the secondary market) of a dollar of new loan,

$$V = [(EP)(1+s)^{-1}] / [L + B] \tag{9}$$

Clearly if (8) holds then V is strictly less than unity. That banks are willing to advance new loans even if $V < 1$ is explained by the fact that this raises the market value of a dollar of old loan from $b(1+s)^{-1} < 1$ to

$$V = [L + bB(1+s)^{-1}] / [L + B] > b(1+s)^{-1} \tag{10}$$

There is a strong incentive for individual banks to free ride: by not providing new funds, they can receive the benefit of increased asset value without paying the cost. I assume for the moment that syndication and implicit penalty provisions make this problem negligible.

Consider the case where (7) does not hold, so that the banks prefer not to advance new loans. If the international institutions (the IMF and the World Bank) can provide part of the new funds at subsidized interest rates, the private banks will have an incentive to join in. To see this, suppose that the IMF proposes to lend αL to the debtor, at the rate of interest $i < s$, provided that the private banks lend $(1-\alpha)L$, and that the debtor country government's scope of economic reform is R^*. Assume, for simplicity only, that i is so low that even in the worst scenario the debtor country is still able to repay in the case $\alpha = 1$:

$$\theta_1 F(L) > (1+i)L$$

I assume that the IMF has priority claim over the private banks. In this case, the amount to be paid to the private banks is:

$$P = (1+r) [B+(1-\alpha)L] \quad \text{if } \theta \geq \theta(\alpha) \tag{11}$$
$$P = \theta F(L)-(1+i)\alpha L \quad \text{if } \theta \leq \theta(\alpha) \tag{12}$$

where $\theta(\alpha)$ is defined by :

$$\theta(\alpha)F(L) = (1+r) [B+(1-\alpha)L] + (1+i)\alpha L \tag{13}$$

Clearly the banks would accept the deal if and only if their expected receipts under this scheme are at least as high as what they would get by refusing to lend. This condition is

$$EP(\alpha) \geq (1+s) (1-\alpha)L+bB \tag{14}$$

where $EP(\alpha)$ is the expected receipt.

Define the banks' expected profit (from lending a fraction $(1-\alpha)$ of L) as

$$\pi(\alpha) = EP(\alpha) - [(1+s)(1-\alpha)L]-bB. \tag{15}$$

It can be verified that π is strictly concave in α:

$$\pi'(\alpha) = -(1+r)LProb[\theta \geq \theta(\alpha)]-(1+i)LProb[\theta \leq \theta(\alpha)]+(1-s)L \tag{16}$$

and hence $\pi''(\alpha) < O$.

Let

$$\beta(\alpha) = Prob[\theta \geq \theta(\alpha)]. \tag{17a}$$

Then β is an increasing function of α, and

$$\beta(0) = Prob(\theta \geq \theta_c). \tag{17b}$$

It follows that $\pi'(0) > 0$ if and only if

$(1+r)\beta(0)+(1+i)[1-\beta(0)] < 1+s.$ (18)

Thus we can state the following result:

Proposition 1: *If (18) holds then the banks welcome intervention (in the forms of subsidized loans) from the international institutions. From the banks' point of view, the best α is positive but less than unity if and only if, in addition to (18),*

$(1+r)\beta(1) + (1+i)[1-\beta(1)] > 1+s.$ (19)

If (19) does not hold, then the best α is unity.

Proposition 1 indicates that, under certain conditions, the banks may wish the international institutions to inject new lending, and it is possible that beyond a certain point the probability of recovering the existing debt is so high that banks would want to have a positive share in the new loans. Thus we have obtained a Laffer curve (from the banks' point of view) as depicted in figure 1 with respect to the extent of participation of the international institutions.

We now relax the assumption that L is fixed. With L a decision variable, we have to modify (13) - (17). The main change is that $\theta(\alpha)$ is replaced by $\theta(\alpha, L)$, where

$\theta(\alpha,L) = [(1+r)[B+(1-\alpha)L]+(1+i)L] / F(L)$ (20)

Also, in order to explicitly consider the effect of a change in R on the banks' expected profits, we write:

$\pi(\alpha,L,R) = EP(\alpha,L,R) - (1+s)(1+\alpha)L-bB.$ (21)

Let F(L) be a strictly concave and increasing function, with $F'(0) = \infty$ and $F'(\infty) = 0$. These assumptions guarantee the existence of an interior equilibrium.

For a given α, the optimal L (from the banks' point of view) must satisfy the condition :

$\pi_L = -\alpha(1+r)\beta(\alpha,L)+I[\theta_1,\theta(\alpha,L)][\theta F'(L)-(1+i)\alpha]g(\theta,R)d\theta = 0$ (22)

where I[x,y] is the integral operator with x and y being lower and upper limits respectively. Note that π_L is negative if L is very large, because F(L) is assumed to exhibit diminishing returns for large L. On the other hand, first order stochastic dominance implies :

$\pi_R > 0$ (23)

Thus, for each α, we can derive a set of iso-profit curves for the banks. One such set is illustrated in Figure 2. The set of points to the right of the curve $\pi(\alpha, L, R) = 0$ will be designated the banks' *acceptance set*.

I shall assume in the following for simplicity that α is a positive *constant*.

Figure 1

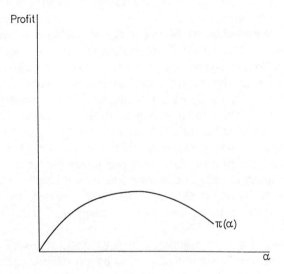

Banks' Laffer Curve

Figure 2

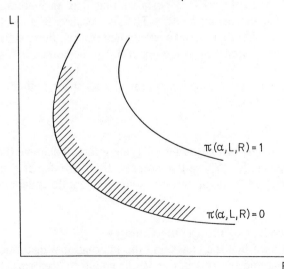

Banks' Isoprofit Curves and Acceptance Set

C. The International Institutions

We have seen that the international institutions, by their ability to provide loans at subsidized rates, may convert an equilibrium with privately negotiated debt relief into one with new lending. Do these institutions have an incentive to do so?

In a critical evaluation of the role of the international institutions in the debt crisis, Anna Schwartz (1989, p. 14) points out that, with the collapse of the Bretton Woods system, the initial functions of the IMF evaporated, and ... "to find a new function, the IMF expanded its activities, principally the Compensatory Financing Facilities (introduced in February 1963) that provide financing in the event of export shortfalls. It also established a new upper tranche Extended Fund Facility, covering a three-year period ... The IMF's expanded activities enable it to extend loans with conditionality provisions to dozens of countries, when previously (under Bretton Woods) it made such loans to only one or two countries a year". Schwartz also remarked that the World Bank similarly sought to enlarge the scope of its activities. In fact, both institutions continually applied for increases in resources.

The motives for any institution to seek expansion are well understood. I propose to present a simplified picture by postulating that the typical institution has a utility function which has, among its arguments, the size of its budget B and the number of staff N. To maintain a given pair (B, N) in an economic environment where threats of funding cuts are frequent, the organisation has to expend lobbying effort, E(B, N). The utility function is increasing in B and N and decreasing in E. In the context of intervention in the debt crisis, I postulate that B is an increasing function of L, and N is increasing in R. This is because if a debtor country government promises to undertake economic reforms, these activities would have to be monitored (to some extent) by personnel of the lending institution.

The reduced form utility function in (L, R) space is then

$$W^I = U^I(L,R) - C^I(E) \tag{24}$$

where

$$E = E(L,R) \tag{26}$$

and $C^I(E)$ is the cost of expending lobbying effort to achieve the levels (L, R). The isoquants for W^I are like ellipses; these are depicted in Figure 3.

I now turn to a different interest group: the rent defenders in the debtor country.

D. Rent Defenders in the Debtor Country

We have seen that the banks and the international institutions have an interest in economic reforms in the debtor country. Reforms, however,

Figure 3

The International Institutions' Indifference Map

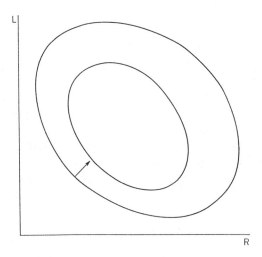

are painful to many groups of individuals. Privatization of public enterprises may mean job losses. Reduction of budget deficits means either
higher taxes or expenditure cuts. Those who are likely to lose because of
reforms will try to defend their rents by political actions. For example,
since expenditure cuts are not normally across the board, one interest group
may try to shift the burden to another group.

A simple model of rent defence can be formulated.[12] I assume that
initially the total rent is K and agent i has a share S_{i0}. The government
announces a cut in total rents by a fraction $(1-\lambda)$, and the new total rent is
λK. The cut is not necessarily across the board, and agent i's new share
is S_i which may be smaller or larger than the original S_{i0}. The agent has
two options: either he resigns from his position and joins the private sector,
in which case he earns an income W and his total utility is U(W); or he
may stay in his position and contend for his share of the reduced total rent.
The outcome of the contention is uncertain. Let $H(t, X_i, X_{-i}, S_{i0})$ denote the
probability that his new share, S_i, exceeds (or at least equals) t, given that
his original share is S_{i0}, his rent-defending effort is X_i, and aggregate rent-
defending effort of his opponents is X_{-i}. It is natural to assume that, for all
$0 < t < 1$,

---

[12] The model is in the spirit of Long and Vousden (1987).

$$H_2 > 0 \, , H_3 < 0 \, , H_4 \geq 0 \, , H_{42} \geq 0 \, , H_{23} < 0 \tag{26}$$

and, in the case $S_{i0}=S_{j0}$ for all (i,j), I assume that H is homogeneous of degree zero in (X_i, X_{-i}) and

$$\lim_{q \to \infty} H_2(t,1,q,S_{i0}) = 0 \text{ where } q = X_{-i}/X_i \tag{27a}$$

and

$$\lim_{n \to \infty} H_2(t,1,n-1,1/n) = 0 \tag{27b}$$

where n is the number of rent defenders.

These restrictions imply that (a) increased rent-defending effort by agent i has a favorable effect on the probability that his new share exceeds t; (b) increased aggregate effort by i's opponent reduces that probability; (c) an agent's effort is more productive if his original share is large ; (d) other agents' effort reduces the marginal product of agent i's effort ; and an agent's marginal product of effort becomes negligible if (e) his effort share is insignificant or (f) his initial share is small.

Let $f(t, X_i, X_{-i}, S_{i0})$ denote the probability density function obtained from H. The expected utility of an agent who stays to fight is

$$V_i = \int_0^1 U(t\lambda K)f(t,X_i,X\text{-}i,S_{i0})dt\text{-}C(X_i) \tag{28}$$

where U is the utility of income and C is the cost of effort. I assume that U is strictly concave and C is strictly convex. An agent will decide to take part in the game if and only if the Nash equilibrium outcome, V_i^*, is not less than the utility obtained from the outside opportunity, $U(W)$.

Notice that in this simple model, each agent takes the size of the cut in total rent as given. Assuming Nash behaviour, each agent's first order condition is

$$\int_0^1 U(t\lambda K)f_2(t,X_i,X_{-i},S_{i0})dt = C'(X_i). \tag{29}$$

Upon integration by parts, (29) becomes

$$(\lambda K)\int_0^1 U'(t\lambda K)H_2(t,X_i,X_{-i},S_{i0})dt = C'(X_i). \tag{30}$$

Consider the simple case where there are n identical agents. In this case, since H is homogeneous of degree zero, H_2 is homogeneous of degree minus one in (X_i, X_{-i}), and (30) can be rewritten as

$$(\lambda K)\int_0^1 U'(t\lambda K)H_2(t,1,n-1,1/n)dt - XC'(X) = 0 \tag{31}$$

where X has replaced X_i because of the assumption of symmetry.

Lemma 1: *A larger cut in total rent (i.e. a decrease in λ) will cause the equilibrium rent-defending effort of each agent to increase [respectively, decrease] if the coefficient of relative risk aversion of U is greater than [respectively, smaller than], unity, provided that the cut is not so large that the equilibrium V_i falls short of the outside utility $U(W)$.*[13]

Next, I want to show that, under certain conditions, total effort tends to be small if the initial rent is widely dispersed.

Proposition 2: *Aggregate rent-defending effort will be smaller the larger is the number of isolated rent defenders, provided that*
$$n_{-1}H_{24} - nH_{23} > [1 + X(C''/C')]H_2.$$

$$(32)$$

Proof:
$$d(nX)/dn = X + n(dX/dn) \tag{33}$$
From (31),

$$X = (\lambda K/C') \int_{0}^{1} U'(t\lambda K)H_2 dt \tag{34}$$

and

$$ndX/dn = n[C' + XC'']^{-1}(\lambda K) \int_{0}^{1} U'[H_{23} - n^{-2}H_{24}]dt < 0. \tag{35}$$

Substituting (34) and (35) into (33), we see that the latter is negative if (32) holds. This completes the proof.

Remark: From (27a) and (27b), as n tends to infinity, (34) approaches zero and (35) tends to minus infinity. Hence (32) holds for large n.

It is clear, then, that if the debtor country government contemplates extensive economic reforms (large R), it should expect a great deal of opposition from rent defenders if they are strongly risk averse, and that the aggregate magnitude of opposition will be large if rents are highly concentrated. I now turn to the utility function of the debtor country government.

E. The Debtor Country Government

The government of the debtor country wishes to maximize its probability of survival. To do so, it balances the interests of rent defenders against those of rent opposers. Generally rent opposers tend to be

---

[13] For the proof, see Long and Vousden (1987).

relatively ineffective. However even the most passive tax payer may voice opposition if economic conditions deteriorate sufficiently. I suppose that the government derives political support from the average tax payer if the latter expects that his living standard will improve as a consequence of government policies. Let $\Phi(L, R)$, the expected economic improvement, be an increasing and concave function of new lending L and of the extend of economic reforms R. It is assumed that

$$\Phi_{21} = 0 \, , \, \Phi(0,0) = 0.$$

Since the improvement is not in the immediate future, a discount factor $(1-\delta)$ will be applied.

The level of discontent D associated with the extent of reforms R depends on L (which may be taken as an indicator of the "tightness" of economic conditions) and on J, an index of concentration of rents. From the above discussion, it is reasonable to assume that

$$D_1(L,R,J) > 0 \, , \, D_{12} > 0 \tag{36a}$$
$$D_2 > 0 \, , \, D_{22} > 0 \tag{36b}$$
$$D_3 > 0 \, , \, D_{23} > 0. \tag{36c}$$

The debtor country government seeks to maximize

$$W^D = (1-\delta)\Phi(L,R) - D(L,R,J) \tag{37}$$

For given L, the optimal extent of reforms is characterized by the first order condition:

$$(1-\delta)\Phi_2(L,R) - D_2(L,R,J) = 0. \tag{38}$$

Equation (38) implicitly defines the reaction function $R=R(L,J,\delta)$. For a given J and δ, this function has a negative slope in (R,L) space:

$$R_L = -[(1-\delta)\Phi_{21}-D_{21}] \, / \, [(1-\delta)\Phi_{22}-D_{22}] < 0. \tag{39}$$

The debtor country government's reaction curve and indifferent map is depicted in Figure 4. Higher values of L give rise to higher utility levels. At points such as A and A´, the slope of the indifferent curve is zero. These points (and hence the reaction curve) move to the left if the concentration index J rises.[14] That is, governments are more reluctant to carry out reforms if rents are concentrated in a few powerful hands. An increase in δ has a similar effect to an increase in J.

Finally, I turn my attention to the creditor country governments.

F. The Creditor Country Governments

A frequently raised argument for intervention by creditor country governments is to maintain the solvency of creditor banks. Another reason

---

[14] This can be seen by differentiating the first order condition (38) with respect to J, treating R as a function of J and keeping L constant.

Figure 4

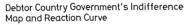

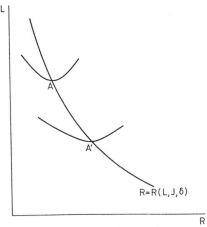

is the aid motive.[15]

In the U.S., it seems that, at least initially, solvency was the main concern. According to Anna Schwartz (1989, p. 13) "... in the 1980s international debt crisis, intervention undertaken by the U.S., the dominant creditor country, was a decision of the monetary authorities. They determined that, to preserve financial stability in the domestic banking system, it was essential to create the facade that foreign borrowers were faced only with a liquidity problem ..." Schwartz's thesis is that the U.S. authorities deliberately engaged in public deception in order to save the U.S. banks. In support of this thesis, she refers to accounting practices that regulators permitted the banks to use to "... hide the fact ..." that loans to troubled debtor countries are " ... bad debts" (p. 19). In her opinion, the whole show was coordinated at first by the Federal Reserve System, and more recently by the U.S. Treasury, with the help of the World Bank and

---

[15] To quote Vernon Ruttan (1989, p. 411), "... two arguments have typically been used in support of transfers that include a grant component. One set is based on the economic and strategic self-interest of the donor country. The second is based on ethical or moral responsibility of the residents of wealthy countries toward the residents of the poor countries".

the IMF.

Without necessarily embracing Schwartz's thesis of public deception, it is clear that the U.S. government has an interest in active intervention in the debt crisis. I have mentioned earlier that there is a risk of free riding by individual banks, unless they are faced with implicit or explicit threats of penalty. The U.S. government had to take the lead in providing new lending to the hard-pressed debtors, via the IMF and other international institutions (these are ultimately supported to a significant extent by revenues raised from U.S. taxpayers).

The creditor-country governments are assumed to have the utility function :

$$W^c = \beta(1-\rho)\Phi(L,R) - \gamma T(L) \tag{40}$$

where $\Phi(L, R)$ is the economic benefit to the debtor country (the same Φ that appears in (37)), $\beta > 0$ is the weight the creditor country governments attached to these benefits, and $\rho > 0$ is the discount rate because the benefits are not immediate, and $\gamma T(L)$ is the tax burden of financing the subsidized loan.

II. STACKELBERG EQUILIBRIUM, COMPARATIVE STATICS AND BARGAINING POSSIBILITIES

For the moment, let us abstract from the possibility of bargaining and focus on Stackelberg equilibrium. Let the coalition of creditor country governments maximize their utility W^c, subject to the banks being in their acceptance set, and subject to a constraint on the utility level of the international institutions. The debtor country government's reaction function

$$R = R(L,J,\delta)$$

is taken as datum. Figure 5 depicts a Stackelberg equilibrium E, with the constraints on the banks and the international institutions holding with strict inequality. At this point, the equilibrium satisfies the first order condition,

$$\beta(1-\rho)[\Phi_1 + \Phi_2 R_L] - \gamma T'(L) = 0. \tag{41}$$

From (41), one sees that an increase in the rate of discount of the creditor country governments will reduce L and move E to E´ (south-west of E):

$$\text{Sign } L_\rho = \text{Sign } [-\beta\Phi_1 - \beta\Phi_2 R_L] = \text{Sign } [-\gamma T'(L)] < 0. \tag{42}$$

Similarly, an increase in the rate of discount of the debtor country government shifts its reaction curve to the left and reduces equilibrium new lending. This is illustrated in Figure 6, where E is shifted to E".

To obtain comparative static results with respect to the index of rent concentration J, I assume that $D(L, R, J)$ is multiplicatively separable with respect to J:

$$D(L,R,J) = M(J)N(R,J). \tag{43}$$

Figure 5

A Stackelberg Equilibrium

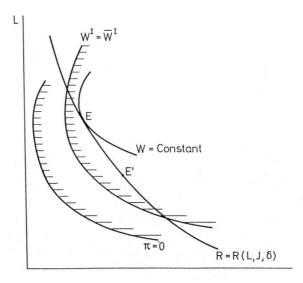

Figure 6

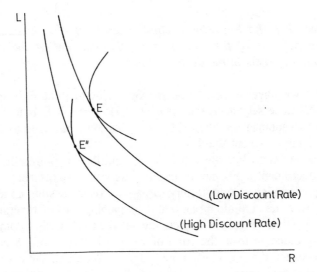

Figure 7

Bargaining Set

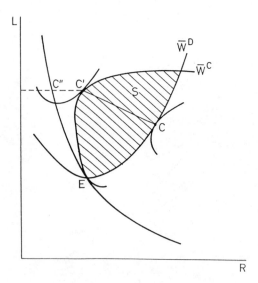

where both M and N are positive valued functions. It can then be shown that an increase in J will reduce the Stackelberg equilibrium level of new lending.

Proposition 3: The Stackelberg equilibrium level of new lending is a decreasing function of the two rates of discount and of the degree of concentration of rents in the debtor country.

So far we have assumed that the Stackelberg point E is inside the banks' acceptance set and is thus feasible. However if E is to the left of the banks' acceptance set, then side-payments must be made to the banks to induce them to accept the deal.

Instead of choosing the Stackelberg equilibrium point, the creditor country government may want to improve its utility by offering the debtor country government an opportunity to bargain over possible combinations of (L, R), with the credible threat that if bargaining fails of reversion to the Stackelberg point. Figure 7 depicts the set S of points that dominate the Stackelberg outcome from the point of view of both parties. S is the area enclosed between the two indifference curves. Within S, the curve CC′ is the contract curve, representing the set of all efficient bargaining outcomes.

The crucial problem is that of the ability to commit to a given deal.

For example, the debtor country government strictly prefers C´ to E. But if both parties agree on C´, and L has to be delivered before R is observed, then there is no guarantee that the debtor will stay at C´. In fact it will prefer C" (the intersection between the debtor's reaction function and the horizontal line passing through C´). To enforce C´, lending and reforms must be carried out simultaneously. In practice this is quite difficult to achieve because of time required for reform measures to be implemented.

III. CONCLUDING REMARKS

The model developed in this paper is an attempt to study the international debt crisis from a political economy perspective that encompasses the incentives of individual agents. Many simplifying assumptions have had to be made to present a basic picture. Certain aspects of the model deserve comment.

The model is static. A multi-period framework provides scope for richer results.[16]

The model is partial equilibrium, neglecting aspects such as terms of trade and endogenous interest rates. This is a common feature of models of the international debt crisis. Some pure aid models (abstracting from debts) have been formulated using a general equilibrium framework[17] and progress on these models may assist in the formulation of a debt crisis model in general equilibrium.

References

Alexander, Lewis S., 1987. "The Legal Consequences of Sovereign Default", Manuscript, Federal Reserve Board, Washington.

Bank of International Settlements, *Annual Reports*, Basle, 1983-85, 1987-88.

Bulow, Jeremy and Kenneth Rogoff, 1989. "A Constant Recontracting Model of Sovereign Debt", *Journal of Political Economy*, 97, 155-178.

Cornes, Richard and T. Sandler, 1986. *The Theory of Externalities, Public Goods, and Club Goods*, Cambridge University Press, New York.

Eaton, Jonathan and Mark Gersovitz, 1989. "Debt with Potential Repudiation: Theoretical and Empirical Analysis", *Review of Economic*

---

[16] See Kenen (1989) and Bulow and Rogoff(1989) for some attempts in this direction). For an intertemporal model of debt without default, see Long and Siebert (1989).

[17] See for example Kemp, Long and Shimomura (1988).

Studies, 48, 289-309.

Froot, Kenneth A., 1989. "Buybacks, Exit Bonds, and the Optimality of Debt and Liquidity Relief", *International Economic Review*, 30, 49-70.

Gale, Douglas and Martin Hellwig, 1989. "Repudiation and Renegotiation: the Case of Sovereign Debt", *International Economic Review*, 30, 3-32.

Guttman, Joel, 1990. "Voluntary Collective Action", chapter 2, this volume.

Helpman, Elhanan, 1988. "Voluntary Debt Reduction : Incentives and Welfare", *NBER Working Paper No. 2692*.

Kaletsky, Anatole, 1985. *The Costs of Default*, Priority Press, New York.

Kemp, Murray, Ngo Van Long and Koji Shimomura, 1988, "On the Optimal Timing of Foreign Aid", Manuscript, University of New South Wales.

Kenen, Peter, 1989. "Debt Buybacks and Forgiveness in a Model with Voluntary Repudiation", *Working Papers in International Economics*, G-89-01, Princeton University.

Krueger, Anne O., 1988. "Resolving the Debt Crisis and Restoring Developing Countries' Creditworthiness", Carnegie-Rochester Public Policy Conference, University of Rochester.

Krugman, Paul, 1988. "Market-based Debt Reduction Schemes", NBER Working Paper No. 2587.

Krugman, Paul, 1989. "Financing vs. Forgiving a Debt : Some Analytical Notes", *Journal of Development Economics*.

Long, Ngo Van and Neil Vousden, 1987. "Risk Averse Rent Seeking with Shared Rents", *Economic Journal*, 97, 971-985.

Long, Ngo Van and Horst Siebert, 1989. "Optimal Foreign Borrowing: the Impact of the planning Horizon on the Half and Full Debt Cycle", *Journal of Economics (Zeitschrift für Nationalökonomie)*, 49, 279-297.

Ruttan, Vernon W., 1989. "Why Foreign Economic Assistance?", *Economic Development and Cultural Change*, 37, 411-424.

Sachs, Jeffrey, 1988a. "Conditionality, Debt Relief, and the Developing Country Debt Crisis", mimeo, Harvard University.

Sachs, Jeffrey, 1988b. "The Debt Overhang of Developing Countries", in the J. B. De Macedo and R. Findlay, editors, *Diaz Memorial Volume*, Wider Institute, Helsinki.

Sachs, Jeffrey and Harry Huizinga, 1987. "U.S. Commercial Banks and Developing-Country Debt Crisis", *Brookings Papers on Economic Activity*, 2, 555-601.

Schwartz, Anna S., 1989. "International Debts: What's Facts and What's Fiction", *Economic Inquiry*, 27, 1989, 1-19.

Chapter 18

FOREIGN-EXCHANGE MARKET LIBERALIZATION:
ANATOMY OF A FAILURE

Ben-Zion Zilberfarb

In May 1977 the Labor Party in Israel lost a general election for the first time since the establishment of the modern state, and the new government set about formulating market-oriented reforms. The new economic policy which was announced was heralded as an "economic revolution". The new policies did not merit this broad description, since liberalization was limited in scope to the foreign exchange market. Nevertheless, the new policy was perceived by the public (and portrayed in the press) as a move toward a free market economy. It is a popular perception that the liberalization program was abandoned in 1984-1985 when foreign exchange controls were reimposed. The attempts at liberalization had, however, effectively come to an end much earlier, in 1979.

This paper investigates why the liberalization program failed.

I. THE POLITICAL BACKGROUND

Prior to 1977, the Labor Party had been the dominant ideological and political force in Israel, with influence extending to the pre-State era. The quasi-government institutions under the British Mandate were controlled by the Party and this dominance continued when the State was reestablished in 1948. The May 1977 elections could therefore have been expected to result in revolutionary change, since Labor was forced into opposition and a government was formed by the Likud, a coalition composed of the Herut and Liberal Parties, the latter of which professed to adhere to free-trade and liberal economic principles. The division of responsibilities in the new government assigned to Herut foreign policy and security issues, and to the Liberal party economic issues. None of the six economic ministries was assigned to Herut. Three of the ministries were assigned to the Liberals, including the most important, the Ministry of Finance.

The election results were a mandate for change. The election platform of the Likud had promised "... to establish a free economy based on efficiency, entrepreneurship, and competition." The Likud would "reduce government intervention and public bureaucracy in economic activity and endeavor gradually to decrease government supervision of economic activity."

Yet the changes in economic policy were not far reaching, but were confined to the foreign exchange market. The attempt at liberalization of the foreign exchange market nevertheless took on a broader symbolic significance. Success or failure was popularly perceived as a test of the applicability of free market principles for the economy of Israel.

II. THE ECONOMIC BACKGROUND

Following the Yom Kippur War and the oil shock of October 1973, the economy of Israel confronted inflation and balance of payment problems. Annual inflation, which had been 12% in 1971-1972, rose to 35% in 1974-1977. The balance of payment deficit increased from $1.1 billion in 1972 to $4.0 in 1975. The latter deficit had been 50% of total exports in 1972, but in 1975 exceeded total exports by 5%.

Resolution of the "crisis" in the balance of payment was assigned priority in economic policy during 1976-1977. To reduce the import surplus, the government resorted to what proved to be an effective short run remedy: economic slowdown. Taxes were raised and government domestic consumption was reduced, slowing down the annual growth rate of GDP from 4.7% in 1973-1975 to 1.7% in 1976-1977. The balance of payment improved, with the import surplus declining by 36% (from $4.0 billion in 1975 to $2.5 billion in 1977). No similar improvement was achieved with regard to inflation. The annual inflation rate in 1977 (35%) was only slightly lower than the 1974-1975 rate (40%).

III. THE ECONOMIC REVOLUTION

The economic policy of the new government, the "economic revolution" which was announced on October 28 1977, focused on the foreign exchange market. This market was the natural focus of a liberalization attempt. Although the Labor Party had lost political power,[1]

---

[1] The Labor party's economic power was based on its special relationship with the Histadrut (or non-state socialist) sector of the economy. The Histadrut has served a dual role in Israel: as an organization of labor unions and a principal employer in the economy. On the role and scope of the Histadrut sector in the economy of Israel, see Hillman (1988).

it still exercised domestic economic power. Changes introduced in the foreign exchange market were in a domain of government policy discretion that avoided domestic political confrontation. There was also a precedent for changes in the exchange rate regime.[2]

Components of the new policy were:

1. Liberalization of the foreign exchange market via abolition of controls on foreign exchange transactions.
2. A change from a crawling peg system to a floating exchange rate.
3. Devaluation (10.35 IL/$ to 15.20 IL/$).
4. Elimination of all direct subsidies, thereby unifying the exchange rate for exporters.
5. Foreign exchange linked accounts (known by their acronym PATAM) were offered to the public.

Under the new regime, the role of the Bank of Israel (BOI, hereafter) in the foreign exchange market was to be limited to offsetting random fluctuations in the supply of or demand for foreign currency.

The most significant part of the program was liberalization of capital-account transactions. For the citizen, the most visible change was permission to purchase $US3,000 per capita at any bank and take that much abroad. Previously (until October 30 1977) Israelis had not been permitted to hold foreign currency, but could purchase up to $500 for foreign travel. Thus, for the citizen, the new policy had immediate consequences: extended freedom to buy foreign currency, and reduced dependence on bureaucratic allocation decisions. These were significant changes for the individual. Hence, in the public's mind the failure of the economic revolution was not evident until 1984-1985, when limits were reimposed on the purchase of foreign currency.

From a political economy perspective the new policy was revolutionary in that bureaucratic discretion was diminished. There was no longer need to apply for permits to buy or transfer foreign exchange.

However, since the economy in 1977 faced high inflation and was overcoming balance-of-payments difficulties, appropriate fiscal policy was contractionary, especially since the devaluation that was part of the liberalization program was inflationary. However, a contractionary fiscal policy was not adopted. The Likud constituency, having being deprived of past access to the ruling agencies, sought to use government allocation towards its objectives. Table 1 shows the share of the government civilian consumption as percentage of GDP. This share which was roughly constant at the beginning of the 1970s (at 10.5%) increased between 1977 and 1979 (to 12.3%).

---

[2] This point is made by Bruno and Sussman (1980).

Under these circumstances, the attempt to slow down the economy took the form of monetary policy.

IV. EXCHANGE-RATE INTERVENTION

For the first weeks following the introduction of the new policy the BOI intervened in the foreign exchange market to fix the exchange rate at 15.2 IL/$. What necessitated this intervention, notwithstanding free-market liberalization intentions? Table 2 provides the values for the effective exchange rate (the official rate plus direct subsidies) for a dollar of value added in exports prior to the new economic plan. The values exhibit a wide variation among the various sectors of the economy. Subsidies for exports were based on the firm's value-added in exports. The higher the value-added, the higher the subsidy. The level of the firm's value added was determined by the Ministry of Industry and Commerce. Table 2 reveals that some sectors of the economy were receiving subsidies that implied a higher value-added than was realized. The new policy of elimination export subsidies thus withdrew benefits that were not uniformally granted in accord with economic criteria. Tov (1988) reports that the revelation to the new finance minister of the magnitude of subsidies that were determined via the discretion of government officials was instrumental in the decision to cancel the export subsidies.

Table 2 reveals that for 20 percent of Israel's value added in exports the effective exchange rate was in excess of 15 IL/$ (textile and clothing, rubber and plastics, and chemicals). Because of the cancellation of direct subsidies to exports, an exchange rate of less than 15 IL/$ would have caused "problems" for these sectors. It was to preempt these problems that the BOI intervened in the foreign exchange market to stabilize the exchange rate at 15.2 IL/$ by buying up the excess supplies of dollars.

One may ask why there should have been an excess supply of dollars. The opportunity for the public to adjust its portfolio to increase the share of foreign assets should have led to an excess demand for foreign exchange rather than an excess supply. However, the public preferred to adjust its portfolio through the PATAM accounts rather than by buying foreign exchange. The excess supply of foreign exchange was limited in magnitude and short lived, and was created by the recipients of restitution payments from Germany who also had been permitted to hold foreign exchange accounts previously. The devaluation yielded the latter a capital gain of 47% on their foreign accounts. The higher valued dollars were sold for domestic currency. With the exception of this one instance where the objective was to prevent a significant appreciation of the Israeli currency, the BOI did not intervene in the foreign exchange market until the end of 1978. What led to BOI intervention in December 1978?

V. CAPITAL MOVEMENTS

As part of the new policy the BOI imposed credit controls that were aimed at preventing speculative capital movements, thereby easing the transition to the new exchange rate system. These temporary controls were cancelled in January 1978.

The increase in economic activity following the elections, linked to the increase in government expenditures and the opening of new possibilities for financial investments (e.g., foreign exchange linked assets), had contributed to an increase in the demand for credit. Thus, when credit controls were lifted, credit expanded leading to deficient reserves in the banking system. Deficient reserves as percentage of required reserves increased from 5% in December 1977 to 15% in January 1978 and 21% in February 1978 (see Table 3). To reduce the deficiency in reserves, banks shifted increasingly to foreign borrowing as a source of domestic lending. While one IL of domestic loans created deficient reserves of .7 IL or more (.7 being the required reserves ratio), a foreign loan improved or did not alter the banks' reserves position.

The inflow of foreign loans reduced the reserve deficiency to only 2% in April 1978 (see Table 3). In addition to their advantage to the banks, foreign loans were also more attractive to the public because of their lower cost. Figure 4 compares the interest rates on domestic and foreign currency loans. The table reveals that throughout 1978 the cost of foreign loans was below the marginal cost of domestic loans, and in the second half of 1978 was below the average cost. The attractiveness of foreign credit manifested itself in an increased share of foreign credit in total free credit, which rose from 42% in the first quarter of 1978 to 46% at the fourth quarter.

VI. THE POLICY PROBLEM

The inflow of foreign capital created a policy problem for the BOI. The following simple model of the foreign exchange market illustrates the problem:

(1) $X = X(hP_x/P , DDP)$
(2) $M = M(hP_m/P , y)$
(3) $Z = Z(h^e + r_f - r)$
(4) $X + Z = M$.

Equation (1) relates exports (X) to their relative price and to domestic demand pressure (DDP), h is the official exchange rate (IL/\$), P_x is the foreign price of exports and P is the domestic price level. The first variable has a positive effect on exports and the second a negative effect.[3]

---

[3] See Zilberfarb, (1980) and Drachman and Zilberfarb (1987) for empirical verification.

The second equation relates imports (M) to their relative price (P_m is the foreign price of imports) and to the level of domestic economic activity Y. The first variable has a negative effect on M, and the second positive.[4] The third equation relates net capital inflows (Z) to interest rate differentials (h^e is the expected depreciation of the domestic currency and r_f and r are the foreign and domestic interest rates, respectively). The higher the cost of borrowing abroad ($h^e + r_f$), with the cost of domestic credit constant, the lower is the net inflow of foreign exchange. Equation 4 is the equilibrium condition: the supply of foreign exchange deriving from exports and net capital inflow equals demand created by imports.

In response to tight domestic monetary policy, banks borrowed abroad, thereby increasing the supply of foreign exchange. The market response in the absence of sterilization would have been appreciation of the domestic currency. This would have left the monetary base unchanged, but via equations 1 and 2 there would have been an adverse affect on the balance of payments.

To prevent balance-of-payments deterioration, the BOI was required to avoid exchange appreciation. This could have been achieved by purchasing the excess supply of foreign exchange. However, the money supply would then have increased, which was contrary to the tight monetary policy.

Another policy option was to limit capital inflow, either via direct controls, or indirectly by reducing the attractiveness of foreign borrowing. However, this would contradict the policy of liberalization of the foreign exchange market.

The policy dilemma confronting the BOI was the consequence of the expansionary fiscal policy. A restrictive fiscal policy would have led to a decline in imports and expansion of exports (see equations 1 and 2). This would have offset the adverse effect of the appreciation of the domestic currency and would have eased the pressure on the BOI to intervene in the foreign exchange market.

VII. THE FAILURE OF LIBERALIZATION
The above policy dilemma persisted throughout 1978. In recognition of the dilemma, the business sector feared (and rightly so) that the BOI would eventually abandon the free market policy and limit capital inflow. As a result, the business sector borrowed $250 million from abroad in the first ten days of December 1978. Converted to domestic currency, this equalled 21% of the monetary base. On December 10, 1978 the BOI imposed a mandatory non-interest earning deposit of 20% on foreign loans. The interest rate on foreign loans was thereby increased from 11% to 14%

---

[4] See Drachman and Zilberfarb (1987) for empirical evidence.

(since interest was paid on 100% of the loan, while the borrower received only 80%). This marked the first departure from a free foreign exchange market. Capital inflows were still not subject to restriction, but a tax had been levied on foreign borrowing.

The intervention of the BOI was too late and too limited to curb capital inflow. The reserve deficiency of the banking system had effectively constrained domestic currency credit, which rose by only 0.9% in the first quarter of 1979 (see Table 5). The BOI also made domestic borrowing more costly by raising the penalty interest rate on deficient reserves (from 22% to 25% in January and to 28% in February 1979). The increased domestic interest rate increased the attractiveness of foreign loans (see Table 4). Foreign borrowing nonetheless continued to expand at an even higher rate -- around 30% per quarter throughout 1979. This increased the share of foreign credit in free total credit from 46% in the last quarter of 1978 to 62% in the last quarter of 1979 (see Table 5).

The BOI took a second step to limit the inflow of foreign capital on March 9, 1979. It increased the required deposit on foreign credit to 30% and imposed a negative 12% interest rate on the deposit. This raised the interest rate on foreign loans from 14% to 25% (see Table 4). Once more the BOI had intervened in the determination of the price of foreign credit. Concurrently the penalty rate on deficient reserves was increased (from 28% to 30%) thereby raising the cost of domestic currency credit (from 63% to 69%).

The demand for foreign credit continued in spite of the rising cost; this was because of expectations regarding the exchange rate (devaluation in 1978 of 23.6% lagged behind inflation of 48.1%). Foreign borrowing permitted diversification of the credit portfolio, and domestic currency credit was effectively unavailable.

A further step in the retreat from liberalization was taken in April 1979. The BOI offered a loan to the banking system to help reduce deficient reserves, but made the loan conditional on freezing foreign credit. The BOI had now intervened in fixing both the quantity and price of capital inflows. In November 1979 the voluntary restrictions on credit were replaced by mandatory limits on credit. Any expansion of credit (domestic or foreign currency) was subject to a prohibitive penalty (over 175% annually). At this point the "economic revolution" collapsed. Free capital inflows could no longer take place and the exchange rate was determined by the BOI and not by the market. Moreover, the Finance Committee of the Knesset held discussions in December 1979 to bring back direct subsidies for exports.

A comparison of the foreign exchange market prior to the "economic revolution" and at the end of 1979 reveals only minor differences. The previous crawling peg exchange-rate system was back, although the changes in exchange rates were daily rather than monthly, and the BOI determined the exchange rate rather than the Finance Ministry.

One difference persisted, the permission for the public to hold $3,000 per capita of foreign exchange in their asset portfolios. Because of this carryover, the failure of the "economic revolution" did not become apparent to the public until four years later. The persistence of this one aspect of the liberalization scheme permitted the finance minister on leaving office on August 11 1979 to ask his successor in a public statement not to withdraw from the liberalization process, when the process had already come to an end during his term in office.

Although not evident to the average citizen, the failure of the liberalization attempt of the foreign exchange market was clear to the economic policy makers of the Likud. This, in addition to their concerns about confrontations with the Histadrut, weakened resolve to introduce further free-market reforms. So much was evident when the liberal finance minister resigned in 1979. The post of Finance Minister was not returned to the Liberal party until five years later. Finance ministers in the years following 1979 were not committed to free-market principles, and were interchangeable in terms of commitment to market principles with prior Labor party counterparts.

VIII. RELATED ISSUES

The literature on liberalization of the capital account suggests that the BOI should have anticipated the events of 1978-1979. The literature predicts events as they took place and recognizes that "... when the prereform domestic interest rate exceeds the depreciation-adjusted world rate, the removal of impediments to private capital movement causes an initial period of real appreciation. A current account deficit emerges upon removing those impediments..." (Obstfeld, 1986, p. 202).

Questions are also raised concerning the responsibility of economic advisors or professional economists in public service. Should they recommend a policy, the success of which is contingent on steps that while clearly specified are unlikely to be implemented? The macroeconomic policies that were required to facilitate the success of a policy of liberalization of the foreign-exchange market were not implemented. The macroeconomic policies that *were* implemented ensured the failure of liberalization.

IX. CONCLUDING REMARKS

The "economic revolution" that took place in Israel in 1977 subsequent to the first change in government to a non-socialist coalition marked Israel's first attempt to apply free-market principles, via liberalization of the foreign exchange market. Also unprecedented was the demonstrated willingness to limit political discretion, by cancelation of sector-specific export subsidies.

Liberalization failed because of inappropriate accompanying macro-economic policy. The appropriate policies were not implemented because of political constraints on the level of government expenditure. However, foreign-exchange liberalization was symbolic of a shift to a free market system. Failure provided a precedent for resisting subsequent market-oriented change.

Table 1 Real government civilian consumption (GC)
1970-1980 (1975 prices)

Period	GC	Percentage of GDP
70	610	10.5
1	641	9.9
2	692	10.0
3	739	10.7
4	769	10.4
5	804	10.1
6	848	10.8
7	873	11.7
8	920	11.6
9	939	12.3
80	928	11.8

Source: Central Bureau of Statistics: Monthly Bulletins.

Table 2 Effective exchange rates* (17.10.77)

	$1 of exports	$1 of value added	Percentage change immediately following the plan
Agriculture	13.62	14.08	8.0
Diamonds	10.97	13.45	13.0
Minerals	13.62	13.39	13.5
Food	13.46	14.40	5.6
Textile and Clothing	13.75	15.14	0.4
Leather	13.15	13.76	10.5
Wood	13.35	14.45	5.2
Paper and Publishing	13.40	13.99	8.6
Rubber and Plastics	13.60	15.82	-3.9
Chemicals	13.58	15.42	-1.4
Basic Metals	12.93	14.14	7.5
Metals and Machinery	13.56	14.63	3.9
Electrical and Electronics	13.48	14.78	2.8
Transportation	13.09	14.20	7.0
Hotels	12.83	13.06	16.4
Knowledge	12.91	12.96	17.3
Total goods	12.61	14.30	6.3
Total services	12.84	10.56	43.9

*Includes direct but not indirect subsidies.

Table 3 Deficient reserves as percentage of required reserves

Month	1977	1978	1979
1	-0.2	15.4	4.2
2	2.5	21.1	17.7
3	9.0	4.8	25.2
4	6.4	2.1	15.7
5	-0.6	13.1	18.7
6	6.3	17.5	26.1
7	9.5	17.8	30.6
8	3.8	18.8	16.9
9	5.8	20.7	24.7
10	22.0	31.4	35.3
11	10.2	21.4	23.0
12	5.0	17.7	22.7

Source: Bank of Israel, Examiner of Banks, Annual Reports.

Table 4 Cost of free credit (annual terms)

| | Domestic Currency | | Foreign Credit | | |
| | Average | Marginal | Foreign | Total cost | |
Period	cost	cost	interest note r_f	(a)	(b)
77.4	49	64			
78.1	49	64	10	49	43
78.2	49	64	11	40	54
78.3	49	64	11	44	24
78.4	52	64	14	25	31
79.1	63	99	14	40	84
79.2	69	102	25	156	141
79.3	92	129	26	115	186
79.4	132	175	29	159	186

Total cost for foreign credit is calculated as: $(1 + r_f) (1 + h) - 1$. h is the devaluation rate: average of period - column (a), or end of period - column (b).

Source: Bank of Israel, Examiner of Banks, Annual Reports.

Table 5 Free Credit

| | | Percentage change | | Percentage of total credit | |
| | | Domestic | Foreign | Domestic | Foreign |
Period	Total	currency	currency	currency	currency
77.1				60.7	39.3
2	2.5	9.1	-7.8	64.7	35.3
3	9.0	10.2	5.1	65.4	34.6
4	33.5	13.4	72.6	55.6	44.4
78.1	11.9	17.0	6.5	58.1	41.9
2	15.1	13.9	16.7	57.5	42.5
3	20.4	22.2	18.0	58.4	41.6
4	13.5	4.1	26.8	53.5	46.5
79.1	14.7	0.9	30.7	47.0	53.0
2	24.0	15.6	28.1	41.0	59.0
3	22.0	13.1	29.0	38.0	62.0
4	22.3	13.1	29.0	38.0	62.0

References

Bruno, M. and Z. Sussman, 1980. "From crawling peg to floating exchange rates, Israel 1977-79 in retrospect," *The Economic Quarterly*, 27, 359-374.

Drachman, R. and B. Zilberfarb, 1987. "An econometric annual model of the real sector in Israel," *Economic Modelling*, 370-376.

Hillman, Arye L., 1988. "Impediments to a competitive environment in Israel," paper presented at *Symposium on American-Israel Relations in Honor of the 40th Anniversary of the State of Israel*, New York.

Obstfeld, M., 1986. "Capital flows, the current account, and the real exchange rate: the consequences of stabilization and liberalization," in S. Edwards and L. Ahamed, editors, *Economic Adjustment and Exchange Rates in Developing Countries*, University of Chicago Press, 201-234.

Tov, I., 1988. "The 1977 economic upheaval - execution of goals," *Economic Quarterly*, 39, 33-47.

Zilberfarb, B.,1980. "Domestic demand pressure, relative prices and the export supply equation - more empirical evidence," *Economica*, 47, 443-450.